PEOPLE AND PLACES IN NORTHERN EUROPE 500–1600

ESSAYS IN HONOUR OF
PETER HAYES SAWYER

This collection of essays deals with the history and archaeology of Northern Europe in the Middle Ages. It looks at Anglo-Saxon England, at its contacts with Francia and Scandinavia, particularly in the Viking age, and at the impact of the Norwegians and Danes on the place-names of the British Isles. It also includes papers which present, in English, the results of recent archaeological and onomastic research in Scandinavia. Two papers deal with the history of women, as recorded in runestones, and as active in law suits during the medieval period. Many of the topics have attracted the attention of Peter Sawyer, formerly Professor of Medieval History at the University of Leeds, in whose honour the volume has been compiled.

Peter Sawyer. Photo by Kaaren Grimstad

People and Places in Northern Europe 500–1600

Essays in Honour of Peter Hayes Sawyer

EDITED BY

Ian Wood and Niels Lund

THE BOYDELL PRESS

First published 1991 by The Boydell Press, Woodbridge

The Boydell Press is an imprint of Boydell & Brewer Ltd
PO Box 9, Woodbridge, Suffolk IP12 3DF
and of Boydell & Brewer Inc.
PO Box 41026, Rochester, NY 14604, USA

ISBN 0 85115 547 2

British Library Cataloguing in Publication Data
People and places in northern Europe 500–1600 : essays in
honour of Peter Hayes Sawyer.
1. Europe to 1453
I. Wood, Ian   II. Lund, Niels   III. Sawyer, P. H. (Peter
Hayes) 1928–
940.1
ISBN 0–85115–547–2

Library of Congress Cataloging-in-Publication Data
People and places in northern Europe, 500–1600 : essays in honour of
Peter Hayes Sawyer / edited by Ian Wood and Niels Lund.
    p.   cm.
Includes bibliographical references.
ISBN 0–85115–547–2 (alk. paper)
    1. Scandinavia – History. 2. Scandinavia – Antiquities.
3. Scandinavia – Relations – Great Britain. 4. Great Britain –
Relations – Scandinavia. I. Sawyer, P. H. II. Wood, I. N. (Ian
N.), 1950– . III. Lund, Niels.
DL61.P46 1990
948–dc20   90–45308

This publication is printed on acid-free paper

Printed in Great Britain by
Woolnough Bookbinding Ltd, Irthlingborough, Northants

CONTENTS

ILLUSTRATIONS

PREFACE

A Festschrift for Peter Sawyer is inevitably a broadly focused volume. He himself is a man of wide scholarly interests, and he has had an impact on many aspects of Medieval scholarship, in Britain, Scandinavia and North America. This collection is intended to pay tribute to those interests and that impact. The contributors reflect the range of Peter Sawyer's influence, and the essays focus on the two main areas of his work; Britain and Scandinavia in the Middle Ages. It was on Domesday Book and on its place-names that he first established his reputation, and these interests are apparent in this volume. So too is his growing concern with Pre-Conquest England, and also with the history of the Scottish Isles. The second half of the book is a tribute to Peter Sawyer's Scandinavian interests, and to his familiarity with and influence on recent Scandinavian historiography. Much of the work that has been done on Denmark, Sweden and Norway in the early Middle Ages is not accessible to English readers, because it is written in one or other of the Scandinavian languages. This Festschrift, therefore, provided the opportunity not only to celebrate Peter Sawyer's sixtieth birthday, but also make available in English some of the recent developments in historical and archaeological scholarship in Scandinavia. For this, Niels Lund translated the contributions of Steen Hvaas, Brita Malmer and Greta Authén Blom, while Birgit Sawyer translated those of Hans Andersson and Thorsten Andersson. It is to be hoped that the resulting volume serves both as a tribute to Peter Sawyer and as a stimulus to the exchange of ideas within the scholarly communities on either side of the North Sea; communities which Peter Sawyer himself has influenced over the last thirty years.

Ian Wood   *Niels Lund*
University of Leeds   *University of Copenhagen*

ABBREVIATIONS

Alf.	Alfred the Great, Laws (ed. F. Liebermann, *Gesetze der Angelsachsen*, 3 vols (Halle, 1903–16)
As.	Athelstan, Laws, see *Alf.*
ASC	*Anglo-Saxon Chronicle*
ASE	*Anglo-Saxon England*
Atr.	Æthelræd, Laws, see *Alf.*
BAR, BS	British Archaeological Reports, British Series
BAR, IS	British Archaeological Reports, International Series
Bede, *HE*	Bede, *Historia Ecclesiastica*
CBA	Council for British Archaeology
CCSL	Corpus Christianorum, Series Latina
Cn.	Canute, Laws, see *Alf.*
DB	*Domesday Book*, gen. ed. J. Morris (Chichester, 1974–87); see also *GDB* and *LDB*
DEPN	E. Ekwall, *The Concise Oxford Dictionary of English Place Names* (Oxford, 1936, 3rd edn. 1960)
DN	*Diplomatarium Norvegicum*, vols 1–21, ed. C. C. A. Lange et al. (Christiania/Oslo, 1847–1972)
DR	*Danmarks Runeindskrifter*, ed. L. Jacobsen and E. Moltke (Copenhagen, 1942)
Edg.	Edgar, Laws, see *Alf.*
Edm.	Edmund, Laws, see *Alf.*
Edw.	Edward the Elder, Laws, see *Alf.*
Edw. and Guth.	The Laws of Edward and Guthrum, see *Alf.*
EHD	*English Historical Documents c.500–1042*, ed. D. Whitelock, 2nd ed. (London, 1979)
EHR	*English Historical Review*
GDB	Great Domesday Book; see also *DB*
In.	Ine, Laws, see *Alf.*
LDB	Little Domesday Book; see also *DB*
MGH	Monumenta Germaniae Historica
Ep	Epistolae
LL	Legum Sectio
SRG	Scriptores Rerum Germanicarum
SRM	Scriptores Rerum Merovingicarum
SS	Scriptores

NHD	*Norske Herredags-Dombøger*, ed. E. A. Thomle, et al., Udg. for det Norske Historiske Kildeskriftsfond, vols 1– (Christiania/ Oslo, 1895–)
NIYR	*Norges innskrifter med de yngre runer* vols 1–6, ed. M. Olsen and A. Liestøl (Oslo, 1941–60)
NPL	*The Northumbrian Priests' Law*, see *Alf.*
NTS	*Norsk Tidsskrift for Spogvidenskap*
PL	Patrologia Latina
PSAS	*Proceedings of the Society of Antiquaries of Scotland*
PRO	Public Record Office
S.	P. H. Sawyer, *Anglo-Saxon Charters: an annotated list and bibliography*, Royal Historical Society Guides and Handbooks 8 (London, 1968)
Saga-Book	*Saga-Book of the Viking Society*
SR	*Sveriges Runinskrifter*
SR G	*Sveriges Runinskrifter* 11–12, *Gotlands Runinskrifter*, ed. S. B. F. Jansson, E. Wessén and E. Svärdström (Stockholm, 1962–78)
SR Sö	*Sveriges Runinskrifter* 3, *Södermanlands Runinskrifter*, ed. E. Brate and E. Wessén (Stockholm, 1924–36)
SR U	*Sveriges Runinskrifter* 6–9, *Upplands Runinskrifter* 1–4, ed. E. Wessén and S. B. F. Jansson (Stockholm, 1940–58)
TRHS	*Transactions of the Royal Historical Society*
Y, YE, YN, YW	Yorkshire (East, North and West Ridings)

PETER SAWYER: AN APPRECIATION

Ian Wood

When Naomi Hurnard asked an astonished Finals candidate during a viva, 'What would you do if you met me in a state of nature?' it was Peter Sawyer who spread the news. Not only was he responsible for circulating the story, but he also inquired of various friends and tutors what their responses would have been if they had been in the place of the unfortunate undergraduate. 'Be nasty, brutish and short', was Roger Highfield's reply. But the answer to which Peter – typically – gave pure alpha was Michael Wallace-Hadrill's 'Form a social contract'.

Among historians Peter has one of the largest funds of anecdotes. Some of them are told against himself, with great delight. Once when staying with Christopher Cheney, his host took out a pack of playing cards and said, 'You don't mind my playing Patience? It gives me something to think about while I'm talking to you.' He recounts such tales without a hint of malice; he roars with laughter when he recalls the applications for travel grants which he and Magnus Magnusson made when undergraduates. He received £25 to visit the museums and galleries of Paris, while Magnus received £50 to eat and drink in the same city. Such anecdotes make Peter one of the most convivial of academics, but there is more to them than entertainment value. *Le style c'est l'homme*, and this anecdotalism is indicative of the importance of contact with other scholars and of the exchange of ideas for Peter's own work.

Essentially he fires and is fired by others in conversation and correspondence. This was true even in his primary schooldays, when his old headmaster, E. A. Greening Lamborn, author of *The Story of Architecture in Oxford Stone*, inspired him with an interest in history and buildings. Nor was he discouraged by Greening Lamborn's curt dismissal of a drawing he had made of Oxford's skyline; 'St Mary's is taller than All Saints'. Among his later mentors were Reggie Lennard, V. H. Galbraith, who encouraged him in his early work on Domesday, and the professors he served under: Christopher Cheney at Manchester, Richard Pares at Edinburgh and John Le Patourel at Leeds. In Scandinavia his greatest mentor was Sune Lindquist, and he was later to learn much from Sture Bolin and Nils Ludvig Rasmusson. Yet he was no single scholar's pupil, and indeed he wrote no doctoral thesis, much to the astonishment of his senior colleagues at Manchester. Rather, he talked to the majority of early medieval scholars, including Sir Frank Stenton, to the chagrin of the old man's wife.

As with mentors, so with colleagues and friends, including Eric John and Geoffrey Martin at Manchester, Bertil Almgren and Bengt Schönbäck at

Uppsala, Stuart Hoyt at Minneapolis, Glan Jones at Leeds, and subsequently a younger generation of British and Scandinavian scholars. In part the range of Peter's interests is mirrored in his contacts and friendships. It was with Glan Jones that he organised the seminars on settlement which formed the basis of the collection of essays on *Medieval Settlement: continuity and change*, which he edited, and which influenced much of his more recent thought on Anglo-Saxon England. Predictably, this is a volume which strays outside the normal confines of history; many of his contacts have been experts in related disciplines, for instance Michael Dolley and Stewart Lyon among numismatists, Gillian Fellows-Jensen among place-name scholars, Michael Lapidge among latinists and Richard Hall and Richard Morris among archaeologists. In recent years it has perhaps been his relationship with the archaeologists which has been most fruitful and also most exciting. Were it not for the fact that he pays more attention to their work than do the majority of historians, his provocative quip that archaeology is an expensive way of finding out what we knew already might have gone down like a satanic verse.

His willingness to explore material which historians have usually left to others is nowhere more apparent than in *The Age of the Vikings*, which is effectively a series of free-standing studies, trespassing on the worlds of the archaeologist and the numismatist, as much as they rampage through the territory of the historian. The result was a book which questioned almost every aspect of received opinion about the Vikings, including their cruelty and the destruction they effected, their technology, their numbers and the scale of their settlement. At the same time, in its study of the Anglo-Saxon Chronicle it raised a series of questions about a document whose reliability had too often been taken for granted. As such it was a trail-blazing book from a number of different perspectives and it transformed the field of debate; inevitably it was controversial. My own tutor thought it was full of error, and told me that it was the only book that he had ever written in, because so much needed correction! In fact such an assertion was unwarranted. Nor did the counterblasts worry Peter; more than most historians he was and is willing to change his mind, if just cause is shown – as the second edition of *The Age of the Vikings* revealed. Indeed, if anything, there he was more prepared than he need have been to follow the advice of others. Thus his first instincts about Trelleborg have been proved to be right. For this, as for other reasons, it has been suggested, with as much reason as wit, that if a third edition were ever needed, a reprint of the first would fit the bill.

In fact, of course, *Kings and Vikings* constitutes a return to the subject matter, but from new perspectives; for Peter, if not for all his critics, debate has moved on from the fields covered in *The Age of the Vikings*. This second approach to the Viking Age is a slim volume, perhaps slimmer than it ought to have been. Nevertheless it covers much that its predecessor omitted. Kings, significantly, feature in the title, reflecting interests encouraged by a circus of lectures on Early Medieval Kingship held at Leeds in 1977, and published in the same year. But Alf Smyth's work had also concentrated his mind on the leadership of the Vikings. In addition there is a greater awareness of the Continent, initiated perhaps by a field trip for students which he and his colleague John Cox organised, and which was his first visit to Normandy. (It was also the occasion of his realisation that Norman architecture was not Anglo-Norman. He was later to have the pleasure of surprising Lucien Musset with the distinctly Anglo-Norman architecture of Southwell.) More important, however, for his appreciation of the Frankish dimension of the Viking Age was Michael Wallace-Hadrill's unusually provocative 'Vikings in Francia', as well as the writings of Jinty Nelson. In addition, Kings and Vikings is littered with the evidence of renewed contacts with the landscape and the scholars of Scandinavia.

Since the publication of Kings and Vikings and his retirement from the Chair of Medieval History at Leeds, both in 1982, Scandinavia has become increasingly central to Peter's work. Developing from his earlier publications, and profiting from his friendship with Niels Lund, is his Da Danmark blev Danmark, which constitutes the third volume of a new multi-volume history of Denmark. Then there is also his response to his new home in the book which he and Bibi wrote, and published from their own Viktoria Bokförlag, Innan Alingsås blev Stad. This latter work amounts to a major essay in local history, and provides an indication of Peter's growing awareness of the interest of the territories of the Götar. It is, however, not just a matter of their interest, but also of their importance. While distancing himself with increasing care from extreme interpretations of Västergötland as 'the cradle of Sweden', he has come to appreciate more and more the contribution of the Götar to the formation of the medieval Swedish kingdom.

But the shift to Scandinavia has not just seen a change of geographical horizons. There has also been an exploration of themes which had hitherto been of neglible significance in Peter's work, in particular that of the spread of Christianity. His concern with this topic was signalled first by a series of seminars organised at Gothenburg University, and subsequently by a symposium at Kungälv, which gathered together scholars from a whole range of disciplines, anthropology, archaeology, history, literature and linguistics, for the purpose of discussing the christianisation of Scandinavia. The result was another volume from Viktoria, providing a report on the symposium and a collection of related essays.

While the chief emphasis of Peter's work in recent years has been on matters Scandinavian, this has not been exclusively the case. From Roman Britain to Norman England appeared in 1978, providing an incisive interpretation of Anglo-Saxon history, which begins with the known, the seventh century, before plunging into the mire of the migration period, a chronological trick he was to use later in starting Kings and Vikings in the twelfth century. Pre-Viking Age England was to some extent virgin territory for Peter, although once again he took care to try out his ideas on numerous friends, in particular David Dumville and Patrick Wormald. The second half of the book meant a return to issues which he had begun to consider in the landscape seminars held at Leeds, and also to matters of economy and society which he had first explored in his paper to the Royal Historical Society on 'The Wealth of England in the Eleventh Century'.

At the same time his interests in British regional history have continued. He has always had a commitment to the history of his immediate environment, perhaps because of the influence of Greening Lamborn; the book on Alingsås is merely the most obvious manifestation of this interest. When he was at Birmingham he was editor for the Worcestershire Historical Society; at Leeds he was an enthusiastic supporter of *Northern History*, and he developed more than a cursory knowledge of the Hebrides when he had a house on Mull. More recently he has been at work on York, Cheshire, for the Victoria (sic) County History, and Lincolnshire. It was work on this last-named county that provided him with his chief evidence for a reconsideration of landholding in the pre-Conquest period, which was the subject of his article in the volume of essays he edited to mark the ninth centenary of Domesday Book. Meanwhile, research on Domesday Cheshire was leading him to similar conclusions, causing him, at the same time, to reconsider the basic issue of the Domesday returns.

Domesday was in fact the subject on which Peter initially flexed his muscles. Indeed, before he was associated with Viking studies, he appears to have been known as 'Domesday Sawyer'. He had been inspired by Galbraith to consider the making of Domesday Book, which he did in his first article, in the *English Historical Review* for 1955. From there he moved to the question of the Domesday manuscripts and their place names, and the text and its historians have fascinated him ever since. He can and does talk about John Horace Round with as much zest as he talks about his own acquaintances, friends and mentors. In particular, he delights in recounting the conflicts between Tait and Round over the Cheshire Domesday, and in recording the latter's discomforture. Yet in his introduction to *Domesday Book: a Reassessment* he gives the great Victorian due praise.

There was something ungenerous about Round, which is alien to Peter's nature, witness the delicate criticism of John Le Patourel over Penenden Heath, carefully tucked away in a footnote. Le P was rash enough to promise to stand Peter a meal for every manuscript of the Penenden Heath plea he could find. There were rather more than he bargained for. And Peter had, and has, a great capacity for working through manuscripts.

To the outsider there may seem to be a rift between the historian who trailed his coat so controversially in *The Age of the Vikings*, and the scholar who edited the *Textus Roffensis* and the charters of Burton abbey, and, above all, who compiled the handlist of Anglo-Saxon charters. This can reasonably be seen as one of the most significant contributions to Anglo-Saxon history of the last half century, and after twenty years the list of addenda and corrigenda is still minute. In a sense there is, indeed, a distinction to be drawn between the iconoclastic articles and surveys and the painstaking labour of the editions and the handlist. And yet there are ways in which the methods of work are similar. Discussion and argument underlie all his oeuvre; *The Charters of Burton Abbey* benefited enormously from his readiness to seek advice from others, among them Michael Lapidge and Simon Keynes, despite his own position as Secretary to the British Academy/ Royal Historical Society Committee on Anglo-Saxon Charters, and his great familiarity with the whole range of charter material. But then Peter is not a man to stand on his own importance or his institutional position, even when he might reasonably do so.

Anglo-Saxon Charters: an annotated list and bibliography has not been the only major bibliographical undertaking with which Peter has been involved. It was as a result of a year spent as Visiting Professor at the University of Minnesota in 1966–7 that he and Stuart Hoyt decided to found the *International Medieval Bibliography*. An office was set up in Leeds, and the first volume appeared in 1968. Since then a group of committed editors and secretaries has ensured that the bibliography has fulfilled the expectations of its founders, in becoming an indispensable tool for research.

The reference works and the editions for which Peter has been reponsible may well prove to be his greatest contribution to scholarship, but his other writings have served dramatically to push debates forward. In so doing they have transformed the historiographical landscape, and have themselves become familiar monuments. They are not, however, monuments which Peter himself is concerned to shore up at any cost. Instead he has turned his hand to creating new vistas, occasionally to the alarm of old sparring partners, like David Wilson, who discover themselves momentarily to be in agreement with him. Moreover, by constantly considering new and reconsidering old ground, he has ensured that his critics are faced with a moving target. Such mobility is both a strength and a weakness – ideas are sometimes sketched rather than worked up; publication of them can fall short of the perceptions which have animated numerous conversations and arguments. But then there is still the other half of the oeuvre, the editions and the handlist.

PETER HAYES SAWYER: A BIBLIOGRAPHY

1955
'The "Original Returns" and Domesday Book', *EHR* 70, pp. 177–97.

1956
'The Place-names of the Domesday Manuscripts', *Bulletin of the John Rylands Library* 38, pp. 483–506.

1957
The Textus Roffensis, vol. 1 (Copenhagen).

1958
'The Density of the Danish Settlement in England', *University of Birmingham Historical Journal* 6, pp. 1–17.

1960
Evesham A, a Domesday Text, Worcester Historical Society, *Miscellany* 1 (Worcester), pp. 3–36.

1962
The Age of the Vikings (London); 2nd edn 1971.
The Textus Roffensis, vol. 2 (Copenhagen).

1965
'The Wealth of England in the Eleventh Century', *TRHS* 15, pp. 145–64.

1968
Anglo-Saxon Charters: an annotated list and bibliography, Royal Historical Society (London).

1969
'The Two Viking Ages of Britain', *Medieval Scandinavia* 2, pp. 163–76, 203–7.

1970
'The Vikings and the Irish Sea', in *The Irish Sea Province in Archaeology and History*, ed. D. Moore (Cardiff), pp. 86–92.

1973
'Baldersby, Borup and Bruges: The Rise of Northern Europe', *University of Leeds Review* 16, pp. 75–96.

1974
'Anglo-Saxon Settlement: the documentary evidence', in *Anglo-Saxon Settlement and Landscape*, ed. T. Rowley, BAR 6, pp. 108–19.

1975

'Charters of the Reform Movement: The Worcester Archive', in *Tenth-Century Studies*, ed. D. Parsons (London), pp. 84–93.

'The Charters of Burton Abbey and the Unification of England', *Northern History* 10, pp. 28–39.

1976

ed. *Medieval Settlement: continuity and change* (London).

'Introduction: Early Medieval English Settlement', in *Medieval Settlement: continuity and change* (London), pp. 1–7.

'Harald Fairhair and the British Isles', in *Les Vikings et leur civilisation*, ed. R. Boyer (Paris), pp. 105–9.

1977

ed. with I. N. Wood, *Early Medieval Kingship* (Leeds).

'Kings and Merchants', in *Early Medieval Kingship* (Leeds).

1978

From Roman Britain to Norman England (London).

The Charters of Burton Abbey (British Academy, London).

'Some sources for the history of Viking Northumbria', in *Viking Age York and the North*, ed. R. A. Hall, CBA Research Report 27 (London), pp. 3–7.

'Wics, Kings and Vikings', in *The Vikings*, ed. T. Andersson and K. I. Sandred (Uppsala), pp. 23–31.

1979

ed. *Names, Words and Graves: Early Medieval Settlement* (Leeds).

ed. *English Medieval Settlement* (London).

'Medieval English Settlement: New Interpretations', in *English Medieval Settlement* (London).

1981

'Conquest and Colonisation: Scandinavians in the Danelaw and in Normandy', in *Proceedings of the Eighth Viking Congress*, ed. H. Bekker-Nielsen, P. Foote and O. Olsen (Odense), pp. 123–31.

'Fairs and Markets in Early Medieval England', in *Danish Medieval History: New Currents*, ed. N. Skyum-Nielsen and N. Lund (Copenhagen), pp. 153–68.

1982

Kings and Vikings (London); Swedish translation, *Kungar och vikingar* (Stockholm, 1985).

'The Vikings and Ireland', in *Ireland in Early Medieval Europe*, ed. D. Whitelock, R. McKitterick and D. Dumville (Cambridge), pp. 345–61.

'The Causes of the Viking Age', in *The Vikings*, ed. R. T. Farrell (London), pp. 1–7.

'The Viking Perspective', *Journal of Baltic Studies* 13 , pp. 177–84.

1983

'The Royal *tun* in Anglo-Saxon England', in *Ideal and Reality in Frankish and Anglo-Saxon Society*, ed. P. Wormald (Oxford), pp. 273–99.

'English Archaeology before the Conquest: a historian's view', in *25 Years of Medieval Archaeology*, ed. D. A. Hinton (Sheffield), pp. 44–7.

'Settlement and Power among the Svear in the Vendel Period', in *Vendel Period Studies*, ed. J. P. Lamm and H.-Å. Nordström (Stockholm), pp. 117–22.

'The Dark Ages', in *The Ages of Britain*, ed. P. Crookston (London), pp. 43–54.

1984

'Boundary Treaties and State Formation', in *Fra Stamme til Stat, Symposium på Sostrup Kloster 23.–25. maj 1984* (Copenhagen), pp. 115–24.

'Vikingar i öst och väst', in *Den dolda historien*, ed. R. Ambjörnson and D. Gaunt (Stockholm), pp. 334–44.

'Ohthere and Viking Age Trade', in *Two Voyagers at the Court of King Alfred*, ed. N. Lund (York), pp. 43–55; Danish version, *Ottar og Wulfstan: to rejsebeskrivelser fra vikingetiden* (Roskilde, 1985), pp. 45–57.

1985

with B. Sawyer, *Innan Alingsås blev Stad: en västsvenskt gränsbygds äldsta historia* (Alingsås).

ed. *Domesday Book: a Reassessment* (London).

'Domesday Studies since 1886', in *Domesday Book: a Reassessment* (London), pp. 1–4.

'1066–1086: A Tenurial Revolution?', in *Domesday Book: a Reassessment* (London), pp. 71–85.

'Birka, the Baltic and Beyond', in *Society and Trade in the Baltic during the Viking Age*, ed. S-O. Lindquist, Acta Visbyensia 7 (Visby), pp. 165–70.

'The Anglo-Norman Village', in *Medieval Villages: a review of current work*, ed. D. Hooke, Oxford Committee for Archaeology, pp. 3–6.

'Fairs and Markets in England and Scandinavia in the Early Middle Ages', *Chronica* 37, pp. 6–11.

1986

'Early Fairs and Markets in England and Scandinavia', in *The Market in History*, ed. B. L. Anderson and A. J. H. Latham (London), pp. 59–77.

'Anglo-Scandinavian Trade in the Viking Age and After', in *Anglo-Saxon Monetary History*, ed. M. A. S. Blackburn (Leicester), pp. 185–99.

'The Anglo-Saxon Inheritance', in *Angli e Sassoni al di qua e al di là del mare*, Settimane di studio del Centro italiano di studi sull'alto medioevo 32 (Spoleto), pp. 863–83.

'The Christianisation of Scandinavia', in *Beretning fra Femte tværfaglige Vikingesymposium*, ed. T. Kisbye and E. Roesdahl (Copenhagen), pp. 23–37.

1987

ed. with B. Sawyer and I. N. Wood, *The Christianization of Scandinavia: report of a symposium held at Kungälv, Sweden, 4–9 August 1985* (Alingsås).

'The process of Scandinavian Christianization in the tenth and eleventh centuries' (Alingsås), pp. 68–87.

with A. T. Thacker, 'The Cheshire Domesday', in *The Victoria History of the County of Chester*, vol. 1, ed. B. E. Harris and A. T. Thacker (Oxford), pp. 293–341.

'Translation of the Text' (of the Cheshire Domesday), in *The Victoria History of the County of Chester*, vol. 1, pp. 342–370.

'Medieval Technology: sources, causes and effects', *Polhem* 5, pp. 141–8.

'The Bloodfeud in Fact and Fiction', *Tradition og Historieskriving*, ed. K. Hastrup and P. Meulengracht Sørensen, Acta Jutlandica 63:2, Humanistisk serie 61 (Århus), pp. 27–38.

'Ethelred II, Olaf Tryggvason, and the conversion of Norway', *Scandinavian Studies* 59, pp. 299–307.

1988

Da Danmark blev Danmark Fra ca. 700 til ca. 1050, Danmarks Historien, ed. O. Olsen, vol. 3 (Copenhagen).

'Parishes and Dioceses in twelfth-century Scandinavia', in *St Magnus Cathedral and Orkney's Twelfth-Century Renaissance*, ed. B. Crawford (Aberdeen), pp. 36–45.

' "Landamæri I": the supposed eleventh-century Boundary treaty between Denmark and Sweden', in *Festschrift til Olaf Olsen* (Copenhagen), pp. 165–70.

1989

The Making of Sweden (Alingsås).

'Knut, Sweden, and Sigtuna', in *Avstamp för en ny Sigtunaforskning*, ed. S. Tesch (Sigtuna), pp. 88–93.

'The effects of Viking activity on Scandinavian society', in *Les Mondes Normandes, VIIIe–XIIe siècles*.

THE FRANKS AND SUTTON HOO

Ian Wood

The discoveries at Sutton Hoo have never been central to the writings of Peter Sawyer, and yet there is much about them which might easily have attracted his attention. They pose problems of archaeological and historical interpretation, they raise issues relating to the history of kingship, and they seem to link England and Scandinavia; all of which are fields in which he has made his mark. Had he directed his attention to the interpretation of the site and its finds, the assumptions that underlie many assertions about them would have been exposed with a clarity that few scholars of his generation have equalled, and the interpretation of seventh-century East Anglia would have been all the more interesting as a result.[1]

Because most literary evidence from the Early Middle Ages concerns kings, the aristocracy and the Church, historians have tended to pay attention to the sites of archaeologists only when they are high-status or feature in the written record, and, equally, it is when their sites are high-status that archaeologists are most inclined to turn to historical texts. There are, of course, moments when Dark Age law casts light on such matters as burial custom, or when grave-finds elucidate matters of social structure, but more often than not history and archaeology have been combined in order to create, or at least shore up, a historical narrative. This has certainly been the case at Sutton Hoo.

For some scholars Mound One has now become, without question, the burial place or cenotaph of Redwald, king of East Anglia; the reasons for this are Redwald's status as 'bretwalda', which is apparently appropriate for the treasure found in the mound, his position as a first generation christian who subsequently lapsed, which explains the mixture of pagan and christian objects in the treasure, and the chronology of the coins, which appear to allow for a burial date around 625. This is said to be compatible with what can be deduced from Bede about the date of Redwald's death.[2]

---

[1] For one of Peter Sawyer's few comments on Sutton Hoo, see *From Roman Britain to Norman England* (London, 1978), p. 40. I am indebted to Martin Carver, Philip Dixon, Angela Care Evans, Richard Morris, Janet L. Nelson, Leslie Webster and Susan Youngs, all of whom read and commented on earlier drafts of this paper; they cannot be held responsible for the more extreme assertions that follow. If responsibility lies with anyone, it is with Peter Sawyer himself, who first encouraged me to write and publish my paper on *The Merovingian North Sea* (Alingsås, 1983), to which this is intended as a sequel.

[2] The clearest statement of this case is R. L. S. Bruce-Mitford, 'The Sutton Hoo ship

At first sight these criteria may seem to present a persuasive case, but each of them is open to question. To begin, there is the problem of the relationship between Redwald's status and the wealth of Mound One. According to Bede he was one of a number of kings 'who exercised authority over all the southern kings of the Angles and their provinces, which are divided by the river Humber and the boundaries adjacent to it from the northern ones'.[3] The word 'bretwalda', which seems to be no more than an attempt by a late ninth-century chronicler to offer a shorthand translation of Bede's phrase,[4] should be avoided, since it appears to institutionalise a type of authority for which Bede may have had no single institutional term. All we know is that Bede regarded Redwald as being one of a number of kings who exercised power over other monarchs.[5] His grave may well have been richer than those of rulers of inferior status, but we lack other royal graves which might allow us to conclude that Mound One really is the burial or cenotaph of a high-king.[6] It is not even certain that it was originally the richest of the Sutton Hoo mounds.

Leaving aside the question of the status and wealth of the man commemorated by Mound One, there is the question of religion. Clearly the presence of christian goods in a grave which has affinities with earlier pagan burials suggests that in religious terms the mound belongs to a period of transition. It is not possible, however, to use the grave-goods to determine the religion of the man they commemorate; the Saulos/Paulos spoons could in theory have been acquired by someone with little or no contact with Christianity.[7] Equally there is nothing in the treasure which could not have been owned by a christian. The notion that the grave reflects exactly the religious attitudes of the backsliding Redwald is not so much an objective observation, as an idea based on modern assumptions about pagan and Christian burial practices, which cannot be substantiated from the historical or the archaeological record.[8] And if the mound and its treasure indicate nothing more than a date in the conversion period, Redwald was by no means the only known member of the royal family to live through the christianisation of East Anglia. His successors were not brought up as christians; according to Bede, Eorpwald was converted by Edwin of Northum-

---

burial; some foreign connections', in *Settimane di Studio del Centro Italiano sull'Alto Medioevo* 32, *Angli e Sassoni al di qua e al di là del mare* (Spoleto, 1986). p. 142; see also pp. 150, 153, 162, 164, 181, 208–9.

[3]   Bede, HE II 5, ed. C. Plummer, *Baedae Opera Historica* (Oxford, 1896).

[4]   *Anglo-Saxon Chronicle* MS A, s.a. 827, ed. J. M. Bately, *The Anglo-Saxon Chronicle: a collaborative edition*, vol. 3, MS A (Cambridge, 1986), p. 42. MS A is the only version to preserve this reading; see p. cxvii, n. 332.

[5]   Bede, HE II 5.

[6]   This was the salutary observation of J. M. Wallace-Hadrill, 'The Graves of Kings', *Studi Medievali* 3rd series, I 1 (1960), pp. 177–94, reprinted with additional comments in id., *Early Medieval History* (Oxford, 1975), pp. 39–59.

[7]   A. C. Evans, *The Sutton Hoo Ship Burial* (London, 1986), pp. 60–3 provides a useful comment on the interpretation of the spoons.

[8]   For some recent general comments on the problem of identifying paganism and christianity in graves, see E. James, *The Franks* (Oxford, 1988), pp. 137–45.

bria,[9] and Sigberct was converted on the continent.[10] Either of these East Anglian kings might have been buried or commemorated with the grave goods appropriate to their status, and if it is objected that Sigberct had been a monk, it
should be remembered that those who would have presided over his exequies
probably included men who dragged him out of his monastery to lead them in
battle against Penda.[11] Indeed, Sutton Hoo is likely to tell us more about those
who organised the burial or commemoration, than about the man buried or
commemorated there. What would have been at stake was the view taken of the
stirps regia and the gens by the living, not by the dead.

Turning to the detailed evidence for Redwald's reign, which, combined with
the dates of the coins, apparently provides the chronological basis for associating
him with Mound One, once again the case is at best one hypothesis among
many. The standard discussion of the coins concludes that the latest of them are
likely to date from c.625,[12] which is said to be the time of Redwald's death. The
date for this last event has to be calculated from Bede's accounts of Redwald's
successors, and of the bishops of the East Anglian kingdom. Of these Boniface
was consecrated by archbishop Honorius, who died in 653;[13] his predecessor,
Thomas, had been bishop for five years, and before him Felix was bishop for
seventeen years; that is Felix must have been consecrated in about 631, and since
he became bishop in the time of Sigberct,[14] the latter must already have been
king by then. Dovetailing nicely with this is the information, first, that Sigberct's
brother or perhaps half-brother, Eorpwald, was converted by Edwin,[15] who is
thought to have been baptised in 627;[16] second, that his conversion was followed
by his murder at the hands of the pagan Ricberht;[17] and third, that this murder
took place three years before Sigberct's accession.[18] Eorpwald's death must, therefore, be dated to 627–8 and Sigberct's accession to 630–1. The date of Eorpwald's
accession, however, remains problematic since that we do not know how long he
ruled as a pagan, whilst the last recorded action of his father and predecessor,
Redwald, is his leadership at the battle of the River Idle, dated to 616/7.[19] To
place the latter's death as late as 625 is pure guesswork.

Further, although the latest coin in the Sutton Hoo purse is said to date from
c.625, other chronologies have been put forward, so that on the one hand there

9   Bede, HE II 15.
10 Bede, HE II 15, III 18.
11 Bede, HE III 18.
12 J. P. C. Kent in R. L. S. Bruce-Mitford, ed., The Sutton Hoo Ship Burial, vol. 1 (London,
1975), pp. 588–607. But see also D. Brown, 'The dating of the Sutton Hoo coins', in D.
Brown, J. Campbell, S. C. Hawkes, eds, Anglo-Saxon Studies in Archaeology and History 2,
BAR BS 92 (Oxford, 1981), pp. 71–86.
13 For what follows see Plummer, ed., Baedae Opera Historica, vol. 2, p. 106; Bede, HE III
20.
14 Bede, HE II 15, III 18.
15 Bede, HE II 15.
16 Bede, HE II 9, 13–14.
17 Bede, HE II 15.
18 Bede, HE II 15.
19 Bede, HE II 12; Plummer, ed., Baedae Opera Historica, vol. 2, pp. 66, 98–9.

is a case for seeing the most recent tremisses as being minted c.622–9, with at least one dating from c.626–9,[20] while on the other there is a strong possibility that all the coins had been minted by 613.[21] If this were the case, the coins could conceivably have been buried with Redwald, even if he did die some while before his traditional death-date of c.625. Nevertheless, 613 only provides a *terminus post quem* for the collection, and it is possible that they were collected and buried at a later date. If, however, the most recent of the coins belonged to the late 620s, they could scarcely have been available in Redwald's reign.

Among the factors which have not been taken into account in concluding that Redwald is the man commemorated in Mound One is the simple one that there were times in the early seventh century when East Anglia was ruled over by more than one king. Bede, for instance, records the joint-rulership of Sigberct and his relative Ecgric;[22] he also reveals that, although Sigberct granted the land of *Cnobheresburg* to Fursey, the buildings of the monastery were erected under the patronage of Anna, who was king of the *provincia*, and by other nobles.[23] Further, Bede recounts the baptism, possibly in Anna's time, of Suidhelm of Essex, whose godfather was Anna's brother, the East Anglian king Ædilwald.[24] Another brother, who succeeded Anna in the kingship, was Æthilhere, one of the casualties at the Winwaed.[25] Alongside this information it is possible to set that of the Anglian genealogies, which list, in descending order, Tyttla, Eni, Ethilric, Alduulf and Ælfwald.[26] Tyttla is recorded as Redwald's father by Bede,[27] who names Anna as being Eni's son,[28] and Alduulf as the son of Hild's sister, Heresuid.[29] It is clear, therefore, that there was a very sizeable royal family, and that rulership was not necessarily confined to one member of it at a time.

If a simple chronological correlation between Mound One and an individual

---

[20] Brown, 'The dating of the Sutton Hoo coins', p. 84.
[21] A. Stahl, 'The date of the Sutton Hoo coins' (forthcoming). I was fortunate enough to hear Alan Stahl deliver his paper at Kalamazoo, and to be able to revise my own ideas before trying them out at the same conference.
[22] Bede, HE III 18.
[23] Bede, HE III 19; on the problem of identifying *Cnobheresburg* see J. Campbell, 'Bede's Words for Places', in P. H. Sawyer, ed., *Names, Words and Graves: Early Medieval Settlement* (Leeds, 1979), p. 36, reprinted in Campbell, *Essays in Anglo-Saxon History* (London, 1986), p. 101; see also the negative evidence of the Burgh Castle excavations; S. Johnson, *Burgh Castle, Excavations by Charles Green 1958–61*, East Anglian Archaeology Report no. 20 (1983), pp. 119–20.
[24] Bede, HE III 22.
[25] Bede, HE III 24; on the punctuation and meaning of this passage see J. O. Prestwich, 'King Æthelhere and the battle of the Winwæd', EHR 83 (1968), pp. 89–95.
[26] D. N. Dumville, 'The Anglian Collection of genealogies and regnal lists', ASE 5 (1976), p. 37.
[27] Bede, HE II 15.
[28] Bede, HE III 18.
[29] Bede, HE IV 23; Plummer, ed., *Baedae Opera Historica*, vol. 2. pp. 106–7, is both confused and confusing here; see F. M. Stenton, 'The East Anglian Kings of the Seventh Century', in P. Clemoes, ed., *The Anglo-Saxons; Studies presented to Bruce Dickins* (London, 1959), pp. 43–52, reprinted in Stenton, *Preparatory to Anglo-Saxon England* (Oxford, 1970), pp. 394–402.

member of the East Anglian royal family is not immediately possible, it may be that there is more to be gained by opening up the area of historical enquiry to make the approach more compatible with that of some of the more general observations of the archaeologists, who, in broad terms, have seen Sutton Hoo in a variety of contexts, Swedish, Kentish and Germanic, while at the same time recognising the importance of the presence of objects from the eastern Mediterranean.[30]

Of these contexts, the first is the one that is least reflected in the historical record. The assertion that the royal dynasty of East Anglia came from Sweden has never been more than a chimera.[31] It depends on the identification of the Wuffingas with the Wylfings of *Beowulf*, and on the assumption that the latter were Svear rather than Geats. Unfortunately *Beowulf* can scarcely be accepted as a historical source relevant to the seventh century,[32] and even if it were to be, there would still be no reason for accepting either proposition; there is nothing in the Anglian genealogies to suggest that the Wuffingas and the Wylfings were one and the same people,[33] nor can the Wylfings be localised in the region around Vendel and Valsgärde.[34] Nevertheless, the parallels between the burials and deposits at those two sites on the one hand and Sutton Hoo on the other do suggest some common background, but one which should be interpreted without recourse to hypotheses concerning the origins of the Wuffingas. The crucial questions here must be those relating to the mobility of craftsmen and high status goods, and to the problems of a common Germanic culture to which both Sutton Hoo and the Vendel period graves belong. Other parallel finds, such as the horse-trappings from Eschwege in Germany,[35] may suggest that the Swedish material at Sutton Hoo is to be understood, at least partially, in a continental context.

The grave goods, however, also point to further, more easily understood, contexts. The complete assemblage of the Sutton Hoo finds suggest that the mounds belong to the same milieu as the other great princely burials of Broomfield, Taplow and Caenby,[36] whilst the garnet and gold work implies particular connections with Kent.[37] Moreover, here the archaeological evidence is complemented by the historical record. Redwald himself is said to have visited Kent,

---

[30] See in particular M. Carver, 'Sutton Hoo in context', in *Settimane di Studio* 32 (1986), pp. 102–8.
[31] Crucial here is R. T. Farrell, 'Beowulf, Swedes and Geats', *Saga-Book* 18 (1970–3), pp. 220–96.
[32] See the discussions in C. Chase, ed., *The Dating of Beowulf* (Toronto, 1981).
[33] Farrell, 'Beowulf, Swedes and Geats', pp. 271–3; for the genealogies, see Dumville, 'Kingship, genealogies and regnal lists', in P. H. Sawyer and I. N. Wood, eds, *Early Medieval Kingship* (Leeds, 1977) pp. 90–1.
[34] Farrell, 'Beowulf, Swedes and Geats', pp. 245–50, 271–2.
[35] K. Sippel, 'Ein merowingisches Kammergrab mit Pferdegeschirr aus Eschwege, Werra-Meissner-Kreis (Hessen)', *Germania* 65 (1) (1987), pp. 147–53.
[36] The parallels with Broomfield and Taplow are drawn by Evans, *The Sutton Hoo Ship Burial*, pp. 39, 66, 69, 78, 82, 98, 111, 112, 114, 115, 116, following the discussions in Bruce-Mitford, *The Sutton Hoo Ship Burial*, 3 vols (London, 1976–83).
[37] M. Carver, 'Sutton Hoo in context', pp. 106–7.

where he was converted,[38] whilst Æthelbehrt, like Redwald after him, was dominant over the other Anglian kings south of the Humber,[39] and it was probably from this position of strength that he induced his East Anglian neighbour to accept christianity. Although nothing can be known for certain about the earliest phase of christianity in the East Anglian kingdom, a juxtaposition of the accounts of Edwin's exile at Redwald's court in Bede and in the Anonymous Life of Gregory the Great suggests that Paulinus was active there, presumably deputed from Canterbury.[40] Later, Sigberct received his bishop, Felix, from archbishop Honorius.[41] The political and religious histories of Kent and East Anglia overlapped.

Perhaps surprisingly, however, the evidence for East Anglian contacts with Merovingian Gaul in the early seventh century is stronger than that for those with Kent, in both the historical and archaeological record. The only objects from Mound One whose precise origins can be determined other than on a typological basis are the coins and the Anastasius dish, the latter coming from Constantinople and the former from the Frankish kingdom.[42] Bede's narrative provides at least some clues to an understanding of the background to the presence of the Merovingian tremisses in the Sutton Hoo purse.

The earliest reference to contacts between East Anglia and Francia comes with the record of the flight of Sigberct to the Merovingian kingdom, occasioned by fear of Redwald, his father or stepfather.[43] This is presumably to be dated to the period before Redwald's conversion, at the instigation of Æthelbehrt, that is to the years before 616, since, according to Bede, the young prince was converted in exile. On his return he determined to christianise his own kingdom. When he turned to Canterbury for help, the missionary sent to him by archbishop Honorius was Felix, a Burgundian.[44] Nor was this the limit of Frankish influence on the new king, who, again according to Bede, instituted a school along Frankish lines with the aid of Felix, here following the traditions of Kent.[45] At an ecclesiastical level it appears that Frankish and Kentish influences were closely intertwined.

Further indications of the Frankish connection can be seen at the end of Sigberct's reign, and during that of his successor. For instance, the Irish monk Fursey left for Francia possibly at the time of Sigberct's death,[46] and he was followed, during the reign of Anna, by his brother Foilan, who went first to his

[38] Bede, HE II 15.
[39] Bede, HE II 5.
[40] Bede, HE II 12; The Earliest Life of Gregory the Great by an anonymous monk of Whitby 16, ed. B. Colgrave (Kansas, 1968); see also pp. 50, 149, n. 63, 150, n. 67.
[41] Bede, HE III 18.
[42] Bruce-Mitford and S. M. Youngs, in Bruce-Mitford, The Sutton Hoo Ship Burial, vol. 3 (London, 1983), pp. 28–32; Kent, in Bruce-Mitford, The Sutton Hoo Ship Burial, vol. 1, pp. 588–607.
[43] Bede, HE III 18.
[44] Bede, HE II 15, III 18.
[45] Bede, HE III 18.
[46] Bede, HE III 19; Vita Fursei 29, ed. W. W. Heist, Vitae Sanctorum Hiberniae, Subsidia Hagiographica 28 (Brussels, 1965); for a discussion of the circumstances of Fursey's depar-

shrine at Peronne.[47] These migrations indicate regular contact with Merovingian Gaul, as also does the presence in Francia of Anna's daughters, Saethryd and Æthilberg, both of whom became abbesses of Faremoutiers-en-Brie,[48] while one more member of the royal family, Heresuid, the sister of Hild and mother of the East Anglian king Alduulf, entered the newly re-established nunnery at Chelles,[49] where Hild contemplated following her.[50] Another English princess to enter Faremoutiers was Earcongota, daughter of Earconberht king of Kent, and perhaps great-granddaughter of the Frankish mayor of the palace, Erchinoald.[51] There were several family links between the Kentish royal family and the Merovingians, to whom Erchinoald was related, but among the Anglo-Saxon princesses in Frankish monasteries Earcongota was unusual in coming from Kent; what is striking about the majority of these ladies is their East Anglian connections.

It may also be that these contacts should be considered alongside the history of the Merovingian queen Balthild. She first appears as an Anglo-Saxon slave in the household of this same Erchinoald, whose daughter apparently married Eadbald of Kent.[52] He was also Fursey's chief continental patron, which suggests an East Anglian connection.[53] Among Fursey's other patrons was the king, Clovis II,[54] whom Balthild later married.[55] As queen, she patronised Faremoutiers and (re)founded Chelles,[56] the very nunneries to which East Anglian princesses were drawn, and she herself entered the second of these foundations after she was deprived of power.[57] All in all there is a very close correlation between the people and places associated with East Anglians on the continent, and those associated with Balthild.

Nor was Balthild the only seventh-century Merovingian queen to be identified as a Saxon; Nanthild, the wife of Dagobert I, is so described in the *Liber Historiae Francorum*.[58] Her name, however, seems to be Frankish, and even if it

---

ture, see D. Whitelock, 'The pre-Viking Age Church in East Anglia', *Anglo-Saxon England* 1 (1972), p. 6.

[47] *Vita Fursei* 30; *Additamentum Nivialense de Fuilano*, ed. B. Krusch, MGH SRM 4 (Hannover, 1902); Plummer, ed., *Baedae Opera Historica*, vol. 2, p. 173; Whitelock, 'The pre-Viking Church in East Anglia', p. 6.

[48] Bede, *HE* III 8; Whitelock, 'The pre-Viking Church in East Anglia', p. 8.

[49] Bede, *HE* IV 23.

[50] Bede, *HE* IV 23.

[51] Bede, *HE* III 8; J. Campbell, 'The First Century of Christianity in England', in id., *Essays in Anglo-Saxon History*, p. 56. On Earcongota's Frankish descent see F. M. Stenton, *Anglo-Saxon England*, 3rd edn (Oxford, 1971), p. 61, and K-F. Werner, 'Les rouages de l'administration', in P. Périn and L-C. Feffer, eds, *La Neustrie* (Créteil, 1985), p. 42. I am indebted to Jinty Nelson for drawing my attention to Werner's persuasive interpretation of the admittedly late evidence.

[52] *Vita Balthildis* 2–3, ed. B. Krusch, MGH SRM 2 (Hannover, 1888), where Erchinoald also tries to marry Balthild; on Erchinoald's other English connections see Werner, 'Les rouages de l'administration', p. 42.

[53] *Vita Fursei* 29.

[54] *Vita Fursei* 29.

[55] *Vita Balthildis* 3.

[56] *Vita Balthildis* 7, 8.

[57] *Vita Balthildis* 10.

[58] *Liber Historiae Francorum* 42, ed. Krusch, MGH SRM 2; in *The Merovingian North Sea*,

were Saxon, her place of origin could have been Saxony rather than England; her husband was certainly interested in the lands east of the Rhine.[59] Nevertheless he also had his contacts with England; Sigberct of East Anglia was in Francia during his lifetime,[60] whilst Edwin's widow sent her children to him for safekeeping.[61] Further, Nanthild was the mother of Clovis II, Balthild's husband,[62] and she herself acted as one of two regents, alongside first Aega and later Erchinoald, Fursey's patron and Balthild's master, during her son's minority.[63] It is possible that she played a role in the development of relations between England and the continent in the period leading up to the arrival of Fursey and the emergence of Balthild.

The Frankish background to the continental associations of the East Anglian Church can usefully be explored further. In part this background is associated with the Irishman Columbanus and his Frankish disciples. Columbanus himself had a bad press in England. A meeting with the Irish bishop Dagan and perhaps with Columbanus was enough to convince Laurentius, Mellitus and Justus that the Irish were no more orthodox than the Britons in some respects, and it induced them to write a letter of admonition to Ireland.[64] Nevertheless it was Columbanus and his successor as abbot of Luxeuil, Eustasius, who inspired Burgundofara to found the nunnery of Faremoutiers,[65] which was to be so influential in the history of English female piety.[66] It may also be that Felix should be seen within the context of Columbanus's disciples, since he came from Burgundy,[67] the north of which was deeply influenced by Luxeuil.[68] If this were so it would help to explain the establishment of links between Faremoutiers and East Anglia.

There is, however, another aspect of the religious developments associated with Columbanus's followers which may be relevant to an understanding of Felix's presence in England. Of those influenced by Columbanus, perhaps the

---

p. 17, where Nanthild is erroneously said to be Chlothar II's wife, I was less sanguine about the possibility of her coming from England. In a personal communication of 1983 Michael Wallace-Hadrill expressed his bewilderment about Nanthild's origins to me, whilst Jinty Nelson has subsequently urged me to reconsider the issue.

[59] Fredegar IV 58, 68, 72, 74–5, ed. J. M. Wallace-Hadrill, *The Fourth Book of the Chronicle of Fredegar* (London, 1960).

[60] Bede, HE III 18.

[61] Bede, HE II 20.

[62] Fredegar IV 76.

[63] Fredegar IV 79–80, 84.

[64] Bede, HE II 4.

[65] Jonas, *Vita Columbani* I 26, II 7, ed. Krusch, MGH SRM 4 (Hannover, 1902).

[66] Bede, HE III 8; Campbell, 'The First Century of Christianity in England', p. 57.

[67] Bede, HE II 15; J. M. Wallace-Hadrill, 'Rome and the early English Church: some questions of transmission', *Settimane di Studio* 7 (2) (Spoleto, 1960), p. 530, reprinted in id., *Early Medieval History*, p. 122; Whitelock, 'The pre-Viking Church in East Anglia', p. 5; Campbell, 'The First Century of Christianity in England', pp. 58–9.

[68] I. N. Wood, 'A prelude to Columbanus; the monastic achievement in the Burgundian territories', in H. B. Clarke and M. Brennan, eds, *Columbanus and Merovingian Monasticism*, BAR, IS 113 (Oxford, 1981), pp. 18–19; see the map in F. Prinz, 'Columbanus, the Frankish nobility and the territories east of the Rhine', ibid., p. 74.

most significant figure was Amandus,[69] who was among the earliest western missionaries to develop an ideology of mission.[70] Known traditionally as the apostle of Belgium, he played an outstanding role in the evangelisation of north-eastern Francia, in which policy he was backed by Dagobert.[71] He is also said to have wished to work as a missionary in England.[72] The chronological coincidence of the careers of Amandus and Felix may suggest that the latter's work in East Anglia should be seen as an extension of the process of evangelisation already underway in the region of the Scheldt. Further, the association of Amandus with Dagobert, husband of the Saxon Nanthild and father of Clovis II, who himself married the Saxon Balthild, might encourage the speculation that the Merovingians themselves had an interest in the expansion of Christianity in East Anglia, and that the interest was originally stimulated by the presence of the exiled Sigberct, who was converted in Francia, and was followed up by the deputation of the Burgundian Felix, who was to become Sigberct's missionary bishop.

Quite separate from all this are the careers of Fursey and his brothers. Although Cnobheresburg was founded with Sigberct's help and endowed by Anna, the father of Saethryd and Æthilberg, later abbesses of Faremoutiers,[73] and although the Irishmen were connected through Erchinoald with the world of Balthild,[74] there is nothing to suggest that their Frankish foundations were in contact with Luxeuil and its offshoots.[75] Fursey's own migration to Francia, and the subsequent movements of Foilan, when juxtaposed against the presence of English princesses at Faremoutiers and Chelles, are thus an indication of the diversity of contacts between East Anglia and the Merovingian kingdom.

None of this material impinges obviously on an understanding of Mound One at Sutton Hoo, but it might provide something of a context for the presence of Merovingian objects in East Anglia. The ecclesiastical evidence, however, relates to the reigns of Sigberct and Anna, and not to those of Redwald or Eorpwald. This is not to say that there was no contact between East Anglia and Francia during Redwald's lifetime. The name Sigberct, essentially the Frankish name Sigibert, common in the Merovingian royal family,[76] may indicate that Redwald married a Frankish princess, as did Æthelberht,[77] or the descendant of

---

[69] I. N. Wood, 'The Vita Columbani and Merovingian hagiography', Peritia 1 (1982), p. 68; J. M. Wallace-Hadrill, The Frankish Church (Oxford, 1983), pp. 72–3.
[70] W. Fritze, 'Universalis gentium confessio', Frühmittelalterliche Studien 3 (1969), pp. 88–96.
[71] Vita Amandi 15, 17, ed. Krusch, MGH SRM 5 (Hannover, 1910).
[72] Vita Amandi ed. B. Krusch, MGH SRM 5, p. 440, n. 2; see Campbell, 'The First Century of Christianity in England', p. 58.
[73] Bede, HE III 19.
[74] Vita Fursei 29–30; Additamentum Nivialense de Fuilano.
[75] I. N. Wood, 'The Vita Columbani and Merovingian hagiography', pp. 69–70.
[76] Cf. Sigibert I, son of Chlothar I, Sigibert II son of Theuderic II, Sigibert III, son of Dagobert I; also the Ripuarian king Sigibert the Lame.
[77] Gregory of Tours, Liber Historiarum IV 26, IX 26, ed. B. Krusch and W. Levison, MGH SRM I 1 (Hannover, 1951); Bede, HE I 25; on the marriage of Æthelberht and Bertha see Wood, The Merovingian North Sea, pp. 15–16.

one, as did Edwin.[78] Sigberct's flight to Francia provides a further indication of such a link,[79] but this event also suggests that in Francia the prince was safe from Redwald's anger, which could be taken to imply that the latter's own relations with the Merovingians had degenerated. If Sigberct's flight did antedate Redwald's conversion, such a cooling of relations is likely to have taken place before 616. The king's subsequent apostasy cannot have helped matters.[80]

Despite the likelihood of hostility between Redwald and the Franks during the later stages of his reign, relations between the Merovingians and the Wuffingas may lie behind the collection of thirty-seven gold tremisses found in Mound One at Sutton Hoo. It is generally accepted that these coins are unlikely to reflect mercantile activity.[81] They should, perhaps, be understood in a political rather than an economic context. That this is likely may be further indicated by the coins themselves. The most peculiar aspect of the whole collection is the fact that they all come from different mints.[82] This can scarcely be chance. Equally, it is difficult to see how such a collection of coins could have been made in East Anglia. The lack of duplicates makes it easiest to envisage the collection as being made on the continent, and indeed in official circles. The thirty-seven tremisses could perhaps be the remnant of a levy taken across the Merovingian kingdom and granted to an East Anglian prince or king. If this were to be so, one crucial point would follow for the chronology of the collection, since the mints represented are scattered across the various Merovingian kingdoms, and it was only on a limited number of occasions during the early seventh century that one king controlled them all.

At this point the internal history of Francia may impinge once again on that of East Anglia. Essentially, in the first half of the seventh century there were only three occasions when one king ruled over the whole of the Merovingian kingdom; there was the period of unitary rule under Chlothar II from 613 to 622/3,[83] and there were two further periods under Dagobert I in 629, before Charibert was established in Aquitaine,[84] and between c.631–3.[85] Although it is possible that Redwald's relations with the Merovingians may have been cordial in 613, this

---

[78] Bede, HE II 9, 20.
[79] Bede, HE III 18.
[80] Bede, HE II 5, 15. It is notable that Bede ascribes Redwald's apostasy to his wife. If Sigberct's mother was, as suggested above, Frankish, she is unlikely to have been the queen responsible for Redwald's renewed paganism. The latter would then have been his step-mother. If this were so, Sigberct's flight may have been related to the matter of the royal succession, which would itself have been an issue of interest to the Merovingians. As regards the date of Redwald's apostasy, since the king apparently condoned Paulinus's presence in East Anglia during Edwin's exile there (Bede, HE II 12; *The Earliest Life of Gregory the Great* 16), it is likely to postdate the battle of the Idle in 616/7. Redwald's renewed paganism cannot, therefore, have been a challenge to Æthelberht.
[81] Bruce-Mitford, 'The Sutton Hoo ship burial; some foreign connections', p. 150.
[82] Kent, in Bruce-Mitford, *The Sutton Hoo Ship Burial*, vol. 1, pp. 578, 607–47. Wood, *The Merovingian North Sea*, p. 14.
[83] Fredegar IV 43, 47.
[84] Fredegar IV 57; for the date see Wallace-Hadrill, ed., p. 47, n. 1.
[85] Fredegar IV 67, 76.

can only have been the case for as short period, if Sigberct's flight is rightly dated to the years before 616. Since, however, the prince was in exile from then until c.630, it is perhaps more likely that the coin collection should be associated with him than with Redwald; indeed one might be tempted to associate the treasure with his return to claim the East Anglian throne, backed perhaps by his Merovingian hosts. If he were the recipient of the coins, then Mound One can scarcely have commemorated Redwald, who had died at least three and possibly as much as thirteen years before Sigberct's return to East Anglia. Moreover, coins collected by the prince are unlikely to have been deposited in the grave of the king from whom he had fled. This is not to say, however, that the mound can be assigned without question to Sigberct, but only that it is not difficult to associate him with the transfer of the Merovingian tremisses to East Anglia. He might have placed some treasure in a cenotaph for his brother Eorpwald, who had been killed three years earlier, during which time a usurper had held the East Anglian throne, leaving little opportunity for providing the dead king with an appropriate burial;[86] equally the gold could have remained in royal hands until the death of Anna. Sigberct is one king among a number who might have been commemorated by Mound One; he could well have owned some of its treasure.

Taken together the historical evidence relating to East Anglia in the early seventh century and the finds from Mound One at Sutton Hoo imply that there is a Frankish background which is worth emphasising. It is a background which encompasses the history of Anglo-Saxon exiles in the Merovingian kingdom, among whom are numbered not only Sigberct, but also, within a few years of his return to England, Edwin's son, daughter and grandson who were sent to be brought up by Dagobert after Eanbald and Oswald seized power in Northumbria.[87] Perhaps if they had not died in infancy they too would have returned to England with Frankish backing.

Alongside this political context there are the religious factors already considered; the monastic expansion in Neustria, which included the nunneries of Faremoutiers and Chelles, as well as Fursey's foundation of Lagny,[88] and the missionary developments which were taking place in north-east Francia in the time of Amandus. Parallel to his work and to that of Felix there is also the activity of Richarius, who is said to have evangelised in the British Isles,[89] although the whereabouts of his mission is nowhere stated. In the middle of the century first Agilbert and then his nephew Leutherius were at work as bishops of Wessex.[90] Both should also be seen in the context of Neustrian spirituality, the former becoming bishop of Paris[91] before being buried in the nunnery of

---

[86] Bede, HE II 15; for a similar suggestion in favour of Æthelhere, see Stenton, 'The East Anglian Kings of the Seventh Century', pp. 400–2.
[87] Bede, HE II 20.
[88] Vita Fursei 29; Bede, HE III 19.
[89] Vita Richarii 8–9, ed. B. Krusch, MGH SRM 4; Campbell, 'The First Century of Christianity in England', p. 58.
[90] Bede, HE III 7.
[91] Bede, HE III 7, IV 1.

Jouarre.[92] And it was this same monastery which provided Balthild with the first inmates for her foundation at Chelles,[93] where Hild's sister Heresuid became a nun.[94]

It is possible that the political and religious contacts between England and Francia are both aspects of the same issue, Merovingian hegemony in the time of Chlothar II and of his son, Dagobert I, the most powerful of all the early Frankish kings, and in that of the latter's own son and successor, Clovis II. Chlothar's influence within England can best be seen in the presence of Peter, abbot of Dover, and Justus, bishop of Rochester, at the Council of Paris in 614.[95] As for Dagobert, his interests stretched well into the Slav lands of central Europe,[96] that is, a good deal further from the Merovingian heartlands than the coast of England,[97] which lay directly across the sea from the territories then being evangelised by Amandus and Richarius, among others. Despite the absence of any specific reference to Merovingian involvement in English politics at this time, it is difficult to believe that Dagobert I and Clovis II after him did not exercise influence in both Kent and East Anglia. The work of Frankish missionaries in England, and especially that of Felix in East Anglia after Sigberct's return, might be one indication of such involvement. If the reign of Redwald did see a cooling of relations with the Merovingians, that of Sigberct saw a dramatic reversal of any anti-Frankish policies. It may even be the case that the presence of East Anglian princesses in Neustrian nunneries is indicative not merely of the spiritual influence of Francia, but also of its political power. Although it would be going too far to see them as hostages, the Anglo-Saxon inmates of Chelles and Faremoutiers were under the direct gaze of the Merovingians, who patronised the two foundations.

The Franks further impinged on the Anglo-Saxon kingdoms in another less benign way.[98] As well as being involved in missionary activity in Britain, Richarius is said to have been involved in the ransom of insular captives,[99] as also was Eligius of Noyon,[100] another bishop from north-east Francia influenced by Columbanan monasticism and associated with Balthild.[101] Further, the *captivos vel pueros transmarinos* ransomed by Amandus may well have been Saxons.[102] The recurrent references to captivity and, by implication, slavery in the lives of these north Frankish saints calls to mind the enslaved condition perhaps of

---

[92] Campbell, 'The First Century of Christianity in England', p. 58.
[93] *Vita Balthildis* 7–8.
[94] Bede, *HE* IV 23.
[95] Council of Paris, 614, ed. F. Maassen, *Concilia Aevi Merovingici*, MGH Concilia 1 (Hannover, 1893), p. 192; Wood, *The Merovingian North Sea*, p. 25, n. 105.
[96] Fredegar IV 58, 68, 72, 74–5.
[97] Wood, *The Merovingian North Sea*, p. 12.
[98] On the Anglo-Saxon Slave trade, see D. Pelteret, 'Slave raiding and slave trading in early England', *Anglo-Saxon England* 9 (1981), pp. 99–114.
[99] *Vita Richarii* 8; Campbell, 'The First Century of Christianity in England', p. 58.
[100] *Vita Eligii* I 10, ed. B. Krusch, MGH SRM 4.
[101] Fritze, 'Universalis Gentium Confessio', pp. 84–8.
[102] *Vita Amandi* 8; see also 13.

Nanthild,[103] and certainly of Balthild, before she attracted the attention of Clovis II, and involved herself in the charitable work of ransoming captives.[104]

It was first and foremost the sea that left south-eastern England open to Frankish influence, and here the maritime nature of the East Anglian kingdom was particularly important. That the kingdom of the Wuffingas was largely a coastal entity is slightly obscured by the significance of the monastery of Ely, founded by Anna's daughter, Æthelthryth. This house, however, was built on an estate conferred on the saint by her husband, Tondbert, princeps of the South Gyrwe.[105] The majority of the early centres of the kingdom of the Wuffingas were, in fact, directly accessible from the sea, as in the cases of Blythborough,[106] Dunwich,[107] Snape,[108] Iken,[109] Rendlesham,[110] Ipswich and Felixstowe. To these should also be added Kingston, which must have been a royal villa in the pre-Viking era.[111] Across the Deben from Sutton Hoo itself, but within sight of the grave field, it has better logical claim to be the centre of the estate to which the mounds were attached, than does the well-known villa of Rendlesham, whose fame depends on Bede's reference to the baptism there of Suidhelm of Essex.[112] With its anchorage on Martlesham Creek, Kingston further emphasises the maritime nature of the East Anglian kingdom.

The religious and political history of northern Francia may, therefore, hold certain keys to developments within East Anglia in the first half of the seventh century. This same history provides a context for the finds at Sutton Hoo. Here it is not just a question of trying to identify the individual commemorated by

103 Nanthild may have been a slave; see Fredegar IV 58, and P. Geary, Before France and Germany; the creation and transformation of the Merovingian World (Oxford, 1988), p. 186.
104 Vita Balthildis 9.
105 Liber Eliensis 4, ed. E. O. Blake, Camden 3rd ser. 92 (London, 1962).
106 Liber Eliensis 7; Whitelock, 'The pre-Viking Church in East Anglia', p. 9.
107 Bede, HE II 15; for the identification of Domnoc as Dunwich see Whitelock, 'The pre-Viking Church in East Anglia', p. 4, n. 2.
108 R. L. S. Bruce-Mitford, 'The Snape Boat-Grave', Proceedings of the Suffolk Institute of Archaeology and Natural History 26 (1952), p. 1, reprinted in id., Aspects of Anglo-Saxon Archaeology; Sutton Hoo and other discoveries (London, 1974), p. 114.
109 S. E. West, N. Scarfe, R. Cramp, 'Iken, St. Botolf and the coming of East Anglian Christianity', Proceeding of the Suffolk Institute of Archaeology and History 35 (1984), pp. 279, 296.
110 R. L. S. Bruce-Mitford, 'Saxon Rendlesham; some preliminary considerations', Proceedings of the Suffolk Institute of Archaeology and Natural History 24 (1949), p. 1, reprinted in id., Aspects of Anglo-Saxon Archaeology, p. 73.
111 N. Scarfe, Suffolk in the Middle Ages (Woodbridge, 1986), pp. 4, 30; that this is a pre-Viking royal estate is suggested by the fact that it was already called Cingestune/Kingestune/Kyngestuna in the eleventh century, by which time it had been out of royal hands for some time; Liber Eliensis 60, 92; Domesday Book, gen. ed. J. Morris, vol. 34 (2), Suffolk, ed., A. R. Rumble (London, 1986), 21 (53). Bruce-Mitford noted the place name, but failed to follow up its implications, in 'Saxon Rendlesham', p. 234, Aspects of Anglo-Saxon Archaeology, p. 80. The presence of the river between the royal villa and the grave field may have been a factor in the practice of boat burial at Sutton Hoo; the separation of villa and cemetery may also have been symbolic. I am indebted to Mike and Bron Carr on whose boat I sailed up the Deben to Woodbridge for prompting these observations.
112 Bede, HE III 22.

Mound One; rather it is the consonance of the objects found at Sutton Hoo with a world dominated by the Franks. The coins are the most obvious illustrations of this, but there are also the typological relationships of the garnet-work, the great gold buckle and the iconography of the purse with known Frankish objects.[113] Indeed, the Wilton Cross, which is thought to be a product of the same workshop as the Sutton Hoo jewellery,[114] was regarded as being of Frankish provenance before 1939.[115]

Further, if Sutton Hoo is indicative of Merovingian hegemony, the more exotic Mediterranean material might be seen as coming via Francia to East Anglia. By far the most likely line of transmission for the Coptic bowl and the Byzantine silver is through the Merovingian kingdom, and it is possible to see the Anastasius dish as reaching the treasury of some Merovingian king before being redistributed to a member of the East Anglian royal family.[116] In addition, the Wilton Cross suggests that the Sutton Hoo jeweller had access to more Byzantine material, in this instance a gold coin of Heraclius, which might well have reached England through Frankish hands.[117] The material of Mound Three, including as it does the remains of a bone casket which can be paralleled by one from Heilbronn, as well as fragments of an eastern Mediterranean bronze vessel and a Roman cameo,[118] is also compatible with the notion that the Byzantine objects at Sutton Hoo could be thought of as reaching East Anglia from the Merovingian kingdom. Francia might even have served as the transmission point for Swedish material; in short, most of the exotic material at Sutton Hoo is likely to have passed through Frankish ports in one way or another.

Looked at from this point of view the history and the archaeology of East Anglia can be seen as being more compatible than is often realised, and both cast light on the kingdom of the Wuffingas and on north-eastern Francia in the reigns of Chlothar II, Dagobert I and their successors. In the historical sources Francia looms large with regard to East Anglian ecclesiastical history, and it is not without its political importance. Equally, in addition to the presence of individual Merovingian objects among the grave finds from Sutton Hoo, the general assemblage suggests that Francia was the transmission point for other pieces as well: Mounds One and Three appear to belong to a world dominated by the kingdom of the Franks.

---

[113] On the Merovingian taste for gold and garnets, see James, *The Franks*, pp. 204, following B. Arrhenius, *Merovingian Garnet Jewellery: emergence and social implications* (Stockholm, 1985); for the great gold buckle, see Bruce-Mitford, *The Sutton Hoo Ship Burial*, vol. 2 (London, 1978), pp. 536–64; J. Werner, 'Das Schiffsgrab von Sutton Hoo', *Germania* 60 (1) (1982), pp. 198–201; see also Bruce-Mitford, 'The Sutton Hoo ship burial; some foreign connections', pp. 176–87.
[114] Bruce-Mitford, *The Sutton Hoo Ship Burial*, vol. 1, p. 709.
[115] T. D. Kendrick, 'St. Cuthbert's pectoral cross and the Wilton and Ixworth crosses', *Antiquaries Journal* 17 (1937), p. 290.
[116] Wood, *The Merovingian North Sea*, p. 14.
[117] Bruce-Mitford, *The Sutton Hoo Ship Burial*, vol. 1, p. 665, no. 18.
[118] G. Grainger and M. Henig, 'A bone casket and relief plaque from Mound 3 at Sutton Hoo', *Medieval Archaeology* 27 (1983), pp. 136–41.

BAPTISMAL PLACES: 600–800

Richard Morris

Infant baptism was the norm to which seventh-century Roman and Frankish bishops were accustomed, and which was introduced into England once conversion had proceeded beyond the adult members of royal households.[1] By the end of the century it was thought desirable to set a time-limit of thirty days within which parents were to ensure that new-born children were baptized.[2] The feasibility of this aim is of course doubtful. Bishops were few in seventh-century England, and in practice responsibility for initiation was divided,[3] and baptismal duties shared between bishops and other clergy.[4] When Paulinus abandoned York in 633 he left James, a deacon, who 'remained for a long time in the church and,

---

[1] Baptism of some infants entered Christian tradition in the second century. The practice increased to the extent that by the sixth century the importance of Easter as the correct time for initiation was being undermined: Council of Macon (585), c. 3, in *Concilia Galliae A.511–A.695*, ed. C. de Clercq, CCSL vol. 148a (Turnhout, 1963), p. 240. Some of the earliest baptisms recorded for seventh-century England show concern for timing. The first baptism mentioned in Northumbria took place at Pentecost (Bede, *HE* II 9). Edwin was baptized on Easter Day (*HE* II 14).

[2] *In. 2.*

[3] The number of diocesans who can be identified as holding office at any one time is seldom more than a dozen. To them might be added peregrine figures like Fursey, who may on occasion have been entrusted with baptismal duties, or undertook them without seeking consent. Bishops living in retirement because of old age (e.g. John *In Derauuda*: Bede, *HE* V 6) or because they had been deprived of their sees (e.g. Winfrith: *HE*, IV 6) may have helped. Some diocesans had suffragans. At York, for instance, there is said to have been an office of *vicedomnus* (deputy bishop) early in the eighth century (Alcuin, *The bishops, kings, and saints of York*, ed. & trans. P. Godman (Oxford, 1982), 11.1217–18). The contribution of British clergy is hard to assess. Bede's account of the two conferences held between Augustine and British bishops states that the performance of baptism was one of the issues upon which they disagreed. An explanation has been sought in the possibility that Augustine regarded baptism within the late sixth-century British Church as being invalidated because the ceremony was on occasion completed not by a bishop but by priests or deacons: C. Thomas, *Christianity in Roman Britain to AD 500* (London, 1981), p. 209. For the division of the rite of initiation see J. D. C. Fisher, *Christian Initiation: Baptism in the West. A Study in the Disintergration of the Primitive Rite of Initiation*, Alcuin Club Collections, vol. 47 (London, 1965).

[4] At the end of the tenth century it was affirmed that deacons, priests, and bishops were empowered to baptize. No distinction was made between a mass-priest and a bishop, except that the bishop alone could ordain priests, consecrate churches, and confirm children: Ælfric's Pastoral Letter for Wulfsige III (993 x c.995), 37, 40–43 (*Councils & Synods* I, ed. D. Whitelock, M. Brett and C. N. L. Brooke (Oxford, 1981), pp. 204–5).

by teaching and baptizing, rescued much prey from the ancient foe'.[5] James's work as a surrogate suggests that pragmatic, as well as canonical, considerations could influence the transmission of episcopal authority. When Cedd returned with the rank of bishop to continue his ministry among the East Saxons, he 'established churches in various places and ordained priests and deacons to assist him in preaching the word of faith and in the administration of baptism'.[6]

The demand for such assistance could lead to the ordination of men who were of meagre accomplishment. John of Beverley, bishop of York (705–18), was credited with securing through a miracle the recovery of Herebald, one of his priests, who had sustained grievous injuries in the course of a horse-racing accident. The miracle was achieved only after John discovered that Herebald's baptism had been ineffective because it had been carried out by an incompetent priest who had been ordered not to exercise this ministry. The episode sheds light upon clerical standards and the condition of ecclesiastical organization in Northumbria early in the eighth century. For although the priest concerned was described by John as being 'so slow-witted that he was unable to learn the office of catechism or baptism' it was John himself who had ordained him.[7] If it was possible for a priest (a priest, moreover, who was destined to become an abbot) in the *familia* of a prominent bishop to be unaware that he had undergone an imperfect baptism at the hands of such a man, the quality of mission towards the *rustici* and their children must be in serious doubt.

By the tenth century the time-limit for baptism had been reduced.[8] This development presumably reflects an increase in the numbers of local churches and priests after 800, with a corresponding improvement of access to baptismal places. But distance was no more of a deterrent to prompt baptism than a demand for payment or the unwillingness of a priest to administer it. The withholding of baptism was a professional irregularity, punishable by both secular and canonical penalties.[9] When Wulfstan was prior to Worcester he used to baptise children without charge. Ostensibly this was in order to combat the greed of priests, although Barlow shrewdly observes that Wulfstan 'may also. . .have been exercising the traditional rights of the old minster'.[10]

The existence of such rights introduces the question of why it should be that there are in England no more than a dozen fonts for which a pre-Conquest date has been claimed.[11] Indeed, with the possible exceptions of the fonts at

---

[5]   Bede, HE II 20.
[6]   HE III 22. See also note 4.
[7]   HE V 6.
[8]   The So-called 'Canons of Edgar' (1005 x 1008), 15, specify seven days; NPL. 10, gives nine. Ælfric may have been nearer to reality when he urged that children be baptized 'as soon as they can most quickly be brought to baptism': First Old English Letter for Wulfstan (c.1006), 177. (Councils and Synods I, pp. 319, 455, 294).
[9]   Edw. & Guth. 3, 1–2; NPL. 8.
[10] William of Malmesbury, Vita Wulfstani 7, ed. R. R. Darlington, Camden Society, 3rd series, XL (1928), pp. 12–13. F. Barlow, The English Church 1000–1066, 2nd edn (London, 1979), p. 199.
[11] H. M. Taylor, Anglo-Saxon Architecture, vol. 3 (Cambridge, 1978) lists eight: Little

Potterne[12] and Deerhurst [13] it seems that none of these items is necessarily older than the tenth century, while the dates of the others could lie towards the end of the eleventh century or even after 1100.[14] This small quota looks all the more extraordinary when it is set against the very large number of fonts which are of post-Conquest workmanship and which have continued in use to the present.[15] The archaeological study of pre-Conquest church interiors is beset by all kinds of lacunae and shortages, some of which might be attributable to exigences of survival. But in the case of fonts a phenomenon of wholesale disappearance is hard to credit.[16] From c.1100 the font was a cherished item. Unless this marks a sharp change in attitude it is reasonable to suppose that if earlier stone fonts existed more of them should have survived. Hence, it is likely that the small total of examples is to be interpreted literally, as indicating that stone fonts did not enter general local use before the eleventh century.

The introduction of fonts might be linked to the building of local churches. But this can scarcely be the whole story, for whereas fonts start to proliferate in the eleventh century there are signs that in many areas the local church was well on its way to becoming a commonplace in the tenth.[17] The widespread introduction of fonts appears to coincide more exactly with the crystallization of the parochial system, and an associated process involving the enlargement in stone of churches which already existed. There are both literary and architectural indications that the two developments went hand in hand. The earliest sources which seem to assume or demand the existence of local fonts date from the tenth century.[18] During the eleventh century canons which refer to baptismal practice begin to feature in codes and the minutes of councils with increasing regularity.[19]

Billing, Cabourne, Castle Frome, Deerhurst St Mary, Holton, Melbury Bubb, Potterne, and Wilne.

[12] The Potterne font bears an inscription taken from Psalm 42. The wording corresponds with that of the so-called Roman psalter. Taylor points out that the four surviving OE psalters which use the Roman wording date from the eighth century to c.950, and consequently he has argued that the inscription belongs to the tenth century or earlier: Anglo-Saxon Architecture, vol. 3, pp. 1064–5. E. Okasha, Handlist of Anglo-Saxon Non-runic Inscriptions, (Cambridge, 1971), p. 149, prefers a date in the later eleventh or twelfth century.

[13] Ornament on the font at Deerhurst points to a date in the later ninth or early tenth century.

[14] The fonts at Melbury Bubb (Dorset) and Wilne (Derbyshire), for instance, may be pre-Conquest only to the extent that they were fashioned from former cross-shafts.

[15] F. Bond, Fonts and Font Covers, new edn (London, 1985), pp. 144–205.

[16] Unless before c.1050 fonts were ordinarily made of wood? This is possible. Bond (Fonts and Font Covers, pp. 123–4) observed that among the earliest stone fonts are examples like that at Little Billing which show signs of skeuomorphism deriving from wooden tubs or barrels.

[17] J. Blair, 'Secular Minster Churches in Domesday Book', in Domesday Book: A Reassessment, ed. P. Sawyer (London, 1985), p. 119.

[18] Ælfric, Pastoral Letter, 129. But Ælfric's discussion of the seven clerical orders, and his assumptions about their literacy and access to books (including a baptisterium) suggests that he had in mind churches of superior status, rather than one-priest churches in the countryside.

[19] See notes 4, 8, 9. Reference to baptism is also given in an early eleventh-century source

At the same time, appreciable numbers of local churches were being extended. The results of archaeological investigation enable us to see that the eleventh century was a period of enlargement for churches which had previously consisted of one or two tiny compartments.[20] Part of the rationale for such expansion could be explained by a growth in the numbers of resident parish clergy, and by a corresponding desire to provide more individualized spaces for different ecclesiastical functions. One of these functions was baptism, although in the eleventh century it appears that superior churches retained control over the provision of chrism to lesser churches.[21] Baptismal innovation would account not only for the sudden multiplication of stone fonts, but also for the increase in emphasis upon the western parts of local churches which becomes noticeable after c.1000.[22]

If this explanation is accepted, it is relevant to ask how, and in what sort of places and surroundings, baptism was administered before the eleventh century. In order to consider these questions it is useful to identify some of the concepts and practices which lay behind medieval attitudes towards baptism.

The water which forms part of Christian initiation embodies a bundle of ideas; a cleansing in *fons vitae*; the crossing of a boundary; an exchange of one life and family for another; and an image of death and rebirth. These concepts came to be reflected in the architectural, locational, and symbolic contexts of baptism. Thus, in a medieval parish church the baptismal ceremony began *ad valvas ecclesiae*. Churches were sometimes positioned close to springs and watercourses, or even superimposed upon them.[23] The idea of baptism as a burial with Christ derived from Paul.[24] It led to a tradition in which the font was regarded as a tomb and the baptistery could resemble a mausoleum.[25] The symmetry of death and rebirth also led to the font being considered as a womb.[26]

On the continent these ideas sometimes found expression in buildings where

on examination of candidates for ordination (*Councils & Synods*, I, 12, p. 425). For baptism in late eleventh-century legislation see Winchester councils of 1070, IX, 7, and 1072, V, 2 (*Councils & Synods*, I, 2, pp. 575, 605).

[20] R. K. Morris, *Churches in the Landscape* (London, 1989), chapters 4–6.

[21] Barlow, *English Church*, pp. 194–5; *The Domesday Monachorum of Christ Church Canterbury*, ed. D. C. Douglas (1944), pp. 5 ff., 77–9. This aspect of the role of superior churches seems to have existed in the northern province as well as southern dioceses: *NPL*. 9.

[22] Taylor, *Anglo-Saxon Architecture*, vol. 3, p. 1065, suggests that 'square west towers which opened to the church through wide arches originally served as baptisteries, just as many of them still do'. Archaeological investigation of the western cell of the tower-church at Barton-on-Humber disclosed traces of a font-base and soakaway, the latter 'unequivocally a primary feature', which have led the excavators to interpet this part of the building as a baptistery. The baptistery was lit by three double-splayed windows, and contained attic rooms above the ground-storey: W. Rodwell & K. Rodwell, 'St Peter's Church, Barton-upon-Humber: Excavation and Structural Study, 1978–81', *Antiquaries Journal* 62 (1982), pp. 296–9, Fig. 6.

[23] G. Binding, 'Quellen, Brunnen und Reliquiengraber in Kirchen', *Zeitschrift für Archäologie des Mittelalters* 3 (1975), pp. 37–56.

[24] Colossians 2. 12.

[25] J. G. Davies, *The architectural setting of baptism* (London, 1962).

[26] J. H. Lynch, *Godparents and Kinship in Early Medieval Europe* (Princeton, 1986), p. 115.

functions of initiations and burial were combined in a single structure. This also appears to have been the case at Canterbury, which is the one place in eighth-century England where evidence for baptismal arrangements is available. When Eadmer described the cathedral at Canterbury as it stood before the rebuilding begun in 1070 by Lanfranc, he noted that a church had been constructed just east of the cathedral in order that baptisms might be celebrated there, and wherein the bodies of archbishops could be buried. This baptistery-cum-mausoleum was dedicated to St John the Baptist. Eadmer thought that it had been built during the pontificate of archbishop Cuthbert (740–60).[27]

No other baptistery of this period is specifically mentioned in written records;[28] nor has any definite example yet been disclosed by archaeological excavation. But a link between water and burial is archaeologically attested, if not yet fully explained, at Repton. Here sometime after c.715 the crypt originated within an existing cemetery as a 'detached, square, semi-subterranean structure with massive ornamental external plinths'. The building has been tentatively identified as a mausoleum. However, 'a drain leading away north-east from below the floor level of the crypt, the presence of a second water channel at a much higher level possibly bringing water in, and the general plan, all suggest that the structure may (also?) have been a baptistery'.[29]

These examples apart, little else is known about the architectual context of baptism in eighth- or seventh-century England. Modern historical writing has tended to stress the role of immersion in rivers during the first stages of conversion. It is possible that this emphasis has been exaggerated. Only four episodes are directly recorded in England.[30] It may be significant that three of them occurred within a period of about six years, and that on each occasion the same bishop – Paulinus – was responsible. If other bishops followed Paulinus's example, we are not told about them. Nor is it clear that the method of baptism which Paulinus used involved total or partial submersion, affusion or aspersion.[31] It is a question whether even a bishop could withstand the cold waters of an English river for any length of time. Moreover, rivers like the Swale and Trent have a strength of current sufficient to convert the prospect of a ritual death into a real one. For reasons both of comfort and safety, therefore, either affusion or aspersion is likely to have been the method which was used. A quantity of water

---

[27] Text and discussion in H. M. Taylor, 'The Anglo-Saxon cathedral church at Canterbury', *Archaeological Journal* 126 (1969), pp. 102, 126.
[28] Though Bede makes a generalized reference to the existence of *baptisteria: HE* II 14.
[29] M. Biddle, 'Archaeology, architecture, and the cult of saints', in *The Anglo-Saxon Church*, eds L. A. S. Butler and R. K. Morris, CBA Research Report 60 (London, 1986), pp. 16, 22. The relationship of the channels to the mausoleum has since been clarified by further excavation. The higher channel pre-dated the mausoleum, and is presumably to be explained as leading *from* another structure which lies beyond the limit of the area under examination. But interpretation of the lower channel which issues from the mausoleum remains unchanged, and the baptistery hypothesis still stands. I am grateful to Birthe Kjølbye-Biddle for her advice on these points.
[30] Bede, *HE* II 14, 16.
[31] J. G. Davies, *The Architectural Setting of Baptism* (London, 1962), pp. 23 ff.

would be poured over the head of a candidate who stood in the shallows, perhaps to no more than ankle or calf depth. This may give a clue to the technique which was employed when initiation was performed within a building.[32]

According to Bede baptism could be administered in a church,[33] an oratory, or baptistery,[34] as well as in the open. Several references to the use of *oratoria* for baptismal purposes may suggest that a class of temporary local structure existed alongside permanent episcopal and monastic provision, and that this preceded the church-founding movement which from the later ninth century seems to have been sponsored by lesser local lords.[35]

Although evidence for alfresco initiation is slight, it is interesting to ask why, or if, particular reaches of certain rivers were thought to be appropriate places for this type of ceremony. In the case of the river Glen an explanation is suggested by the presence nearby of a *villa regia*. Catterick, too, was a royal vill.[36] Neither the location nor the status of *Tiowulfingacaestir* are known, but Bede's designation of the place as *civitas*, and his description of the baptism of *multam populi turbam* in the presence of King Edwin, might suggest that this place too enjoyed royal status.[37]

These are not the only indications that in the seventh century the geography of initiation was closely wedded to the pattern of royal centres. Swithhelm, for instance, was baptized by Cedd *in vico regio qui dicitur Rendlaesham*.[38] Sigeberht was baptized a the *villa regia* of *Ad Murum*.[39]

To some extent, of course, these occurrences may simply reflect the tendency for written records to focus upon the initiation of kings, their families and associates, and hence to give prominence to the types of place which they frequented. But a related reason why *villae regales* loom large in accounts of early initiation arises from the exploitation of the idea of spiritual kinship as a means

---

[32] A phrase such as *Nolumus . . . fontem illum intrare . . .* (*HE* II 5) seems to imply that in seventh-century England a font could be a feature or structure into which the candidate stepped. At some sites (e.g. Leicester, Bath) the presence of former Roman bath buildings might have fulfilled this need. But the role of affusion/aspersion also suggests that there is a particular category of ecclesiastical artefact which awaits recognition.

[33] Bede, *HE* I 26.

[34] *HE* II 14.

[35] Bede makes several references to the use of oratories for baptismal purposes. The wooden structure erected in York by King Edwin while he was a catachumen is the best known of these. This was later enclosed by a permanent church built of stone. The following statement that churchmen in Northumbria *nondum enim oratoria uel baptisteria in ipso exordio nascentis ibi ecclesiae poterant aedificari* (*HE* II 14) strongly implies that oratories were used as places of baptism. Incidental references to the existence of local oratories elsewhere in Bede's writings (e.g. in connection with Dryhthelm's vision of the underworld: *HE* V 12) suggest that the seventh/eighth-century *oratorium* forms a category of structure which has been underestimated.

[36] P. H. Sawyer, 'The Royal *Tun* in pre-Conquest England', in P. Wormald, ed., *Ideal and Reality in Frankish and Anglo-Saxon Society* (Oxford, 1983), p. 292.

[37] Bede, *HE* II 16.

[38] *HE* III 22.

[39] *HE* III 22.

for the reinforcement or extension of royal power.[40] Sigeberht was baptized not in his own kingdom of the East Saxons but in Northumbria. Æthelwealh, king of the South Saxons, is said by Bede to have been baptized 'in the kingdom of Mercia at the suggestion and in the presence of Wulfhere, who, when Æthel-wealh came forth from the font, received him as a son'.[41] The conquest of the Isle of Wight by Caedwalla was succeeded by a baptismal campaign directed towards its inhabitants. This included the conversion of two young princes, brothers of the former king of the island, whose baptism was immediately followed by their execution.[42]

Oswald's sponsorship of Cynegisl in faraway Wessex (traditionally at Dorchester-on-Thames) may illustrate something both of the nature of this process and its geographical implication. Following instruction by bishop Birinius, Cynegisl

> . . .was cleansed from his sins in the waters baptism together with all his people. It so happened that at the same time Oswald . . .was present and stood godfather for him. . .well-pleasing to God was their relationship; that same man whose daughter Oswald was later to receive as his wife, that day, after his new birth and dedication to God, was received by Oswald as his son.[43]

The interest of this episode lies not only in the political dimension of spiritual kinship, but also in the frontier location of the ceremony. Although we are not told where Cynegisl was baptized, Bede adds the curious detail that *both* kings gave the bishop (Birinius) a *civitas* called *Dorcic* as a place in which to establish his episcopal see. A boundary would be an appropriate place for kings to meet, and for one of them to assert authority over another. Following the lapsing of the sees of Leicester and Lindsey this helps to account for Dorchester's anomalous position in the eleventh century as a see on the periphery of a vast diocese extending from the Humber to the Thames.

Dorchester's liminal location may also be considered in an economic context, the nature of which has been defined by Peter Sawyer himself: 'Boundaries were appropriate locations for markets because people could gather from both sides without having to travel through strange territory'.[44] This leads us to ask whether *villae regales* may also have been suitable as sites for mass initiations during the conversion period because they were already places where large num-bers of people were accustomed to assemble in the presence of the king. The size of the crowds that flocked 'from every village and district' to Paulinus at Yeaver-ing may have had less to do with the bishop's reputation as a preacher than with

---

[40] A. Angenendt, 'Taufe und Politik im frühen Mittelalter', *Frühmittelalterliche Studien* 7 (1973), pp. 143–168.
[41] Bede, *HE* IV 13.
[42] *HE* IV 16.
[43] *HE* III 7.
[44] P. H. Sawyer, 'Fairs and Markets in Early Medieval England', in *Danish Medieval History. New Currents*, eds N. Skyum-Nielsen and Niels Lund (Copenhagen, 1981), p. 162.

the existing status of Yeavering as a place of seasonal assembly. Some other seventh-century royal vills may have stood at or close to places which were of long standing as places of gathering. The judicial role of such sites might also be remembered. At Canterbury the conjunction has been noted of burial and baptism in the eighth-century church dedicated to St John the Baptist. This building was also used for certain judicial trials. It is worth asking if some of the functions which hitherto had been performed at *villae regales* were at this time coming to be refocused in ecclesiastical sites, or even to be formalized within the co-location of their architectural components.

The reasons why men and women congregated at certain sites and times can only be guessed at, but archaeology delivers clues which point to trade and festivity as well as religion. With typical prescience, Sawyer has already pointed to the correlation which exists between locations of early medieval fairs and markets, and places which possessed early monasteries or churches. This closes a circle, because nearly all of these churches were of superior status: that is, they were precisely those institutions which by the tenth and eleventh centuries are found to have been exercising, amoung other things, a supervisory role in relation to baptism.

It is a question whether the *congregationes* which sometimes seem to have been associated with baptismal places occurred as a function of their pre-existing status, or as a consequence of their role as places of initiation. The first possibility itself divides into two further questions: in the seventh century were these places where people gathered to the king, or places to which English kings had attached themselves because they were already traditional sites of assembly? It may of course be that both sets of circumstances contributed locations which became places of baptism, and that archaeology may in due course help us to differentiate between the two.

A prudent author would stop there. The material correlates of an early medieval place of assembly have yet to be defined. But a cautious note hardly seems appropriate at the end of an essay which honours Peter Sawyer. Hence what follows is recklessly speculative. With this in mind, it is interesting to re-read lines in the concluding paragraph of Sawyer's seminal essay on fairs and markets in early medieval England: '. . .we may be confident that there were assemblies for worship and entertainment as well as for buying and selling long before the English were converted, even before the Romans came, and we may suspect that some Christian churches were founded at old cult centres'.[45]

One indicator of gatherings which becomes available from the eighth century is provided by finds of coins. The frequency with which sceattas occur 'on Roman sites and hill forts (useful for herding and cattle-fairs)' has been noted.[46] It might also be added that out of some 113 recorded provenances of English finds of sceattas, excluding hoards, some 34 per cent of finds have been made

[45] Sawyer, 'Fairs and Markets', p. 164.
[46] S. E. Rigold & D. M. Metcalfe, 'A Check-list of English finds of Sceattas', *British Numismatic Journal*, 47 (1977), p. 32.

within or in the near vicinity of ecclesiastical sites. These include important episcopal and monastic centres such as Elmham, York, Rochester, Dorchester-on-Thames, Reculver, Selsey, Breedon, Bradwell, Jarrow, Southwell, and Abingdon. In most cases the fines are too few, or the circumstances of their making too vague, to provide any sort of basis for speculation about seasonal assemblies or fairs. But the large assemblage from Reculver, and appreciable totals from other Shore Forts which were made over to monastic use in the seventh century, might be considered in such terms.

Another charcteristic of meeting-places may be the presence of some marked natural or man-made feature. In the former category may be sites like Augustine's Oak, or the mustering-place at *Wilfaraesdun* near Catterick. Prehistoric monuments sometimes fulfilled such purposes. The church at Knowlton, Dorset, for instance stands within a prehistoric henge which became a hundredal meeting-place.[47] The wapentake of Dickering (YE) took its name from the great prehistoric ringwork on Paddock Hill. This was reoccupied in the eighth and ninth centuries AD, when part of the interior was set aside for use as a cemetery. Nearby was a timber hall, indications of judicial killings, and traces of a structure which is interpreted as an oratory or chapel.[48] Elsewhere in Yorkshire it is interesting that substantial henge monuments and/or cursus are associated with the rivers Swale, Ure, Wharfe and Aire, and that in several cases the sites concerned lay in close proximity to places which in the seventh century AD had become centres of royal or ecclesiastical importance.[49]

A factor which sometimes links enclosed areas, traditional places of gathering, and places of consequent ecclesiastical (and therefore baptismal) prominence could be sought in the herding and trading of animals. The suitability of former Roman enceintes for such purposes has been mentioned. The 'great enclosure' at Yeavering is most plausibly to be interpreted in similar terms.[50] A more tentative example is Wharram Percy (YE), where the church of St Martin ruled a large parish and was of baptismal status at least from the eleventh century. It was once assumed on the evidence of finds of eighth- and ninth-century coins, and of pre-Conquest sculpture, that this church had its genesis in the eighth or ninth

[47] M. W. Beresford & J. K. St Joseph, *Medieval England: an aerial survey*, 2nd edn, (Cambridge, 1979), pp. 49–52.
[48] Yorkshire Archaeological Society Prehistory Research Section: *Thwing. Excavation and Field Archaeology in East Yorkshire* (1985; 1986: The Anglo-Saxon Cemetery).
[49] In each case the monuments lie a short distance east of the western flank of the Pennines. Catterick is close to the cursus at Scorton, near the Swale. A complex of henges lies at Thornborough, not far from the Ure, between Ripon and Aldborough (the latter a former Roman *civitas* capital, which by the eleventh century is found to be a crown demesne manor, and the site of a *matrix ecclesia* which dominated an exceptionally large *parochia*). The henge at Newton Kyme is close to the Wharfe and to Tadcaster – presumably the *Kaelcacaestir* of Bede (*HE* IV 23), which contained some sort of religious community. Another henge lay at Ferry Fryston, close to the river Aire. Only the river Nidd – which gave its name to a seventh-century synod – has yet to be associated with one of these monuments.
[50] B. Hope-Taylor, *Yeavering: and Anglo-British centre of early Northumbria*, (London, 1977), pp. 78–88, 205–9.

century.[51] An Eadberht sceatta was recovered from St Martin's churchyard in 1964. A pre-Conquest cross fragment is dated on art-historical grounds to around AD 800. Yet present thinking discounts any direct relationship between the origin of the church and either the coin-finds or the sculpture. The cross fragment was not found on the site of the church, and there are archaeological reasons for supposing that the church is no older then the tenth century.[52] Other reasons must therefore be sought to explain the coins finds, and the existence of pre-Scandinavian sculpture.

The position of the church at Wharram has yet to be satisfactorily explained. The site lies apart from the manorial foci of the settlement, on a terrace within a narrow, steep-sided valley. This area saw intensive use in the prehistoric period, but (unlike other parts of the site) has yielded comparatively little evidence for settlement between the fifth and tenth centuries AD. One reason for this could be that the valley was being used for another purpose: such as the periodic penning or trading of animals. Valleys of similar configuration were employed in a similar way in the Cotswolds in the fifteenth and sixteenth centuries, for the washing and clipping of flocks of sheep. At Wharram the presence of running water and the natural boundaries provided by the valley offered advantages for animal management. It may be to this sort of context that the sceatta belongs, and to which the church was subsequently attached. Even the dedication of the church would suit. Martin's feast day on 11 November coincided with the winter cull of cattle. In some places he was a patron saint of butchers.

Speculation aside, we have seen that there is reason to postulate the existence of places in Middle Saxon England where people were accustomed to participate in seasonal gatherings under the direction of local leaders. For present purposes it scarcely matters whether such places were continuously frequented for millenia, or whether their precise functions were intermittently revised or reinvented. The argument of this essay is simply that places of congress in seventh-century England are likely to have been natural targets for missionaries, and that a proportion of such places may have been venues which were already old. Centres which acquired ecclesiastical attributes because of their previous status in their turn acted as attractors of people, and hence of commercial activity and associated settlement.

[51] J. G. Hurst, 'The Wharram Research Project: Results to 1983', Medieval Archaeology 28 (1984), p. 89.
[52] R. D. Bell, M. W. Beresford and J. C. Thorn, Wharram, a Study of Settlement on the Yorkshire Wolds: Wharram Percy the Church of St Martin (Society for Medieval Archaeology, Monograph Series 11, 1987), pp. 52, 60.

IN SEARCH OF KING OFFA'S 'LAW-CODE'

Patrick Wormald

The difficulty, and the fascination, of the study of European history in the early Middle Ages is that it is in important ways not history but prehistory. The near-contemporary publication of Peter Sawyer's re-assessment of phenomena hitherto ascribed to waves of invading Vikings, and of Grahame Clark's seminal critique of the 'The Invasion Hypothesis' in British prehistory, is a reminder that even the most epoch-making events in northern Europe's post-Roman 'Iron Age' can be as obscure and as vulnerable to drastic revisionism as developments in the La Tène era.[1] It is a commonplace that history is distinguished from prehistory by the availability of written evidence. The student of Offa, confronted with a massive 'public work' and an elaborate coinage, but without any documentation as to how either was managed, is not so differently placed from the student of Cunobelinus.

Yet it is an open question whether the pattern of surviving evidence is in both cases a fair reflection of what once existed. There are mounting indications of the sheer efficiency of government in Anglo-Saxon England. At some point in time between Domesday Book and Stonehenge, the notion that effective administration demands the use of writing reduces itself to absurdity. But a lively current debate in Anglo-Saxon studies (now that Viking fleets have, no doubt temporarily, receded somewhat from the intellectual horizon) divides those who argue that England before 1066 was run by virtue of very extensive documentation from those who maintain that many of the most basic functions of government were conducted orally.[2] For believers in pre-conquest bureaucracy, it

---

[1]   G. Clark, 'The Invasion Hypothesis in British Archaeology', *Antiquity* 40 (1966), pp. 172–89; P. H. Sawyer, *The Age of the Vikings* (London, 1962). Not the least of my own debts to Professor Sawyer (among which that signalled in n. 3 below and his literally indispensable *Anglo-Saxon Charters, An Annotated List and Bibliography* (London, 1968) are only the most obvious) has been the experience of a friendship that survived – even throve on – my disagreements with his celebrated thesis; his capacity to sustain *amicitia* in the midst of controversy was in itself a revolutionary contribution to Anglo-Saxon studies. This paper owes much to the advice and criticism of David Ganz, Simon Keynes, Jinty Nelson and above all Donald Bullough, none of whom should thereby be held responsible for its perversities; also, as ever, to the perceptions and encouragement of Jenny Wormald.
[2]   The strongest statements of the case for a vanished pre-conquest bureaucracy are those of J. Campbell, 'The Significance of the Anglo-Norman State in the Administrative History of Western Europe', in W. Paravicini and K-F. Werner, eds, *Histoire Comparée de l'Administration (IVe–XVIIIe Siècles), Beihefte der Francia* 9 (Munich, 1980), pp. 117–34,

is axiomatic that large quantities of written evidence have been lost; they note that even Domesday Book survives by a relative hairsbreadth (although, if it had gone down with King John's baggage in the Wash, the profusion of 'satellites' would still show that something remarkable had been happening). Adherents of the 'word-of-mouth' school deny not the fact but the extent of losses, believing that what is now available offers some sort of guidance as to what was originally extant. Happily, today's early medieval historian is encouraged to speculate as well as merely to know. But there is a testing course to be steered between the two temptations of indulging a Neo-Platonist faith in evidence that is perfect but invisible, and of running amok with Occam's razor.

This paper, somewhat tardily keeping a promise made over ten years ago in a volume inspired and produced by the honorand and the co-editor of this book, concerns perhaps the most notorious of alleged pre-conquest *deperdita*, the 'law-code' of King Offa of Mercia.[3] It must be admitted at once that early medieval legislation could get lost. In England, this is seemingly true of *friđgewritu* between Wessex and the Danish-ruled enclaves of the north and east, to which Edward the Elder refers in his second code, of Edgar's terrible law on the mutilation of thieves, apparently known only from reports of the miracles of St Swithun, and of Æthelred's *gemot* at *Bromdune*, to which he harks back in this 'first' and 'third' codes. On the other hand, it should also be noted that the making of written law did not come naturally to all early medieval Europe's powerful rulers: the most obvious absentees from the hall of legislative fame are the Ottonians and Salians, a point that later caused Frederick II some embarrassment.[4] North of the Alps

reprinted in his *Essays in Anglo-Saxon History* (London, 1986), pp. 171–89, at pp. 173–9 (see also his 'Some Agents and Agencies of the Late Anglo-Saxon State', in J. C. Holt, ed., *Domesday Studies: Papers read at the Novocentenary Conference of the Royal Historical Society and the Institute of British Geographers, Winchester, 1986* (Woodbridge, 1987), pp. 201–18, at pp. 212–15); and of S. D. Keynes, 'Royal Government and the Written Word in Late Anglo-Saxon England', in R. McKitterick, ed., *The Uses of Literacy in Early Medieval Europe* (Cambridge, 1990), pp. 226–57. The opposite view is represented (in effect) by P. Chaplais, 'The Anglo-Saxon Chancery: From the Diploma to the Writ', *Journal of the Society of Archivists* 3 (1966), pp. 160–76, reprinted in F. Ranger, ed., *Prisca Munimenta: studies . . . presented to A. E. J. Hollaender* (Manchester, 1973), pp. 28–42; by M. T. Clanchy, *From Memory to Written Record: England 1066–1307* (London, 1977), pp. 12–17; and by my 'Uses of Literacy in Anglo-Saxon England and its Neighbours', *TRHS*, 5th series 27 (1977), pp. 95–114. My *The Making of English Law* (Oxford, forthcoming) offers a modified version of this case, and other topics for which fuller argumentation may be sought there include those reflected in nn. 4, 7, 9, 20, 32, 38, 40–1.
[3] 'Lex Scripta and Verbum Regis: Legislation and Germanic Kingship from Euric to Cnut', in P. H. Sawyer and I. N. Wood, eds, *Early Medieval Kingship* (Leeds, 1977), pp. 105–38, at p. 112, n. 40.
[4] *II Edw.* 5.2, *I Atr.* 1.2, *III Atr.* 4, edited by F. Liebermann, *Gesetze der Angelsachsen*, 3 vols (Halle, 1903–16), vol. 1, pp. 144–5, 216–17, 228–9 (references to Anglo-Saxon codes are henceforth to the pages and abbreviations of this edition). M. Lapidge, *The Cult of St Swithun*, Winchester Studies 4.2 (Oxford, forthcoming) edits the *Translatio et Miracula Sancti Swithuni*, whose chapter 26 reveals the source of the story of Edgar's drive against theft, hitherto available only in *Frithegodi . . . Breviloquium vitae Wilfredi et Wulfstani Cantoris narratio metrica de Sancto Swithuno*, ed. A. Campbell (Zurich, 1950), pp. 154–7.

and Pyrenees (up to a point, even south of them), legislation tended to be issued in bursts over three or four generations, almost as if it were a matter of cultural fashion, or – less pejoratively – of a self-generated momentum that could not be sustained because of a lack of corresponding response in law as it was actually experienced. Whatever it was, Offa's 'code' is unique in its apparent isolation by a century on either side from what came before and after.

The main evidence for a lost code of Offa is Alfred's acknowledgement, in the preface to his own, of the debt he owed to Ine, Offa and Æthelberht, the first and third of whose laws do survive (if barely).[5] Courageous attempts have therefore been made to find Offa's law beneath the Alfredian surface. It has been noted that the word *boldgetal* (for 'district' or 'province') in Alfred's thirty-seventh law is otherwise found only in a Mercian context, and that *lefnesse* ('permission' – clauses eight and twenty) is likewise Mercian in form and provenance. More ambitiously, it has been suggested that Alfred's important clause on the entailing of bookland to the kindred – one of the very few Anglo-Saxon laws on property – may also have originated in Offa's code, because charters which do this are first extant in Offa's time.[6] One has the impression here of clutched straws. Alfred 37 is actually based on Ine 39, which had used *scir* in the same context. At a time when (it can be argued) *scir* was changing its jurisdictional sense, Alfred might well have cast about for an alternative; and it so happens that the other evidence for *boldgetal* is the translation of Gregory's *Dialogues* made by his close adviser, Bishop Wærferth! Similarly, *lefness* is elsewhere recorded in the 'Old English Bede'; it has long been known that this is not Alfred's own work, but there remains a strong temptation to link it with Mercians in his court circle. However the king's code was composed, 'Mercian' features are easily explained.[7] As for the

---

For a suggestion about *Bromdun*, see my 'Æthelred the Lawmaker', in D. Hill, ed., *Ethelred the Unready: Papers from the Millenary Conference* BAR, BS 59 (Oxford, 1978), pp. 62–3. For Frederick II on the lack of a German legislative tradition, see *Constitutiones et Acta Publica Imperatorum et Regum*, ed. L. Weiland (MGH, LL 4 (Hannover, 1896), no. 196, II, p. 241.

[5] *Alf.* Prol. 49.9, pp. 46–7. The first formal registration of the loss of Offa's code was by Sir Francis Palgrave, *The Rise and Progress of the English Commonwealth*, 2 vols (London, 1832), vol. 1, p. 47; his suggestion that Mercian MSS of Alfred's code would have been accompanied by Offa's laws, as it was in West Saxon MSS by Ine's, was effectively rebutted by M. H. Turk, *The Legal Code of Alfred the Great* (Halle, 1890), p. 40 – part of a discussion which, *pace* Liebermann's several criticisms, remains the best treatment of these and other aspects of Alfred's law-book.

[6] D. Whitelock, in *Councils and Synods with other Documents relating to the English Church: I, 871–1204*, ed. D. Whitelock, M. Brett and C. N. L. Brooke, 2 vols (Oxford, 1981), vol. 1, p. 18; J. Campbell, 'Bede's Words for Places', in P. H. Sawyer, ed., *Names, Words and Graves* (Leeds, 1979), pp. 35–54, reprinted in his *Essays* (as n. 2), pp. 99–119, at pp. 113–14, n. 19; Simon Keynes, in *Alfred the Great: Asser's Life of Alfred and other contemporary sources*, translated with an introduction and notes by Simon Keynes and Michael Lapidge (Harmondsworth, 1983), pp. 305–6 and cross-references (it is fair to say that Dr Keynes, and to a lesser extent Professor Whitelock, already envisaged the hypothesis presented in this paper).

[7] *Alf.* 37, *In.* 39, pp. 70–1, 106–7; *Bischofs Wærferth von Worcester Übersetzung der Dialoge Gregors des Großen*, ed. H. Hecht (Bibliothek der Angelsächsischen Prosa V, gen.

law on bookland: aspects of property law (like the 'triple obligation' of bridge, fortress and army service) could take centuries to be transferred from charter to code. If inspiration was sought for the provision that entails to kindred must be respected, Alfred needed to look no further than the bequests of his grandfather which he was careful to observe in his own will.[8] Besides, in laws where Alfred is very probably following a lead given by Æthelberht, such as that on the king's *mund*, verbal echoes are non-existent.[9] It is doubtful whether any further progress can be made from this angle.

The quest for Offa's legislation ought, instead, to set out from the nearest one can get to a contemporary vantage-point. A letter of Alcuin (c.797) instructs an unnamed English 'Patrician', whom William of Malmesbury later identified as Osberht, that he

admonish all the people of the Mercians that they diligently observe the good, moderate and chaste customs (*mores bonos et modestos et castos*), which Offa of blessed memory established (*instituit*) for them.[10]

Scholars since Jaffé have thought this a further reference to those 'laws of Offa' whose inspiration was claimed by Alfred. *Mores bonos et modestos et castos* is not, perhaps, the most obviously apposite label for any early medieval legislation. But if this is what Alcuin had in mind, there is one legislative transaction known to have taken place in Offa's Mercia when Alcuin was actually present, and for which his phrase might not have been unsuitable. These are the decrees laid down in the course of the famous legation sent to England by Pope Hadrian I in 786.

Many, if not all, the circumstances of this episode have long been familiar. The story is told in a letter to Hadrian by one of the two legates, who does not give his name in the document itself, but who can be identified as Bishop George of Ostia from its heading in the sole extant manuscript, confirmed by a letter of Pope Leo III twelve years later, encouraging King Cenwulf to persist with the annual gift to St Peter that Offa had promised in the presence of George and Theophylact, *nostri fidelissimi missi*.[11] The heading also refers to 'the synod that

---

eds C. M. W. Grein and R. P. Wülker, Leipzig, 1900), p. 45, where *boldgetalum* translates *provinciis* (the later version of this translation substitutes *scirum*); *The Old English Version of Bede's Ecclesiastical History of the English People*, Part I, ed. T. Miller, 2 vols (Early English Texts Society, xcv–xcvi, Oxford, 1900–1), e.g. vol. 1, pp. 112–13, translating *licentiam*.
[8] V Atr. 26.1, VI Atr. 32.3, pp. 242–3, 254–5, on the triple obligation. Alfred's Will: *Select English Historical Documents of the Ninth and Tenth Centuries*, ed. F. E. Harmer (Cambridge, 1914), no. xi, pp. 19, 52, with Keynes & Lapidge, *Alfred*, pp. 178, 309.
[9] *Alf*. 3, *Abt*. 8, pp. 50–1, p. 3.
[10] *Alcuini sive Albini Epistolae*, ed. E. Dümmler, *Epistolae Karolini Aevi* II, MGH, Ep. 4 (Berlin, 1895), no. 122, pp. 178–80, at p. 180; translated in *EHD*, no. 202, pp. 854–6. Cf. *Willelmi Malmesbiriensis Gesta Regum* i 94, ed. W. Stubbs, 2 vols (Rolls Series 90, London, 1887–9), vol. 1, p. 94. See also below, n. 24.
[11] The best text of the 786 report is *Alcuini . . . Epistolae* no. 3, pp. 19–29; a significantly inferior text was first printed by the 'Magdeburg Centuriators' VIII, cap. ix, cols 574–87, and reprinted, despite Wasserschleben's interim discovery of the Wolfenbüttel MS that

was held in Anglorum Saxonia', and dates it not only A.D. but also by the regnal year of Charlemagne rather than Hadrian. Both features suggest a Frankish provenance for the text, and this was taken to argue its composition by Abbot Wigbod, whom Charlemagne sent to accompany the legates, until Levison showed that George himself had moved in Frankish circles for a generation and been bishop of Amiens since 768.[12] George's report describes how Bishop Theophylact of Todi had brought him letters from Hadrian, containing *saluberrima statuta et omni sanctae ecclesiae necessaria*, with the further instructions that they were to proceed together to England in order to root out the tares that had grown up among the crop sown by Pope Gregory. What followed can be broken down into three phases.

The legates were first received by Archbishop Jaenberht of Canterbury, whom they advised as to 'what was necessary', and then at the court of Offa, who proceeded to meet King Cynewulf of the West Saxons in a council, at which both kings, suitably impressed by the Pope's 'holy writings', promised to carry out the necessary reforms. The second phase opened with the legation splitting up, Theophylact journeying into the kingdom of Mercia and Wales, while George and Wigbod went north to King Ælfwold and Archbishop Eanbald of York.[13] The king called a council of 'all the ecclesiastical and secular leaders' of Northumbria, where it emerged that 'other, no less serious vices (*reliqua vicia non minima*)' required correction. So, 'we wrote a *capitulare* concerning the various matters and put it forward, all in order, in their hearing'. The council promised obedience, and were '**then (tunc)**' given the papal letters. George at this point sets out the *capitula* which he had proferred. Their gist is as follows:

I.   The Nicene Creed to be observed by all; bishops to examine their priests in annual synod, as to mastery of, and devotion to, the faith approved in six universal councils.

II.   Baptism to be as canonically ordained; all to know Creed and Lord's Prayer. Godparents to take responsibility for teaching their charges these prayers when they grow up.

III.   Two councils to be held per year *secundum canonicas institutiones*; each

the Centuriators used (see below, n. 37), in *Councils and Ecclesiastical Documents relating to Great Britain and Ireland*, ed. A. W. Haddan and W. Stubbs (3 vols, Oxford, 1871), vol. 3, pp. 447–62. Leo III's letter is *Alcuini . . . Epistolae* no. 127, pp. 187–9, and *Councils and Ecclesiastical Documents*, pp. 523–5. EHD translates the one in part and the other in full: nos 191, 205, pp. 836–40, 861–2.

[12] The case for Wigbod was argued by A. Dove, 'Das älteste Zeugnis für den Namen Deutsch', *Sitzungsberichte der philosophisch-philologischen und der historischen Classe des königlichen bayrischen Akademie der Wissenschaften* (Munich, 1895), pp. 223–35 (it is the fact that it provides the oldest instance of *theostisce* – see below, p. 32 – that has attracted most attention to this text hitherto). Levison's characteristically effective intervention was in *England and the Continent in the Eighth Century* (Oxford, 1946), pp. 127–9.

[13] The report (p. 20) has Theophylact setting off to visit the *regem Merciorum* – somewhat nonsensically in the light of what had already been transacted with Offa; should we read *regnum*?

bishop to perambulate his diocese annually, arranging *conventicula* where all can hear the word of God: to preach, confirm, separate the incestuous, repress pagan practices. Pastors to act as vigilant shepherds, thinking not of earthly gain, fear or favour but of heavenly reward. [Isaiah 40:9; Jeremiah 1:17; Ezechiel 13:3, 5, 18–19; Matthew 25:21; John 10:11; II Timothy 4:1–2; Jude:12.].

IV. Bishops to see that all canons live *canonice*, and all monks or nuns *regulariter; discretio* between canon, monk and secular. Bishops, Abbots and Abbesses to set good examples to their followers. The six universal councils and papal decretals to be re-read and used to guide the Church aways from innovation or schism. [I Peter 5:3].

V. Successors to abbots and abbesses to be chosen, if need be from another community, with the 'counsel' of the local bishop. [Luke 12:35].

VI. Bishops to ordain only those of proven life as priests and deacons, and to stick to the *titulo* to which they were consecrated, *ita ut nullus de alterius titulo presbiterum aut diaconum suscipere presumat absque causa rationabili et literis commendaticiis.*

VII. Churches to keep the canonical hours.

VIII. Ancient privileges given to churches by the Roman see to be preserved; but what is agreed to be *contra canonica statuta* must be rejected.

IX. Priests not to go in for simulated fasting, like whited sepulchres. [Matthew 6:1; 23:27].

X. Mass not to be celebrated with bare legs; the offerings of the faithful to be bread, not *crusta*; chalice and paten not to be made of ox-horn, *quia sanguineae sunt*; bishops not to judge *secularia* in their councils, but 'to pray that God conserve [the Church] immaculate for the praise and glory of his name, *in omnia secula seculorum, Amen.* [II Timothy 2:4]

XI. *Ad reges et principes*: to rule with *disciplina*; to obey bishops; to have *consiliarios prudentes, Dominum timentes, moribus honestos.* [Deuteronomy 32:7; Psalms 2:12; 88:20, 24; 98:4; 104:14–15; Hosea 8:4; Malachi 2:7; Luke 10:16; Acts 13:22; I Corinthians 4:3; 6:3; Hebrews 13:17].

XII. *In ordinatione regum*, kings to be legally chosen by priests and the elders of the people, not born of adultery or incest: an adulterer can no more be the *christus Domini rex totius regni . . . heres patriae* than he can be a priest; honour due to kings from all; **in necem regis nemo communicare audeat, quia christus Domini est**; bishops guilty of such a crime to be degraded and cast out of their holy inheritance, as Judas was ejected from apostolic rank; all assenting to such sacrilege to be associated with the traitor Judas and burned in eternal fire; consent to a deed incurs punishment of the deed itself; reference to the hanging of two eunuchs who plotted to kill King Artaxerxes, to David's refusal to kill Saul (*christum Domini*) when at his mercy, and to his execution of him who boasted of killing Saul; 'for it has often been proved by examples among you (*apud vos*) that whoever have caused the death of their lords ended their lives in short order and lost both divine and earthly rights (*utroque iure caruerunt*)'. [I Samuel 24:5; 26:11; II Samuel 1:15; Esther 2:23; Ecclesiastes 10:20; Daniel 4:22; Romans 1:32; 13:1–2; I Peter 2:13, 17].

XIII. Rich and powerful to give just judgements; no favour to rich, contempt for poor, taking of bribes. [Exodus 20:17; Leviticus 19:15–16; Psalms 57:2; 81:4; Isaiah 1:17–18; 5:8–9; 58:6, 8; Matthew 7:2; 18:65; 25:34].

XIV. *Tributa* imposed on churches to be no greater than in 'Roman Law and the ancient custom of earlier emperors, kings and princes'; *sit concordia et unanimitas inter reges et episcopos, ecclesiasticos et laicos*. [John 13:35].

XV. Prohibition of 'unjust marriages': see below, pp. 38–9.

XVI. Disinheritance of sons of whores, adulterers and nuns: see below, pp. 38–9. [Romans 6:16; I Corinthians 3:17; 7:21; Ephesians 5:5; Galatians 4:30].

XVII. Tithes as in scripture; quotation of a *sapiens* (probably Caesarius of Arles) that *hoc plerumque contingit, ut qui decimam non tribuit, ad decimam revertitur*; ban on usury; just and equal weights and measures for all. [Exodus 22:29; Deuteronomy 14:22; Psalms 10:8; 14:1, 5; Proverbs 20:10; Malachi 3:10–11; Matthew 6:2; also *Augustine Sermo VIII vii 8*.].[14]

XVIII. Christians to keep their vows and promises to God. [Genesis 4:4–8; 5:24; 6:8ff; 14:18–20; 22:18; Judges 13; Psalms 75:12–13; 115:12; Proverbs 1:26; Ecclesiastes 5:3–5; Romans 2:5; Hebrews 10:31; James 2:23].

XIX. Christians to repudiate relics *ex ritu paganorum* – e.g. tattooing(?), *vestimenta more gentilium quos . . . patres vestri de orbe armis expulerunt*, mutilation of horses' nostrils, ears and tails; use of *sortes gentilium* in lawsuits; horse-eating. [I Corinthians 14:40].

XX. Urgency of conversion, confession, penance, eucharist; imminence of death, after which those in sin may not be prayed for. [Ecclesiasticus 5:8; Joel 2:12; Zacharias 1:3; Luke 3:8; James 5:16; I John 1:8].

George then repeats that he put these *decreta* before king, archbishop and all bishops, abbots, 'senators', dukes and people of the land; they vowed to accept them, 'confirmed them in our hand in your stead with the sign of the Holy Cross, and afterwards wrote with a careful pen on the parchment of this page, affixing the sign of the Holy Cross thus'. What follow are the attestations, charter-style (though without a cruciform mark in the MS as it stands), of Archbishop Eanbald, King Ælfwold, the bishops of Hexham, Lindisfarne, Whithorn, Mayo and an unidentified see, Sigha 'the patrician', and Ealdormen Alric and Sigewulf and Abbots Ealdberht and Ecgheard.

---

[14] *Caesarii Arelatensis Sermones*, no. xxxiii, ed. G. Morin, 2 vols, CCSL, 103–4 (Turnhout, 1953), vol. I, pp. 144–5 (where, however, the echo is not precise); S. *Aurelii Augustini Sermones ad populum* viii 7(8), PL 38, cols 70–1. Scriptural citations (as originally identified by Dümmler) are given throughout this digest of the *capitula*, because they form a crucial part of the author's train of thought; in canons 11–13, 16–18, they not only support but actually form the argument. Cf. n. 43.

In phase three of the mission, George returned south, the *lectores* Alcuin and Pyttel travelling with him as *legati* of the king and archbishop, and 'bringing the same *decreta* with them to the Mercian council'. There, Offa and the 'senators of the land', together with Archbishop Jaenberht and the other bishops, heard the '*singula capitula* read out in a clear voice, and lucidly expounded **both in Latin and in the vernacular (***tam Latine quam theodisce***)**, so that all could understand'. Again, all promised obedience, making the sign of the cross *in manu nostra in vice dominii vestri* and on the *presentem chartulam* itself. Again, the archbishop attested first, then the king (Offa is alone among both sets of attestations in professing to subscribe 'statutes'), a full complement of southern bishops (Hygeberht at their head, but as bishop of Lichfield), four abbots, the *duces* Brorda, Eadbald and Brihtwold and the *comes* Eadbald. The document then breaks off abruptly.

Before the argument proceeds any further, certain comments on this text are called for. In the first place, the report may be lacking its valediction, but there is no reason to believe that the capitulary is other than a complete record of synodical proceedings. The issue here has been complicated by the ingenuity of the 'northern' compiler of the *Anglo-Saxon Chronicle*'s D-E text. His sources comprised the famous A-B-C text annal for '785' recording the 'stormy (*geflitfullic*)' synod at Chelsea, when Archbishop Jaenberht lost half his province to the new archbishopric of Lichfield, and Ecgfrith was 'consecrated king'; and a 'Northumbrian' annal for 786 describing the papal legation. What he did was to add the second to the first under the year 785, thus confronting modern historians with the possibility that the synod which met the legate was the same as that which created the province of Lichfield and anointed Ecgfrith, and that the date in the *Chronicle* (corrected to 787) should be preferred to the triplicate dating in the heading of George's report itself.[15] But there is no reason to suppose that the legatine and *geflitfullic* synods were the same. Nothing in the report places the former at Chelsea. Nothing in any case excludes the possibility of major councils at the same place in successive years; indeed, this is what Archbishop Theodore had demanded at Hertford, and it happened more than once in this most conciliar of Anglo-Saxon ages.[16] The references in canon 12 to the

---

[15] See *Two of the Saxon Chronicles Parallel*, ed. J. Earle and C. Plummer, 2 vols (Oxford, 1892, 1899), vol. I, pp. 52–5; and *Historia Regum*, ed. T. Arnold, *Symeonis Monachi Opera Omnia*, 2 vols, Rolls Series 75 (London, 1882–5), vol. 2, p. 51 (there is likewise no reason to identify the northern council held before the legates with that of *Pincahala*, dated by this contemporary source to the following year). The identification of the Legatine and Chelsea councils goes back to Sir Henry Spelman, *Concilia, Decreta, Leges, Constitutiones in Re Ecclesiarum Orbis Britannici* (London, 1639), p. 291, whence Stubbs, *Councils*, pp. 445–6. H. Vollrath-Reichelt, *Königsgedanke und Königtum bei den Angelsachsen bis zur Mitte des 9. Jahrhunderts* (Cologne/Vienna, 1971), pp. 33–9, revives it, but her interesting discussion in *Die Synoden Englands bis 1066* (Paderborn, 1985), pp. 162–70, seems to stage a tactical retreat. It is surely relevant that Hygeberht does *not* attest the report as archbishop, and bishops of Lichfield usually head lists of episcopal witnesses at this date.

[16] Bede *HE* iv 5 (canon vii), ed. B. Colgrave and R. A. B. Mynors (Oxford, 1969), pp. 352–3. Good examples of English practice are the two great councils of Clovesho meeting

christus domini might seem to tie up neatly with the consecration of Ecgfrith, but a papal legate with a Frankish background had ample reason for using such language by 786, whatever Offa had in mind for his son.[17] Nor is Pope Leo's later mention of Offa's promise before papal legates to pay what would one day become 'Peter's Pence' proof of business omitted by the legatine report; Leo could be referring to Offa's first meeting with them, when he received papal letters 'with great joy and honour because of his reverence for the blessed Peter'.

Secondly, while George and Theophylact may have brought *saluberrima statuta* with them in their baggage, the decrees they drew up and reported back can hardly be equated with these. The report makes it relatively clear that the capitulary was a response to the *reliqua vicia* the legates heard about in the north. The papal letters were something else which the Northumbrian council was shown *tunc*, i.e. thereafter. If the two had been the same thing, there would have been no need, after the legates' return from Northumbria, for a second session with the Mercian authorities, who had already endorsed the pope's 'holy writings'. Many of the *capitula* are standard canon law, and the provision for two annual synods was in fact contrary to English usage; a few others, like that on *tributa*, seem to bespeak papal initiative. But some do seem to have specific local reference, implying a degree of English input.[18] One example is no. 12, with its all too well-informed reference to lord-slaying *apud vos*. Another could be no. 10, where conventional prohibitions on wooden altar furniture have been re-directed at what sound like Heorot-style drinking-horns. And especially intriguing is no 19: 'those whom your fathers expelled by arms from the country' might be Britons, but the use of the words *paganorum* and *gentilium* rather suggest Picts, as does the reference to tattooing (if this is what was meant); thus understood, the decree may have some significance for the ongoing chicken-egg debate about Picto-Northumbrian art.[19]

---

in 824 and 825: S. 1433–7; see also S. Keynes's list of Anglo-Saxon church councils in E. B. Fryde *et al.*, eds, *Handbook of British Chronology*, 3rd edn, (London, 1986), pp. 587–9.

[17] For the link with the unction of Charlemagne's sons by Hadrian in 781, see Levison, *England and the Continent*, pp. 118–19; F. M. Stenton, *Anglo-Saxon England*, 3rd edn (Oxford, 1971), p. 219 (part of a generally shrewd discussion of the whole episode); J. L. Nelson, 'Inauguration Rituals', in Sawyer and Wood, eds, *Early Medieval Kingship*, pp. 50–71, at p. 52; and N. Brooks, *The Early History of the Church of Canterbury: Christ Church from 597 to 1066* (Leicester, 1984), pp. 117–20.

[18] Vollrath-Reichelt, *Synoden Englands*, pp. 162–70, takes the opposite view, though she does note the idiosyncracy of chapter 10.

[19] The Picts were of course no longer pagan, but they had ceased to be so a lot more recently than the Britons, and aspects of their culture might very well have struck an outsider as unregenerate, just as they might reasonably, if inaccurately, seem victims of Northumbrian expansion. For the Picto-Northumbrian art debate, see opposing views in I. Henderson, *The Picts* (London, 1967), pp. 117–34; and R. B. K. Stevenson, 'Sculpture in Scotland in the C6th to C9th A.D.', in V. Milojovic, ed., *Kolloquium über spätantike und frühmittelalterlichen Skulptur*, 2 vols (Heidelberg, 1971), vol. 2, pp. 65–74, at pp. 67–70. The depiction of horses on some Meigle stones bear further examination in the light of the mutilations criticized in canon 19: J. Romilly Allen and J. Anderson, *The Early Christian Monuments of Scotland* (Edinburgh, 1903), Part III, figs 311B, 313B, 314B, 344, 345A; Mrs

The last and not the least point to make is that, by the standards of the 780s, the legatine decrees are sophisticated stuff. Divided as they are into ten canons directed at churchmen (concluding with 'Amen') and ten for laymen (concluding *qui vivat et regnat in secula seculorum*), it is in this respect the first of what would become a long Carolingian – and eventually an English – tradition; indeed, the capitulary has a much more significantly 'secular' content than all other ostensibly ecclesiastical legislation in the Anglo-Saxon period.[20] The decree on monks and canons is earlier than almost any comparably clear statutory distinction in the early medieval West.[21] Treason legislation in this biblical style had not previously featured in northern European law.[22] The twelfth canon is also, if problematically, by far the earliest attempt to establish a legislative difference between legitimately and illegitimately born princes.[23] The antecedents, if any, of this impressive capitulary, and its links with what was soon to follow under Charlemagne deserve a much more extensive exploration than they can possibly receive here; the pioneering researches of such as Professor Mordek will doubtless open them up in due course. What is already clear is that Bishop George had associated the ruling establishments of northern and southern England with law-making which emphatically belongs to the great age of legislation in Church and State then dawning.

It is also clear that these essentially exhortatory *capitula* could indeed be

Henderson kindly informs me that she would date cases of 'docked tails (*caudas amputatis*)' to the ninth century.

[20] The earliest Frankish example seems to be the Capitulary of Thionville (805): *Capitularia Regum Francorum*, ed. A. Boretius and V. Krause, MGH LL 2, 2 vols (Hannover, 1883–97), nos. 43–4, vol. 1, pp. 120–6 (citations of *Capitularia* are henceforward by number and page from this edition); the Capitulary of Mantua (*Capitularia* 92–3, pp. 194–8) was re-dated to 813, on the basis of a MS unknown to Boretius, by F. Patetta, 'Sull' introduzione della Collezione d' Ansegiso . . .', *Atti della R. Accademia delle Scienze di Torino* XXV:15 (1889–90), pp. 876–85, at pp. 883–4 (a reference I owe to Chris Wickham). The clearest English examples are *II–III Edg.*, *IV Edg.* and *I–II Cn.*, pp. 194–215, 278–371.

[21] See my discussion, with references, 'Æthelwold and his continental counterparts: contact, comparison, contrast', in B. Yorke, ed., *Bishop Æthelwold: His Career and Influence* (Woodbridge, 1988), pp. 16–18, 37–8. The nearest early counterpart to the 786 decree is canon 11 of the Council of Verneuil (755): *Capitularia* no. 14, vol. 1, p. 35. This capitulary is also closest to the 786 decrees in overall range; it may be significant that Bishop George is found 'assenting' to the Compiègne decree two years later: *Capitularia* no. 15 ch. 14, vol. 1, p. 38.

[22] Cf. the conspectus available in F. S. Lear, *Treason in Roman and Germanic Law* (Austin, 1965), esp. pp. 32–3, 40–1, 82–5, 181–9, 205–7, 235–8 (it has to be said that Lear's studies largely ignore the possible impact of biblical prescription in this field).

[23] Cf. P. Stafford, *Queens, Concubines and Dowagers: The King's Wife in the Early Middle Ages* (London, 1983), pp. 62–71. I suggested in J. Campbell, ed., *The Anglo-Saxons* (Oxford, 1982), pp. 116–17, that there may be some sort of connection between the attitudes of the legates to this problem and the appearance of the 'Anglian' collection of English royal genealogies (with their Welsh offshoot) at about this time. Another possible 'first' for the 786 capitulary was its decree (no. 2) on the duties of godparents: cf. J. Lynch, *Godparents and Kinship in Early Medieval Europe* (Princeton, 1986), pp. 318–28. There may well be more yet.

characterized as *mores* in the usual sense ('conduct', 'behaviour') that Alcuin gave the word. Such a reminder would moreover have been well-targeted if, as has been plausibly argued, his letter was addressed not to the obscure Osberht but to Brorda, right-hand man to Offa and his son for almost forty years, and himself a witness of the 786 proceedings. But particularly significant are the two sentences which immediately follow the reference to the *mores . . . quos . . . Offa . . . instituit*:

> And that the bishops and servants of God serve Christ in integrity and moderation, and that they preach to the people in the piety of the holy religion, and set an example for good, that they may deserve to be heard by the Lord God Almighty in holy prayers for the people. And require the lay magnates (*potentes laicos*) to make just judgements for the people and lawful marriages; and that they be faithful to their lord (*ut fideles sint ad dominum suum*), and in unanimity and concord among themselves.[24]

Such principles are liberally distributed throughout the cornucopia of advice with which Alcuin showered the great men of England and Francia in his day. The demands made of 'bishops and servants of Christ' could have been penned by anyone with the most nodding acquaintance with Gregory's *Liber Regulae Pastoralis*. The qualities expected of laymen are, with one important exception, the stuff of Carolingian 'mirrors of princes', not least Alcuin's *Liber de Virtutibus et Vitiis* addressed to Count Guy.[25] But the exception is important. Fidelity to lords is not a virtue that figures prominently in the *speculum* tradition; and 'Osberht's' is one of only two letters in which Alcuin urges it. This is also the only letter in which the 'lay' *desiderata* of justice, chastity, fidelity and concord are so neatly packaged. Again, it is almost alone in its bi-polar balance between instructions for clerical and secular potentates. If one discounts tithe, a subject on which Alcuin had notoriously mixed feelings, and the 'pagan' fashions in tattooing and costume, which he may have thought more specifically relevant to Northumbria, Alcuin's sentences are in fact a reasonably faithful rehearsal of the main points in the capitulary read out before Offa and the Mercian council in 786.[26] The vagueness of his summary is easily explained if he no longer had

[24] See n. 10. A. T. Thacker, 'Some Terms for Noblemen in Anglo-Saxon England, c.650–900', in D. Brown, J. Campbell and S. C. Hawkes, eds, *Anglo-Saxon Studies in Archaeology and History* 2 BAR, BS 92 (Oxford, 1981), pp. 201–36, at pp. 218–20. In view of the other debts which this paper owes to Professor Bullough, it is fair to say that he 'would find it difficult to identify *mores . . . castos* with the synodal decrees'.
[25] [Alcuini] *De Virtutibus et Vitiis Liber ad Widonem Comitem*, PL 101, cols 613–38. Cf. H. H. Anton, *Fürstenspiegel und Herrscherethos in der Karolingerzeit* (Bonn, 1968), pp. 85–107.
[26] Alcuini . . . *Epistolae* (as n. 10) no. 16, p. 43, addressed to King Æthelred of Northumbria, is a possible echo of 786 on 'pagan' fashions, as noted by the percipient C. J. B. Gaskoin, *Alcuin: His Life and Work* (London, 1904), pp. 62–4. For Alcuin on tithe (admittedly for the **newly converted**), see *Epistolae* nos. 107, 110–13, pp. 153–4, 156–66. As regards fidelity and the 'Mirror' tradition, the famous remarks of the Lady Dhuoda (cf. F. L. Ganshof, *Feudalism*, trans. P. Grierson, 3rd edn (London, 1964), pp. 33–4) are the exception that proves the rule. But Alcuin (and Charlemagne) did of course commend fidelity in other ways: e.g. *Epistolae* nos. 101, 231, pp. 147, 376.

access to the text, and was recalling its general tenor from the part he had played in proceedings eleven years before.

Two other letters of Alcuin are worth a glance in this context. One is addressed to King Æthelred of the Northumbrians, together with the 'patrician', Osbald, and the *dux*, Osberht (presumably a Northumbrian rather than the supposed recipient of the admonition on Offa's *mores*). It is one of a series inspired by the Lindisfarne disaster of June 793. Appreciably longer than the Mercian letter, it covers the same sort of ground and contains Alcuin's other specific injunction on fidelity to lords. It ends with the observation that it is for bishops 'to put right monasteries, to arrange the life of servants of God, to preach the word of God to the people, and diligently educate the folk subject to them', while laymen should 'obey preaching, be just and merciful'. But the call to peace, mercy and justice, chastity and fidelity, had come earlier on; and in general, the presentation of instructions in this letter is much more rambling and repetitive. Its original inspiration looks more like Pseudo-Cyprian than the 786 decrees. If, moreover, the parallels still seem striking, it may be recalled that the 786 capitulary was first submitted to the Northumbrians, as Alcuin was well placed to know. If there is no corresponding association here between the decrees and Northumbrian royalty, Ælfwold had been responsible for Æthelred's expulsion from the throne in 779, and to draw attention to his possible role in their promulgation would not have been tactful.[27]

The other letter is to King Cenwulf and is contemporary with the Mercian patrician's. It too has a possible hint of Offa's 'laws':

> Always bear in mind the excellent customs (*optimos . . . mores*) of your most noble predecessor, his moderation in way of life and zeal for correcting the life of the Christian people.

After a guarded allusion to Offa's darker deeds, and their probable consequence in his son's premature death, Cenwulf is told to

> have prudent counsellors, fearing God, loving justice, desiring peace with friends, showing faith and holiness in pious living (*consiliarios prudentes, Deum timentes, iustitiam amantes, pacem cum amicis desiderantes, fidem et sanctitatem in conversatione pia ostendentes*).

This might almost be a verbal quotation from the last sentence in the eleventh of the 786 decrees. The echo in Alcuin's letter to Æthelred is even stronger: there is an additional reference to the *honestis moribus* of ideal advisers. Elsewhere, notably in two letters to Charlemagne's heir and namesake, the qualities to be

---

[27] *Alcuini . . . Epistolae* no. 18, pp. 49–52; cf. *De Duodecim Abusivis Saeculi*, ed. S. Hellmann, Texte und Untersuchungen zur Geschichte der altchristlichen Literatur, 34, 1; 3, iv(1) (Leipzig, 1909), pp. 51–3, and J. M. Wallace-Hadrill, *Early Germanic Kingship in England and on the Continent* (Oxford, 1971), pp. 105, 119–20. In *Epistolae* no. 16, p. 43, the process of moral degeneration in Northumbria is alleged to have got under way in King Ælfwold's time.

looked for in councillors come to much the same thing but are differently phrased.[28] Seen in isolation, the sentiments in Cenwulf's letter could hardly be traced back to the legatine decrees. Viewed alongside similar threads in the letters to 'Osberht' and Æthelred, they might seem to make a pattern. There remains a temptation to set all these passages aside as platitudinous conventions. Yet it can be cancelled out by the consideration that Alcuin's exposure to the 786 legislation antedates almost his entire correspondence and could well have been formative. And Alcuin was likewise formative for the whole Carolingian 'mirror of princes' tradition.[29]

The sentences in Alcuin's letter to 'Osberht' may after all have no direct relation to the preceding endorsement of Offa's *mores*, just as these *mores*, whether in that letter or Cenwulf's, may be a matter not of Offa's law-making but of the general example he set. But the context does at least suggest a connection between what Offa 'instituted' and the qualities that Alcuin went on to advocate. The implications are important. Even if the *mores* were a law-code other than the legatine decrees, Offa's 'real' legislation is seen to follow the same lines as those laid down by the papal legates (as is anyway intrinsically probable). If, however, it was the 786 capitulary that was thus described, then a witness of proceedings before the Mercian council evidently regarded them as in some sense Offa's responsibility. It follows that Alfred could have done so too.

We can now turn back to the historiographically more influential, if chronologically secondary, evidence of King Alfred. An important first point is that Alfred does *not* specify a code as such:

> But those which I found which seemed to me most just, either **in the time of** my kinsman, King Ine, or of **Offa, king of the Mercians**, or of Æthelberht, who first among the English received baptism (*on Ines dæge, mines mæges, oððe on Offan Mercna cyninges, oððe on Æthelbryhtes, þe ærest fulluhte onfeng on Angelcynne*), I collected herein.

The antecedent of this sentence, is (some way back) the whole legislative history of Christendom since the Council of Jerusalem:

> When it came about that many peoples had received the faith of Christ, many synods (*seonoðas*) were assembled throughout all the earth, and likewise throughout the English (*geond ealne middangeard, 7 eac swa geond Angelcyn*) . . . of holy bishops and also of other distinguished wise men (*oðerra geðungenra witena*); they then established . . . that secular lords (*weoruldhlafordas*) might . . . receive . . . compensation in money (*fiohbote*)

---

[28] *Alcuini . . . Epistolae* no. 123, pp. 180–1. Cf. nos. 18, 188, 217, pp. 51, 315, 361. There remains the problem that Alcuin's letters to Offa himself (nos. 64, 101, pp. 107, 146–8) contain no such echoes; but this is a difficulty on any interpretation of the *mores . . . quos . . . Offa instituit.*

[29] Dümmler was tempted to see Alcuin as in some sense responsible for the composition of the 786 decrees: 'Zur Lebensgeschichte Alchuins', *Neues Archiv* XVII (1892), pp. 53–70, at pp. 61–2. Dr C. Cubitt makes a good case for this in chapter 7 of her Cambridge Ph.D. thesis, 'Anglo-Saxon Church Councils c. 650–c. 850' (1990).

for almost every misdeed at the first offence, which compensation they fixed; only for treachery to a lord (*hlafordsearwe*) they dared not declare any mercy, because Almighty God adjudged none for those who scorned him, nor did Christ . . . adjudge any for him who gave him over to death (*nane ne gedemde þe hine to deaðe sealde*). They then in many synods fixed the compensations for many human misdeeds, and they wrote them in many synod-books, here one law, there another (*on monegum senoðum monegra menniscra misdæda bote gesetton, 7 on monega senoðbec hie writan, hwær anne dom hwær operne*). But those which . . .[30]

The judgements laid down 'in the time of . . . Offa king of the Mercians' thus belonged to a longer and wider tradition than that represented merely by the legislation of Æthelberht and Ine. It was a reasonable deduction of Liebermann's that they took the same form as the codes of Æthelberht and Ine. But one might just as reasonably observe that a '*senoðboc*' '*gesetton*' by 'holy bishops' and '*oðerra geðungenra witena*' '*on . . . dæge . . . Offan Mercna cyninges*' is exactly what the 786 capitulary is.[31] And if it does not contain the sort of *menniscra misdæda bote* that dominate earlier English codes as well as Alfred's own, it does 'declare no mercy' for *hlafordsearwe*, with specific reference to Judas among other biblical examples. Indeed, this was the only English precedent behind the treason law which Alfred went on to include in a code where, by his own claim, 'I dared not presume to set in writing at all many [laws] of my own'.[32]

Treason legislation, however, was widespread in 'barbarian' codes and capitularies by the end of the ninth century; unless Alfred were as insular as many of his subsequent admirers he need not have found the requisite *foregenga* in 786. But another of his laws bears a more compelling resemblance to the legatine capitulary. Discussing the case of nuns brought out of their monasteries without royal or episcopal leave (*lefnesse*), Alfred orders:[33]

If she outlives him who brought her out, she is to have nothing of his inheritance (*ierfes*). If she bears a child, it is not to have any of that *ierfes*, any more than the mother.

This may be compared with the fifteenth and sixteenth of the 786 *decreta*:

We forbid unjust and incestuous marriages to all whether with handmaids of God and other disallowed persons, or with relatives and kin or the wives of others . . . By law (*decreto*) legitimate inheritance is denied to the children of prostitutes. We declare by apostolic authority that the sons of adulterers and nuns are altogether spurious and adulterous. For we do not

---

[30] *Alf*. Prol. 49.7–9, pp. 44–7. Turk, *The Legal Code of Alfred the Great*, p. 39 rightly took *þas* in the first line of 49.9 as referring back; Liebermann's grounds for dissent (*Gesetze* vol. 3, p. 50, *ad loc*.) amounted to a denial on principle that Alfred had been influenced by *Synodbücher*!

[31] Liebermann, *Gesetze* vol. 2, p. 600 (*s.v.* Offa).

[32] *Alf*. Prol. 49.9, 4–4.2, pp. 46–7, 50–1.

[33] *Alf*. 8–8.2, pp. 54–5.

hesitate to declare that a virgin who has vowed herself to Christ and put on in imitation the garment of holy Mary is the bride of Christ.

Alfred's laws look like an application of the principles set out by the papal legates. And the crucial point is that in this respect the provisions of 786 and of Alfred's code stand not only together but also alone.

The illegitimacy of prostitutes' offspring was standard Roman Law; this was perhaps what the legates meant by *decreto*. Likewise, the earliest papal legislation had of course borne heavily on any sort of breach in the chastity vows of women. A decretal of Innocent I (401–17), duly codified by Dionysius Exiguus, made just that extrapolation from earthly to heavenly marriages which underlies the argument of 786.

> If it is principle among men that whoever marries another when her husband lives is held an adulteress debarred from penance unless one of the two men dies, how much more should this be held of one who previously joined herself to an immortal troth, and afterwards moved over to human marriage?[34]

The nearest parallel to the further extension of this argument lies in laws of Liutprand's eleventh year (723). After another comparison between the conjugal rights of Christ and of lesser bridegrooms, Liutprand orders that the errant nun's entire property be forfeit *ad potestatem palatii*. His next law but one goes on to the offpsring of uncanonical marriages (stepmother, stepdaughter, brother's wife, wife's sister), who are denied legitimate inheritance. The similarity between these provisions and the 786 *capitula* may be thought close enough to suggest that one influenced the other. But even if this is so, and despite the fact that Liutprand's law was renewed by the Carolingian rulers of ninth-century Italy, the *capitula*, consecutive rather than separated, and providing for disinheritance rather than forfeiture, remain much the more plausible source of inspiration for Alfred himself.[35] There is, in any event, no other parallel. Visigothic law is concerned to establish the rights of apostates' legitimate children; so also, Chlothar II's edict following the Council of Paris (614). The comprehensive 'Ecclesiastical Capitulary' of Louis the Pious (818/19) was content to quote the normative decretal of Gelasius (492–6). Ninth-century Frankish legislation went little further, even when Archbishop Hincmar was confronted with a gross specific scandal at the Council of Douzy (874). Especially interesting, because

---

[34] *Iustiniani Digesta* XXIII ii 41–8, ed. Th. Mommsen and P. Krüger, 16th edn (Berlin, 1954), vol. 1, pp. 332–3 – a collection of commentaries on Augustus' '*Lex Iulia et Papia*'; cf. *Codex Theodosianus* IV vi 3, ed. Th. Mommsen and P. M. Meyer, 2nd edn (Berlin, 1954), vol. 1(2), p. 176 – Constantine's characteristic Augustan echo. *Decreta Innocentii Papae* xix, in *Collectio Decretorum Pontificum Romanorum auctore Dionysio Exiguo*, PL 67, cols 244–5.

[35] *Liutprandi Leges* 30, 32, ed. F. Bluhme, *Leges Langobardorum* MGH, LL in fol. 4 (Hannover, 1868), pp. 122–3, and cf. *Liutpr. Leg.* 76 (726), p. 138; *Capitularia* 157 c. 5, 158 c. 6, 168 c. 7, 210 c. 12, vol. 1, pp. 317, 319, 336; vol. 2, p. 83.

almost contemporary with Alfred's code, was the Council of Tribur (895). The council itself followed Gelasius' decretal with earlier pronouncements to the same effect by Pope Siricius (384–99) and the Council of Chalcedon (451), adding that there should be an appropriate division between the guilty parties. The 'capitulary' versions, subsequently taken up by Regino of Prüm, elaborated upon this last point: any communal money or lands was to be 'dispersed' to avoid scandal.[36] Two points thus seem relatively clear. Given the disinheritance of offspring from any conventionally adulterous liaison, the logical leap to the consequences of cuckolding Christ could have been made by any sub-Roman legislator, so that the legates of 786 and King Alfred could have come to the same conclusion independently. Yet in actual fact, the legates of 786 and King Alfred were the only ones who did so; and this is, at the very least, an interesting coincidence.

Possible references to Offa's 'law-code' have hitherto been found in a letter of Alcuin and in Alfred's code. In each, there are echoes of the 786 capitulary. These *capitula* could fairly be called both 'good, moderate and chaste customs', and a 'synod-book written down in Offa's time'. A final question, then, is whether the *statuta* that Offa subscribed could also be said to have been 'instituted' by him? Everything here depends on the form in which they were presented to their English audience.

The capitulary is extant only as part of Bishop George's report to the Pope. A copy of the whole report was incorporated into a canonical collection of the later-tenth or early-eleventh century, which is probably from Hildesheim, and is now at Wolfenbüttel. The collector's access to it is most easily explained if Bishop George left a copy at his Frankish see of Amiens; significantly, perhaps, the Wolfenbüttel collection contains the decrees of a Roman council of 769 at which George was also present.[37] In any event, the 786 decrees themselves must

---

[36] *Lex Visigothorum* III iv 12, v 2, ed. K. Zeumer, MGH, LL I, (I) (Hannover, 1902), pp. 151–2, 159–60; *Edictum Chlotharii* c. 18, ed. C. de Clercq, *Concilia Galliae*, CCSL 148A (Turhout, 1963), p. 285; *Capitularia* no. 138 c. 25, vol. 1, p. 279 (cf. *Decreta Gelasii Papae* xx (as n. 34), col. 308); *Concilium Duziacense*, Mansi, *Sacrorum Conciliorum nova et amplissima collectio* XVII, col. 288; *Capitularia* 252 c. 23, vol. 2, pp. 225–6 (cf. *Epistola Decretalis Papae Siricii* vi (as n. 34), col. 234; *Regulae Ecclesiasticae . . . a Chalcedonensi . . . concilio* xvi (ibid.), col. 174).

[37] On this collection, in Wolfenbüttel MS Helmstadensis 454, see P. Fournier and G. Le Bras, *Histoire des Collections Canoniques en Occident depuis les Fausses Decretales jusqu'au Décret de Gratien*, 2 vols (Paris, 1931), vol. 1, pp. 300–5. Its discovery was first signalled by H. Wasserschleben, *Beiträge zur Geschichte der vorgratianischen Kirchenrechtsquellen* (Leipzig, 1839), pp. 29–30, 162–5. His attribution of the collection to Archbishop Rotger of Trier (+ 930) appears to have been a guess. It was taken up in the Wolfenbüttel catalogue (O. von Heinemann, *Die Handschriften der herzoglichen Bibliothek zu Wolfenbüttel: I, Die Helmstedter Handschriften*, vol. 1 (Wolfenbüttel, 1884), no. 488), and has hence influenced other writers (e.g. Dove, as in n. 12); but it was exposed as error by L. Weiland, 'Zwei ungedruckte Papstbriefen aus der Kanonensammlung des sogenannten Rotgers von Trier', *Zeitschrift für Kirchenrecht* 20 (1885), p. 100. I owe to Professor Bullough the information that this was the MS used by the Magdeburg Centuriators, and that it 'is almost certainly an early-eleventh-century Hildesheim ms., one of a group which is currently the subject of a thesis by Herr Schuffels (Göttingen)'.

have had an original existence independently of their inclusion in George's report: it is hardly to be supposed that the *pagina/chartula* which Alcuin and Pyttel 'brought with them' from Northumbria, and which was then proclaimed and 'subscribed' at the southern English council, was the report itself. Now, it happens that the legatine decrees can be shown to have had a specifically 'Anglo-Saxon' history as late as the tenth century, when they were extensively excerpted for the 'Chapters' of Archbishop Oda (942/6).[38] Oda might theoretically have read a copy of George's whole report, re-exported to England; but it is surely more likely that he used a version of the capitulary extant in its own right and descended from that which the legates must have left behind. This would presumably have been supplied with some sort of prologue giving an English account of the circumstances in which the decrees were composed and promulgated. If the records of the Councils of *Clovesho* (747) and Chelsea (816) are any guide, such a prologue would have stressed the presidency of the archbishop and merely noted the presence of the king.[39] Yet Alcuin, writing after eleven further years experience of Charlemagne's forceful ways with the Church, and Alfred, anxious to emphasize his law-book's debts to the traditions of all the kingdoms subject to him, each had reasons for highlighting the role of Offa.

The reason why scholars have barely considered the hypothesis put forward in this paper hitherto is that they have been looking for a code in the mould of Æthelberht's, Ine's and Alfred's own. One reason why it may remain unacceptable is the sense that the 786 decrees are quite different, in form and content, from law-making as the early Middle Ages understood it. This view takes insufficient account of the sheer variety of early medieval legislation. In form, the text we have is indeed anomalous, but it has to be remembered that this is not likely to be the form in which it was originally promulgated. If, as is possible, there were a written text of what was expounded *theotisce*, that would not stand out too sharply in the corpus of pre-conquest legislation *for Gode 7 for worlde* (it is possible that one reason why the decrees were read out in the vernacular was that this was already established as the proper medium for laws with wider application than the Church alone).[40] Its content is not so very different from the pious exhortations, equally unleavened by pertinent sanctions (and significantly dismissed as 'pseudo-legislation'), which Archbishop Wulfstan drafted for Æthelred

---

[38] G. Schoebe, 'The Chapters of Archbishop Oda (942/6) and the Canons of the Legatine Councils of 786', *Bulletin of the Institute of Historical Research* 35 (1962), pp. 75–83; cf. *Councils and Synods*, ed. Whitelock, no. 20, vol. 1, pp. 67–74. A trace has also been detected in the *Regularis Concordia* (T. Symons, 'Regularis Concordia: History and Derivation', in D. Parsons, ed., *Tenth-Century Studies: Essays in Commemoration of the Millenium of the Council of Winchester and Regularis Concordia* (Chichester, 1975), pp. 37–59, at p. 44); but not, anyway as yet, in the reading or writing of Archbishop Wulfstan.

[39] Haddan and Stubbs, *Councils and Ecclesiastical Documents*, vol. 3, pp. 362, 579; cf. Vollrath-Reichelt, *Synoden Englands*, pp. 132–44, rightly correcting some sloppy observation on my part.

[40] Bede, *HE II* 5, ed. Colgrave and Mynors, pp. 150–1, for Æthelberht's laws *conscripta Anglorum sermone.*

II; indeed, Wulfstan's Latin *Relatio* of the legislation approved at Enham in 1008 has several points of similarity with the 786 report as it now stands.[41]

There is another parallel which is just as striking and much nearer in date. Only three years after the papal legation to England, Charlemagne issued his great *Admonitio Generalis*. Its prologue, with its explicit comparison between Charles himself and 'Holy Josiah', who, 'as we read in the Books of Kings, strove to recall the kingdom given to him by God to the worship of the true God by travelling about correcting and admonishing', gives the *Admonitio* all the appearance of the most solemn royal law-giving. It remained inspirational for many of Charlemagne's subsequent capitularies, and stood at the head of the capitulary collection made by Ansegisus *ad christianam religionem conservandam atque concordiam pacis et dilectionis in aecclesia catholica tenendam*. This seems a far cry from the legatine capitulary of 786 as it now survives. But the first 59 chapters of the *Admonitio* consist of excerpts from the so-called *Dionysio-Hadriana*, the code of canon law which Pope Hadrian I had sent Charlemagne fifteen years before; here is a quite explicit case of a European king in the 780s making papal legislation his own.[42] The remaining thirty-one chapters of the *Admonitio* go on to cover much the same ground as the 786 capitulary, with several of the same biblical quotations: appropriate preaching, peace and concord, just judgement, honouring of father and mother, prohibitions of blasphemy, idol-worship, homicide, theft and *iniusta connubia* (the inspiration hereabouts is unmistakably the Decalogue), episcopal administration of standards in the local churches of their dioceses, monastic vows, weights and measures, and so on.[43] Nowhere in 789 any more than in 786 is there a hint of either customary adjustment or punitive enforcement; *Lex Salica* (which was nonetheless to be reissued twice in the next decade and a half, on the second occasion with supplementary *capitula* in the appropriate

[41] VI *Atr.*, pp. 247, 249, 251, 253, 255, 257. The parallels include explicit scriptural citation such as is very rarely found in vernacular codes; indeed, the 786 report could itself be described as a *Relatio*: K. Jost, *Wulfstanstudien*, Schweizer Anglistische Arbeiten 23 (Bern, 1950), pp. 30–1.

[42] *Capitularia* no. 22, vol. 1, pp. 52–62; cf. nos. 28, 35, 37, 59, and *Ansegisi Abbatis Capitularium Collectio* (*ibid.*), vol. 1, pp. 75–8, 102–4, 107–9, 146, 397–405. Cf. H. Mordek, 'Dionysio-Hadriana und Vetus Gallica – historisch geordnetes und systematisches Kirchenrecht am Hofe Karls des Großen', *Zeitschrift der Savigny-Stiftung für Rechtsgeschichte, kanonistische Abteilung* 55 (1969), pp. 39–63.

[43] Biblical citations used to similar effect in each include: Exodus 20:17 (c. 66), Proverbs 20:10 (c. 74), Ecclesiastes 5:4 (c. 73), John 13:35 (c. 62), II Timothy 4:1–2 (c. 82). The argument set out here is of course materially strengthened if, as seems more than possible, Alcuin was heavily involved in the composition of the second half of the *Admonitio*: see F-C. Scheibe, 'Alcuin und die *Admonitio Generalis*', *Deutsches Archiv* 14 (1958), pp. 221–9; defended (with additional evidence from scriptural quotations) by D. A. Bullough, 'Alcuin and the Kingdom of Heaven: liturgy, theology and the Carolingian Age', in U-R. Blumenthal, ed., *Carolingian Essays: Andrew W. Mellon Lectures in Early Christian Studies* (Washington, 1983), p. 22, n. 44; and by W. Hartmann, 'Die karolingische Reform und die Bibel', *Annuarium Historiae Conciliorum* 18 (1986), pp. 58–74 at pp. 62–3 (with some valuable remarks on the comparison between 786 and 789). No less pertinent is the possibility of Bishop George's influence on the *Admonitio*, for which (and much else to the point) see Chapter III of Professor Bullough's forthcoming book on Alcuin.

idiom) might be a world away. This does not of course show that Offa in 786 legislated as Charlemagne did in 789. It does show that a king whom both Alcuin and Charlemagne admired for his religious zeal as well as his martial prowess might have done.[44] There was no one mould for early medieval legislation. Nor is it merely a matter of variety. For the ruling elites of early medieval Europe, the warrior people of Israel were both binding example and awful warning. In their law-making, whatever their customary *fiohbote*, nothing could be more relevant than the tones of Moses, Samuel, David, Solomon and Isaiah.

The case presented in this paper is not conclusive and does not claim to be. The evidence admits up to four possibilities. The first is the orthodox view: the laws referred to by Alfred and perhaps Alcuin had no significant connection with 786, and represented a lost code of the normal earlier Anglo-Saxon type. Its virtue is that it raises only one real difficulty, the disappearance of so important a text, which, given the fate of so many other possible Offan memorials, is scarcely a difficulty at all. Secondly, the laws issued by Offa could have been a vernacular code more or less strongly influenced by what the papal legates laid down at his council; or thirdly, they could have been a written text of the vernacular exposition which the 786 capitulary is known to have received in Mercia but not Northumbria. Both these possibilities would allow for this paper's arguments for the links between the legatine *decreta* and what Alcuin and Alfred cited, while at the same time preserving the possible echoes of Mercian law that previous scholars have found in Alfred's code (*Boldgetal* could have appeared in place of *titulo* in a translation or adaptation of canon 6; *Lefness* actually occurs in Alfred's law on nuns). Finally, there is the hypothesis defended here: what Alcuin meant by the 'customs which Offa instituted', and Alfred by the 'judgements established in the time of King Offa', was simply the papal legates' Latin text. This mildly revolutionary suggestion paradoxically represents the least speculative position. There survives legislation of a sort that is known to have been promulgated before Offa and his council. At least one of Alfred's laws is quite probably taken from it. In a letter referring to the 'customs which Offa instituted', Alcuin rehearses its general gist. A text of it can anyway be shown to have been available in pre-conquest England. If this document had appeared with a prologue in the name of *Karolus rex Francorum*, it would not seem at all out of place in the Carolingian capitulary series. The exceptional circumstances of the papal visit explain what is itself exceptional, the appearance of a royal code at a date so widely separated from those of Ine and Alfred. Does the presence in Alfred's code of occasional features for which their derivation from a code of Offa is by no means the only possible explanation entitle us to believe in the existence of anything else?

Judgements made by historians can be influenced by their temperament to a degree which most would be loath to admit. What is 'orthodox', is often no more

---

[44] *Alcuini . . . Epistolae* nos. 64, 100, 123, pp. 107, 145, 181; cf. Wallace-Hadrill, *Early Germanic Kingship*, pp. 113–20.

than the assumption or speculation that was first in the field. In the penumbra of prehistory, where historical certainty is more elusive than ever, 'orthodoxy' ought to be less secure than in Anglo-Saxon studies it usually has been. For the case of Offa's 'law-code', counter-factual historiography may thus have some value. If scholars had taken their cue not from Alfred's prologue, in an intellectual climate treasuring all that seemed most vernacular and so 'archaic' in Anglo-Saxon law, but from Alcuin's *mores bonos et modestos et castos*, in the light thus cast by the spiritual and cultural aspirations of the Carolingian Renaissance, would not attention have been directed to the 786 *capitula*, with which Alcuin himself had a known connection? And once it had been thereby concluded, rightly or wrongly, that these *capitula* as circulated in southern England were considered to have been 'instituted' by Offa, would historians have looked anywhere else for Alfred's source?

In the event, the answers to these only partly rhetorical questions have little bearing on the debate whether Anglo-Saxon government depended on a plethora of lost documents or worked largely by word of mouth – whether it was actually or just apparently prehistoric. The text of the 786 capitulary used by Oda has itself been lost. Our knowledge of it depends on one continental collection compiled in the interest of papal 'legitimacy'. Whether or not this was Offa's 'law-code', the survival of something so significant by so tenuous a thread might seem to make the case for exponents of the Written Word school just as well as the prevailing view that the code is lost. In the course of the discussion, however, another issue has also arisen which may ultimately be more important. The legates' own representation of their role, as renewing the ancient bond between the papacy and the English, is often quoted, and rightly. What was not said then or since is that the English kingdoms were thus brought, however fleetingly, within the tradition of vigorously pastoral legislation that sought to equip Europeans for the struggle to be true warriors of God in a world encompassed by his enemies. If the argument presented here on Offa's behalf is accepted, it should not be forgotten that we are by the same token offered a unique example of Northumbrian legislation. What could have been the 'code of Ælfwold' deserves to be set alongside the welter of self-spilt blood that is the dominant image of northern English government and society after Bede. Assessments of Offa himself have been drastically affected by the paucity of evidence associated with him and by the nature of what evidence there is. How often do we read in students' essays (and not only there) that he was essentially a **warrior** who established his hegemony by force, whereas Alfred was a **statesman** who did so by consent! Yet Alcuin's letters suggest a dedicated and cultured monarch, who possessed a copy of Bede's *History* and had learned some of its lessons about the proper discharge of Christian kingship: a king, that is to say, not unlike what Alfred himself would seem in default of Asser and the king's own translations. Even the creation of the Lichfield archbishopric might fairly be thought more than just a political manoeuvre at the expense of hostile Canterbury; the motive (*propter vastitatem terrarum . . . et extensionem regni*) quoted in the papal letter that suppressed the scheme, is exactly what conscientious Carolingian re-organizers of church-government would have adduced.[45] Offa could have been Carolingian in more than just his coinage. The perception of 786 proposed here serves to deepen this perspective. Offa was associated with legislation similar in scope and spirit to the *Admonitio Generalis*, and three years earlier. As Peter Sawyer knows better than most, it is a good question whose fault it was that the 'Carolingianization' of English kingship had to begin all over again a century later. But it was assuredly not Offa's.

---

[45] For the archbishopric, see *Alcuini . . . Epistolae* no. 127, p. 188; cf. Levison, *England and the Continent*, pp. 86–8, 95–6; and D. A. Bullough, 'The dating of Codex Carolinus 95, 96, 97, Wilchar and the beginnings of the Archbishopric of Sens', *Deutsches Archiv* 18 (1962), pp. 223–30, at pp. 228–9. On Offa's 'culture', see *Epistolae* nos. 64, 101, pp. 107, 148 (pupils of Alcuin at Offa's court), and Levison, pp. 244–6 (Offa's copy of Bede). Cf., overall, my comments in *The Anglo-Saxons*, ed. Campbell, pp. 106, 110–12.

RECONSTRUCTING A ROYAL FAMILY:
REFLECTIONS ON ALFRED,
From Asser, chapter 2

Janet L. Nelson

Peter Sawyer has inclined many minds to many interesting tracks. On two where his guidance has been especially valuable, this paper attempts some further exploration: Anglo-Scandinavian interaction in the Viking Age, and early medieval kingship.[1] On both, the reign of Alfred occupies a critical point. Yet Alfred himself remains a curiously enigmatic figure. Asser's *Life*, with its account of Alfred's secret piety, and unidentified chronic illness, in some ways deepens the mystery.[2] In describing Alfred's youthful prayers for heaven-sent affliction to help him curb the lusts of the flesh, and then recording the onslaught of a second illness during Alfred's wedding feast, Asser hints at Alfred's anxieties about his own sexuality. A charter of the king's successor, Edward, reveals that Alfred had deprived a thegn of the benefice he held of the bishop of Winchester on grounds of the thegn's sexual misconduct (*stuprum*); but it goes on to say that Alfred thereafter returned the land to the bishop on receipt of a large payment.[3] Can

---

[1] The scale of Peter Sawyer's achievement is reflected throughout the present volume. Repeated references to 'S.' numbers in the notes below indicate my debt to *Anglo-Saxon Charters, An Annotated List and Bibliography* (London, 1968). Special acknowledgement is due here for *The Age of the Vikings* 2nd edn. (London, 1971), *Kings and Vikings* (London, 1982), and 'The royal *tun* in pre-Conquest England', in P. Wormald ed., *Ideal and Reality. Studies in Frankish and Anglo-Saxon Society presented to J. M. Wallace-Hadrill* (Oxford, 1983), pp. 273–99. But Peter has always trailed inspiration *et verbo et scripto*, and this is the place to thank him for many years' worth of both. For their help and criticism on the present paper, I am very grateful to Matthew Blows, Iain Fenn, Simon Keynes, Pauline Stafford, and Patrick Wormald, and also to John Gillingham and Ian Wood. Any remaining errors are of course mine.
[2] Asser, *De Rebus Gestis Ælfredi*, ed. W. H. Stevenson (Oxford, 1904), reprinted with a note by D. Whitelock on recent work (Oxford, 1959), translated S. Keynes and M. Lapidge, *Alfred the Great* (Harmondsworth, 1983). All page-references below are to Stevenson's edition and the translation of Keynes and Lapidge. Since 1983 the one important study on Asser has been J. Campbell's in C. J. Holdsworth and T. Wiseman, eds, *The Inheritance of Historiography* (Exeter, 1986), pp. 115–35. Despite Asser, and his exegetes, it remains true that, as W. J. Sedgefield wrote in his introduction to *King Alfred's Version of the Consolations of Boethius* (Oxford, 1900), p. vii, 'to very many intelligent people [Alfred is] a distinctly nebulous character'.
[3] S.374. Loss of lands was the penalty for adultery in a clause tacked on to the Alfred-Ine Code in the now-burnt Cotton MS Otho B XI: see D. Whitelock's note to F. M. Stenton,

these be termed the acts of a puritan, or a cynic? We need to shun such anach-ronistic labels if we want to reconstruct Alfred's motives, and the politics of ninth-century Wessex. Some of the complexities and contradictions in the heart of the West Saxon royal family, and within Alfred's own family-life, have left traces in Asser, still to be seen and chased up.

Asser himself says that he wrote up the *Life* in 893, which means that the last years of Alfred's reign, so poorly-documented in other sources too, are thus not directly covered.[4] But there are obvious advantages for us in being able to pin down Asser's information to a particular point in an ongoing political story which, through internal as well as external pressures, was subject to frequent change. Further, Asser wrote within the royal *familia* (household), close to the king and his kin. From there, and from then, Asser gives a view of a recent past through which Alfred's own changing priorities can be glimpsed. For it was Alfred himself who provided Asser with 'the truth' about the history of the West Saxon royal family in the period before 866 when Asser arrived in Wessex; and it was to Alfred that Asser dedicated his work.[5] We shall not get much closer to Alfred than this.

Thanks to recent scholarship, we now know quite a lot about Alfred and his brothers, his father, and paternal grandfather.[6] We know a lot less, however, about the rest of Alfred's kin: his antecedents and coevals on his mother's side, and also his children's generation. Asser tells something; but he certainly does not tell all – which is to say that his patron and source may have been economi-cal with the truth. If so, conflicts in the heart of the royal family – that acid test of early medieval kingship – may help explain why.

Though Asser's first chapter, on the paternal ancestry of Alfred, has often been commented on, chapter two, on Alfred's mother and maternal ancestry, has been relatively neglected. Like much of what Asser purveys, it is found nowhere else; it is hard to check, and hard to interpret.

> His mother was named Osburh, an extremely pious woman, noble in character and noble by birth: she was the daughter of Oslac, King Æthel-wulf's famous butler. Oslac was a Goth by nation, for he was sprung from Goths and Jutes, namely from the seed of Stuf and Wihtgar, two brothers

Anglo-Saxon England, 3rd revised edn. (Oxford, 1971), pp. 309–10, n. 5. The date of the addition *could* be early in the tenth century. My thanks are due to Patrick Wormald for clarification on this text.

4   The hole in the evidence for Alfred's last years has not attracted enough attention; but its size can be gauged by a glance at Keynes and Lapidge, *Alfred*, pp. 120, 191.

5   Asser, pref., c.13, pp. 1, 12 (Keynes and Lapidge, *Alfred*, pp. 67, 71).

6   See, notably, D. Dumville, 'The Ætheling', *ASE* 8 (1979), pp. 1–33; P. Stafford, 'The king's wife in Wessex', *Past and Present* 91 (1981), pp. 3–27; P. Wormald, in J. Campbell ed., *The Anglo-Saxons* (London, 1982), pp. 132–59; N. Brooks, *The Early History of the Church of Canterbury* (Leicester, 1985), pp. 145–7, 197–200; and references in Keynes and Lapidge, *Alfred*, p. 314, n. 3. See also J. L. Nelson, ' "A king across the sea": Alfred in Continental perspective', *TRHS* 5th series 36 (1986), pp. 45–68; and 'Wealth and wis-dom: the politics of Alfred', in J. Rosenthal ed., *Kings and Kingship*, Center for Medieval and Early Studies, State University of New York, *Acta* 11 (1986), pp. 31–52.

and also companions in arms, who received control over the Isle of White from their uncle King Cerdic and Cynric his son, their cousin, and slew the few Britons who inhabited that island, those they could find there, at the place which is called Guuitgaraburhg.[7]

Stuf and Wihtgar, whose names Asser gives in their OE forms, are persons familiar to any reader of the *Anglo-Saxon Chronicle*, which records, under the year 514, their arrival and victory over the Britons, and under the year 534, that they were younger kinsman of Cerdic and given the Isle of Wight (*Wiehte ealond*).[8] The name Stuf is not attested elsewhere. The OE word closest to it is *stofn*: stem, or progeny. Wihtgar means spear-man.[9] The pair look like mythical founding fathers. Asser's editor thought that Asser got these names from the ASC; and it used commonly to be assumed that the ASC here, as elsewhere in the earliest annals dealing with the settlement of Wessex, preserved the memory of genuine historical persons and events.[10] Asser's account of the activities of Stuf and Wihtgar on the Isle of Wight does indeed show strong affinities with the information given in the ASC under the years 530 and 534. But this need not mean that Asser took his material from the ASC: both could have drawn on a common source, which need not have been very old when Asser used it.[11]

The story of Stuf and Wihtgar rooted Alfred's mother's ancestors firmly in the Isle of Wight. It may not be coincidence that Alfred's daughter, and younger son, were bequeathed lands on the Isle of Wight in Alfred's Will, perhaps lands that had come to his from his mother.[12] Asser's Guuihtgaraburhg, which the ASC calls Wihtgara byrg: 'the burh of the dwellers of Wight', may not, after all, be Carisbrooke; but the place was apparently on Wight and familiar to a ninth-

---

[7] Asser, c. 2, p. 4. There is a striking similarity here with the *Life* of Louis the Pious by Thegan, ed. G. H. Pertz, MGH SS 2 (Hannover, 1829) pp. 585–604, where too the first and second chapters deal with the subject's paternal, then maternal, ancestry, and Louis' mother is praised in c. 2 as *nobilissimi generis* and *beatissima.*

[8] *Anglo-Saxon Chronicle*, s.a. 514, 534, ed. C. Plummer, *Two of the Saxon Chronicles Parallel*, 2 vols (Oxford, 1892, 1899), vol.1, pp. 14, 16; *The Anglo-Saxon Chronicle: a collaborative edition*, vol. 3, MS A, ed. J. Bately (Cambridge, 1986), p. 21. References hereafter are to ASC, and, unless otherwise specified, to Plummer's edition.

[9] Stevenson, *Asser*, p. 173 and n.1.

[10] Ibid., pp. 170–1; Stenton, *Anglo-Saxon England*, pp. 23–4. Cf. J. N. L. Myers, *The English Settlements* (Oxford, 1986), p. 146.

[11] Asser in c. 1 draws on a genealogy of Alfred's paternal line which circulated independently of the ASC. His version contains a significant variant which distinguishes it from that in ASC MS A: see below, p. 63, and n. 87. Asser's explanation in c. 2 of the relationship between Cerdic and Cynric, and Stuf and Wihtgar, is incompatible with the grandfather-grandson relationship between the first two men asserted in c. 1. In ASC, MS A, s.a. 534, Stuf and Wihtgar are termed *nefan* ('grandson' or 'nephew') of Cerdic and Cynric, which squares with the father-son relationship of the latter two in A's genealogy.

[12] Alfred's Will, trans. Keynes and Lapidge, *Alfred*, pp. 175, 177, and 321. Wellow, Isle of Wight, is identified here as the bequest to Alfred's youngest daughter Aelfthryth (rather than the Wellow in Hampshire left to his eldest daughter Æthelflaed), and the first estate left to Æthelweard, Alfred's younger son, is identified ibid. p. 319, as Arreton, Isle of Wight.

century audience.[13] This, said Plummer, 'shows that Wihtgar is a mere abstraction to account for the place-name . . . [which] throws some light on the historical value of these traditions'.[14] Quite.

But suppose we assess 'historical value' in another way? Suppose we abandon the attempt to sift this material for nuggets of sixth-century fact, and instead, treat it as evidence for ninth-century fiction? David Dumville has demonstrated that reconstruction of the Cerdicing genealogy, and of the early history of Wessex, was under way in the ninth century.[15] Stoutly resisting the temptation to speculate on the reasons for such revisionism, Dumville hints that the chronologists were not immune to contemporary political pressures.[16] Some temptations are worth yielding to; and Dumville's hints are worth pursuing through Asser's chapter 2. Even historians sceptical about the factual reliability of the early annals of the ASC seem to have believed that the descent of Alfred's mother from 'the seed of Stuf and Wihtgar' was an oral tradition in her family well-established by the ninth century. This inference has been that repeated mentions of Stuf and Wihtgar were inserted into the ASC (and adapted thence by Asser) to draw flattering attention to Alfred's maternal kin.[17] But how traditional was this 'tradition'? Asser shows (and he had Alfred's word for it) that another ninth-century 'custom', namely the denial of queenly status to the West Saxon king's wife, had been formed in the course of just two generations – *moderno tempore*.[18] In Alfred's maternal *genealogia* might be seen another recent invention of tradition, its purpose to establish a distant collateral link between the house of Cerdic and Alfred's mother's family: Stuf and Wihtgar might, for instance, have been understood to be Cerdic's sister's sons.[19] Women believed (or alleged) to be distant kin were perhaps preferred royal spouses, rather than simply hard to avoid.[20] The main beneficiaries of such beliefs were one branch of the Cerdicings, who needed every bit of ancestral charisma they could lay claim to, not least to distinguish them from other branches of that sprawling line. In other words, the story of Stuf and Wihtgar and of Osburh's descent from their seed, may tell us more about the concerns of Osburh's son (and perhaps of her husband too) than about those of her own natal family.

But the oddest thing about Asser's depiction of Stuf and Wihtgar is the one I

13 Plummer, Saxon Chronicles, vol. 2, p. 14, accepted the identification with Carisbrooke. So too does Myers, Settlements, pp. 145–6. But Stevenson, Asser, p. 174, showed that this cannot be right. See also P. Sims-Williams, 'The settlement of England in Bede and the Chronicle', ASE 12 (1983), pp. 1–41, at p. 30, n. 130.
14 Plummer, Saxon Chronicles, vol. 2, p. 14. Cf. Sims-Williams, 'The settlement of England', pp. 25, 30.
15 D. Dumville, 'The West Saxon genealogical regnal list and the chronology of early Wessex', Peritia 4 (1985), pp. 21–66.
16 Dumville, 'The West Saxon genealogical regnal list', pp. 42, n. 55; 52, n. 83, 56–8; 59, n. 114; 60–1; 64–5.
17 Sims-Williams, 'The settlement of England', pp. 30, 37. Cf. K. Sisam, 'Anglo-Saxon royal genealogies', Proceedings of the British Academy 39 (1953), pp. 287–348, at 337.
18 Asser, cc. 13, 14, pp. 11–2. See Stafford, 'The king's wife', pp. 3–4, 7 and passim.
19 Stevenson, Asser, p. 171; Stenton, Anglo-Saxon England, p. 24.
20 Cf. Stafford, 'The king's wife', pp. 14–6.

have so far left unmentioned: they are Goths. The first difficulty is that this seems to contradict the ASC, whose annal for 514 is sometimes translated:

In this year, the West Saxons Stuf and Wihtgar, came to Britain.[21]

This is not actually what any manuscript says: rather, a distinction is made between the first statement, that West Saxons came to Britain and landed at *Cerdicesora*, and the second statement, that Stuf and Wihtgar fought with the Britons and put them to flight. The gentile origin of Stuf and Wihtgar is thus not specified here. But why does Asser identify them as Goths? And why his apparent identification of Goths with Jutes? Is Asser trying to accommodate Bede with an oral tradition (as Dumville suggests in other contexts the West Saxon genealogists may have been)?[22] Or is Asser merely muddled? While Stenton thought '[Asser's] statement . . . good evidence that Stuf and Wihtgar were Jutes', Stevenson took a different view: Asser was the victim of his 'foreign origin' and proneness to be 'led by learned associations'(!). 'Such a confusion could scarcely be made by an Englishman in the time of King Alfred', according to Stevenson, for Alfred was clear on the distinction between Gotan, 'without the erroneous *th* of the classical forms', and Jutes.[23] But though the OE Bede translated the former Gotan, the latter Geatan, Stevenson had to admit that Jutland nevertheless appears in the OE Orosius as Gotland, and ninth-century OE pronunciation could have aided a confusion.[24] Ninth-century 'Englishmen' may not have thought of Orosius' or Boethius' Goths as so remote from themselves in time or space.

In their note on Asser's statement that Alfred's maternal grandfather was a 'Goth', Keynes and Lapidge crisply observe: 'Asser is probably trying to convey the information that Oslac was of ultimately Danish extraction'.[25] Their point is well made – and more important than their lack of further comment implies. A. C. Murray has recently, and persuasively, argued that the addition of Scyld and Scef to the West Saxon royal genealogy in the late ninth century amounts to an 'attribution of "Danish" ancestors to the West Saxon kings', and that 'the Danish

---

[21] ASC, s.a. 514, p. 14; cf. also Bately, ed. cit., p. 20 and notes. The translation quoted is Stenton's, *Anglo-Saxon England*, pp. 20–1, and also that of G. N. Garmonsway, *Anglo-Saxon Chronicle* (London, 1953), p. 14. For a correct translation, see D. Whitelock *et al*, *The Anglo-Saxon Chronicle. A revised translation* (London 1961), p. 11. Dumville, 'The West Saxon genealogical regnal list', p. 44, n. 63, points out that 'there is no necessary association (such as is generally assumed) between this arrival [of the West Saxons] and the following notice of the activities of Stuf and Wihtgar.

[22] Dumville, 'The West Saxon genealogical regnal list', pp. 28 and n. 15, 41–2 and n. 55; 53–4 and n. 85, 66.

[23] Stenton, *Anglo-Saxon England*, pp. 23–4. Stevenson, *Asser*, p. 167. Cp. ibid. p. 170, for 'a great Scandinavian scholar' who seems to have been more 'confused' then Asser!

[24] Stevenson, *Asser*, p. 169. For early medieval views on the Goths and their origins, see J. M. Alonso-Nunez, 'Jordanes and Procopius on Northern Europe', *Nottingham Medieval Studies* 37 (1987), pp. 1–16, esp. p. 8 and references in n. 11, for confusion of *Getae* with *Gothi*.

[25] Keynes and Lapidge, *Alfred*, p. 230, n. 8.

presence in England was in some way a stimulus' to this genealogical creation.[26] Murray goes on: 'A Danish background was intended to give them prestige and leverage among the petty and disunited Scandinavian kings and earls of northern England and to support the claim of West Saxon suzerainty [sic] over the north . . . The Danish invasions and settlements did not lead Englishmen to disassociate themselves from the Scandinavian heroic age. On the contrary, the heroic North attracted them'.[27] This is rather less persuasive, for it smacks a little of anachronism. Not the least of Asser's advantages is his firm location at Alfred's court in the early 890s. From there, from then, did the Danes look any more 'petty', 'disunited', or indeed 'heroic', than the political scene that confronted Alfred at home?

That home scene had three important features. First, it included Scandinavians. Asser tells of *pagani* – meaning Scandinavians – enrolled at his monastic foundation at Athelney.[28] For Asser, then, the very term *pagani* was on the way to losing its religious connotation: alongside 'many Franks, Frisians, Gauls, Welshmen, Irishmen and Bretons', are the *pagani* in Alfred's household.[29] There is no evidence that conversion to Christianity as entry requirement posed any problem for Scandinavian warlords and their men.[30] Like contemporary Carolingians, Alfred needed to attract and hold a multigentile, polyglot following which then exerted a pull of its own. Hence, if Asser tells his readers that Alfred's maternal grandfather Oslac was of Scandinavian origin, he is presumably making Oslac's grandson more acceptable to local and contemporary Scandinavians, actual or potential recruits to Alfred's *familia*. Os- was of course a perfectable acceptable leading-name among contemporary Scandinavians: the ASC mentions a Danish earl Osbearn in 871, and a Scandinavian king Oscytel in 875.[31]

The second feature of the period around 893 is Alfred's new concern with areas beyond his 'English' kingdom: with Wales, with East Anglia and with the North. It is not the ASC but Asser (supported by the late tenth-century Æthelweard) who reveals this reorientation.[32] If one person of 'foreign origin' helps us here, so does another: the Continental Saxon Hrotsvitha. She believed that Alfred's granddaughter Edith was descended from the seventh-century Northumbrian king Oswald, and in celebrating Edith's marriage to Otto, son of the East Frankish king Henry I, in 929/30, Hrotsvitha claimed that Oswald's was a *stirps beata* ('blessed lineage') and that 'the whole world sang his praise'. Plummer

---

[26] 'Beowulf, the Danish invasions, and royal genealogy', in C. Chase ed., *The Dating of Beowulf* (Toronto, 1981), pp. 101–111, at 105.

[27] Ibid.

[28] Asser, c. 94, p. 81: 'paganicae gentis'. Keynes and Lapidge, *Alfred*, p. 103, translate: 'of Viking parentage'.

[29] Asser, c. 76, p. 60: 'pagani'. Keynes and Lapidge, *Alfred*, p. 91, translate: 'Vikings'.

[30] This point is made by P. Sawyer, *Kings and Vikings*, pp. 137–8. See also S. Coupland and J. L. Nelson, 'The Vikings on the Continent', *History Today* 38 (December, 1988) pp. 12–19, at 15.

[31] ASC, s.a. 871, 875, pp. 70, 74.

[32] Asser, cc. 80, 81, pp. 66–8; Æthelweard, *Chronicle*, s.a. 893, 894, 895, 899, translated Keynes and Lapidge, *Alfred*, pp. 190–1.

remarked: 'That [Edith's descent] is not genealogically correct only makes the testimony the more striking'. Plummer suggested no explanation for the 'error'.[33] But a tenth-century Continental Saxon might well have derived it as an inference from the reappearance of the saint-king's leading name among Edith's close kin. With Alfred recruiting Old Saxons and East Franks into his *familia*, and Oswald's cult already known on the Continent, it could well be that a claim like Hrotsvitha's was already being made and exploited by Alfred's entourage. In Northumbria too, which had once been Oswald's kingdom, and where the ealdorman of Somerset was sent to intervene at York in 894, Alfred might have acquired lustre from his maternal grandfather's name, Oslac – the same name as may have been borne by Oswald's own brother.[34] Os- had continued to be one of the commonest leading-names in the Northumbrian royal dynasty until its extinction in 867: the very hallmark of a *gecyndne cyning*, that is, one of the royal line.[35] It was to be Alfred's daughter Æthelflaed, lady of the Mercians, who translated Oswald's relics from Bardney to Gloucester.[36] The suggestion has been made that Alfred named his eldest daughter after Æthelflaed, daughter of the Northumbrian king Oswy and niece of Oswald.[37] Had Alfred hoped to dedicate his daughter to God as a thank-offering for victory over pagans just as Oswy did? In any event, the reappearance of an old Northumbrian royal name, and name-element, in Alfred's family might have been expected to appeal to late ninth-century Northumbrians in search of a latter-day *bretwalda*.

Heightened tensions within the royal family constitute, I think, a third feature of Wessex in the early 890s. Such tensions, ever-present, tended to surface when a king lived long enough for the next generation to challenge his position:

---

[33] Hrotsvitha, *Gesta Ottonis*, ll. 94–7, ed. P. Winterfeld, *Hrotsvithae Opera*, MGH SRG in usum scholarum, 2nd edn. (Berlin, Zurich, 1965), p. 207; Plummer, ed., *Baedae Opera Historica* (Oxford, 1896), vol. 2, p. 160, under the heading 'Miscellaneous' evidence for the cult of Oswald on the Continent. Oswald married the daughter of the West Saxon king Cynegils, Bede, *HE* III 7, but Bede gives no indication that this direct line continued beyond his son Oidilwald, *HE* III 24. K. Leyser, 'Die Ottonen und Wessex', *Frühmittelalterliche Studien* 17 (1983), pp. 73–97, at 78, has important observations on Hrotsvitha's assertion, but does not say it is an error. Perhaps Oswald *did* have descendants, who fled to their mother's kin in Wessex: note the appearance of a West Saxon *aetheling* called Oswald, ASC, s.a. 728, p. 42.

[34] Plummer, ed., *Baedae Opera Historica*, vol. 2, p. 99. It is possible, however, that the relatively late source, MS 'E' of the ASC, has been influenced by post-seventh-century appearances of the name Oslac (?including Asser, chapter 2).

[35] ASC 867, p. 68: the Northumbrians rejected King Osbryht and accepted Ælla, an *ungecyndne* king. The Os- leading name also appears in the Mercian royal line: ASC, s.a. 755, p. 50. See Sims-Williams, 'The settlement of England', pp. 22–3. For OE leading-names ('protothemes') in general, see C. Clark, 'English personal names ca. 650–1300', *Medieval Prosopography* 8 (1987), pp. 31–60, at 33–4.

[36] ASC 'C' (the Mercian Register), ed. Plummer, p. 94.

[37] The suggestion was C. S. Taylor's: see Plummer, *Saxon Chronicles*, II, p. 118, though, as Patrick Wormald reminds me, Oswy's daughter was called Ælfflaed, according to Bede. The name Eadweard given by Alfred to his son could have recalled a leading-name (Ead-) of the Northumbrian royal dynasty; but (Ead-) is also a common Kentish royal name-element. The name's appearance in the Cerdicing line anyway needs an explanation.

his *familia* would be exposed to the rival attractions of younger men's lordship, and his kingdom threatened by outside interventions concerted with insiders' pressures for a reallocation of power. In Alfred's case, we should be alerted to such possibilities, rather than deterred from investigating them, by the very fact that the evidence for the last years of his reign is unusually scarce. But before focussing on the 890s, we need to establish the broader context of family politics in the period.

Asser offers a rare opportunity to glimpse the role of maternal kin, and also the limits of that role, in Alfred's world. For it is thanks to Asser's chapter 2 that we know the names not only of Alfred's maternal grandfather Oslac but of his mother herself. Osburh's function in Asser's narrative is already established in her first appearance: her noble lineage accentuates and confirms her son's already illustrious birth, giving him a double link with Cerdic. Asser says that she, like her husband, favoured Alfred above their other sons: the book-memorising competition she sets them serves to highlight Alfred who, though the youngest, is the winner.[38] Osburh has no further part in Alfred's story, as Asser presents it. But the location of the book-competition in the narrative, after the account of Alfred's father's second marriage to the Carolingian princess Judith, has been thought by some commentators to make it possible that Osburh was still alive after that event, and perhaps outlived her husband: in other words, that King Æthelwulf in 856 was not a widower but a bigamist. Asser's ordering of events is not always chronological, but, despite Stevenson's hot denials, the possibility remains open that Æthelwulf repudiated, or relegated, Osburh in order to make his Carolingian alliance.[39] If Asser does not quite leave Alfred's childhood in the obscurity with which Einhard shrouded Charlemagne's, he leaves enough unclear to suggest that Osburh's story was in process of reconstruction at the time he was writing, in the late ninth century.

By specifically mentioning that Æthelwulf, 'contrary to custom', sat his Carolingian wife Judith on a throne alongside him, Asser suggests that Osburh had had no such status. Asser does not call Judith 'queen', but implies that that title was associated with enthronement.[40] The ASC explicitly says that Judith

---

[38] Asser, c. 23, p. 20 (Keynes and Lapidge, *Alfred*, p. 75).

[39] This was suggested already by J. M. Lappenberg, *Geschichte von England*, (Hamburg, 1834), vol. 1, p. 294; and rebutted by R. Pauli, *The Life of Alfred the Great*, trans. B. Thorpe (London, 1853), pp. 52–3 ('in all probability, Osburgha died before her husband set out for Rome. Her death was quiet, as her whole life had been: she had lived as the mother of her children, and not as a queen'), and by Stevenson, *Asser*, pp. 222–3 ('there is not the slightest evidence that Æthelwulf treated her in this brutal way, and his well known religious character renders the supposition that he did so a very unlikely one'). The treatment of Osburh by nineteenth-century scholars, and their difficulties in crediting Judith ('that light Frankish princess', Stevenson p. 223) with interest in her stepsons' education, reveal more about Victorian values than Anglo-Saxon attitudes. But for an exception, see the Bishop of Bristol (G. F. Browne), 'Alfred as a religious man and educationalist', in A. Bowker, ed., *Alfred the Great* (London, 1899), pp. 71–99, at 77–8, noting Judith's background at the cultivated court of Charles the Bald.

[40] Asser, c. 13, p. 11.

was given Æthelwulf *to cuene-* 'as queen'. [41] Osburh's lack of queenly status is even more broadly hinted at in the West Frankish *Annals of Saint Bertin*: 'Æthelwulf . . . conferred on Judith the title of queen, something which had been until then unfamiliar to him and to his people'.[42] The author of these *Annals* is evidently retailing information given to the Franks by Æthelwulf and his entourage in 856: the West Saxons were anxious to stress the special mark of honour accorded to their new royal bride. Pauline Stafford has argued for an otherwise consistent demotion of the status of the king's wife in ninth-century Wessex, and offered a plausible explanation in terms of a preference for fraternal, 'horizontal', succession over the 'vertical' succession of sons or nephews.[43] But changing circumstances ensured that the preference was neither consistent nor unanimous. Memories of earlier queens were not lost: even the 'highly unusual event' of Seaxburh's one-year reign (672) was not deleted from the ASC or from the West Saxon regnal list, perhaps because it was 'well known in West Saxon oral tradition'.[44] According to both Asser and the ASC, Eadburh, wife of King Beorhtric of Wessex (786–802), had been a queen.[45] Of Egbert's consort(s) nothing is known. In Alfred's own generation, one brother, Æthelbald, married his stepmother, Queen Judith, after his father's death, while another brother, Æthelred, had a wife called Wulfthryth who is accorded the title *regina* in a charter of 868 (the year of Alfred's own marriage).[46] Thus, in the period before Alfred's own reign, Osburh is the only West Saxon king's wife whose lack of a queenly title is clear. If Æthelwulf did plan to repudiate and replace her in 855/6, it could have suited him very well to emphasise to the Franks her lowliness and their glory through the honourable status reserved, by contrast, for the Carolingian king's daughter. By the late 880s, Osburh's sole surviving son may well have felt the whole episode in need of explaining – or explaining away: hence 'the truthteller' himself 'often' told Asser the story of the wicked Eadburh and the West Saxons' ensuing 'perverse custom' of denying the title of queen to the king's wife.[47] At

---

[41] ASC, s.a. 855, p. 66.
[42] *Annales de Saint-Bertin*, ed. F. Grat, J. Vielliard and S. Clemencet (Paris, 1964), s.a. 856, p. 73. In my forthcoming translation of this work, I discuss the possibility that this passage was interpolated into the 856 annal of Hincmar. See meanwhile Nelson, 'The Annals of St Bertin', in M. Gibson and J. L. Nelson eds., *Charles the Bald: Court and Kingdom*, revised edn. (London, 1990), pp. 23–40. The political context, and consequences, of Æthelwulf's Frankish marriage have been illuminated by Stafford, 'Charles the Bald, Judith and England', ibid., pp. 139–53.
[43] Stafford, 'The king's wife', pp. 7–12, 15. Though she recognises (p. 12) that 'succession practices change with circumstances', Stafford sees continuity 'during the ninth century', with Judith the exception that proves the rule.
[44] Dumville, 'The West Saxon genealogical regnal list', p. 53 and n. 85.
[45] ASC, s.a. 836, p. 62; Asser, c. 13, p. 11: Eadburh was a '*pertinax et malevola regina*'.
[46] S.340. Stevenson, *Asser*, p. 201, n. 4, says this charter's source, the Winchester Cartulary, is 'highly suspicious'. But the witness-list seems usable. Immediately after Wulfthryth's attestation comes that of Wulfhere *princeps*: see below n. 58. If genuine, Wulfthryth's title seems designed to open up the possibility of vertical succession, that is, to assert the claims of her sons. Cf. Nelson, ' "A king across the sea" ', pp. 55–7.
[47] Asser, c. 13, p. 12. Asser adds that Alfred told him that *his* informants in turn were

the same time, Alfred may have wanted to suggest that his mother's lack of queenly status was more than compensated for by exceptional piety, ancient lineage, and a Cerdicing connexion. Hence the construction of Osburh's illustrious *genealogia* could have postdated not only her union with Æthelwulf, but her youngest son's succession: could have been, in other words, the marriage's effect, rather than its cause.

Nevertheless, it is likely, given the high value placed on maternal kin in this society, that Æthelwulf chose a wife of noble rank with politically useful connexions. If Osburh's son Æthelbald was old enough to fight alongside his father in 851, and her daughter to marry in 853, this could imply a date for the parents' union before 839, that is, when Æthelwulf was still only sub-king of Kent.[48] Osburh's father Oslac may have been related to an important Kentish noble family in which the Os- leading-name appears in the late eighth and early ninth centuries.[49] If so, this could well have recommended him further to Æthelwulf in the mid-830s. As for the linkage of Oslac's ancestors with the Isle of Wight, this could only have been encouraged by Bede's specific statement that *Cantuarii* and *Victuarii*, that is, Kentishmen and men of Wight, were alike 'of Jutish origin'.[50]

Oslac may have died soon after his daughter's marriage, since there is no record of his attesting any of Æthelwulf's charters.[51] Oslac's post of royal butler (*pincerna*) seemed problematic to Stevenson: he thought there was virtually no 'English' evidence for holders of this office during or before the ninth century, and hence no warrant for regarding it *per se* as a mark of 'loftiest birth', while 'the *pincerna* was an officer of somewhat subordinate importance in the [ninth-century] Frankish court', and hence if Oslac really was a 'great noble', his alleged job seemed an anachronism.[52] But the early evidence for 'English' butlers is better than Stevenson realised, while on the other side of the Channel, the *de Ordine Palatii* places the butler fourth, after the chamberlain, the count of the palace and the seneschal, among the officers of the Carolingian royal household,

---

veredici, that there were many of them, and that some of them were able to recall the event itself.

[48] ASC, s.a. 851, 853, pp. 64, 66. Pauli, *Alfred*, p. 42, suggests that the mother of Æthelstan, Æthelwulf's eldest son, may have been a woman other than Osburh.

[49] The death of an Ealdorman Osmod is mentioned in ASC, s.a. 836, p. 62. If he is the Osmod attesting in S.270, 271, he probably belonged to the Kentish family documented in S.1188, 1439.

[50] HE I 15. Note also the appearance of Oslac *dux* of the South Saxons granting land in Sussex in S.1184 (dated 780). Cf. S.44, 48, 49, for Osmund *rex* of the South Saxons a generation before. For Alfred's bequests in Sussex, see below, pp. 59–60.

[51] *Pace* Keynes and Lapidge, p. 229, n. 7, the Oslac who attests S.328 seems too low (ninth) on the list of lay attesters, and the date, 858, too late, for identification as the then king's maternal grandfather to seem likely. But, as Simon Keynes kindly points out to me, this is a Kentish charter.

[52] Stevenson, *Asser*, p. 164, with references to earlier literature (though slightly misrepresenting H. Brunner, *Deutsche Rechtgeschichte*, 2 vols, 2nd edn. (Munich and Leipzig, 1906, 1928), vol. 2, p. 140). An exceptional attestation of an 'English' butler in the eighth century occurs in S.57 (which, *pace* Sawyer's comment here, is not listed as 'spurious' by Stevenson at the place cited).

and all these posts were certainly held in the ninth century by men of high birth, often at an early stage in their careers.[53] The best parallel for Oslac is Odo, butler to Louis the Pious in 826, and kinsman of Count Bernard of Septimania. Odo was in an ideal position to benefit from the realignment of court factions that resulted in Bernard's appointment as chamberlain in 828: Odo himself became count of Orleans and married into the family of the counts of Paris. His daughter in turn married Louis the Pious' son Charles the Bald. (Hence the Frankish princess Judith was Odo's granddaughter.)[54] It is a coincidence that both Charles the Bald and Æthelwulf married butlers' daughters? Was Odo's example known of, or even followed, on the other side of the Channel?[55] Like Odo, Oslac attained a Königsnähe ('closeness to the king'), which noble birth on its own could not assure: in both cases, what the butler saw was a privileged access-route to the centre of political power. Like Odo, Oslac may have died too young to enjoy this access for long.[56]

Whatever happened to Osburh's father, evidence may exist to show another of her kinsmen as a beneficiary of her royal marriage. In 847, Osric princeps subscribed a West Saxon charter after King Æthelwulf and the ætheling Æthelbald. The unusual title, and Osric's exceptionally high placing, suggest the possi-

---

[53] 'English' butlers appear in S.348 (and see now Keynes and Lapidge, Alfred, p. 181, with comments at pp. 326–7 and 330, n. 15), where Sigewulf pincerna may be the same man as the Sigulf dux who attests S.350 (dated 898), and S.1515, the Will of King Eadred (946–56) where the listing of discthegn, hraelthegn and biriele echoes that of the de Ordine Palatii, c. 23, ed. T. Gross and R. Schieffer, Fontes Iuris Germanici Antiqui (Munich, 1980), pp. 74–6. On the problem of de Ordine's authorship and date (c.820 x c.880), see Nelson, 'Legislation and consensus in the reign of Charles the Bald', in Wormald ed., Ideal and Reality, pp. 91–116, at 105–6. Useful general comments on Carolingian household-officers in the ninth century can be found in K. F. Werner, 'Missus-marchio-comes', in W. Paravicini and K. F. Werner eds., Histoire comparée de l'administration (IVe–XVIIIe Siècles), Beihefte der Francia 9 (Munich, 1980), pp. 191–239, at pp. 209 and n. 73, 236–7 and nn. 166–168; cf. Nelson, 'Public Histories and private history in the work of Nithard', Speculum 60 (1985), pp. 251–93, at pp. 257, n. 22 (Adalard), and 281, n. 126 (Vivian); and below, n. 55. A thorough prosopographical study has never been undertaken.
[54] For Odo's career, see L. Levillian, 'Les Nibelungen historiques, II', Annales du Midi 50 (1938), pp. 5–66, at 31–46; Werner, 'Untersuchungen zur Frühzeit des französischen Fürstentums (9.–10. Jht.)', Die Welt als Geschichte 50 (1959), pp. 146–93, at 163, n. 72. Whether or not Odo was already a count in 821, he was referred to as puer in 826: Ermold, Poème sur Louis le Pieux, ed. E. Faral (Paris, 1932), 1.2346, p. 178. His daughter Ermentrude married Charles the Bald in 842: Nithard, Histoire des fils de Louis le Pieux, ed. P. Lauer (Paris, 1926), IV, 6, p. 142.
[55] Odo's countship, and his kinship with Bernard, but not his office of butler, are mentioned by the Astronomer, Vita Hludowici, ed. G. Pertz, MGH SS 2, cc. 44, 45, p. 633, an author whom Asser may have known: see references in Keynes and Lapidge, Alfred, p. 222, n. 115. That Odo was known by his office-title may be suggested by an instruction given by Emperor Louis to missi in 826, Capitularia Regum Francorum 1 ed. A. Boretius, MGH LL 2 (Hannover, 1883) no. 155, p. 314, c. 6: 'Odo buticularius de foreste sua interrogandus est'. (Was forest-management part of the butler's official duties?)
[56] Odo was killed in 834: Nithard, Hist. 1, 5, p. 20, fighting for the Emperor, and to recover his countship.

bility that this man was Osburh's brother.[57] The title was also used in the late 860s by Wulfhere, who was perhaps the brother-in-law of the then king, Æthelred.[58] Osric might be further identified with the ealdorman of Dorset mentioned in the ASC for 845, and/or with the ealdorman of Hampshire mentioned in the same source, under the year 860.[59] Did he hold two ealdormanries at the same time? If so, this would begin to look like a budding territorial principality in the hands of a man who knew how to exploit his special *Königsnähe*.[60] But the asset had a time-limit: there is no record of Osric attesting as *princeps* after the 840s. In 856, he is third down the list of ealdormen, and it is tempting to link his 'demotion' with Osburh's.[61] Only in 860, in his last charter-appearance, does Osric attest second in the list of ealdormen: this is the first extant charter of Æthelberht's reign and it may be that Judith's departure allowed her predecessor's brother a brief and partial recovery of his former influence.[62] By 868, whatever position he had held at Æthelwulf's court was occupied by Wulfhere at Æthelred's.

But we can perhaps pick up one more echo of Osric, and of the characteristic leading-name of Alfred's maternal kin. The ASC, in a unique and striking narrative inserted into the 757 annal, reports the death in 786 of King Cynewulf of Wessex at the hands of his kinsman Cyneheard. The story's climax is the refusal of the king's thegns to accept any terms offered by Cyneheard, despite the fact that some of their kinsmen were with him: 'They replied that no kinsman was dearer to them than their lord, and that they would never follow his slayer'.[63] The chief of these loyal thegns is named as 'Ealdorman Osric'; and a second

---

[57] S.298. Unfortunately, all the other charters bearing Osric's attestation are of doubtful authenticity, yet even in these, his very high place on lists of attesters may be significant: S.305, 313, 1274. It should be noted that Osric's title of *princeps* is not unique in S.298's list: the title is also given to Ceorl, presumably the ealdorman of Devon mentioned in ASC, s.a. 851. p. 64. But I take the arrangement of the names in the MS, BL Cotton Charter viii, 36, to indicate that Osric is higher-placed than Ceorl. It is even possible that Ceorl's name, and title, were added later, Osric may make another appearance as *princeps* in S.319 (dated 874 but possibly altered from the original's 844), but the witness-list here is jumbled, the abbreviations used for titles are not consistent, and though other priests attest here as *prsb* or *p*, it is unclear whether *prs* too means *presbyter*.

[58] S.340, 341, and cf. 336. I raised this possibility in ' "A king across the sea" ', p. 55. It is tempting to wonder if 'Oswulf princeps' of S.39, 1439, was the brother-in-law of King Cuthred of Kent. Other men with the title 'princeps' appear in spurious charters: S.290, 292, 299, and 300. But if S.301 is reliable, 'Tuddan princeps' would repay further investigation.

[59] ASC, s.a. 845, 860, pp. 64, 68.

[60] The parallel that comes to mind to here is Charles the Bald's brother-in-law Boso: for his and other cases, see K. Schmid, 'Über die Struktur des Adels im frühen Mittelalter', *Jahrbuch für frankische Landesforschung* 19 (1959), pp. 1–23, translated T. Reuter, *The Medieval Nobility* (Amsterdam, 1979), pp. 37–59. The prospects of such territorial formations on the Continent in this period are coolly assessed by J. Dunbabin, *France in the Making, 843–1180* (Oxford, 1985), chapter 4.

[61] S.317. Cf. also the spurious S.308, and 307.

[62] S.327, dateble to 860. My suggestion depends on the rejection of S.326, 1274 as untrustworthy.

[63] ASC, s.a. 757, on events in 786.

instance of his exemplary conduct is given a few lines further on, when Cyneheard and all his men 'were slain, all except one who was the ealdorman's
godson, and he spared his life'. The highlighting of Osric's role is no more
coincidental than the emphasis on the loyalty expected of king's thegns and the
obligations of spiritual kinship. These themes surely reflect Alfred's priorities in
the early 890s when the ASC was being put together: a point to which I return
presently.

Another probable kinsman of Alfred's on whom the characteristic Os- leading
name of his mother's *genealogia* was bestowed, is the Osweald *filius regis* who
attests a charter of 875 in third place after Alfred and the archbishop of Canterbury. Stevenson identified him as 'the son of one of Alfred's brothers'.[64] Keynes
and Lapidge suggest that he was a son of Æthelred, but it is noteworthy that the
account in Alfred's Will of the inheritance-dispute at the time of Alfred's own
succession shows only two sons of Æthelred ('the older and the younger'),
presumably the Æthelhelm and Æthelwold mentioned later in the Will, which
would mean that Osweald was not a contender along with them in 871.[65] We
have no information about other legitimate sons of any of Alfred's three elder
brothers. Osweald *filius regis* also attests two charters of 868.[66] Could he have
been an illegitimate son (or perhaps, more accurately, a son born to a woman of
low, even unfree, status), of either Æthelbald or Æthelberht? If so, he could have
been a young adult by 868; and in any case, tenth-century charters show West
Saxon aethelings attesting when still very young.[67] But if Osweald was well-
placed at Alfred's court in the early years of the reign, he was out of the running
(dead, or exiled?) by the time that Alfred made his Will, for he is not mentioned
among Alfred's beneficiaries. In any event, Osweald is a significant figure: here is
a king's son of whose existence we should have had no inkling but for the
fortuitous survival of three charters, and who, despite his possible illegitimacy,
was given the 'official' title used by such other, legitimate, kings' sons as his own
uncle and cousins. How many *æthelings* have sunk without trace?

One more kinsman of Alfred's appears prominent later in the reign: Osferth.
He is mentioned, notably, in Alfred's Will, which in its present form seems to
date from the late 890s.[68] Osferth is left eight estates, all in Sussex: considerably

---

[64] Asser, p. 299, n. 4 *a propos* S.1203.

[65] Keynes and Lapidge, *Alfred*, p. 322, n. 79. Cf. Alfred's Will, ibid., pp. 175, 177. See also
Dumville, 'The Ætheling', p. 11.

[66] S.340, S.1201. The 'Oswald *miles*' who attests S.348 (dating to 892) seems too low on
the list, and the charter too late, for emendation to, and identification with, Osweald to be
feasible.

[67] E.g. in S.569, 570, 745, 893. See also Dumville, 'The Ætheling', p. 14. For the
suggestion of an age-gap between Æthelbald and Æthelberht on the one hand, and
Æthelred and Alfred on the other, see Nelson, ' "A king across the sea" ', p. 55. For a
Carolingian example of youthful paternity, cf. Louis the Pious, who fathered a son and a
daughter in his early teens, before his marriage: see Werner, 'Die Nachkommen Karls des
Grossen', in W. Braunfels and H. Beumann eds., *Karl der Grosse, Lebenswerk und Nach-
leben*, 5 vols. (Dusseldorf, 1965–8), vol. 4, pp. 403–79, at 445–6.

[68] As implied by Keynes and Lapidge, *Alfred*, p. 174, rightly pointing out, p. 173, that the
reference to Archbishop Æthelred (died 888) provides a *terminus ante quem* only for the

more than Alfred's brother's son Æthelwold, and a much more compact bloc than the other nephew Æthelhelm. Was the bequest to Osferth in fact the core of a South Saxon subkingdom? Clearly Osferth was not, like Æthelwold and Æthelhelm, a brother's son: he, unlike them, is identified by the term *maegd* (kinsman).[69] He appears again in another document whose date, 898, may be close to that of the Will: this is the Kentish charter is which Edward attests as king.[70] Here, Osferth is second on the list of *ministri*, following Beorhtsige who is probably identifiable with Brihtsige, the son of a Mercian *ætheling*.[71] In 901, Osferth, without any title, attests next after King Edward, and in 903, again without title, immediately after Edward's younger brother Æthelweard.[72] In a doubtful charter of 909, Osferth attests next after Edward's son (and before all the ealdormen) with the title *propinquus regis*.[73] After the gap in the charter series later in Edward's reign, Osferth reappears in Athelstan's early years (thus during the period when the dynasty's descent from the saint-king Oswald was being touted) as an ealdorman at, or very near, the top of the list of lay attesters, from 926 until 934.[74] Clearly Osferth held an exceptionally prominent position at the courts of three successive kings. It is a sobering thought that none of the narrative sources mentions him at all.

What was Osferth's kin-relationship to Alfred? The one charter-attestation to specify his place in the family calls him *frater regis* in relation to Edward the Elder – 'mistakenly', comment Keynes and Lapidge, with a briskness worthy of the late Dorothy Whitelock herself.[75] But is it really out of the question that Osferth was Edward's half-brother, and thus Alfred's illegitimate son? In view of Osferth's

---

first three paragraphs of the Will. Two additional reasons for dating the Will to the very last years of Alfred's reign are: (i) his title in paragraph 4, 'king of the West Saxons', may be compared with that in S.350 (dated 898), on which see below, p. 64, n. 90; (ii) the Ecgwulf mentioned in the Will in terms which imply he is no longer living (Keynes and Lapidge, p. 175: '. . . property which I entrusted to Ecgwulf . . .) may be the horse-thegn whose death is mentioned in ASC, s.a. 896, p. 90 (as noted by Keynes and Lapidge, p. 289, though without the possible implications for dating the Will). If so, the bequest of this property to Winchester may have been for the good of Ecgwulf's soul. For a Carolingian parallel, see the grant of Charles the Bald to St Lucien, Beauvais, in return for prayers for the soul of Wido 'fidelis ac carissimi nobis vassalli': G. Tessier ed., *Receuil des Actes de Charles II le Chauve*, 3 vols. (Paris, 1944–55), vol. 2, no. 325, p. 217.
[69] Keynes and Lapidge, *Alfred*, p. 177.
[70] S.350.
[71] Dumville, 'The Ætheling', p. 4.
[72] S.364, 367.
[73] S.378. C. Hart, *The Early Charters of Northern England and the North Midlands* (Leicester, 1975), p. 355, notes the parallel with a phrase used in reference to Athelstan Half-King. The other charters cited by Hart as attested by Osferth (S.376, 378, 381, 382, 383) are at best dubious.
[74] In S.396 (dated 926), Osferth attests third of the *duces*; in S.400, 401, 402, 403, 412, 413, 418, 422, 393, Osferth tops the list of lay attesters; in S.407, 416, 417, 425, he attests second. Was Osward, King Edgar's *propinquus* in S.803, a descendant (?son) of Osferth?
[75] Keynes and Lapidge, *Alfred*, p. 322, *a propos* S.1286, where both Æthelweard 'filius regis' and Osferth 'frater regis' are listed above the archbishop! Cf. Hart, *Early Charters*, p. 355: the identification of Osferth here is 'certainly a mistake'.

place in Alfred's Will, and his sustained high position in the witness lists of Edward's reign and Athelstan's early years, that possibility is surely worth considering. More work needs doing on Anglo-Saxon royal naming habits. Contemporary Continental evidence shows that some names denoted greater throne-worthiness than others. Perhaps, once the criterion of legitimacy had increasingly been adopted and the circle of eligibles thus more closely drawn, to call a son by a leading-name from the father's *maternal* line was an indication of diminished suitability on grounds of illegitimate birth.[76]

It is true that Asser makes no mention of Osferth, any more than he mentions Alfred's nephews. What he offers, instead, is a picture of Alfred as the happy father of a tidy nuclear family, with just one bed-fellow – his wife – and two sons only, both legitimate, one the 'obedient' Edward, the other apparently destined for the Church. Why should Asser tell the whole story? If Osferth was a bastard son of Alfred, his existence belied the image of the chaste king portrayed in Asser's chapter 74. And yet, at the same time, it would explain the earnestness with which Alfred prayed for an illness that would inhibit sexual activity.

In the twelfth century, when lawyers were making the distinction between legitimate and illegitimate offspring more clear-cut than ever, when realms and lordships were solidifying, and when the exclusion of illegitimate sons from inheritances was becoming accepted custom, the philandering of a Henry I need produce no brood of claimants to shares in a divided realm. In the seventh and eighth centuries, kings were prolific and half-brothers fought fiercely, while the pleas of a few moralists had little effect. But the ninth century saw new tensions, new contradictions: between the persisting ways of the past, and more sustained and generalised attempts on the part of kings and noblemen as well as moralists to differentiate between legitimate and illegitimate sons and to impose stricter controls on sexual behaviour. Demographic shifts – a higher birth rate, and/or an improved survival rate for infants – and economic pressures resulting from reduced opportunities to extract plunder and tribute, are hypotheses that explain the phenomena as well as any.[77] In the Carolingian world, the claims of bastards recurrently tore apart patrimonies, kingdoms and the Frankish realm itself. Ninth-century observers did not ignore the risks of overly-narrowed descent lines, but saw too the danger of proliferating sons. There could be too much

---

[76] A possible Carolingian example of the use of a name from the father's maternal line for an illegitimate son, is Hugh son of Lothar II: Lothar's maternal grandfather was called Hugh. Thankmar, son of the East Frankish king Henry I, is another possible example. What is certain is that such names as Bernard and Hugh were used for Carolingians' illegitimate sons. For examples, see Werner, 'Die Nachkommen'. On the naming of daughters, see C. Bouchard, 'Patterns of women's names in royal lineages, ninth-eleventh centuries', *Medieval Prosopography* 9 (1988), pp. 1–32.

[77] Compare the explanations invoked by J. Wollasch, 'Parenté noble et monachisme reformateur', *Revue Historique* 264 (1980), pp. 3–24, and D. Herlihy, *Medieval Households* (Harvard, 1985), pp. 83–7, in reference to the eleventh and twelfth centuries. I hope to discuss this problem more fully in a forthcoming paper on Gerald of Aurillac.

nobilitas, too many noble youths with claims to 'equality of birth, rank and power'.[78] Among the landed elite, chastity began to be preached with a new vigour, and not only by churchmen: the noble lady Dhuoda exhorted her son 'to do service in the marriage bed', or to opt for virginity, but at all costs to avoid 'inlicita stupra'.[79] No doubt many Franks failed to live up to such prescriptions, just as many English did. But the interesting thing is that the ideal was insistently proposed, and that some laymen, at least, tried to practise it.[80] According to Asser, chapter 74, the young Alfred prayed earnestly for an illness that would keep him from lust, and, once married, was a model of fidelity. Even if Alfred was unable to avoid an occasional lapse, he aspired to chastity.

Alfred's aspiration, discussed by previous historians in terms of his individual psychology, could also be understood as a reponse to contemporary social and political pressures. Reading between the lines of the ASC, and making the most of Asser, we can glimpse those pressures in the recurrent succession-crises of ninth-century Wessex. The generation before Alfred's had seen a series of responses to the problems of acute fraternal rivalry and filial unrest: the creation of a subkingdom, rebellion, a division of the realm, stepmother-marriage. Alfred's succession to an undivided realm was not just a matter of luck. Both the ASC and, especially, Asser present Alfred in the late 860s as successor-in-waiting, and his brother's designated heir. Both the ASC and Asser neglect to mention Alfred's nephews whose claims to succeed their father Alfred set aside in 871. Both the ASC and Asser also leave out Osferth. Nor does the ASC as written up in 892 say anything about Alfred's son Edward, though by then he was probably aged over twenty. What this means is that the view from 892/3 of a narrowed-down succession line, and a future which Alfred could control, was also an aspiration rather than a reality.

Alfred's Will is explicit about its own reference to a particular point in time: there have been other wills, it says, which are now declared superseded. Implicitly Alfred acknowledges that *this* Will may also be ephemeral. Asser too reveals a moment in time: he presents Alfred, in 893, aligning Edward for the succession, but the depiction of Edward as 'obedient' reminds us of Asser's own earlier depiction of an *ætheling* who was not obedient: the 'wicked and grasping' Æthelbald who rebelled against his ageing father.[81] In other words, where Asser reveals conflict within the royal family in the previous generation, he suppresses it in

---

[78] Regino of Prüm, *Chronicon*, ed. F. Kurze, MGH SRG in usum scholarum (Hannover, 1890), s.a. 888, p. 129; but cf. the anxieties expressed by Regino s.a. 880, p. 116–7.

[79] Dhuoda, *Manuel pour mon fils*, ed. P. Riché (Paris, 1975), IV, 6, p. 228.

[80] See Wormald, 'Æthelwold and his Continental counterparts: contact, comparison, contrast', in B. Yorke ed., *Æthelwold* (Woodbridge, 1988), pp. 13–42, at 20, 35–7; and Nelson, 'A tale of two princes', *Studies in Medieval and Renaissance History* 11 (1988), pp. 105–40.

[81] Asser, c. 12, pp. 9–10: 'quaedam infamia' (Keynes and Lapidge, *Alfred*, p. 70: 'a disgraceful episode'). I follow Keynes and Lapidge in translating *pertinax* as 'grasping'.

Alfred's. Alfred is different: papally-anointed; parentally-preferred; the nobility's choice even before his brother's death.[82]

But Asser's is not the only story, even in 893. Against the ASC's silence is Æthelweard's account of the battle of Farnham in that year, in which Edward's military prowess, and popularity with a following of young warriors, are high-lighted.[83] Plans for the succession must surely have been revised more than once in the course of Alfred's reign. Alfred's Will throws light on the scene in the late 890s: here Edward is lined up to inherit most of Alfred's personal property in Somerset, as well as some estates in Wiltshire and Hampshire, but no fewer than four other kinsmen of Edward's generation (his brother Æthelweard, his two cousins Æthelwold and Æthelhelm, and Osferth) are assigned parts of Alfred's personal inheritance, both in Old Wessex, where Æthelweard, not Edward, inherits estates in Dorset and the Isle of Wight, and in the acquired regions to the east, Surrey and Sussex, where again Edward received almost nothing. Edward, on the other hand, is to receive 'all my booklands in Kent'.[84] This distribution suggests that a subsequent re-partition of the expanded realm remained on the cards. The Will records a dispute between Alfred and his nephews over a particular piece of shared inherited property, probably in 871, and hints, further, at Alfred's disputed succession to the realm itself. A charter whose witness-list could suggest a date not many years after 871 actually has Alfred's nephew the *ætheling* Æthelwold attesting above his son Edward.[85]

In 897 or 898, Alfred 'invested' his little grandson Athelstan in what has been understood as a ritual of designation to succeed eventually to Alfred's expanded, composite kingdom. This may have signalled a far-sighted plan for the trans-mission of an undivided realm through the succeeding two generations. It may have been designed with Edward's connivance, indeed, at his insistence, for it certainly implied a narrowed descent-line excluding Edward's own brother.[86] But there is an alternative explanation: the designation of a grandson may have been Alfred's own project, its purpose to bypass Edward at least as far as the succession to Wessex itself was concerned. Dumville has observed that there are alternative versions of Alfred's genealogy at the critical point of Cerdic's successor: some include Cerdic's son Creoda, while others delete him, jumping straight from Cerdic to Cynric. Dumville comments: 'It is perhaps just conceivable that in Alfred's or Edward's reign the legitimate succession of a grandson might be thought to create an unfortunate model for Æthelwulf's other grandsons to follow'.[87] Dumville was evidently thinking of the conflicting claims of Edward

---

[82] Asser, cc. 8, 22, 42, pp. 7, 19, 32.
[83] Æthelweard, *Chronicon*, ed. A. Campbell (London, 1962), p. 49 (Keynes and Lapidge, *Alfred*, p. 189.
[84] See Keynes and Lapidge, *Alfred*, pp. 175–7, and map, p. 176.
[85] S.356.
[86] As I implied in ' "A king across the sea" ', p. 56, following a suggestion of Lapidge, 'Some Latin poems as evidence for the reign of Athelstan', ASE 9 (1981), pp. 61–98, at 79–81
[87] Dumville, 'The West Saxon genealogical regnal list', p. 59, n. 114.

and his cousin Æthelwold, who was, of course, also a grandson of Æthelwulf. But it is possible that the genealogists' discrepancy hints, instead, at conflict between Edward's expectations, and his own father's plans involving his grandson.[88] Alfred himself may have chosen, and perhaps dowered, Edward's first spouse, Ecgwyna (Athelstan's mother), for him, and sought thus to control her offspring. Edward seems to have married another woman, Ælfflaed, very soon after his father's death.[89] The divergent forms of the Cerdicing pedigree could reflect the views of rival camps in the mid-890s: one favouring Edward's sole succession, the other his partial exclusion in favour of his own son – that is, a redivision of the realm such as Edward himself was to try to engineer for the next generation.[90]. We know that Athelstan was brought up in Mercia by his aunt Æthelflaed: but whose idea was that – his father's, or his grandfather's? In the 890s there were several possible ways of reslicing the cake. One that had been tried before (and would perhaps be tried again by Edward for one of his own sons) was to recreate a kingdom in Kent.[91] A Kentish charter of 898 is attested by Edward as 'rex', while Alfred's title here, *rex saxonum*, seems to imply a more limited authority than the 'Anglo-Saxon' kingship asserted during the previous decade and more.[92] In this same charter, Osferth attested for the first time: he was probably behind Edward in a political as well as a diplomatic sense. Hungry *æthelings* were indeed beginning to prowl.[93] And when *æthelings* prowled, a king needed, above all, to keep the loyalty of his own thegns. Here, in the last years of Alfred's reign, was his Achilles heel: for, as the ASC poignantly records, the worst problem he confronted in 896 was the loss of 'many of the best king's thegns that were in the land'.[94] Even the bonds of spiritual kinship, pointedly mentioned in the 893 annal, as in the Osric episode recounted under 757, could not be counted on to hold.[95]

---

[88] For paternal intervention in an adult son's affairs to influence the royal succession in the second generation, compare Charles the Bald's attempt to disinherit his own grandsons by making Louis the Stammerer repudiate his wife and marry another woman: Regino of Prüm, *Chronicon*, s.a. 878, 879, p. 114, and Werner, 'Nachkommen', pp. 437–8. Charles at this point was hoping to beget a new son of his own, and also conferring *Königsnähe* on the kin of Louis's new wife.

[89] On Edward's marriages, see Stafford, 'King's wife', p. 13, and my comments in 'The Second English Ordo', in J. L. Nelson, *Politics and Ritual in Early Medieval Europe* (London, 1986), p. 367. Pauline Stafford kindly points out to me that Alfred might have sought to secure Ecgwyna's status, had he wanted to promote her son, and that Carolingian evidence shows kings choosing their sons' brides and providing the morning-gifts.

[90] See Nelson, ' "A king across the sea" ', p. 57.

[91] Kent had been ruled as a sub-kingdom by Æthelwulf during Egbert's lifetime, then by Athelstan during Æthelwulf's: Keynes and Lapidge, *Alfred*, pp. 15, 231–2. Edward the Elder may have planned for his third son, Edwin, to rule Kent: Plummer, *Saxon Chronicles*, 2, pp. 137–8.

[92] S.350. I am grateful to Iain Fenn for this point.

[93] I borrow (not for the first time!) the inimitable phrase of K. Harrison, *The Framework of Anglo-Saxon History* (Cambridge, 1976), p. 92.

[94] ASC, s.a. 896, p. 90: 'during those these years' – i.e. 893–6.

[95] ASC, s.a. 893, p. 86, in the context of the sons of Haesten. For earlier examples, see ASC, s.a. 878 (Guthrum-Athelstan), and Asser, c. 80, p. 67 (Anarawd ap Rhodri).

I have left to the last another problematic king's wife. Though Alfred was anxious to assert his own mother's rank (if not her queenly status), he was apparently indifferent to that of his own consort. The ASC does not mention his marriage; Asser does, but omits the name of the bride, though he says she was descended through her mother from the Mercian royal line.[96] Neither source tells us anything of Alfred's wife's activity during her husband's reign. Nor does she attest any charter of Alfred's. His Will seems to be the only document produced during his lifetime to give her name – Eahlswith; but she is not identified here even as wife, let alone queen, and in the list of kin who are Alfred's beneficiaries, she comes last of all, behind Osferth. Of the three estates bequeathed to her, two may have been already 'earmarked for the support of royal women'.[97] Thus, at the time the Will was drawn up, Ealhswith's stock with her husband seems not to have been particularly high. In 892/3, the silence of the ASC and Asser tells a similar tale.

Conversely, the ASC indicates Ealhswith's emergence from obscurity after 899, when Alfred died: her brother's death is recorded under the year 902 (recte 901), and her own death under 904 (recte 902).[98] Though only one possibly genuine charter of Edward's carries her attestation, as 'king's mother', a record of her endowment of the Nunnaminster at Winchester also survives.[99] She seems to have left her landed property to her son Edward.[100] It is tempting to suggest that Ealhswith was a consistent supporter of Edward, and to account thus for her absence in the early 890s from an historical record that was tilted against her son. When Asser says that the onset of Alfred's second, unidentifiable, illness at his wedding-feast was attributed by some contemporary observers to witchcraft, he may have been projecting back, significantly to that occasion, the atmosphere of 893.[101]

Hence perhaps the dilemma facing Alfred, and Asser, over the status of the king's wife in ninth-century Wessex. Much as Alfred wanted to cast a retrospective aura around his mother's name, in the early 890s strictly contemporary circumstances required that his own wife be kept in the background. Had Alfred at that time wished to secure the 'vertical' sole succession of his own elder son, there would have been every reason to affirm Ealhswith's status. Instead, what

---

[96] Asser, c. 29, p. 24.
[97] Keynes and Lapidge, *Alfred*, p. 323; cf. Stafford, 'The king's wife', p. 22.
[98] ASC, s.a. 902, 904, pp. 92, 94.
[99] S.363, 1560. On the record of bounds of land at Winchester, see M. Parkes, 'a fragment of an early tenth-century Anglo-Saxon manscript and its significance', ASE 12 (1983), pp. 129–40, at 131–2.
[100] Keynes and Lapidge, *Alfred*, p. 325.
[101] Asser, c. 74, p. 55: 'multi ... favore et fascinatione circumstantis populi hoc factum esse autumabant' (Keynes and Lapidge, *Alfred*, p. 89: '. . . spells and witchcraft of the people around him'). For a comparative view of witchcraft accusations in 'the intimate, ambiguous hot-house atmosphere of the court', see E. Peters, *The Magician, the Witch and the Law* (Philadelphia, 1978), pp. 9–10, 16, 112–25, esp. p. 116, noting the effect of the arrival of a new queen into a court. Paul Kershaw and Neville Wylie kindly drew my attention to the possible significance of Asser's words.

the evidence points to is a growing tension between Alfred and Edward, and (whether as cause or effect) attempts on Alfred's part to keep open his options on the succession. In that context, hungry *æthelings* had their advantages. Not before 898, it seems, was Edward able to secure the Kentish kingdom. In his father's Will, Edward received Alfred's booklands in Kent, and a landed base in Old Wessex too. Other *æthelings* bided their time. By 898, Asser had stopped work, and the ASC for the moment was hardly being kept up. While Edward lived on to gain immortality through a new generation of annalists after 900, prime victims in the 890s of his ambition, and of the historians' silence, were the king's wives of the preceding century.

CRIME AND PUNISHMENT IN
THE REIGN OF KING ÆTHELRED THE UNREADY

Simon Keynes

King Æthelred the Unready was about twelve years old when he came to the throne, following the murder of his half-brother Edward the Martyr in 978, and he ruled England for the next thirty-eight years, until his death aged about fifty in 1016. It was a long reign by any standards, and the prevailing impression is that it was a period of political mismanagement, domestic dissension, widespread lawlessness and military disaster, all proceeding from and exacerbated by the incompetence and weakness of the king himself. The primary sources from which this view of Æthelred's reign is derived include the *Anglo-Saxon Chronicle* (with its tale of defeat, treachery and bad government), Archbishop Wulfstan's *Sermo ad Anglos* (a catalogue of the abuses which pervaded English society), King Æthelred's own legislation (regarded by some as vague, loquacious and futile), and several of his charters (which describe crimes leading to the forfeiture of a given estate into the king's hands); as Sir Frank Stenton remarked, 'the historians who regard Æthelred's reign as a time of national degeneracy have good contemporary opinion behind them'.[1] One could not deny that in the conditions which prevailed at the end of Æthelred's reign the fabric of society was coming apart at the seams, and no amount of special pleading on the king's behalf could excuse the humiliation which the English suffered at the hands of their Danish conquerors. It will, however, be my purpose to put the incidence of crime and punishment in Æthelred's reign into some kind of historical context: by asking whether his predecessors had experienced difficulty in the enforcement of law and order; by considering, against this background, whether Æthelred's reign was a period of particular lawlessness, or perhaps a period when particular kinds of crime were rife; and also by considering whether his own enforcement of the law betrays any special weakness of his regime.

A king's duty to maintain the rule of law was enshrined in the threefold promise which he made at his coronation: to ensure that God's church and all the Christian people hold true peace; to forbid acts of robbery and all wrong-

---

* I express just one aspect of a long-standing debt to Peter Sawyer every time I cite a charter. I am otherwise indebted to Patrick Wormald for much stimulating discussion of Anglo-Saxon law, and to Janet Nelson for her valuable comments on a draft of this paper.

[1] F. M. Stenton, *Anglo-Saxon England*, 3rd ed. (Oxford, 1971), p. 394.

doing to every kind of person; and to enjoin justice and mercy in all judgements.[2] Yet the problems which a king had to overcome in fulfilling the terms of his coronation oath are apparent already in the reign of King Alfred the Great, and only multiplied thereafter as the size of the kingdom increased and as the internal structures of authority became more complex. The law-code of King Alfred himself was conceived and executed in the grand manner: very formal and self-conscious, covering a wide variety of subjects, and intended to impress not least by its scale. It would have been inappropriate in such a context for the king to deal explicitly with current malpractices, but it emerges from Asser's *Life* of Alfred that the king often had occasion to intervene in disputed judgements, and that he was much exercised by his ignorant, biassed and bribable judges.[3] Theodulf of Orleans' satire on the judicial malpractices which prevailed during the age of Charlemagne would clearly have been quite apposite in Alfred's reign.[4]

The surviving 'law-codes' issued during the reigns of King Alfred's successors in the tenth century do not approach his own in scope, and were quite different from it, and to some extent from each other, in their general intent; indeed, to categorise them as 'law-codes' in the first place is probably misleading, except in so far as they were pronouncements on legal matters apparently issued in written form, and circulated to the parties or courts concerned.[5] The surviving texts include: injunctions addressed by the king to officials responsible for enforcing the law, specifically the king's reeves;[6] decrees made at meetings of the king and his councillors for wider publication, some of which are on particular matters of current concern,[7] while others range over a variety of practices and seem have been intended to enforce the good customs through which the people would

---

[2]   For the coronation *ordo* current in the late tenth century, see *The Claudius Pontificals*, ed. D. H. Turner, Henry Bradshaw Society 97 (London, 1971), pp. 89–97; and for the Old English version of the coronation oath, see *Memorials of Saint Dunstan*, ed. W. Stubbs, Rolls Series 63 (London, 1874), pp. 355–7. See also J. L. Nelson, 'The Second English *Ordo*', in her *Politics and Ritual in Early Medieval Europe* (London, 1986), pp. 361–74.

[3]   Asser, ch. 106: see *Asser's 'Life of King Alfred'*, ed. W. H. Stevenson (Oxford, 1904), pp. 92–5 (text), and S. Keynes and M. Lapidge, *Alfred the Great: Asser's 'Life of King Alfred' and other Contemporary Sources* (Harmondsworth, 1983), pp. 109–10 (translation).

[4]   See *Poetry of the Carolingian Renaissance*, ed. P. Godman (Norman, Oklahoma, 1985), pp. 13–15 and 162–7. See also Charlemagne's *Admonitio generalis* (789), c. 63 (*Capitularia Regum Francorum* I, ed. A. Boretius, MGH LL 2 (Hannover, 1883), no. 22; trans. P. D. King, *Charlemagne: Translated Sources* (Kendal, 1987), pp. 214–15).

[5]   On the publication of law in the tenth century, see S. Keynes, 'Royal Government and the Written Word in Late Anglo-Saxon England', *The Uses of Literacy in Early Medieval Europe*, ed. R. McKitterick (Cambridge, 1990), pp. 226–57. Laws are cited below from *Die Gesetze der Angelsachsen*, ed. F. Liebermann, 3 vols (Halle, 1903–16); see also *The Laws of the Earliest English Kings*, ed. F. L. Attenborough (Cambridge, 1922), and *The Laws of the Kings of England from Edmund to Henry I*, ed. A. J. Robertson (Cambridge, 1925). The following abbreviations are used in references to particular codes: *Alf.* (Alfred), *Edw.* (Edward the Elder), *As.* (Æthelstan), *Edm.* (Edmund), *Edg.* (Edgar), *Atr.* (Æthelred the Unready) and *Cn.* (Cnut).

[6]   I *Edw.*, I *As.*, (King Æthelstan's) *Ordinance on Charities*, and VI *As.* 11; see also VIII *Atr.* 32, *Cn.* 1020, 11, and *Cn.* 1027, 12.

[7]   E.g. II *Edw.*, II *As.*, V *As.*, III *Edm.*, II *Edm.*, and the *Hundred Ordinance* (= 'I *Edg.*').

hope to deserve God's favour;[8] and documents produced by local bodies concerning their own implementation of the law, whether produced in the form of a report to the king,[9] or simply for the record.[10]

It is abundantly clear from all this material that the tenth-century kings experienced considerable difficulties in maintaining the rule of law and order. Indeed, some kings had occasion to complain in general terms about the failure of their subjects to observe their commands. Edward the Elder exhorted his councillors at Exeter 'to consider how their public peace (*frið*) could be kept better than it had been, because it seemed to him that his previous orders had not been carried out so well as they ought to have been'.[11] King Æthelstan, also at Exeter, complained that the public peace had not been kept to the extent either of his own wishes or of his decrees issued previously at Grately, adding that his councillors had told him that he had suffered this too long,[12] and explaining further that all the oaths, pledges and sureties given at Grately had been disregarded or violated,[13] a point which needed to be repeated in a later code issued at Thunderfield;[14] the king's concern to remedy abuses is reflected again in the injunctions which he made to his councillors at Whittlebury, and one who was present on that occasion declared that if the laws were observed 'our public peace will be better than heretofore'.[15] And King Edmund introduced his legislation designed to curb the blood-feud by expressing his dismay at the 'illegal and manifold conflicts which take place among us'.[16]

It is apparent, however, that the fault lay as much with the kings' reeves, in their failure to enforce the law, as with the people themselves, in their failure to respect it. The law-codes of Edward and Æthelstan in particular are replete with injunctions aimed at reminding reeves of their obligations in connection with the administration of justice, and warning them of the penalties which they will incur for neglect of their duties. Thus King Edward commanded his reeves to pronounce just judgements, and to observe correct procedures in the hearing of suits;[17] and King Æthelstan had to contend with reeves who took more than was the king's due or their own,[18] with reeves who were reluctant to carry out what they were commanded to do,[19] with reeves who took bribes and thereby per-

---

8 E.g. *I Edm.*, *II–III Edg.*, and *IV Edg.*
9 *III As.*, being a report of the Kentish shire-court to the king.
10 E.g. *VI As.* 1–8, being the regulations of the London 'peace-guild'.
11 *II Edw.* Prol.
12 *V As.* Prol.
13 *V As.* Prol. 3.
14 *IV As.* 3.2.
15 *VI As.* 12.4.
16 *II Edm.* Prol. 2. Cf. the *Capitulare missorum generale* (802), c. 32 (*Capitularia* I, no. 33; trans. H. R. Loyn and J. Percival, *The Reign of Charlemagne: Documents on Carolingian Government and Administration* (London, 1975), pp. 77–8, and King, *Charlemagne*, pp. 240–1), on Charlemagne's efforts to curb similar misconduct.
17 *I Edw.* Prol., and *II Edw.* 2 and 8.
18 *I As.* 5.
19 *Ord. on Char.* 2, *II As.* 25, *IV As.* 7, *V As.* 1.2, *VI As.* 8.4, and *VI As.* 11.

verted the course of justice,[20] and with reeves who permitted secret settlements out of court.[21] In cases of improper activities, the reeve might be deprived of his office and would be liable to pay a fine of 120 shillings for *oferhiernes* (disobedience to the king).[22]

Another recurrent theme in tenth-century legislation is the difficulty which the public authorities evidently experienced in bringing certain men to justice. King Æthelstan seems to have been confronted with men so rich or belonging to so powerful a kindred that they could not be restrained from crime or prevented from harbouring criminals; his answer was to have them driven with their families and possessions to some other part of the kingdom, and to forbid them ever to return to their native district.[23] Provision was made in other ways for persistent offenders, or for those who persistently evaded the due process of law.[24] Edward the Elder decreed that a man who withheld certain rights from another man was liable to pay a fine of thirty shillings to the king on the first occasion, thirty shillings again on the second occasion, and 120 shillings on the third.[25] According to King Æthelstan's Grately code, a lord who was an accessory to a theft committed by one of his slaves lost the slave and forfeited his wergild on the first occasion, and everything he owned on the second.[26] In the same code we read of the heavy fine imposed on one who refused to ride on a mission to seize the property of a man who had himself refused to pay the fine for failure to attend an assembly three times,[27] a situation which was still envisaged during the reign

[20] V As. 1.3.

[21] VI As. 11.

[22] See II *Edw.* 2, I As. 5, II As. 25, IV As. 7, V As. 1.2–3, VI As. 8.4, and VI As. 11; the same fine was payable by others for a variety of offences against the king's authority. The theme of the wicked reeve can be traced in later tenth-century legislation: see, e.g., III *Edm.* 7.2, III *Edg.* 3, IV *Edg.* 1.5, and IV *Edg.* 13.1; see also *EHD* no. 238 (p. 923). For a Carolingian analogy, see the *Capitulare missorum in Theodonis villa datum secundum, generale* (805), c. 12 (*Capitularia* I, no. 44; trans. Loyn and Percival, *Reign of Charlemagne*, p. 89, and King, *Charlemagne*, p. 249).

[23] V As. Prol. 1, III As. 6, and IV As. 3; cf. VI As. 8.2. King Æthelstan's policy may be compared with Charlemagne's provision for the resettlement of malcontents: see *Capitulare Haristallense* (779), c. 22 (*Capitularia* I, no. 20; trans. Loyn and Percival, *Reign of Charlemagne*, p. 49, and King, *Charlemagne*, p. 205), and cf. *Capitulare Saxonicum* (797), c. 10 (*Capitularia* I, no. 27; trans. Loyn and Percival, *Reign of Charlemagne*, p. 56, and King, *Charlemagne*, pp. 231–2).

[24] The persistent offender was a perennial problem; in early-ninth-century Mercia, a malefactor caught three times was to be delivered to a royal estate (S. 180 and 1861).

[25] I *Edw.* 2.1, and II *Edw.* Prol. 3. The principle of escalating fines for repeated offences pervades Carolingian legislation: see, e.g., *Capitulare Saxonicum* (797), c. 4 (*Capitularia* I, no. 27; trans. Loyn and Percival, *Reign of Charlemagne*, p. 55, and King, *Charlemagne*, pp. 230–1); *Capitulare legibus additum* (803), c. 2 (*Capitularia* I, no. 39); and *Capitulare de latronibus* (804 x 813), c. 5 (*Capitularia* I, no. 82).

[26] II As. 3.1.

[27] II As. 20.2. Charlemagne similarly made provision for repeated refusals to answer a summons to court: see *Capitulare legi Ribuariae additum* (803), c. 6 (*Capitularia* I, no. 41; trans. Loyn and Percival, *Reign of Charlemagne*, pp. 85–6); *Responsa misso cuidam data* (802 x 813), cc. 4–5 (*Capitularia* I, no. 58; trans. King, *Charlemagne*, pp. 267–8); and *Capitula de missorum officiis* (810), c. 3 (*Capitularia* I, no. 66). See also P. Fouracre, ' "Placita" and the

of King Edgar.[28] An escalating scale of fines was applied to those who persistently ignored the authority of the hundred: thirty pence to the hundred on the first occasion, sixty pence on the second, half a pound on the third, and the loss of everything (and outlawry) on the fourth.[29] In much the same way, thegns or reeves who violated Æthelstan's Grately decrees were made to pay five pounds (300 shillings) on the first occasion, the sum equivalent to their wergild (1200 shillings) on the second, and to forfeit everything on the third;[30] similar provisions probably applied thereafter, though when next they surface in the surviving laws the scale of fines is the wergild on the first occasion, twice that on the second, and (should a man be so presumptuous – dyrstig – as to persist in his misconduct) again everything on the third.[31]

It would be mistaken to imagine that the tenth-century kings were wholly successful in achieving their purpose, or any more so than the generality of their medieval contemporaries; after all, one does not have to look far in (say) the legislation of the Frankish kings to find evidence of corrupt judges, persistent offenders, uncontrolled blood-feuds and contempt of legal procedures.[32] But if in

Settlement of Disputes in Late Merovingian Francia', *The Settlement of Disputes in Early Medieval Europe*, ed. W. Davies and P. Fouracre (Cambridge, 1986), pp. 23–43, at 27–9.

[28] *III Edg.* 7.2; see also *II Cn.* 25. For an illustration of the treatment of certain people who had ignored repeated summonses to a court, apparently during the reign of Edward the Martyr, see the *Libellus Æthelwoldi Episcopi* (below, n. 42), c. 34 (*Liber Eliensis*, ed. E. O. Blake, Camden 3rd series 92 (London, 1962), pp. 97–8).

[29] *Hundred Ordinance* ('I Edg.') 3. Compare the provisions which operated for repeated non-payment of rent: the heirs of a certain Alfred (who leased an estate from the New Minster, Winchester, during the reign of King Æthelstan) were required to pay 60 pence (on top of the rent itself) for a first offence, 30 shillings for a second, and would lose the land if they failed to pay a third time (S. 1417); and similarly, for repeated failure to render dues in respect of an estate leased from Glastonbury (S. 509, dated 946). See also *IV Edg.* 1.1–2, and King Edgar's provisions for repeated non-payment of church dues (*II Edg.* 4.1–3, and *IV Edg.* 1.3–4).

[30] *II As.* 25.2.

[31] *II Cn.* 83. One might add that it is laid down in the Statutes of Trinity College, Cambridge, that 'if any Fellow of the College pertinaciously offend against the discipline of the College or wilfully violate or neglect to comply with any of the Statutes of the College, it shall be the duty of the Council . . . to admonish him and (if necessary) to repeat the admonition; and if notwithstanding the repeated admonition he contumaciously persist in such misconduct, it shall be competent for the Council . . . to suspend him from the enjoyment of the benefits and advantages of his Fellowship for one year, and if he still continue contumacious to deprive him altogether of his Fellowship'.

[32] The point (implicit in nn. 4, 16, 22, 23, 25 and 27 above, and n. 41 below) is best appreciated by perusing the corpus of Charlemagne's capitularies (*Capitularia* 1, *passim*; trans. Loyn and Percival, *Reign of Charlemagne*, pp. 46–105, and King, *Charlemagne*, pp. 202–68); see also F. L. Ganshof, *Frankish Institutions under Charlemagne* (New York, 1970), pp. 71–97, and J. L. Nelson, 'Dispute Settlement in Carolingian West Francia', *Settlement of Disputes*, ed. Davies and Fouracre, pp. 45–64. On the crucial question of the relationship between Frankish capitularies and Anglo-Saxon laws, see J. Campbell, 'Observations on English Government from the Tenth to the Twelfth Century', *Essays in Anglo-Saxon History* (London, 1986), pp. 155–70, at 159, and P. Wormald, 'Æthelred the Lawmaker', *Ethelred the Unready: Papers from the Millenary Conference*, ed. D. Hill, BAR, BS 69 (Oxford, 1978), pp. 47–80, at 71–3.

Æthelstan's reign men allowed their cattle to wander freely 'owing to their over-confidence in the public peace',[33] King Edmund was moved to thank his people 'for the immunity from thefts which we now enjoy',[34] and King Edgar expressed his pleasure with his subjects 'because you are so eager about public peace'.[35] King Edgar, indeed, has always enjoyed a reputation as one particularly strong on law and order,[36] and the effectiveness of his regime stands in stark contrast to the alleged weakness of that of his son Æthelred the Unready. Of course there are plenty of incidental references to crimes committed during Edgar's reign, which only serve to remind us that human nature is what it is: for example, an estate was forfeited by a woman and her son who drove an iron pin into a scale model of a certain Ælfsige, for which act of witchcraft the woman was drowned at London Bridge and her son (who escaped) made an outlaw;[37] the property of one Ecgferth who committed some serious crime was declared forfeit 'by the sword which hung on his hip when he drowned';[38] and a layman called Eadwold forfeited his land to the king when convicted of flagrant piracy.[39] Yet contemporaries must have had good reason for applauding King Edgar's effective maintenance of the peace, and it is not difficult to see by what means it was maintained. In his *Translatio et Miracula S. Swithuni*, written in the closing years of Edgar's reign, Lantfred of Winchester tells of the officious (or perhaps merely zealous) king's reeve who was so determined to see a slave hang for a petty crime that he refused to accept legal composition in respect of the offence, and instead subjected the slave to the ordeal of hot iron;[40] and Lantfred also tells how King

---

33 'for þam ofertruan on þam friðe': *VI As.* 8.7.

34 'ðæs friðes ðe we nu habbað æt ðam ðyfðam': *II Edm.* 5.

35 'for ði þe ge swa georne ymbe frið syndon': *IV Edg.* 16. At Pîtres, in 864, Charles the Bald had thanked those present for their attendance 'fully and in peace', adding 'even if not all of you, as we wanted, have been keeping the peace since our last assembly, still most of you have' (see J. L. Nelson, 'Legislation and Consensus in the Reign of Charles the Bald', *Ideal and Reality in Frankish and Anglo-Saxon Society*, ed. P. Wormald (Oxford, 1983), pp. 202–27, at 220).

36 The reputation was already well-established within a few years of Edgar's death: see, e.g., Bishop Æthelwold's tract on the establishment of monasteries (*EHD* no. 238); Wulfstan Cantor's *Narratio metrica de S. Swithuno* II, lines 440–65 (for which see D. Whitelock, 'Wulfstan Cantor and Anglo-Saxon Law', *Nordica et Anglica*, ed. A. H. Orrick (Mouton, The Hague, 1968), pp. 83–92, at 83–4); Ælfric, in his *Life of St Swithhun* (*EHD* no. 239g) and in *Judges* (*EHD* no. 239i); B's *Life of St Dunstan*, c. 25 (*Memorials*, ed. Stubbs, pp. 36–7; *EHD* no. 234, p. 902); and Wulfstan of York, in the *Anglo-Saxon Chronicle*, MS. D, s.a. 959, and *VIII Atr.* 37 and 43, etc. King Edgar would clearly bear comparison in this respect with his contemporary Otto I: see K. J. Leyser, *Rule and Conflict in an Early Medieval Society: Ottonian Saxony* (London, 1979), pp. 35–8.

37 S. 1377: *Anglo-Saxon Charters*, ed. A. J. Robertson, 2nd ed. (Cambridge, 1956), no. 37, and *EHD* no. 112.

38 S. 1447: *Charters*, ed. Robertson, no. 44.

39 S. 753.

40 Lantfred, c. 25: see M. Lapidge, *The Cult of St Swithun*, Winchester Studies 4.2 (Oxford, forthcoming). Lantfred's prose account of the miracles of St Swithhun was the basis of Wulfstan Cantor's *Narratio metrica de S. Swithuno* (written in the early 990s), and Wulfstan's version of the story of the officious reeve is discussed by Whitelock, 'Wulfstan Cantor', pp. 87–92.

Edgar introduced comprehensive mutilation as a deterrent against all manner of crimes, and how it was practised on a certain innocent man.[41] Further insight into what was perhaps the somewhat overbearing nature of Edgar's regime is afforded by consideration of the so-called 'anti-monastic reaction' associated with the reign of his successor, Edward the Martyr: it emerges that the attacks on monasteries by those who resented the burgeoning wealth of the monks were just one aspect of a rather different phenomenon, which might itself be characterised as a period of general disorder precipitated by King Edgar's death and exploited by those who saw personal advantage in undoing what had been done before, but who may not have dared behave as they did during King Edgar's lifetime.[42]

Such, then, is the necessary background to a consideration of crime and punishment in the reign of Æthelred the Unready: it emerges that his predecessors in general had to contend with corrupt reeves, persistent offenders and men who could not be brought to justice, and that if Edgar in particular enjoyed some measure of success in restraining lawlessness it was by virtue of a regime which (from his subjects' point of view) might have verged on the oppressive. The question remains: against this background, was Æthelred's reign really a period of social disorder?

The *Anglo-Saxon Chronicle* certainly yields examples of internal dissension, military incompetence and treachery, and in his *Sermo ad Anglos* Archbishop Wulfstan waxes rhetorical on the proliferation of crime, on injustices and abuses of various kinds, and on God's punishment in the form of Viking attacks. Both of these sources were, however, written under the conditions which prevailed at the very end of the reign, and both must therefore be treated with all due circumspection;[43] it is to Æthelred's laws and charters that we should turn in the hope of gaining a more balanced view of the state of affairs during the course of his reign as a whole.

It would appear that King Æthelred himself promulgated new legislation on the occasion of a meeting of his *witan* at *Bromdun*, perhaps in the 980s, but the earliest surviving law-codes issued in his name belong to the 990s.[44] II *Æthelred* is a treaty with the Viking army, drawn up in 994; but though a remarkable

---

[41] Lantfred, c. 26; see Whitelock, 'Wulfstan Cantor', pp. 83–7, for discussion of Wulfstan's version of the same story, and S. Keynes, 'A Tale of Two Kings: Alfred the Great and Æthelred the Unready', *TRHS* 5th series 36 (1986), pp. 195–217, at 212. Charlemagne had laid down a scale of mutilation for persistent thieves: see *Capitulare Haristallense* (779), c. 23 (*Capitularia* I, no. 20; trans. Loyn and Percival, *Reign of Charlemagne*, p. 49, and King, *Charlemagne*, p. 205).

[42] A principal source for the 'anti-monastic reaction' is the *Libellus Æthelwoldi episcopi*, a twelfth-century work based on a late-tenth-century vernacular record of the endowment of Ely abbey; see *Liber Eliensis*, ed. Blake, between pp. 79 and 110. The *Libellus* will be edited, with translation and commentary, in S. Keynes and A. Kennedy, *Anglo-Saxon Ely: Records of Ely Abbey and its Benefactors in the Tenth and Eleventh Centuries* (Woodbridge, forthcoming).

[43] See S. Keynes, 'The Declining Reputation of King Æthelred the Unready', *Ethelred*, ed. Hill, pp. 227–53, and 'Tale of Two Kings', pp. 201–5.

[44] See Wormald, 'Æthelred the Lawmaker', pp. 61–3, and S. Keynes, *The Diplomas of King Æthelred 'the Unready' 978–1016* (Cambridge, 1980), pp. 196–7.

document in its own right, it is not strictly relevant in the present context. *I Æthelred* is legislation for 'English' England, issued at Woodstock c.997: it lays down the procedure when a man is accused, and how he might clear himself by oath or by submission to the judicial ordeal. And *III Æthelred* is legislation for the territory of the Five Boroughs, issued at Wantage c.997: it deals with the matters covered in *I Æthelred* (with some significant variations in detail), but it also covers other things besides and in general offers a valuable insight into the distinctive practices which had arisen in this part of the Danelaw. There is nothing in any of this legislation which suggests that the bonds of social order were beginning to break already under the first onslaught of the Viking invaders in the 980s and 990s, and indeed, the general impression created by these codes is of a king who was perfectly capable of taking requisite and appropriate action in response to traditional tenth-century concerns.

The tone of Æthelred's legislation changes, however, in the last decade of his reign, from a strictly pragmatic approach towards the administration of justice to an obsession with the purification of society through adherence to the principles which should govern a Christian people. It may seem that this later legislation, which is known to have been drafted by Archbishop Wulfstan of York, was nothing if not vague, loquacious and futile,[45] but it can also be read as moving testimony of the effect which the Vikings were having by this stage, forcing the king and his councillors to affirm again and again that it was only through good conduct that the English could hope to earn God's favour and support in their struggle.[46]

The great interest of Archbishop Wulfstan's legislation in the present context is the glimpse it affords of the abuses which arose in the later years of Æthelred's reign, when the country was enduring the worst of the Viking attacks. In one of the codes issued in the king's name in 1014, Wulfstan expresses his view that since the days of King Edgar 'Christ's laws have waned and the king's laws dwindled'.[47] The most specific indication of what he might have meant by this reference to the dwindling of the king's laws is provided by a series of clauses in one version of *V Æthelred*, a code promulgated at Enham in 1008.[48] Wulfstan appeals for an end to the abuses (*unlaga*) which the king himself had repeatedly ordered to be suppressed: namely, the practices of disreputable men in the west, in connection with the attaching of property;[49] the disregard of the testimony of

[45] H. G. Richardson and G. O. Sayles, *Law and Legislation from Æthelberht to Magna Carta* (Edinburgh, 1966), p. 27.
[46] Thus *VII Atr.* is, in effect, a programme for public prayer and penitence, ordained at a time of acute distress; see Keynes, *Diplomas*, pp. 217–19. Yet it differs little in conception from, e.g., the *Capitulare episcoporum* issued by Charlemagne's bishops in 793 (*Capitularia* I, no. 21; trans. King, *Charlemagne*, pp. 223–4), from King Æthelstan's insistence on the performance of charitable acts and the saying of prayers for the king (see Keynes, 'Written Word', p. 237 and n. 48), and from such codes as *I Edm.* and *IV Edg.*
[47] 'Cristes lage wanodan 7 cyninges laga litledon': *VIII Atr.* 37. Cf. *Leges Edwardi Confessoris* 34.3 (*Gesetze*, ed. Liebermann, I, pp. 663–4).
[48] *V Atr.* 32–32.5, in Cambridge, Corpus Christi College 201.
[49] Cf. *II Atr.* 8–9.

witnesses, properly given;[50] the bringing forward, against an heir, of claims which had never been made against his predecessor;[51] and the practice, said to prevail in the north, of bringing an accusation of homicide against an innocent person, and of holding it to be valid if made on the very day of the alleged crime. Wulfstan does, of course, inveigh against other abuses elsewhere in the legislation which he drafted for King Æthelred,[52] but it is interesting that he should have been so concerned about these abuses in particular, and that he should have felt that their incidence varied from one part of the country to another; moreover, Wulfstan states that the king had stopped the last-named abuse, adding 'May he do more'.

One doubts, somehow, that Æthelred would have been able to do much in the years following 1008, when the country was subjected first to the invasion of Thorkell the Tall (1009–12) and then to the invasion of Swein Forkbeard (1013–14); and one suspects, indeed, that under such circumstances matters could only get worse. But on his return from temporary exile in 1014, undertakings were made which amount to a reaffirmation of the bonds between a king and his people: Æthelred pledged to be a gracious lord, and to reform all the things which they all hated, and in return they swore to turn to him without treachery.[53] It was evidently felt that Æthelred's government had been unjust, and it is from a section in one of the law-codes which Wulfstan drafted for Cnut that we gain an understanding of what needed to be reformed.[54] The section is introduced as being the mitigation (lihtingc) by which Cnut wished 'to protect all the people from what they were hitherto oppressed with all too greatly',[55] and it is clear that Wulfstan is addressing practices which had come to prevail in the last few years of Æthelred's reign. They are, by and large, practices of precisely the kind which one would expect to arise in a country torn apart by the inevitable effects of war, among a people whose natural loyalties were under strain, and at a time when normal standards of behaviour would be thrown to the winds.

---

[50] Cf. III Atr. 2–3.

[51] Cf. III Atr. 14. For an instance of this malpractice, during the reign of King Edgar, see the Libellus Æthelwoldi episcopi, c. 27; there are many other indications in the Libellus of the importance of holding land without counterclaim (cc. 9, 14, 28, 38, 39, 42, 45, 57 and 60).

[52] In addition to predictable complaints about heathen practices and various manifestations of disrespect for the Church, the abuses implicit in Wulfstan's legislation include the selling of innocent men to the pagans (V Atr. 2, VI Atr. 9, VII Atr (Lat.) 5; cf. II Cn. 3), the condemnation of men to death for too trivial offences (V Atr. 3, VI Atr. 10; cf. II Cn. 2.1), desertion from an army under the personal command of the king (V Atr. 28, VI Atr. 35), and plotting against the king's life (V Atr. 30, VI Atr. 37; cf. II Cn. 57).

[53] See D. Bethurum Loomis, 'Regnum and Sacerdotium in the Early Eleventh Century', England before the Conquest, ed. P. Clemoes and K. Hughes (Cambridge, 1971), pp. 129–45, at 138.

[54] II Cn. 69–82; see P. Stafford, 'The Laws of Cnut and the History of Anglo-Saxon Royal Promises', ASE 10 (1982), pp. 173–90, at 176–8.

[55] 'eallon folce gebeorgan, ðe hig ær ðyson mid gedrehte wæron ealles to swyðe': II Cn. 69.

They concern unjust exactions by the king's reeves,[56] the scale of heriots payable in the event of a man dying intestate and the proper distribution of his property,[57] the right of heirs to enjoy their property if no claims had been brought against their predecessor,[58] the law that a widow must not remarry for a year and then only a husband of her own choice,[59] the (limited) liability of the rightful owner in the case of a crime committed with a stolen weapon,[60] the (limited) liability of wives or children in the case of crimes committed by their husbands or fathers,[61] various considerations in respect of men on military service,[62] and other miscellaneous matters.[63] This passage in Cnut's law-code certainly lends substance to the more generalised indictment of contemporary behaviour in Wulfstan's *Sermo ad Anglos*, and there can be no doubt that in his sermon Wulfstan was responding, albeit in his inimitable rhetorical style, to what he perceived as a dire situation; but the point is, of course, that when placed in the context of the entire corpus Æthelred's legislation the malpractices which upset Archbishop Wulfstan are seen to be a feature, not of the whole reign, but rather of its closing years.

I turn finally to the evidence of King Æthelred's charters. It is a distinctive feature of these charters that they quite often contain some account of how the land concerned had come into the king's possession, and was thus his to give away; and in several cases this involves reference to crimes committed by a previous owner, in consequence of which the land had been forfeited to the king.[64] One does not find this kind of material in such profusion before and after Æthelred's reign, so the impression it creates is of a sudden crime-wave during his reign, which is thought to be in accord with the traditional picture of national degeneracy and bad government.[65] Yet the evidence should be handled

---

[56] II Cn. 69.1–2; cf. VII Atr. (Lat.) 6.3, II Cn. 8.2, and Cn. 1027 12. For Wulfstan's views on the malpractices of reeves, since the death of King Edgar, see his *Institutes of Polity*, c. 10 (*Die 'Institutes of Polity, Civil and Ecclesiastical'*, ed. K. Jost, Swiss Studies in English 47 (Bern, 1959), pp. 81–2; *Anglo-Saxon Prose*, ed. M. Swanton (London, 1975), pp. 130–1). Their behaviour never improved: see J. Green, 'The Sheriffs of William the Conqueror', *Anglo-Norman Studies 5*, ed. R. A. Brown (Woodbridge, 1983), pp. 129–45.

[57] II Cn. 70–71a.5; for discussion of heriots, see N. P. Brooks, 'Arms, Status and Warfare in Late-Saxon England', *Ethelred*, ed. Hill, pp. 81–103, at 87–90 (demonstrating that the rates recorded in *II Cn.* had apparently been in force since the late tenth century).

[58] II Cn. 72 (and above, n. 51).

[59] II Cn. 73–4; cf. V Atr. 21.1 and VI Atr. 26.1.

[60] II Cn. 75.

[61] II Cn. 76.

[62] II Cn. 77 (desertion on military service), 78 (remission of heriot for death in battle) and 79 (rights of those who properly perform military service in respect of their land).

[63] II Cn. 80 (hunting rights), 81 (inviolability of gifts) and 82 (entitlement of men to peace, whenever going to and from a meeting).

[64] See F. M. Stenton, *The Latin Charters of the Anglo-Saxon Period* (Oxford, 1955), pp. 74–82; Keynes, *Diplomas*, pp. 97 and 200–2; Wormald, 'Æthelred the Lawmaker', p. 48; and P. Wormald, 'A Handlist of Anglo-Saxon Lawsuits', ASE 17 (1988), pp. 247–82, at 277–8 and 281. For comparable material from Ottonian Saxony, see Leyser, *Rule and Conflict*, pp. 36–7.

[65] Thus Whitelock remarks of Æthelred's charters in general that they indicate 'general disorder and bad government' (*EHD*, p. 47); in particular, she says of S. 877 (*ibid.* no. 120)

with care. The law-codes of Alfred and his successors in the tenth and eleventh centuries show that there were various circumstances in which land could be forfeited into the king's hands by the due process of law;[66] and there seems no reason to doubt that there was a steady flow of estates coming in this way into the king's possession.[67] Moreover, such estates would then account for a fair proportion of the land which kings distributed or sold to others during the course of their reigns; but as it happens, it was only during Æthelred's reign that the draftsmen of charters gave details of the crime which had led to the forfeiture. It has been said that the charters of Æthelred thus 'give away his sense of insecurity and his need for self-justification',[68] but the phenomenon could be explained in other ways. It may simply be a matter of fashion, to be compared (for example) with the very distinctive practices adopted by the draftsman of a group of Æthelstan's charters, which include giving precise details of the date and place of issue and the provision of remarkably full witness-lists;[69] or it could have been occasioned by a desire to strengthen the new owner's title to the estate, in the light of general experience, since forfeited estates would be precisely those most likely to attract claims by the previous owner or members of his family;[70] or it could have been an extension of the interest apparently shown at this period in the process known as *team*, i.e. vouching to warranty,[71] by which the possessor of property claimed by someone else would cite the person from whom he had himself acquired it to prove that the property had been that person's to give or sell in the first place.

Whatever the explanation, it remains a fact that the surviving charters of King Æthelred afford about twenty instances of the forfeiture of land into the king's hands, as a consequence of criminal activity. In several cases the exact nature of the crime is not specified,[72] and in the other cases the crimes involved

---

that its major interest 'is the picture it gives of the weakness of Æthelred's regime' (*ibid.* p. 575), and of S. 939 (*ibid.* no. 121) that 'it shows the measure of disgust with Ethelred's rule' (*ibid.* p. 579). Elsewhere she cites a papal letter as supporting evidence 'for the lawlessness of the reign of Ethelred the Unready' (*ibid.* p. 895).

[66] E.g. *Alf.* 4, 4.2 (cf. *II As.* 4); *II Edm.* 1.3, 6; *Hund. Ord.* 3.1; and *II Cn.* 13.1, 77.

[67] For earlier instances of forfeiture, see, e.g., S. 362 (Ealdorman Wulfhere and his wife, for desertion), 1445 (Helmstan, for theft) and 1211 (Goda, for unexplained reasons), during the reigns of Alfred and Edward the Elder; *Libellus Æthelwoldi Episcopi*, c. 54 (Waldchist, for unspecified crime), during the reign of Edmund; and S. 1447 (Ecgferth, for unexplained reason), 753 (Eadwold, for flagrant piracy), 1377 (a widow and her son, for witchcraft), 1457 (Brihtwaru, for complicity in theft), and *Libellus Æthelwoldi Episcopi*, cc. 5 (Wulfwine *cocus* and his wife Ælfswyth, for unspecified crime), 29 (Oslac, for unexplained reasons), and 45 (unnamed person, for theft), during the reign of Edgar. All the attested cases of forfeiture in the ninth, tenth and eleventh centuries are included in Wormald, 'Handlist of Lawsuits', *passim*.

[68] Whitelock, in *EHD*, p. 47; cf. Stenton, *Latin Charters*, p. 75, and *Anglo-Saxon England*, pp. 394–5.

[69] See S. Keynes, 'Regenbald the Chancellor (*sic*)', *Anglo-Norman Studies* 10, ed. R. A. Brown (Woodbridge, 1988), pp. 185–222, at 186 n. 4.

[70] See Stenton, *Latin Charters*, p. 82, and Keynes, *Diplomas*, pp. 200–1.

[71] E.g. *II Atr.* 8–9 (but cf. Wormald, 'Æthelred the Lawmaker', p. 60), and *III Atr.* 6.1.

[72] S. 842 (Lufa), 896 and 937 (Ealdorman Ælfric), 869 (unnamed person), 918 (Wulf-

range from sexual misconduct,[73] through theft or appropriation of other people's property,[74] to fighting or killing[75] and various forms of defiance of royal authority, including disregard of the king's orders,[76] killing a king's reeve,[77] harbouring a fugitive,[78] and treachery.[79] By and large, the crimes are not remarkable in themselves, for examples of criminal behaviour of similar kinds could be cited from other periods in the tenth and eleventh centuries; and certainly there would be no warrant on this evidence alone for supposing that Æthelred's was a reign when the law had broken down. It is rather the special quality of the evidence in Æthelred's charters which sets his reign apart from other periods: not only do we have particularly vivid accounts of the crimes themselves, as it happens in greater quantity than before or after, but we also gain unusually detailed views of how the malefactors were brought to justice.

Two or three of the individual cases do, however, seem to reflect badly on Æthelred's government, and it may be worth looking at them more closely. The crimes of a certain Wulfbald are recorded in a charter (dated 996) by which King Æthelred gave some of the forfeited property to his mother Queen Ælfthryth.[80] At first sight, the account strikes one as a fairly damning indictment of the quality of Æthelred's regime.[81] We are told that on his father's death, Wulfbald went to his stepmother's land and seized all the goods he could find; two times the king ordered him to pay back the stolen goods, but on each occasion Wulfbald paid no attention, and on each occasion his wergild was duly assigned to the king (in other words, he was fined the sum equivalent to his wergild, presumably 1200 shillings). Wulfbald then seized the estate belonging to his kinsman Brihtmær of Bourne; two times the king ordered him to vacate the land, but on

geat and Ælfgifu), 927 (Leofric) and 1223 (unnamed person); see also S. 937 (Æthelweard and his brother) and 923 (a certain *matrona*).

[73] S. 901 (unnamed woman, for her 'crime of fornication'), ? 911 (a certain *matrona* called Leoftæt, for her improper behaviour), and 927 (Leofric, for crimes which included adultery).

[74] S. 877 (Wulfbald seized his stepmother's property, and then his kinsman's property), 886 (Æthelsige stole swine belonging to Æthelwine), 893 (Æthelsige committed various acts of theft and plunder), and 927 (Leofric indulged in outrageous plundering).

[75] S. 877 (Wulfbald's widow killed her husband's cousin and fifteen of his companions), 883 (three brothers fought others from whom a bridle had been stolen), and 892 (Wistan forfeited land 'for unlawful killing'); see also below, n. 77.

[76] S. 877 (Wulfbald ignored the king's repeated orders to pay back plundered goods).

[77] S. 893 (Æthelsige killed the king's reeve who was defending the king's property), and 916 and 926 (Ealdorman Leofsige killed the king's reeve Æfic 'in his own house without warning').

[78] S. 926 (*matrona* called Æthelflæd rendered assistance to her brother, Ealdorman Leofsige, after he had been declared an exile).

[79] S. 934 (Wulfgeat colluded in schemes with the king's enemies) and 927 (Leofric rebelled against the king's forces on military service); see also S. 939 (Æthelric allegedly involved in plot to receive Swein in Essex).

[80] S. 877: *EHD* no. 120.

[81] Thus Whitelock says of the charter that it reveals 'the extraordinary feebleness of the government he (Wulfbald) defied for so long' (*EHD*, p. 47); see also her comment on the charter quoted above, n. 65.

each occasion Wulfbald paid no attention, and on each occasion his wergild was duly assigned to the king. In a 'great meeting' at London, Wulfbald's property and his life were placed at the king's disposal. Wulfbald seems to have been spared, and yet we are told that he made no amends for his crimes up to the time of his death. Once he had died, Wulfbald's widow went to Bourne, and killed Eadmær (Wulfbald's cousin) and fifteen of his companions; when a 'great synod' was held at London, c.990, Wulfbald's property was again assigned to the king. Several points of interest should be noted. In the first place, the account of Wulfbald's crimes had apparently been written down on the occasion of the London meeting c.990 (given the detailed witness-list), for preservation thereafter in the king's archives as evidence of the forfeiture which had brought him the land. Indeed, it is likely in general that such accounts of crimes in the charters were derived from written records made when the case was settled, and that the draftsmen of the charters either incorporated them more or less verbatim, or re-cast them into the body of the text;[82] we should expect, therefore, that the accounts represent what was in effect the official point of view, and may thus be rather one-sided. Secondly, the crimes committed by Wulfbald and his widow evidently arose from a family dispute about inheritance, and are not especially remarkable in themselves; it may appear that the great meetings at London were held specifically to deal with their offences, but of course the case would have been just one of the many which the councillors discussed on each occasion. Thirdly, the final settlement took place c.990, which places Wulfbald's activities in the 980s; thus if the account is indicative of weakness of any sort, it is a weakness in the opening decade of Æthelred's reign, which may not necessarily have obtained thereafter. And fourthly, Wulfbald's repeated disregard of royal commands reminds one of the difficulties which earlier tenth-century kings had experienced in bringing certain powerful men to justice, and of the provision which they made for persistent offenders; so it is possible that Wulfbald's defiance of authority reflects weaknesses inherent in the legal system itself, rather than the inability of a particular king to enforce the law.

Two charters refer in some detail to the activities of Leofsige, ealdorman of Essex from about 994 until his banishment in 1002. In the first of them, dated 995, we hear of Æthelwig, the king's reeve in Buckingham, and of Wynsige, the reeve in Oxford, who gave Christian burial to two brothers who had been killed in a fight; Ealdorman Leofsige came to the king and accused the reeves of acting wrongfully in this respect, but the king upheld their action because he did not wish to sadden Æthelwig, who was 'dear and precious' to him. It is interesting to find that the newly-appointed ealdorman of Essex was prompted to intervene in a matter of this nature on what must been the periphery of his own (territorial) jurisdiction, and indeed, it is difficult to believe that it was simply to protect the principle of Christian burial. About seven years later Ealdorman Leofsige again clashed with a reeve, and this time he went too far: he is said to have killed the king's (high-)reeve Æfic 'in his own house without warning', and was duly

[82] E.g. S. 877 and 886, in the vernacular; S. 883, 893, 896 and 926, in Latin.

declared an exile with his accomplices.[83] Leofsige was not the only ealdorman exiled in Æthelred's reign, for Ælfric of Mercia (appointed in 983 following the death of Ealdorman Ælfhere) had been banished in 985 for (unspecified) crimes against God and the king's authority;[84] and while the incidents of Leofsige's career may simply exemplify King Æthelred's supposed lack of judgement in the choice of reliable men, it is also possible that they illustrate the friction which must often have arisen between those in high office,[85] in which case it is of some interest that Æthelred's loyalties should have been towards the reeves who were his personal representatives and not to the ealdorman with perhaps more vested power. It is worth adding that Leofsige was not the only person to clash with the king's reeves, for we read in another charter of a reeve who was killed defending the king's property against a disreputable thegn.[86]

If it would be mistaken to make too much of the individual cases of Wulfbald and Leofsige, at least as instances of problems peculiar to Æthelred's reign, the same may not be true of the recorded cases involving treachery to the king. Æthelric of Bocking, for example, was accused of complicity in a plot to receive Swein Forkbeard in Essex when first he came there with a fleet (presumably a reference to the invasion of 991), but the matter was still not settled when Æthelric died several years later. It is not clear what construction to put upon this: perhaps it was reluctance on the king's part to press the charge while Æthelric was alive to defend himself, with the implication that the king was not prepared to give him a fair trial;[87] or perhaps the case proved difficult to resolve because the charge was only a matter of general suspicion, placing the onus on Æthelric to clear himself by oath or ordeal.[88] Whatever the explanation, we are told that the king wished to raise the matter of the outstanding charge when the widow brought Æthelric's heriot to him, but in the event he was persuaded to drop it and to confirm the bequests made in Æthelric's will. Two attested cases of treachery from near the end of the reign are more straightforward. A certain Leofric is said to have forfeited his property for, among other things, desertion on military service,[89] and a thegn called Wulfgeat lost his lands because 'he colluded in schemes with the king's enemies'.[90] The charters which record these forfeitures

---

[83] For Leofsige's activities, see S. 883 and 926 (and S. 916); for the extent of his jurisdiction, see C. Hart, 'The Ealdordom of Essex', An Essex Tribute, ed. K. Neale (London, 1987), pp. 57–81, at 76. If his sister Æthelflæd, who suffered forfeiture of her own property for helping her disgraced brother (S. 926), is the Æthelflæd who bequeathed land in Essex and Hertfordshire to St Paul's (S. 1495), it would seem to follow that her will was not, in the event, allowed to stand: see Anglo-Saxon Wills, ed. D. Whitelock (Cambridge, 1930), p. 176.

[84] S. 896 and 937.

[85] The Fonthill letter (S. 1445) affords another, much earlier, instance of a clash between ealdorman and reeve.

[86] S. 893.

[87] See Whitelock, in EHD, p. 579.

[88] Cf. R. Bartlett, Trial by Fire and Water: the Medieval Judicial Ordeal (Oxford, 1986), pp. 29–31.

[89] S. 927.

[90] S. 934. It is conceivable that the Wulfgeat who forfeited his property for treachery, in

are, in fact, the only ones which afford instances of forfeiture for treachery, and they are dated 1012 and 1015 repectively; it is only to be expected that the incidence of such crimes would increase as the Viking onslaught drew to its climax, and as certain people began to put their own interests above those of the king.

While it is easy, therefore, to see how one might get the impression that the reign of King Æthelred was a period when lawlessness prevailed, such an impression would, on this evidence, be arguably mistaken. The king himself has been regarded as one prone to acts of spasmodic violence, and might be supposed to have set a bad example to his subjects; but it has been suggested elsewhere that the acts in question would have seemed different to contemporaries aware of their true nature and context.[91] The other evidence of wrong doing in King Æthelred's reign needs to be approached with the same respect for historical perspective. The law-codes of Æthelred's predecessors in the tenth century serve to expose the difficulties which any king faced in the maintenance of law and order, and it is simply the special quality of his charters which provides us with the graphic illustration of these difficulties which we happen not to have for other reigns. There can be no doubt, however, that manifold abuses arose in the closing decade of Æthelred's reign, when social order was evidently compromised to a degree not seen before; in Archbishop Wulfstan's view of the world, God duly sent in the Vikings to punish the English for their crimes, but perhaps in this respect Wulfstan had confused the effect with the cause.

or sometime before 1015 (S. 934), was the same person as the Wulfgeat who forfeited his property for unspecified crimes, in or sometime before 1008 (S. 918), and that both can be further identified as the Wulfgeat whose forfeiture (for unspecified reasons) is recorded in the *Anglo-Saxon Chronicle* for 1006; see Keynes, *Diplomas*, pp. 210–11, and Wormald, 'Handlist of Lawsuits', p. 256 n. 29. Yet the Wulfgeat who fell from grace in 1006 was arguably the victim of political machinations (Keynes, *Diplomas*. pp. 211–13), and seems previously to have been well disposed towards Abingdon abbey (S. 937; *ibid.* p. 192), so on the face of it the Wulfgeat of S. 918, who held property in the abbey's despite, is unlikely to have been the same person; moreover, a thegn called Wulfgeat attests a charter in 1009 (*ibid.*, Table 8). It might seem difficult to entertain the existence of two or more thegns called Wulfgeat, but equally it would be dangerous to resolve them all into one.

[91] See Keynes, 'Tale of Two Kings', pp. 211–13.

SOURCES FOR PRE–CONQUEST YORK

R. A. Hall

While incumbent of the Chair of History at Leeds University, Peter Sawyer's interests inevitably brought him frequently to York to gain first-hand news and views of the work of York Archaeological Trust.[1] The Trust in turn capitalised on his knowledge by inviting him both to contribute to its publications[2] and to join its governing Council, where his advice often helped direct the course of our research. Trust staff are now studying the material retrieved over the last decade or so, which includes that excavated in 1976–81 at 16–22 Coppergate, the first substantial body of data for the Anglo-Scandinavian town of *Jorvik*, and that from 46–54 Fishergate, excavated 1985–6, where part of a seventh to ninth century Anglian settlement was discovered. With these projects in train, it is an appropriate time to offer to Peter Sawyer a tribute on behalf of York Archaeological Trust in the form of some reflections on the interplay of documentary and archaeological source material in the elucidation of the pre-conquest city.

It remains true that it is the earliest part of the post-Roman era – the fifth, sixth and seventh centuries – which is most obscure in York's history. There is no body of published archaeological data to infill the almost complete historical *lacuna*; it is to be hoped that this may change with the report of excavations below York Minster, carried out by Derek Phillips of York Minster Archaeology Office. Meanwhile, the layers within and overlying the latest Roman features on each site excavated in and around the Roman military and civilian nuclei must be scrutinised most carefully in the hope of gaining some clue – structural, artefactual or environmental – to what happened in the decades, generations and centuries following the withdrawal of the Roman military presence and the consequent break-up of the established Romano-British economic and social order. At present, however, it seems impossible to predict areas likely to be especially productive of information about this period, which remains truly a 'dark age' in York.

The re-introduction of Christianity to York in 627 (there had been a Roman

---

[1] I am pleased to acknowledge the stimulus and co-operation of my colleagues at York Archaeological Trust, and of Dr Terry O'Connor of the Environmental Archaeology Unit in the Department of Biology at York University; I am also most grateful to the Trust's Illustrator, Peter Marshall, for preparing the accompanying plan. Dr Ian Wood and Richard Morris also made helpful comments on a preliminary draft of the text.
[2] P. H. Sawyer, 'Some sources for the history of Viking Northumbria', in *Viking Age York and the North*, ed. R. A. Hall (London, 1978), pp. 3–7.

bishop from at least 314) heralds a period for which not only the volume of written evidence but also the amount of excavated information increases, and there is clearly room for further interdisciplinary approaches to many of the problems.

There can be few more important ecclesiastical sites in the country than the cathedral, first built by King Edwin for his baptism, and the complementary monastic establishment. The pre-Norman cathedral has not been found in the excavations below and around York Minster (1) (bracketed numbers refer to the plan on p. 85), but pre-Viking scupltural fragments do support the long-held view that this was indeed the site of Edwin's church.[3] One possibility is that the earliest church occupied the courtyard of the old Roman *principia* or headquarters building, which was reportedly still standing at the time of the Vikings' take-over.[4] This courtyard was almost certainly the largest space unoccupied by Roman buildings within the walls of the Roman fortress; could it have formed the *platea populi*, the 'public square', mentioned in passing by the early eighth century author of the *Anonymous Life of Gregory the Great*?[5]

The reference comes in a passage concerning King Edwin's pre-baptismal instruction, where the king is described as leaving a hall (*aula*), where he and others had been exhorted to change their way of life, and hurrying to the church (*ad ecclesiam*) by way of the *platea populi*. Is this brief topographical allusion to be given any credence at all; should any weight be placed on this early eighth century Whitby writer's anecdotal phraseology concerning the early seventh century layout of York, or was he borrowing both the spirit and the letter of some earlier and topographically unrelated source? Further historical discussion of this point would be helpful, but it may be suggested that the relative proximity of the writer's monastery to York, and the prime importance of the locale, both provide some reason to believe that the terminology may reflect at least early eighth century York if not that of a hundred years earlier.

Morris has suggested that this passage provides a picture of the juxtaposition of secular and religious foci,[6] and this may be so, although the *aula* is not stated to be in royal possession; but what of the *platea populi*? What function would this have? The related phrase *popularis platea* occurs in a context of 934–9 at Winchester, and has been translated as 'the market place'.[7] There, however, it relates to a block of land outside the west gate, and to a time in the tenth century when there is much more evidence, both documentary and archaeological, for town-

---

[3] For a contrary view see D. M. Palliser, 'York's West Bank: medieval suburb or urban nucleus?', in *Archaeological Papers from York presented to M. W. Barley*, ed. P. V. Addyman and V. E. Black (York, 1984), pp. 104–5.

[4] D. Phillips, 'Excavations at York Minster 1967–73', *Friends of York Minster 46th Annual Report* (1975), p. 24.

[5] ed. B. Colgrave (Cambridge, 1968), pp. 96–7.

[6] R. K. Morris, 'Parish Churches', in *Urban Archaeology in Britain*, ed. J. Schofield and R. Leech, CBA Research Report 61 (London, 1987), p. 188.

[7] M. Biddle and D. J. Keene, 'Winchester in the Eleventh and Twelfth Centuries', in *Winchester in the Early Middle Ages*, Winchester Studies 1, ed. M. Biddle (Oxford, 1976), p. 265.

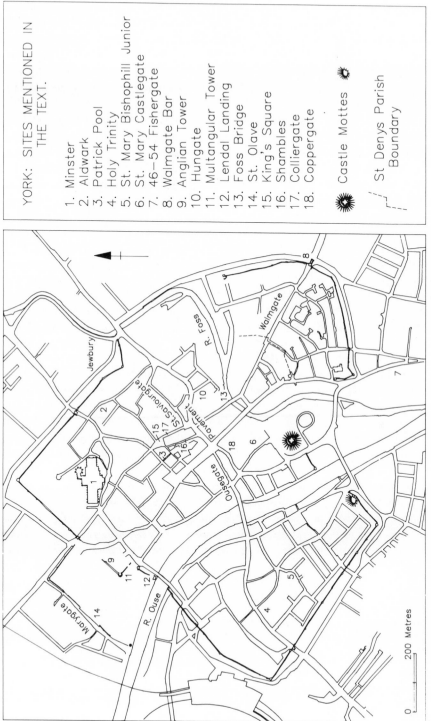

YORK: SITES MENTIONED IN
THE TEXT.

1. Minster
2. Aldwark
3. Patrick Pool
4. Holy Trinity
5. St. Mary Bishophill Junior
6. St. Mary Castlegate
7. 46–54 Fishergate
8. Walmgate Bar
9. Anglian Tower
10. Hungate
11. Multangular Tower
12. Lendal Landing
13. Foss Bridge
14. St. Olave
15. King's Square
16. Shambles
17. Colliergate
18. Coppergate

⁂ Castle Mottes

St Denys Parish
Boundary

based commerce. If the *platea populi* at York was indeed a market place in the courtyard of the *principia*, its separation from the recently discovered commercial/ manufacturing area (below, p. 87) is of considerable interest, raising questions about the role of royalty and the church in trade and exchange. Or should *platea populi* be translated in a different way as 'place of assembly' or 'public square', again begging the interesting question of a relationship with the putative palace and the church?

Whatever the correct translation, the notion of any sort of early eighth-century meeting place here, whether commercial or social, must be investigated while bearing in mind the current lack of virtually any archaeological evidence, either artefactual or structural, for secular occupation of the fortress at this time. This negative evidence can be supplemented by environmental analyses of samples from the north-eastern sector of the fortress in Aldwark (2), which have dates that centre on the early eighth century, and which point to a largely neglected and somewhat marshy area hereabouts.[8] (Perhaps the nearby Roman rampart, a bank of near impervious soil, blocked the natural drainage pattern; a similar circumstance may have led to the creation of the feature which gave its name to Patrick Pool (3), now the name of a street similarly adjacent to the fortress wall some 350m to the south). These strands of evidence point to lack of occupation in the vicinity, but although at least this part of the fortress area seems to have been semi-derelict there was a resident population about one kilometre away to the south-east (below, p. 87); thus the concept of a meeting place at this time has some validity.

While at least the general position of the cathedral church is clear, the location of the *monasterium* is very uncertain. Recently, however, the vicinity of the priory of Christchurch/Holy Trinity (4) has been suggested as its whereabouts on the basis of a variety of historical inferences.[9] The earliest archaeological evidence from Holy Trinity itself is decorated stonework of ?eleventh century date, but at the nearby church of St Mary Bishophill Junior (5), although the earliest parts of its existing fabric probably date to the third quarter of the eleventh century,[10] there were burials immediately to its north in the early tenth century,[11] and sculptural fragments of Anglian date indicate that its foundation may go back to that period. It could then in theory have formed part of an ecclesiastical agglomerate hereabouts. As with the cathedral, however, it seems that documentary evidence has been taken to the limit of inference, and that the

---

[8]   H. K. Kenward, A. R. Hall and A. K. G. Jones, *Environmental evidence from a Roman Well and Anglian Pits in the Legionary Fortress. The Archaeology of York* 14/5, ed. P. V. Addyman (London, 1986), pp. 268 ff.

[9]   R. K. Morris, 'Alcuin, York and the *alma sophia*', in *The Anglo-Saxon Church*, ed. L. A. S. Butler and R. K. Morris, CBA Research Report 60 (London, 1986), pp. 80–9.

[10]   C. M. Briden and D. A. Stocker, 'The Tower of the Church of St Mary Bishophill Junior', in *St Mary Bishophill Junior and St Mary Castlegate. The Archaeology of York* 8/2, ed. P. V. Addyman (London, 1987), pp. 122, 146.

[11]   L. P. Wenham and R. A. Hall, 'St Mary Bishophill Junior: Excavation to the North of the Church', in *St Mary Bishophill Junior*, p. 80.

location and investigation of the *monasterium* will be advanced through archaeological examination.

It can be noted in passing that the only possible structural evidence for a pre-Viking church in York comes not from either of these sites but from the church of St Mary Castlegate (6), where substantial architectural fragments have been recorded.[12] These are unlike Roman work, and find their best parallels in the column bases/capitals of the seventh century church at Reculver,[13] and in an undated pair of even larger stones of similar form at Ripon cathedral, which are generally believed to be pre-Norman and which might indeed have formed part of Wilfrid's work.[14] Tenuous though these comparisons are, the early development of the St Mary Castlegate site, before the tenth century church indicated by other sculptural finds, is of great potential interest.

The cathedral and *monasterium* are notable if small-scale examples of the basic requirement to explore and amplify the documentary evidence for the form, layout and development of pre-conquest York. The larger scale of the problem is demonstrated by the fact that until recently archaeological evidence for the secular aspects of Anglian York, *Eoforwic*, referred to or implied in the documents, was almost totally elusive. This situation has been altered by excavations at 46–54 Fishergate (7), at the confluence of the rivers Ouse and Foss, approximately 1 km downstream from the Roman centres, which have located some 2500 square metres of seventh to ninth century occupation and activity. The area is traversed by metalled roads, and a series of timber buildings averaging 15m x 5m has been recognised despite the often scanty nature of their remains. The siting of this settlement beyond the earlier focus recalls the phenomenon long recognised at *Hamwic* (Saxon Southampton) and more recently diagnosed at *Lundenwic*, and both the regular, planned appearance of the settlement and the relatively spacious inter-relationships of the buildings recall the layout of *Hamwic*, the only one of the handful of pre-Viking towns in England which is tolerably well known. *Hamwic* is recognised as a regional centre of manufacturing and trade, and the newly discovered York site may similarly represent the commercial quarter of the Anglian city. Certainly there is evidence for inter-regional contact on the site, as well as the waste from a number of industrial activities including both non-ferrous and ferrous metalworking and perhaps glass-working.

It must now be a priority to define the extent of this part of Anglian York. Exiguous traces of contemporary activity recognised in 1972 in limited excavations some 250m away may suggest a north-eastward extension of this settlement; it might even have spread beyond to the medieval Walmgate Bar (8), a further 250m to the north, where trenching below the Norman city rampart revealed no sign of pre-conquest defences but did unearth signs of Anglian activity. Alternatively, these discoveries, which have yet to be evaluated in

[12] T. C. F. Blagg, 'Architectural Fragments', in R. A. Hall, 'St Mary's Church, Castlegate: Observations and Discoveries', in *St Mary Bishophill Junior*, pp. 154–5.
[13] C. R. Peers, 'Reculver, its Saxon church and cross', *Archaeologia* 77 (1927), p. 246 and fig. 5.
[14] Hall, 'St Mary's Church, Castlegate', p. 153.

detail, may represent separate, smaller foci of occupation and activity within a very different pattern, representing a very different social and economic order. To establish the exact position, area and layout of this broad component of the pre-Viking settlement is fundamental to understanding its role and function. Only when a sufficiently large and representative sample of it is investigated will it be possible to be confident about understanding its relationship to other possible nuclei of contemporary occupation within the Roman fortress or *colonia*, including the scatter of mid-Saxon ceramic evidence along the banks of the River Ouse.[15]

A preliminary examination of the coin series from the Fishergate site suggests that it was deserted in the mid ninth century, at a time which may correspond to the attested sack and subsequent takeover of York by the Vikings. This event, and the ensuing long drawn out struggle between the kings of Wessex and numerous Viking contenders for the throne of York, served to multiply contemporary references to the city, and these provide a starting point for a discussion of the limits of Viking-age *Jorvik*. Alfred's biographer Asser, writing c.893 of the Northumbrian counter-attack on Viking-held York in 866, relates that

> Christiani . . . etiam intra urbis moenia eos persequi, et murum frangere instituunt quod et fecerent; non enim tunc illa civitas firmos et stabilos muros illis temporibus habebat

> [the Northumbrians pursued their enemies inside the city defences, and began to break down the wall; for in those days that city did not possess strong and well-built walls][16]

Referring to the decision of part of the Viking army to settle permanently in Yorkshire in 876, the anonymous author of *Historia Translationum Sancti Cuthberti* wrote at some date after 1122[17]

> nam Eboracae civitatis moenia una ex his restauravit, regionemque in circuitu incolens, ibidem pausavit

> [for one of these (sections of the army) restored the defences of York and, settling in the area, stayed there].[18]

In this he was clearly following the anonymous *Historia de Sancto Cuthberto*, a Durham production of c.1050[19] which recorded

> una Eboracam civitatem re-aedificavit, terram in circuitu coluit, et ibi remansit

[15] A. J. Mainman, 'Pottery from 46–54 Fishergate', in *The Archaeology of York* 16/6, ed. P. V. Addyman (London, 1991).
[16] Asser, *De Rebus Gestis Ælfredi* 27, ed. W. H. Stevenson (Oxford, 1904).
[17] C. F. Battiscombe, *The Relics of St Cuthbert* (Oxford, 1956), p. 3.
[18] *Capitula de Miraculis et Translationibus*, ed. T. Arnold, in *Symeonis Monachi Opera Omnia*, 2 vols, Rolls Series 75 (London, 1882–5), vol. 1, p. 229.
[19] *EHD*, p. 119.

[one rebuilt the city of York, cultivated the land around, and remained there][20]

The early twelfth century writer, William of Malmesbury, describing Athelstan's recapture of the city for the English in 927, says

Ethelstanus interea castrum, quod olim Dani in Eboraco defirmaverunt, ad solum diruit, ne esset quo se tutari perfidia posset; praeda quae in castro reperta fuerat, et ea quidem amplissima, magnifice et viritim divisa

[Meanwhile Athelstan razed to the ground the fortress which the Danes had formerly fortified in York, so that it should not be a place where treachery could shelter; the large amount of booty which had been found in the fortress was generously divided up amongst everyone][21]

No more is heard of the city's defences throughout the political upheavals of the second quarter of the tenth century, and the next mention of fortification is in the *Anonymous Life of St Oswald* written c.1000, where York is described

quae quondam erat nobiliter aedificata et firmiter muris constructa; quae nunc est dismissa vetustati

[Once nobly built and strongly walled but now decayed through age][22]

Finally, *Domesday Book* records that

Hamelin ht. 1 mans in fossato urb.

[Hamelin has one dwelling in the city ditch].

It is not clear if the ditch referred to is of pre- or post-Norman date, and there is no indication of which particular part of the city is concerned.

Ostensibly these references provide a coherent picture of a city which was in poor defensive repair in 866, which was restored by the Vikings and then destroyed by Athelstan, and which by the eleventh century was again in disrepair. But there must be some doubt about the reliability of Asser, the anonymous historians of St Cuthbert, and William of Malmesbury, at least, since all in varying degrees were separated by time or space from what they describe. How much Asser, in the south of England, knew about the state of York twenty five years earlier, to what extent the Cuthbert community was glossing the bare historical framework of the Viking army's actions in 876, or indeed what, if any, reliable sources William of Malmesbury was drawing upon, are all unanswerable

---

[20] *Historia de Sancto Cuthberto* 14, ed. T. Arnold, in *Symeonis Monachi Opera Omnia*, vol. 1, p. 204.

[21] William of Malmesbury, *De Gestis Regum Anglorum*, II 134, ed. W. Stubbs, 2 vols, Rolls Series 90 (London, 1887–9), vol. 1, p. 147.

[22] *The Historians of the Church of York and its Archbishops*, ed. J. Raine, 3 vols, Rolls Series 71 (London, 1879–94), vol. 1, p. 454.

questions. It is equally uncertain whether the anonymous monk of Ramsey who wrote St Oswald's biography was referring to the Roman defences of the city or to more recent works when he described the walls' decay. In sum, these various sources are of dubious value, and should be treated with caution.

Of the many questions which can be raised on the basis of these references, the most basic must be 'did late Anglian and Viking-age defences exist at all, where were they, what did they consist of and how big an area did they defend?'. These questions must be taken together. If the newly discovered Anglian settlement follows the *Hamwic* pattern, it will turn out to be an undefended site, and thus not an appropriate setting for the enactment of the events of the late ninth and early tenth centuries catalogued above. All that can be said at present on this score is that there is no indication in the topography of the Fishergate area to suggest the former presence of defences.

The obvious location for those events is, however, one or other of the Roman *enceintes*. Although recent excavations near the northern limit of the *colonia*, in Wellington Row, have revealed traces of what could be a late Roman riverward defence, the walls of the *colonia* are hardly known, and there has been no opportunity to chart their subsequent transformation into the medieval defended circuit south of the river Ouse. On the north bank of the river, in contrast, the defensive sequence has been observed and recorded on a number of occasions, and evidence for a series of refurbishments to the Roman walls has been discovered at several points along their north-west and north-east sides where they are directly overlain by the later medieval walls. Yet even here there is no indisputable proof of any attention to the defences in the four and a half centuries between Roman military withdrawal and Viking arrival. Even the dating evidence for the so-called 'Anglian Tower' (9), which fills a breach in the Roman walls, is minimal and ambiguous, and it could conceivably be of late Roman, Anglian or late ninth to tenth century construction.

These doubts, however, are relatively insignificant when compared to the questions which still surround the disappearance of defensive potential along the lines of the south-west and south-east sides of the Roman fortress, and the equally vexed question of their replacement. The date at which the fortress walls were abandoned has not been established in excavation, usually because the evidence has been destroyed by 'robbing trenches' dug to facilitate the salvaging of the Roman facing stones for re-use, often in the twelfth and thirteenth centuries. This era was not necessarily the time when the defences lapsed into decay, however.

The establishment of new defensive lines is equally problematic. Excavation and analysis by York Archaeological Trust has demonstrated that theories involving a putative Viking age wickerwork stockade running off the south corner tower of the fortress and swinging northwards in a loop along the bank of the Foss can now be discounted; another element in this supposed line of defence, a riverside 'embankment' uncovered at Hungate (10) in 1950–1, can also be plausibly re-interpreted as a flood defence created to safeguard land threatened with inundation by William the Conqueror's damming of the Foss to flood his castle ditches. If these elements are subtracted from the putative pre-Norman defences, there remains no evidence whatever for the north-eastern limits of the pre-conquest town.

Yet it seems likely that the defensive line had been extended eastwards before the Normans' arrival, to include the heavily built-up area around the crossing point over the Ouse. If this is so, the most obvious suggestion is that the later medieval rampart and wall in the Jewbury area originated in the Anglo Scandinavian period, and that the Foss, wherever precisely it flowed at this time, formed a natural barrier, perhaps augmented by other man-made features which have yet to be recognised. Similarly, at the opposite side of the city, the length of medieval rampart and wall running the short distance from close to the Multangular Tower (11) down to the River Ouse at Lendal Landing (12) may also be a later medieval reflection of a new defence of the Viking Age, extending and replacing the south-west fortress defences, and safeguarding the western end of the city's principal waterfront.

The Foss itself raises another major topographical problem concerning the Anglo-Scandinavian city. There was surely a crossing, probably a bridge, at some point, and the most likely place is on or near the present Foss Bridge (13). This is approached from the city by a continuation of one of the principal Roman streets, and crosses to Walmgate, a spine road in this area of the city, which is mentioned in a document originating in the late eleventh century[23] and is thought to be a pre-Norman creation. Any bridgehead here was of considerable importance, and it is possible that a defensive line east of the Foss may have existed. Excavations had shown that the later medieval defences surrounding the Walmgate area were a new creation of the Norman period, and attention was therefore focussed upon the theory that the arc-shaped parish boundary of St Denys, which enclosed a rather smaller area around the bridge, originated in and perpetuated a defensive work of the Viking Age. An opportunity in 1987 to test this did not yield any conclusive results, and the question of a defended Walmgate area in the pre-conquest period therefore remains open, and with it the problem of charting the size of the Anglo-Scandinavian city.

Whatever its size, the population of the pre-conquest city was clearly stratified, with the documentary sources dwelling principally on those of the first rank, the kings, earls and archbishops. The location and characterisation of their palaces would be of considerable interest, and the general position of the earls' palace is indicated by two strands of historical evidence. Firstly, there is the record by the eighteenth century historian Francis Drake that the area of Marygate was formerly known as *Earlsburh*; and, secondly, the record of the *Anglo-Saxon Chronicle* that when Earl Siward died in 1055 he was interred in the church dedicated to St Olaf which he himself had built. This church, now known as St Olaves (14), also lies in Marygate, and the archaeological remains of Siward's residence are unlikely to be far away.

[23] F. Liebermann, 'An English Document of about 1080', *Yorkshire Archaeological Journal* 18 (1905), pp. 412–6.

Three other palace sites have been proposed within Anglian or Anglo-Scandinavian York. The residence of the pre-conquest archbishops, although not pin-pointed in any document, may be presumed to have lain below the palace of their Norman and later successors, which lay to the west of the Minster. Of the other two, the first is a matter of conjecture; with the great basilican cross-hall of the Roman *principia*, supposedly still standing for several centuries after the Roman withdrawal, it has seemed likely to some that King Edwin and his line utilised this impressive and prestigious building, and that the reason for the foundation of the cathedral hereabouts was the proximity of the royal palace. This proposition remains to be proved. The second proposal relies on place–name evidence for support. King's Square (15) lies at an important road junction which marks the *porta principalis sinistra* of the Roman fortress, the site of a gatehouse. An alternative name for the vicinity is King's Court, recorded in c.1270 as *Kuningesgard*, and this faithfully echoes the Old Norse form *Konungsgarðr*.[24] The suggestion here has been that by the mid ninth century any royal palace at the *principia* had been abandoned, either because of structural decay or because the area had been given over absolutely to the church, and that the Viking kings took over or established a palace based upon the remains of the Roman gatehouse. It is remarkable to have four possible palace sites in the city, none of which fulfils that function today, and where in theory it would be possible at some time to investigate the urban setting from which the leaders of the Anglian and Anglo-Scandinavian church and state ruled. Urban palaces of these periods remain unknown in Britain except for incidental references, and any opportunity to study the structural/architectural pretensions of the rulers and the material remains of their cultural milieu must be seized eagerly.

The multiplicity of secular palace sites can itself perhaps be explained by extending the hypothesis given above for a movement from the *principia* to King's Square. The latter was on the edge of the Roman fortification, and thus well placed to control one of the entry points to the city and, as a corollary, to be more readily defensible and to have immediate access to a line of retreat should that be required. With the redundancy of the south-east fortress wall, however, and the establishment of a new north-south main axis incorporating Ousegate-Pavement-Saviourgate, King's Court became encapsulated within the city and lost the advantages of a peripheral position. The establishment of the earls' residence at the other side of York could thus be interpreted as a move to re-establish these advantages, and the factor that directed the move to Marygate rather than elsewhere was perhaps a desire to make use of the remains of a walled Roman annex to the fortress which may have occupied this area. This trend to the periphery was, of course, continued by William the Conqueror in the siting of his twin motte and bailey castles.

A final instance of the interplay of documentary and archaeological approaches to York can be chosen from the record in Domesday Book of the city's first recorded street-name. It comes in connection with the holdings of the

---

[24] D. M. Palliser, 'The Medieval Street Names of York', *York Historian* 2 (1978), p. 8.

Count of Mortain, which included *ii bancos in macello*. This is usually translated as 'two stalls in the meat market', and equated with the street now called Shambles (16), which in the later middle ages was known as *Flesshamelles*. The nature of the *bancos* and their setting are uncertain. The area of the Shambles was also known as *Marketskyre* in the fourteenth century,[25] and this name may reflect the subdivision of the city into seven shires at the time of the Norman conquest, although it is impossible to determine whether the Anglo-Scandinavian administrative arrangements survived the intervening two and a half centuries unaltered.

It has been suggested that Marketshire got its pre-conquest name through containing two triangular market areas which were subsequently fossilised in the street system.[26] The triangle bounded by Shambles, Colliergate (17) and Pavement has not been subject to archaeological excavation, but the precocious archaeological records made by the architect George Benson when a part of the other triangle between High Ousegate and Coppergate (18) was redeveloped in 1902–3 can now be re-interpreted to suggest that the full width of the block was taken up by buildings from the late tenth century, if not before.[27] Futhermore, excavations in 1976–81 at the nearby 16–22 Coppergate site demonstrated that frontages hereabouts were built up from c.900; an open market place is therefore exceedingly unlikely. Whether or not this is true of the Shambles area remains to be seen. If the Shambles frontage too was built up relatively early, the Domesday *bancos* are unlikely to have been independent free-standing market stalls, but may rather have been the immediate predecessors of the integral benches or stalls which are perpetuated to this day at the front of some of the shops in Shambles.

If the physical setting of the *bancos* in Shambles is uncertain, it must be said that the very existence of a butchery trade in Viking-age York is not indicated by a study of contemporary animal bones. It is true that the data currently available is virtually confined to only four of the approximately one thousand eight hundred tenements which existed within mid eleventh century York, but these tenements at Coppergate are those of representative artisans, and they are positioned within only 125m of Shambles. Dr T. P. O'Connor's (1989) study of these bones has brought to light several strands of evidence which indicate non-specialist butchery, including the presence of poleaxed cattle and pig skulls, and the unsystematic, even clumsy, nature of the butchery. These and other features, described in full in Dr O'Connor's fascicule *Anglo-Scandinavian Animal Bones from 16–22 Coppergate*, suggest rather that beasts were bought in and slaughtered as required, perhaps being shared by several households.

At what is an early stage in Anglo-Scandinavian animal bone studies in York

[25] A. H. Smith, *The Place-Names of the East Riding of Yorkshire*, English Place-Name Society 14 (Cambridge, 1937), p. 293.
[26] H. G. Ramm, 'The growth and development of the city to the Norman Conquest', in *The Noble City of York*, ed. A. Stacpoole (York, 1972), p. 250.
[27] R. A. Hall, 'Observations at 5–7 Coppergate', in *The Archaeology of York* 8/3, ed. P. V. Addyman (forthcoming).

this interesting divergence of the historical and archaeological evidence may be more apparent than real. The more explicit street-name evidence from Winchester, where a *Flaescmangere straet* is recorded in 996, affirms the existence of specialist butchers there by the end of the tenth century; is it simply that in York their counterparts did not exist until almost immediately before the conquest, and are thus not represented in the predominantly tenth century bone groups which form the bulk of Dr O'Connor's evidence? This would itself be a useful insight into the chronology of the origins of the urban provision market in York. Or could the York butchers perhaps have catered only for more wealthy households than those of Coppergate? These wealthy households, however, are more likely to have been supporting themselves by farming the lands around the city. Was it then the artisans of Coppergate who eked out a living with food from small-holdings? Whatever scenario turns out to be correct, it must surely adjust and refine our view of life in York before the conquest. In this particular, as in so many others, it is the inter-linking of a range of disciplines to study the city's history, an approach exemplified in Peter Sawyer's work, which should prove exponentially fruitful.

THE IDEAL OF MEN DYING WITH THEIR LORD IN *THE BATTLE OF MALDON:* ANACHRONISM OR *NOUVELLE VAGUE*

Roberta Frank

> He that fights and runs away
> May live to fight another day.
> > Anonymous English proverb[1]
>
> Qui fugiebat, rursus proeliabitur.
> > Tertullian, *De Fuga in Persecutione,* §10
>
> Vir fugiens, et denuo pugnabit.
> > Erasmus, *Adagia,* I.x.40
>
> Demosthenes dist que l'home fuyant combatra
> de rechief.
> > Rabelais, *Pantagruel,* IV.v.

It is occasionally acknowledged that there is no historical or literary continuity between Tacitus' first-century Germans, who thought it a lifelong disgrace and infamy to survive their leader by retreating from the battlefield, and Byrhtnoth's retainers who – nine centuries later – affirm, one after the other, that they will not leave the field now that their beloved leader lies dead.[2] But for every Hans Kuhn, who in the 1950s doubted the utility, Germanity, and reality of this 'ideal', there was a Dorothy Whitelock insisting that there had been no break in tradition, that the *comitatus* ideal referred to by Tacitus had never ceased to be expressed in Anglo-Saxon England; or, for the continent, Hermann Conrad reporting that 'Als Schande wurde es angesehen, seinen Herrn in der Schlacht zu verlassen und ihm nicht in den Tod zu folgen. Die Geschichte liefert uns eine Reihe von Beispielen, dass das Gefolge dieses Gebot, das Schicksal des Herrn zu teilen, in die Tat umgesetzt hat.'[3] Kuhn did not find history quite so forthcoming.

---

[1] On the uncertain origin of this proverb, see T. Raylor, 'The Source of "He that fights and runs away" ', *Notes & Queries* 33/4 (1986), pp. 465–466.

[2] *De Origine et Situ Germanorum,* ed. J. G. C. Anderson (Oxford, 1938), 14: *Iam vero infame in omnem vitam ac probrosum superstitem principi suo ex acie recessisse.* Line references to the Old English poem are to D. G. Scragg, ed., *The Battle of Maldon* (Manchester, 1981).

[3] H. Kuhn, 'Die Grenzen der germanischen Gefolgschaft', *Zeitschrift der Savigny-Stiftung für Rechtsgeschichte,* Germanistische Abteilung 73 (1956), pp. 1–83, reprinted in Kuhn,

Cases of men fighting to the death after their lord was slain were open to other explanations than the fulfillment of an abstract obligation: 'Es fällt mir trotzdem schwer, diese harte Forderung als verbreitet anzusehn. . . . Da, wo Gefolgsleute oder auch andre nach dem Fall ihres Herrn bis zum eigenen Tode weiterkämpften, kann der Grund ein anderer sein, so das Ehrgefühl, das Waffenstreckung und Flucht untersagt, oder momentaner Schmerz und Verzweiflung, oder die Überzeugung, das es keine Schonung und kein Entrinnen gab, und schliesslich die Hoffnung, doch noch zu siegen oder wenigstens den Tod des Führers zu rächen.'[4] Nevertheless, Walter Schlesinger, responding to Kuhn, pleaded for continuity (1963), and accused his countrymen of, among other things, ignoring what English scholars, notably Chadwick and Whitelock, had been saying.[5]

In an influential article of 1976 that seems untouched by the German debate, Rosemary Woolf argued that the obligation of a warrior not to outlive his lord was not a traditional commonplace of Germanic heroism; it occurs, outside Germania, only in the Danish Bjarkamál, and would have struck the audience of Maldon as something new and strange.[6] She concluded that the English poet must have derived the ideal from the Old Norse poem – a possibility suggested in 1929 by Bertha Phillpotts.[7] Woolf assumed that Bjarkamál, which portrays the last stand of Hrólfr kraki's retainers after the fall of their lord, was brought to England in the tenth century by Danish settlers. The sudden emergence, nine silent centuries after Tacitus, of the ideal exemplified in Maldon seemed, therefore, explicable: 'It was in the long unconverted Scandinavian countries that highly primitive traditions survived into the Christian literary era' (p. 80). The theory of Germanic continuity, ostensibly squashed in the body of her article, is here alive and kicking. Woolf's theory has won cautious acceptance from Anglo-Saxonists, getting favorable notice in, for example, A New Critical History of Old English Literature: 'The closest literary parallel containing the idea of dying with one's lord seems to be the Bjarkamál – extant mainly in the twelfth-century summary of Saxo Grammaticus. It has been suggested as the source for the poet's inspiration, and thus the poem exhibits a deliberate antiquarianism rather than an ongoing live tradition – see Phillpotts 1929 and Woolf 1976.'[8] Peter Sawyer accepts Woolf's point that literature, not life, inspired the Anglo-Saxon poet: 'In

---

Kleine Schriften: Aufsätze und Rezensionen aus den Gebieten der germanischen und nordischen Sprach-, Literatur- und Kulturgeschichte, ed. Dietrich Hofmann (Berlin, 1969–78), vol. 2, pp. 420–483; D. Whitelock, The Beginnings of English Society (Harmondsworth, 1952), pp. 29–38; H. Conrad, Deutsche Rechtsgeschichte, vol.1 (Karlsruhe, 1954), p. 37.

4   'Grenzen' in Kleine Schriften, vol. 2, pp. 424–425.

5   'Randbemerkungen zu drei Aufsätzen über Sippe, Gefolgschaft und Treue', Alteuropa und die Moderne Gesellschaft: Festschrift für Otto Brunner, ed. Historische Seminar der Universität Hamburg (Göttingen, 1963), pp. 11–59 (esp. pp. 21–41 on Kuhn, pp. 26–27 on suicidal fighting).

6   'The Ideal of Men Dying with their Lord in Germania and in The Battle of Maldon', ASE 5 (1976), pp. 63–81.

7   'The Battle of Maldon: Some Danish Affinities', Modern Language Review 24 (1929), pp. 172–90.

8   Ed. S. B. Greenfield and D. G. Calder (New York, 1986), p. 157, n. 58.

imaginative literature many of the ideals may well be literary rather than real, and it has recently been suggested that the theme of the poem on *The Battle of Maldon*, the ideal of men fighting to the death beside their fallen lord, owes more to literary tradition than to any contemporary code of conduct (Woolf, 1976).[9] A problem arises only if 'literary tradition' is identified as Bjarkamál, for, these days, that poem is sporting a noticeably younger and trimmer look.

Bjarkamál survives as two Old Norse stanzas quoted by Snorri Sturluson (c.1230), and as a Latin poem by Saxo Grammaticus in 298 hexameters (c.1200), which Axel Olrik at the turn of this century reconstructed as thirty-five modern Danish stanzas.[10] For his own patriotic reasons, Olrik decided that Saxo based his version not on twelfth-century Icelandic material but on Danish heroic poetry of the tenth century: Bjarkamál was the most loved, famous, and praised of Norse poems ('Nordens mest elskede og hædrede digt', p. 42; 'Nordens berømteste digt', p. 84), and also one of the very oldest ('et af de ældste nordiske kvad', p. 109). Olrik's artistry, passion, and vision carried the day. In 1903 Andreas Heusler and Wilhelm Ranisch confidently placed Bjarkamál in the 'older period of Norse heroic poetry', noting that it had to be composed no later than 1030 when, according to several sagas, it was recited before the battle of Stiklarstaðir.[11] E. V. Gordon reported in his 1927 *Introduction to Old Norse*, and repeated thirty years later in the second edition, that 'the old Bjarkamál was composed around 900, probably in Denmark, and was one of the most famous of the old heroic poems'.[12]

In recent decades, however, the general consensus has been challenged. František Graus expressed doubts about the great age of Bjarkamál in 1959: 'Jedenfalls haben wir hier mit einem sehr späten Zeugnis zu tun, und ich kann nicht einsehen, warum gerade hier etwas "Urgermanisches" zu finden sein sollte'.[13] In 1976, the year of Woolf's article, Klaus von See assigned the poem as transmitted – that is, the Old Norse text that underlay Saxo's version – to the twelfth

---

9 From *Roman Britain to Norman England* (London, 1978), p. 169.

10 *Danmarks Heltedigtning*, vol.1 (Copenhagen, 1903), pp. 28–222 (Danish reconstruction in 35 stanzas, pp. 46–59; Saxo's Latin text, pp. 344–352); English translation by L. M. Hollander, *The Heroic Legends of Denmark* (New York, 1919), pp. 66–216 (reconstruction, pp. 90–98; Latin, pp. 100–136). An English translation of Saxo's poem in *Gesta Danorum*, II 53–61, is available in *Saxo Grammaticus: The History of the Danes*, trans. P. Fisher (Cambridge, 1979), vol.1, pp. 56–63. The two Old Norse stanzas cited by Snorri (*Heimskringla*, *Óláfs saga helga*, c. 208) are usually compared to the Old English *Finnsburh Fragment*, not to *Maldon*: see, e.g., *Sources and Analogues of Old English Poetry II: The Major Germanic and Celtic Texts in Translation*, trans. D. G. Calder et al. (Cambridge, 1983), p. 142.

11 *Eddica Minora: Dichtungen eddischer Art aus den Fornaldarsögur und anderen Prosawerken* (Dortmund, 1903), p. xxiii. (The two editors are indebted to Olrik's reconstruction of Bjarkamál in *Danske Oldkvad i Sakses Historie* (Copenhagen, 1898)). The four thirteenth-century works that mention the recitation of Bj. in 1030 are the *Legendary Saga of St. Olaf*, *Heimskringla*, *Separate Saga of St. Olaf*, and *Fóstbrœðra saga*.

12 (Oxford, 1927), p. 216; 2nd ed. (Oxford, 1957), p. 237.

13 'Über die sogenannte germanische Treue', *Historica* I (1959), p. 84.

century.[14] He eliminated the 1030 *terminus ad quem* by arguing that the story of its recitation before the battle of Stiklarstaðir was ultimately inspired by William of Malmesbury's early twelfth-century account of the singing of the *Roland* before the battle of Hastings. Hallvard Lie, in a 1977 article written before he had read von See's, also concluded that *Bjarkamál* was both relatively late ('heltediktnings sluttfase', col. 122) and overvalued ('B.'s populære estime kan . . . neppe ha berodd på diktets kunstneriske egenverdi', col. 123).[15] Hans Kuhn, responding to von See's argument, urged the retention of the Stiklastaðir connection and noted that thematically the poem fits rather well into an early eleventh-century context.[16] Von See countered with thematic resemblances between *Bjarkamál* and other twelfth-century compositions, pointing out that in 1897 Ferdinand Detter thought Finnur Jónsson would have dated the poem late had the Stiklarstaðir anecdote not gotten in the way.[17] Solid ground seems unattainable: internal semantic, stylistic, thematic, or socio-political evidence standing in the way of an early date can always be attributed to Saxo's active hand. But though not producing certainty about the age of *Bjarkamál*, a century of speculation has shown that the traditional dating of the poem to the early viking age rests not on science but – to borrow Eric Stanley's phrase – on 'a conspiracy of romantic hopes'.[18]

A major contribution of Woolf's article was her demonstration that the ethical code of *The Battle of Maldon* was different from that governing the conduct of retainers in, for example, Jordanes, Gregory of Tours, Bede, and Paul the Deacon, in the *Anglo-Saxon Chronicle*, in *Beowulf*, and in the *Heliand*, in Welsh heroic poems such as the *Gododdin*, and in early medieval Latin epics such as the *Waltharius* – all works that contain striking examples of other heroic acts of loyalty. The *Maldon* ideal was, she claimed, 'uncharacteristic of Old Norse literature' and 'without echo in the *chanson de geste*' (p. 72). Now that *Bjarkamál*

---

[14] 'Hastings, Stiklastaðir und Langemarck: Zur Überlieferung vom Vortrag heroischer Lieder auf dem Schlachtfeld', *Germanisch-romanische Monatsschrift* 57 (1976), pp. 1–13; reprinted in von See, *Edda, Saga, Skaldendichtung: Aufsätze zur skandinavischen Literatur des Mittelalters* (Heidelberg, 1981), pp. 259–271.

[15] *Kulturhistorisk leksikon for nordisk middelalder* 21 (1977), cols. 121–124.

[16] 'Uns ist Fahrwind gegeben wider den Tod: Aus einer grossen Zeit des Nordens', *Zeitschrift für deutsches Altertum und deutsche Literatur* 106 (1977), pp. 147–162.

[17] 'Húskarla hvǫt: Nochmals zum Alter der *Bjarkamál*', in *Speculum Norroenum: Norse Studies in Memory of Gabriel Turville-Petre*, ed U. Dronke et al. (Odense, 1981), pp. 421–431; reprinted in von See, *Edda, Saga, Skaldendichtung*, pp. 272–282. Detter tried to gauge Finnur Jónsson's feelings in 'Zur *Ragnarsdrápa*', *Arkiv for nordisk filologi* 13 (1897), p. 366: 'Besässen wir die Nachricht über Þormóðr nicht . . . so hätte es F. Jónsson gewiss erst im zweiten Bande seiner Litt. Geschichte zusammen mit den Krákumál, den Starkað-Liedern u. a. besprochen'. Jónsson responded in 'Bjarkemåls alder', *Arkiv for nordisk filologi* 15 (1899), pp. 267–268. See now Joseph Harris, 'Eddic Poetry', in *Old Norse-Icelandic Literature: A Critical Guide*, ed. C. Clover and J. Lindow, Islandica 45 (Ithaca, N.Y., 1985), pp. 118–119, who relates Bj. to a tradition of applied poetry and sees 'no reason why the Þormóðr incident should not be historically true'.

[18] *The Dating of Beowulf*, ed. C. Chase, Toronto Old English Series 6 (Toronto, 1981), p. 101, n. 3.

has been offered a home in the twelfth century, Maldon is left very isolated indeed. My goal in the pages remaining is to find this lonely poem some company more nearly its own age.

It has been observed that 'as a literary product, the poem harkens not so much back to the likes of Finnsburh and Hildebrand but forward to the Roland'.[19] The Maldon poet is not the only author in Anglo-Saxon England at the turn of the millennium to strike observers as peculiarly 'advanced' for his time. English writers of the late tenth and early eleventh century seem, on the whole, to have been unusually quick to produce theoretical arguments for the new political and social realities. One such reality was the gradual integration and blurring of the secular and ecclesiastical spheres, of the militia saecularis and the militia Christi.[20] When Ælfric wanted to justify the practice of kings delegating military command and not themselves leading armies, he found a precedent in Constantine's use of his general Gallicanus, the latter not only a successful warlord but also, before his death, a holy man.[21] Nicholas Brooks has observed that 'in the writings of Archbishop Wulfstan and others there were even ideas about the ordering of society and about the duties of thegnship that were capable of development in much the same way that reforming ecclesiastics of the later eleventh century contributed to the development on the continent of the concept of a separate and chivalric knightly order'.[22] James Campbell wonders whether 'the legislation of the later years of Æthelred [is not] similar in some respects to that produced abroad in connection with the Peace of God'.[23] It is in the laws of Cnut, penned between 1020 and 1023 by Wulfstan, that the loyalty owed to a lord is made

[19] A. N. Doane, 'Legend, History and Artifice in The Battle of Maldon', Viator 9 (1978), p. 43.
[20] See C. Erdmann, Die Entstehung des Kreuzzugsgedankens, Forschungen zur Kirchen- und Geistesgeschichte 6 (Stuttgart, 1935), esp. ch. 2. English trans. by M. W. Baldwin and W. Goffart, The Origin of the Idea of Crusade (Princeton, 1977). Also J. Flori, L'Idéologie du glaive: Préhistoire de la chevalerie, Travaux d'histoire éthico-politique, 33 (Geneva, 1983). K. Leyser, 'Early Medieval Canon Law and the Beginnings of Knighthood', in Institutionen, Kultur und Gesellschaft im Mittelalter. Festschrift für Josef Fleckenstein zu seinem 65. Geburtstag, ed. L. Fenske et al. (Sigmaringen, 1984), pp. 549–566, finds traces of Christianized warfare in the legislation of the ninth and tenth centuries, when noblemen could be described as milites in contexts stressing courage, loyalty, and camaraderie. Niels Lund has drawn my attention to an entry in the early ninth-century Annales quae dicitur Einhardi s. a. 782: . . . aliorumque clarorum atque nobilium usque ad viginti interfecti, praeter ceteros, qui hos secuti potius cum eis perire quam post eos vivere maluerunt (up to twenty other distinguished and noble men were killed, besides the others – their followers – who preferred to perish at their side rather than survive them). See R. Rau, Quellen zur karolingischen Reichsgeschichte, I (Berlin, 1955), p. 44.
[21] See M. Godden, 'Ælfric's Saints' Lives and the Problem of Miracles', Leeds Studies in English, N. S. 16 (1985), pp. 83–100, esp. pp. 94–95. Godden cites other passages indicating that Ælfric saw parallels between the days of the early martyrs and the persecution of the English by the vikings.
[22] 'Arms, Status and Warfare in late-Saxon England', in Ethelred the Unready: Papers from the Millenary Conference, ed. D. Hill, BAR, BS 59 (Oxford, 1978), p. 97.
[23] 'England, France, Flanders and Germany in the Reign of Ethelred II: Some Comparisons and Connections', in Ethelred the Unready, p. 257. Reprinted in Campbell, Essays in Anglo-Saxon History (London, 1986), p. 194.

explicit for the first time in Anglo-Saxon legislation: for the desertion of his lord during a military campaign, a soldier is to forfeit life and property (*II Cn* 77); but if he falls in battle in the presence of his leader, his heirs need not restore his heriot (*II Cn* 78).[24] Right devotion to a lord brings more than worldly rewards, for 'God will be loyal to the man loyal to his lord' (*I Cn* 20.1).[25] In the years around 1000, it is the personal, individual character of the man/lord bond that seems to impress observers as both admirable and unusual enough to mention.[26] The anonymous monk of St Bertin's or St Omer's, Flanders, who c.1039–42 in the reign of Hǫrðaknútr composed the *Encomium Emmae Reginae*, reports in praise of Cnut's father, Sveinn Forkbeard, that his retainers were so loyal that they would rush into battle at his command even if it meant certain death: 'So that you may realize how highly he was regarded by his men, I can strongly affirm that not one of them would have recoiled from danger owing to fear of death, but, unafraid, would have gone out of loyalty to him against innumerable enemies alone, and even with bare hands against armed men, if only the royal signal should be given to them as they went'.[27]

---

[24] Texts and German translations can be found in the edition of the Anglo-Saxon laws by F. Liebermann, *Die Gesetze der Angelsachsen* (Halle, 1903–16), vol. 1, pp. 364–365; English translations in *EHD*, p. 466. P. Wormald, 'Aethelred the Lawmaker', in *Ethelred the Unready*, p. 59, mentions the possibility that the secular part of Æthelred's law code (*VIII Atr.*) may be buried without trace in Cnut's code. The first datable code (c.1008) drafted in the style of Archbishop Wulfstan imposes the death penalty on anyone deserting 'from an army that the king himself is with'; but if the king is absent, the deserter gets off with a fine of 120 shillings (*V Atr.* 28; Liebermann, vol. 1, pp. 244–45; *EHD*, p. 445).

[25] Liebermann, vol.1, pp. 300–301; *EHD*, p. 455.

[26] G. Duby, *La Société aux XIe et XIIe siècles dans la région maconnaise* (Paris, 1953), p. 145, notes that such personal ties of loyalty were customary among the maconnais aristocracy at the end of the tenth century. E. Delaruelle, 'Essai sur la formation de l'idée de croisade', *Bulletin de littérature ecclésiastique* 45 (1944), p. 26, is struck by Abbo's portrait of the English king Edmund as a feudal lord surrounded by his men (*armiger, miles, fideles, famuli*) and solicitous for the welfare of his *coloni*. A useful edition of Abbo's *Vita* is in *Three Lives of English Saints*, ed. M. Winterbottom (Toronto, 1972), pp. 67–87.

[27] *Encomium Emmae Reginae*, ed. A. Campbell, Camden 3rd Series 72 (London, 1949), I, i. 22–25 (Campbell's translation). On the date and purpose of the *Encomium*, see now F. Lifshitz, 'The *Encomium Emmae Reginae*: A 'Political Pamphlet' of the Eleventh Century?' in *The Haskins Society Journal: Studies in Medieval History*, 1 (1989), pp. 39–50. The passage has been cited in connection with *Maldon* and the Jómsvikings by E. R. Anderson, 'The Battle of Maldon: A Reappraisal of Possible Sources, Date, and Theme', in *Modes of Interpretation in Old English Literature: Essays in Honour of Stanley B. Greenfield*, ed. P. R. Brown et al. (Toronto, 1986), pp. 247–272. On the new professionalism and discipline of the viking armies that visited Ethelred's England, see E. John, 'War and Society in the Tenth Century: The Maldon Campaign', *TRHS* 5th ser. 27 (1977), pp. 173–195; also N. Lund, 'The Armies of Swein Forkbeard and Cnut: *leding* or *lið?*', *ASE* 15 (1986), pp. 105–116. The notice given to the devotion of personal retainers in eleventh-century England (e.g., Cnut's housecarls, Godwin's men during the threatened rising of 1051, Harold's hearth troop at Hastings) also seems to be something new. On the likelihood of reciprocal innovation here, see R. Chazan, *European Jewry and the First Crusade* (Berkeley, 1987), who sees in the behavior of the Jewish martyrs of 1096 a mirror image of many of the themes of crusading martyrdom, a novel response disguised as a reassertion of the old.

Similar statements about a retainer's willingness to die for his lord occur in stanzas composed by Icelandic poets born around the time of the battle of Maldon. The skalds Þormóðr and Sighvatr, for example, declare to their respective kings, St Óláfr and his son Magnús: 'I want to live and die with you' (256, 285).[28] Þormóðr relates that he was so overjoyed at his acceptance into the Norwegian king's service that he thought himself 'in possession of the entire world' (285). The tears shed by retainers at the death of a lord are now worth noting (272, 355). There is a corresponding rise in emotional temperature on the battlefield, as in the following stanza from Sighvatr's memorial ode on St Óláfr (261):

> Bjǫrn frá'k auk af œrnu
> endr stǫllurum kenndu
> hug, hvé halda dugði
> (hann sótti framm) dróttin;
> fell í her með hollum
> hann verðungar mǫnnum
> (leyfðr's) at hilmis hǫfði
> hróðrauðigs (sá dauði).

> I heard, too, that Bjǫrn made
> his courage abundantly known again
> to the king's marshalls, how he served
> his lord; he went forward.
> He fell in the host with the loyal
> men of the king's bodyguard
> at the head of his renowned lord;
> praised is that death.

Skaldic stanzas, brief and intense, portray characters acting in a single situation in a single significant moment, without reference to position in a sequence of incidents. The thirteenth-century *Heimskringla* and *Separate Saga of St. Olaf* cite Sighvatr's verse as evidence that Bjǫrn was slain in battle trying to protect his king; in the next stanza quoted, Óláfr has been felled. Snorri Sturluson, the author of both works, has probably for his own narrative purposes reversed the original order of the two stanzas, for *Ágrip* – the oldest extant vernacular history of Norway, compiled there in the 1190s – relates that (as logic suggests) Óláfr was slain *before* Bjǫrn fell at his head and Þorsteinn at his feet.[29] The stanzas,

---

[28] The number following each skaldic verse cited gives its page in the first volume of *Den norsk-islandske skjaldedigtning*, ed. F. Jónsson, A. Tekst efter håndskrifterne (Copenhagen, 1908). The *Encomium Emmae* II.23 reports that Cnut's subjects, too, were so upset by his death that the majority wanted to die with him 'if this would not have been at variance with the divine plan', ed. Campbell, p. 39.

[29] *Ágrip af Nóregs konunga sǫgum*, ed. F. Jónsson, Altnordische Saga-Bibliothek 18 (Halle, 1929), p. 32 (c. 31.8); new ed. by B. Einarsson, Islenzk Fornrit 29 (Reykjavík, 1985), p. 30 (c. 30).

when transposed, provide a parallel for both *Maldon*, in which three retainers fall alongside their lord and another declares his intention to lie down next to him, and *Bjarkamál*, in which Bjarki and Hjalti resolve to lie respectively at the head and foot of their king.

But it is another skaldic poem, Arnórr Þorðarson's memorial ode on St Óláfr's half-brother, Haraldr harðráði (c.1067), that repeats in miniature the sequence of events (and emotions) in *Maldon*. If Arnórr's *drápa* has not yet been brought to bear on *Maldon* matters, when almost everything else from Quintus Curtius Rufus to Shakespeare has, it is probably because the first two of his relevant four stanzas (351–352) are found not in the much admired and translated *Heimskringla* but in *Morkinskinna* (c.1220), the least studied and accessible of the kings' sagas. The lines in question are devoted to Haraldr's last, fatal battle at Stamford Bridge. The king's carefree *uppganga* 'landing' (*Maldon* 87: *upganga*) is described in stanza 12; his *ofrausn* 'rash magnificence' (Finnur Jónsson's Danish translation: *overmod*), the approximate cause of his fall and that of so many others, is mentioned in stanza 13; stanza 14 praises the king's courage and swordplay; his death in battle is reported in the first half of stanza 15, while the second half concludes:

> heldr kuru meir ens milda
> mildings, an grið vildi,
> of folksnaran fylki
> falla liðsmenn allir.

> All the warriors of the generous ruler
> chose rather to fall
> around the battle-swift king
> than to accept peace.

Morkinskinna provides a context: 'Harald Godwinsson offered peace to his brother Tostig and all the survivers. But they all shouted back at once and said that they would never accept a truce. They said they would have victory over their enemies or lie there, all of them, around their king'.[30] The half stanza is very much in the idiom of *Maldon* (cf. *grið*, 35; *lidmenn*, 99, 164; *ceosan*, 113; even *folc* 'battle', 259), but this time with the vikings as good losers. That the *Maldon* poet's praise may have been directed as much at Byrhtnoth as at his retainers is suggested by the message of loyalty telegraphed by the skald, which spends four of its precious words on the fallen leader (*mildr mildingr, folksnarr fylkir*), only one on his troops. Arnórr cut his way through the mangled limbs and meanness of the actual battle to commemorate a worthy action, one that redounded to the credit of king and *comitatus* alike.

W. P. Ker observed in 1897 that the system of vassalage evolving in the eleventh century brought with it a new heroic mode, a literature that eyed with special keenness the emotional bond between man and lord and the lengths to

---

[30] *Morkinskinna*, ed. F. Jónsson, Samfund til Udgivelse af Gammel Nordisk Litteratur 53 (Copenhagen, 1928–32), p. 278.

which it might be stretched: 'Feudalism did not invent, neither did it take away, the virtue of loyalty that has so large a place in all true epic, along with its counterpart of defiance and rebellion . . . It intensified the poetical values of both motives, but they are older than the *Iliad* . . . It glorified to the utmost, it honoured as martyrs those who died fighting for their lord'.[31] The *chansons de geste* allude again and again to the intense loyalty of retainers even to unworthy lords. Roland knows his duty:

> Pur sun seignor deit hom susfrir destreiz
> Et endurer et granz chalz et granz freiz.
> Si'n deit hom perdre en del quir et del peil.

> For his lord one must suffer hardships
> And endure both great heat and great cold.
> For him one must lose hide and hair.
>   *La Chanson de Roland*, 1010–12

Doon de Mayence meditates on the ways and means:

> Se me sire est ochis, je voeil estre tués,
> Et se il est pendu, avec li me pendés;
> Se il est ars en feu, je voeil estre bruslés,
> Et se il est noié, avec li me getés.[32]

> If my lord is killed, I want to be killed,
> And if he is hanged, hang me with him.
> If he is scorched at the stake, I want to be burned,
> And if he is drowned, throw me after him.

Garin le Loherain manages to turn loyal soldiers into martyrs:

> Lor autres mors ont toz en terre mis.
> Crois font sor aus, qu'il erent droit martir:
> Por lor seignor orent esté ocis.[33]

> They have placed all the other dead in earth.
> They make the sign of the cross over them because they were
>   true martyrs:
> They had been slain for their lord.

There is only one *chanson de geste*, however, that dramatizes, like *Maldon*, the loyalty owed a *fallen* lord, and that is the fragmentary, probably late eleventh-century *Gormont and Isembard*.[34] Having been unjustly treated by King Louis,

---

[31] *Epic and Romance: Essays in Medieval Literature* (London, 1897), pp. 52–53.
[32] Ed. F. Guessard, *Les anciens poètes de la France* (Paris, 1858–70), 2, p. 276.
[33] Ed. P. Paris (Paris, 1833–35), 2, p. 88.
[34] For recent scholarship, see J. B. Ashford, 'État présent des recherches sur *Gormont et Isembard*', *Olifant* 10/4 (1984–85), pp. 188–209. The best edition is still A. Bayot, *Gormond et Isembard, fragment de chanson de geste du XIIe siècle* (Paris, 1914). H-E. Keller,

Isembard, a Frank, crosses the English Channel and enters the service of the pagan king Gormont, just before the latter invades France. About halfway through the fragment, Gormont has been killed, Louis mortally injured, and the pagans are fleeing to their waiting ships. Isembard finds the body of Gormont on the field, utters a lament, and reproaches his fellows for their flight (lines 436–63). Repeating all three actions again (lines 464–98), he affirms his intention not to retreat now that his lord lies dead:

> Je ne faudrai a sa meisnee,
> pur tant cum pusse ceindre espee.

> I will never desert his service
> as long as I can gird on sword.   (487–88)

Isembard incites the warriors around him to make one last heroic effort. When this remnant, too, runs for cover, he fights on alone until, lying on the grass under an olive tree, he dies, his face turned to the east and with God on his lips. The idea that 'God will be loyal to the man loyal to his lord' can apply, it seems, even to an apostate in the service of a pagan king.

As late and as far away as thirteenth-century Iceland, promising material could be shaped in the heroic *Maldon/Bjarkamál* mold. The earliest account of the death in 1086 of Knútr Sveinsson the Saint was inscribed c.1095 on the *Tabula Othiniensis*, a metal plaque that listed by name the seventeen loyal retainers who died as martyrs with Knútr and his brother Benedikt.[35] Aelnoth's *Gesta et Passio* (c.1120), preceded by the anonymous *Passio sancti Kanuti regis et martyris* (c.1095), reports that there were those among Knútr's men who slipped away and saved their lives (117). Yet the king's most loyal retainers, even after he had been slain, 'not only did not surrender to the enemy but, indeed, exhorted each other in turn to keep up courage, to exert strength, to rush eagerly against those pouring in through the openings, to meet steel with steel, and to give requital to the slayers; they chose rather to fall with glory than, having lost so great a prince, to survive' (121).[36] Saxo (c.1200) tells of the loyalty and self-

---

'Changes in Old French Epic Poetry and Changes in the Tastes of Its Audience', in *The Epic in Medieval Society: Aesthetic and Moral Values*, ed. H. Scholler (Tübingen, 1979), says *Gormont et Isembard* 'represents probably the oldest epic poem which has come down to us' (p. 161).

[35] On Knútr's martyrdom, see M. Cl. Gertz, *Knud den Helliges Martyrhistorie* (Copenhagen, 1907), which contains editions of the early texts. On the now-vanished *Tabula*, and for English translation of and commentary on Saxo's account of the king's last stand (*Gesta Danorum*, Book XI), see E. Christiansen, ed. and trans. *Saxo Grammaticus, Books X–XVI*, BAR, IS 84 (Oxford, 1980), I, pp. 52–88, 216–258. Both hagiographic texts, authored – like the *Tabula* – by Englishmen, are available in *Vitae Sanctorum Danorum*, ed. M. Cl. Gertz (Copenhagen, 1908–12), I, pp. 34–38 and 77–136 respectively. H. Brix, 'Bjarkemaalet, Analyser og Problemer', *Undersøgelser i den ældre danske Litteratur* (Copenhagen, 1935), 2, pp. 5–32, notes parallels between the death of Hrólfr kraki as recounted in the 'Danish' poem and the murder of Knútr IV.

[36] *Constantissimi uero commilitones duce interempto non modo hostibus non cedere, uerum*

sacrifice of Knútr's men, but keeps the king alive until his subordinates have fallen: 'As many of his warriors as could dash through the enemy got to the king, for they wanted to share his danger and made his peril theirs; although they could have saved themselves deserting him, they sought to face the danger, and became famous by their deaths, rather than run away to safety . . . even when they had every opportunity of fleeing'.[37] The author of *Knytlinga saga*, working a half-century later, also confirms that the king's loyal supporters did not desert but fought until they dropped.[38] But by having the king die first, he creates an opportunity for dialogue and genuine choice among the retainers: 'After this there were loud mutterings amongst the king's men, many saying that it was every man for himself and they should get out any way they could'.[39] Knútr's brother Eiríkr escapes with several others and urges Benedikt to join them. The latter replied: 'Everyone has to do as he thinks best. Those who wish to escape must do so, but let them fight on who think it more fitting. Hail and farewell, brother, until we meet in Heaven'. The saga author commends Benedikt's doomed stand: 'Though they were great champions, they were overwhelmed by the odds against them and the old saying was proved true, a man can't beat a multitude. So Benedikt and all those with him were killed there, earning such renown that their courage and tenacity will be praised for evermore'. The 'ideal' that Rosemary Woolf saw as a 'born again' Germanic survival seems here – as in *Maldon* – the by-product of individual, voluntary Christian fidelity, of a loyalty that is only truly tested when its object has been physically extinguished.[40]

The theme of men dying with their lord can be adapted to many different contexts and purposes. As a literary motif, it is relatively free floating rather than firmly linked to a particular genre or to one form of social organization. Only its affective value seems constant. The *Maldon* 'ideal' is never sensible, worldly, or rational, never reflects 'general opinion' like the proverbs heading this essay. It attests to the existence of paradoxes and wonders, to moments of consciousness in which man seems illumined by a divine or demonic force. The sentence that Coleridge uses as the epigraph to *The Ancient Mariner* urges readers to contemplate a universe of invisible spirits, lest the mind, enmeshed in daily trivia, become 'narrow, and sunk entirely into mean thought'.[41] The man/lord devotion

---

etiam adinuicem exhortando animos incitare, uires exercere, per aperta irruentibus haud segniter occurrere, armis arma uiriliter referre, cedentibus uicem rependere, gloriose magis occumbere quam tanto principe amisso eligentes superuiuere. Professor Niels Lund was kind enough to draw these lines to my special attention.

[37] Christiansen, *Saxo Grammaticus*, p. 84.

[38] *Knytlinga* has now been edited by B. Guðnason in *Danakonunga sǫgur*, Islenzk fornrit 35 (Reykjavík, 1982), pp. lxxi–clxxxvii, 91–321.

[39] *Knytlinga Saga: The History of the Kings of Denmark*, trans. H. Pálsson and P. Edwards (Odense, 1986), pp. 93–94.

[40] For a recent look at Christian resonances in *Maldon*, see R. Hillman, 'Defeat and Victory in *The Battle of Maldon'*, *English Studies in Canada* 11/4 (1985), pp. 385–395.

[41] T. Burnet, *Archaeologiae Philosophiae, sive, Doctrina antiqua de rerum originibus* (London,

featured in *Maldon*, in the skaldic memorial odes, in *Gormont and Isembard*, in Aelnoth, and in *Knytlinga saga* is similarly mind-opening: it draws attention to a Boethian world in which bad fortune is better than good, and life won by its loss; it posits a military class imbued with notions of Christian service and sacrifice. *Maldon*, 'the only purely heroic poem in Old English',[42] peers, not backward through the mists to Germania, but just around the corner, to an eleventh-century Europe in which the profession of warrior was a way of achieving religious perfection and a martyr's crown.

1692), p. 68: . . . *ne mens assuefacta hodiernae vitae minutiis se contrahat nimis, et tota subsidat in pusillas cogitationes.*
[42]　E. V. Gordon, *The Battle of Maldon* (London, 1937), p. 25.

OF DANES – AND THANES – AND DOMESDAY BOOK

Gillian Fellows-Jensen

Although it is now thirty years since Peter Sawyer's controversial study of the density of the Danish settlement in England burst upon the field of Viking studies with the impact of a hungry cat let loose among the pigeons, the feathers are still flying in the onomastic dovecots around the North Sea. Sawyer argued in this paper that it was wrong to consider that all Scandinavian place-names in England had been formed, or transformed, by Scandinavians or their immediate descendants, for many, perhaps even most, of the names could have been coined at much later dates by men of English descent who bore Scandinavian personal names and whose language had been enriched with Scandinavian loanwords. In support of this argument he compared the effect of the Scandinavian settlers on the nomenclature of the Anglo-Saxons with the transformation of the personal nomenclature of England brought about in the century and a half following the Norman Conquest. This was an ill-advised comparison, however, for there is a difference in kind between the relatively few Norman names introduced by the aristocracy, which became immensely popular and were able to displace from favour names of native origin, and the much more varied and vital Scandinavian nomenclature that flourished side by side with English names in the pre-Conquest period. Feeling that Sawyer had misunderstood the evidence of the personal names, name-scholars tended to be unwilling even to contemplate the possibility of accepting his conclusion that of the approximately 220 place-names in -bý recorded in Domesday Book for the East Midland counties, 'there does not seem to be any good reason for believing that more than perhaps twenty were formed in the ninth century'.[1]

That Peter Sawyer's views in 1958 on the evidence of place- and personal names ought not to have been dismissed so lightly should, however, have been clear to anyone who had read the acute study he had published two years earlier of the spellings of place-names in Domesday Book and its related texts.[2] In this, Sawyer had demonstrated that the earlier stages of the Domesday inquiry generally had more reliable name-forms than Domesday Book itself, while there was a tendency in Great Domesday Book for the orthographical peculiarities that

---

[1]   P. H. Sawyer, 'The density of the Danish Settlement in England', *University of Birmingham Historical Journal* 6 (1958), pp. 1–17.
[2]   P. H. Sawyer, 'The place-names of the Domesday manuscripts', *Bulletin of the John Rylands Library* 38 (1956), pp. 483–506.

could be attributed to French scribes in the Exon Domesday to be replaced by a more normal English orthography. There can have been few other scholars active at the time who had such a profound knowledge of the name-forms in Domesday and its satellites and hence the necessary background for judging the significance to be attached to the evidence the names could provide about settlement.

In a book published in 1982, Peter Sawyer discussed the dating of the Scandinavian settlement names in England once again, reiterating his belief that few of the names were coined by the first colonists in the ninth century and arguing that 'the main period of Scandinavian name production was in the early years of the tenth century'.[3] His argument was now based on the fact that areas which had already been recovered by the English soon after 900 have few names of Scandinavian origin so that it seems reasonable to assume that the Danes did not begin to coin names until the old estates began to be broken up. This fragmentation Sawyer would associate with a number of major defeats suffered by the Danes in the first half of the tenth century, defeats which must have weakened the authority of the Danish aristocracy and made it easier for small landowners to claim fuller rights of ownership over their holdings and to mark their claims by giving these holdings new names incorporating their own personal names. Sawyer noted that a very high proportion of these personal names were of Scandinavian origin and seemed implicitly to accept this fact as evidence in support of a tenth-century date for the coining of the place-names.

It is therefore ironic that recent research conducted by Peter Sawyer in a different field should have led me by a roundabout route to the conclusion that some at least of the place-names consisting of a Scandinavian personal name plus -bý are unlikely to have acquired the form in which they are recorded in Domesday Book much before the eleventh century. It will be the aim of the present paper to show how I have consequently been forced to modify my earlier view that Domesday place-names in -bý in eastern England which have Scandinavian personal names as their specifics 'contain for the most part the names of Danish colonists who settled in England between c875 and c925'.[4]

To mark the ninth centenary of the making of Domesday Book, Peter Sawyer embarked upon a detailed examination of the Domesday texts with a view to illuminating the tenurial conditions reflected in these documents.[5] His painstaking examination of the texts enabled him to identify many of the subordinate tenants and to reconstruct a large number of pre-Conquest lordships and reveal that the changes brought about by the Norman Conquest were less dramatic than had commonly been supposed. Sawyer considered that it would be more correct to speak of a change of tenants after the Conquest than of a tenurial

---

[3] P. H. Sawyer, Kings and Vikings. Scandinavia and Europe AD 700–1100 (London, 1982), pp. 103–7; cf. id., 'Conquest and colonization: Scandinavians in the Danelaw and in Normandy', Proceedings of the Eighth Viking Congress (Odense, 1981), pp. 123–31.
[4] G. Fellows Jensen, Scandinavian Personal Names in Lincolnshire and Yorkshire, Navnestudier 7 (Copenhagen, 1968), p. xxxiii.
[5] P. H. Sawyer, '1066–1086: A Tenurial Revolution?', in id., Domesday Book. A Reassessment (London, 1985), pp. 71–85.

revolution. In the course of this research Peter Sawyer had become aware that several of the name-forms in Domesday Book had hitherto been misinterpreted. He drew my attention, for example, to the fact that the names of several identifiable individuals in Lincolnshire appear at different places in Domesday Book in forms so disparate that they had been treated as separate names by Olof von Feilitzen in his study of the names of the pre-Conquest tenants[6] and, where relevant, by me in my study of the names of Scandinavian origin in the county.[7] On the basis of the material which Peter Sawyer generously placed at my disposal and with the painstaking assistance of many of my onomastic colleagues, I was able to show that many different factors could contribute to the representation of one man's name in several different forms and that it was inadvisable to try and construct an etymology for every individual name-form as it occurred.[8] Whenever possible, a name-form recorded in the account of a fief of a tenant-in-chief in one county should be compared with references to the same under-tenant in the fiefs of the same tenant-in-chief in other counties or in the fiefs of other tenants-in-chief or in the texts containing earlier stages of the Domesday survey, for example Exon Domesday for the south-western counties.

After the publication of my paper in 1985, Peter Sawyer drew my attention to the fact that neither Olof von Feilitzen nor I had made it clear that the *Tochi filius Outi* (GDB 336a, 337a)[9] who held property in the city of Lincoln and had sake and soke and toll and team in Lincolnshire was the same man as the *Tochi filius Otta* (GDB 298b; C/36) who had sake and soke and toll and team in Yorkshire. This man with the typically Danish name of *Tóki* is shown by the Lincolnshire entries to have been the son of a man with another typically Danish name, *Auti*, who himself held land in the city of Lincoln (GDB 336a).[10] The form *Otta* taken by *Tóki*'s patronymic in the Yorkshire entry was explained by both von Feilitzen and me as the Danish personal name *Otti*, itself probably a loan from Continental Germanic *Otto*,[11] while Margaret L. Faull and Marie Stinson have recently explained *Otta* as a reflex of the Scandinavian name *Óttarr*, which is in fact borne by a tenant in the East Riding (*Otre*, GDB 301a (3x); 1E17, 25, 36). Since it is clear that *Tochi filius Otta* is to be identified with *Tochi filius Outi*, the form *Otta* can hardly be explained otherwise than as a scribal

[6] O. von Feilitzen, *The Pre-Conquest Personal Names of Domesday Book*, Nomina Germanica 3 (Uppsala, 1937).

[7] Fellows Jensen, *Scandinavian Personal Names*.

[8] G. Fellows Jensen, 'On the Identification of Domesday Tenents in Lincolnshire', *Nomina* 9 (1985), pp. 31–40.

[9] GDB 336a, 337a; C. W. Foster and T. Longley, *The Lincolshire Domesday and the Lindsey Survey*, Lincoln Record Society 19 (Lincoln, 1924), pp. 2/3, 13. References to sections in *Domesday Book* relating to counties other than Lincolnshire are to the edition of J. Morris (Chichester, 1974–86).

[10] Foster and Longley, *The Lincolnshire Domesday*, p. 4/13; von Feilitzen, *Pre-Conquest Personal Names*, pp. 169, 385; Fellows Jensen, *Scandinavian Personal Names*, pp. 43–4, 287–8.

[11] von Feilitzen, *Pre-Conquest Personal Names*, p. 342; Fellows Jensen, *Scandinavian Personal Names*, p. 208.

error for *Outa*, in which *Ou-* has replaced *Au-* and final *-i* has been anglicised to
-a.

Yorkshire Domesday has a section of *Clamores* or Claims and this provides a
form of control of some of the spellings employed in the main text. An under-
tenant of the Count of Mortain in Sandall in the West Riding appears as *Scotecol*
(GDB 307b; 5W11). This form has been explained as representing the name
Skotakollr, which makes a few appearances as a by-name in West Scandinavian
sources.[12] The first element of this name is probably the genitive of the folk-
name *Skotar* 'Scots, Irish', while the second element is *kollr* m. 'head, shaven
crown', perhaps used in an extended sense for 'man'. Hans Bekker-Nielsen has
argued persuasively that the by-name may originally have been given to a man
whose bald head or characteristic hairstyle recalled the Celtic form of tonsure
and that the name is to be attributed to the Atlantic cultural sphere in which
Icelanders, Faroese and Norwegians had regular contacts with the Celts of Ireland and Scotland.[13] It is possible that *Skotakollr* was a man from the Western
Isles who had come with Norwegian settlers to north-west England and then
made his way across the Pennines to Yorkshire. A man with the same name,
although spelt *Scotcol* (GDB 315b; 9W40), was an under-tenant of Ilbert de Lacy
in Owston not far from Sandall and it seems likely that *Scotecol* and *Scotcol* were
one and the same man. It is therefore perhaps significant that one of *Scotcol's*
fellow tenants in Owston was a man called *Glunier*, who held several manors in
the West Riding and whose name has been explained as an Irish adaptation,
Glúniairn, of a Scandinavian by-name *Iarnkné*.[14] It is tempting to think that both
Glunier and *Scotcol* may have come to the West Riding from the Western Isles.
However that may be, there is an entry about land in Sandall in the *Clamores*,
where an interlinear addition says that the church had belonged to *Sotecol* (GDB
373b; CW11). This name-form, which seems to have been overlooked by von
Feilitzen, was explained by me as an otherwise unrecorded Scandinavian by-
name **Sótakollr* 'black-head', a name which is semantically plausible, being
identical in meaning with the well-recorded *Svartkollr*. I would nevertheless now
prefer to explain the *Sotecol* of the *Clamores* as the same man as the *Scot(e)col* of
the main text and to explain *Sotecol* as simply a scribal error for *Scotecol* (cf. the
note to CW11).

Whereas a tenant named in the main text of Domesday can generally be
identified with reasonable certainty with a tenant bearing the same or a similar
name in an entry in the *Clamores* dealing with the same manor, it is often
impossible to be confident about an identification of a Domesday tenant with a
man named in some more or less contemporary but unrelated source. It seems

---

[12] von Feilitzen, *Pre-Conquest Personal Names*, p. 366; Fellows Jensen, *Scandinavian Personal Names*, p. 252.
[13] H. Bekker-Nielsen, 'Skotakollr', *Fróðskaparrit* 18 (1970), pp. 145–50.
[14] C. J. S. Marstrander, *Bidrag til det norske sprogs historie i Irland* (Kristiania, 1915), p. 45; E. Ekwall, *Scandinavians and Celts in the North-West of England* (Lund, 1918), p. 86; A. H. Smith, 'Some aspects of Irish influence on Yorkshire', *Revue Celtique* 44 (1927), p. 43; von Feilitzen, *Pre-Conquest Personal Names*, p. 262.

inherently likely, for example, that the Vlf who set up the sundial in Aldbrough church in the East Riding 'for himself and the soul of Gunvor' at some time in the eleventh century is to be identified with the Vlf who is recorded in Domesday as holding land in Aldbrough (GDB 324a; 14E11).[15] The name Ulf was a common one, however. There were several men of that name holding land in Yorkshire in the eleventh century.[16]

Similarly, it is tempting to identify the Orm Gamal suna who set up the sundial at Kirkdale church in the North Riding between 1055 and 1065 with the Orm who, in 1065, held a number of Yorkshire manors, including Kirby Moorside, whose parish church is the one at Kirkdale (GDB 327a–327b; 23N7, 17, 19, 22, 23, 25)[17] and it may even be that Orm's father Gamal is to be identified with the Gamel filius Orm who is reported by Symeon of Durham to have been killed by Earl Tosti in York in 1064[18] and with the Orm who was also a pre-Conquest tenant in the North Riding.[19] The Scandinavian names Ormr and Gamall are both, however, of common occurrence in Yorkshire[20] and it is not certain that the proposed identifications are correct, although they are certainly plausible.

In the case of the identification of several of the men recorded in a list of festermen for a man called Ælfric in a document dating from about 1050 with pre-Conquest tenants of Domesday estates in Yorkshire, it is the occurrence of their names in connection with estates either expressly named as the place of origin of the festermen or lying in the neighbourhood of such places which forms the basis for the identifications proposed by William Farrer.[21] He considered that the places named in the list of festermen were to be identified as Barmby on the Marsh in the East Riding (Barnabi, Bærnabi), Cawood (Ca'), Kirkby Wharfe (Cir'), Hambleton (Há'), Burton Salmon (Burhtun), Brotherton (Broðortun), Brayton (Braiþatun) and Hillam (Hillum), all in Barkston Ash Wapentake in the West Riding. The only two of these places for which tenants are named in Domesday Book are Kirkby Wharfe, where one manor was held by Forne (GDB 315b; 9W30), who can perhaps be identified with the festerman Forna, and Hambleton, where the tenant Alchel (GDB 315b; 9W25) is probably to be identified with Alfcetel in Há'. The chief reasons for the lack of information in Domesday Book about the tenants of the other vills named in the list of festermen are that Domesday did not treat separately the berewicks under the Archbishop of York's estate of Sherburn and that it omitted to account for the royal Soke of Snaith. If the names of the festermen are compared with the names of

[15] E. Okasha, Hand-List of Anglo-Saxon Non-Runic Inscriptions (Cambridge, 1971), p. 47.
[16] Cf. Fellows Jensen, Scandinavian Personal Names, p. 323.
[17] Okasha, Handlist, p. 88.
[18] Symeonis Monachi Opera Omnia, ed. T. Arnold, Rolls Series 75, 2 vols (London, 1882–5), vol. 2, p. 178; note to GDB Yorkshire 8N2.
[19] R. H. Skaife, 'Domesday Book for Yorkshire', Yorkshire Archaeological Journal 14 (1898), p. 269 n. 30.
[20] Fellows Jensen, Scandinavian Personal Names, pp. 91–5, 205–6.
[21] W. Farrer (ed.), Early Yorkshire Charters vol. 1 (Edinburgh, 1914), p. 28; W. H. Stevenson, 'Yorkshire Surveys and other Eleventh-Century Documents in the York Gospels', EHR 27 (1912), pp. 12–3.

the Domesday tenants of vills in the wapentake of Barkston Ash and adjoining districts, then a large number of plausible identifications can be made, as shown by William Farrer and Harald Lindkvist in the first quarter of this century.[22]

If these various identifications are, in fact, accepted, it will be seen that the forms taken by the names in the list of festermen are closer to the original Old English (OE) or Scandinavian forms of the names than are the forms recorded in Domesday Book. Some of the variations are merely orthographical. The old letters þ and ð survive in the list, for example Þór, Þorcetel, Eðastan, Arðor, Farðain, Barað, Halwærð, whereas Domesday replaces these letters with t or d (e.g. Tor GDB 329a; 25W3), Torchil (308a; 5W19), Adestan (326b; 21W2), Artor (316a; 9W48), Fardan (329a; 25W2), Baret (315a; 9W20), Aluuard (315b; 9W27). The Old English diphthong eo survives in the list in the name Leofnoð, whereas in Domesday this has been replaced by e, Leuenot (318a; 9W140). OE æ is represented by e in the list, e.g. Elfric, Elfwine, Eðastan, but by a in Domesday, e.g. Aluric (315b; 9W26), Aluuine (316a; 9W42), Adestan (326a; 21W2). Scandinavian Ás- is represented by As- in the list, e.g. Ascetel, Asmund, whereas it has been anglicised to Os- in Domesday Book, e.g. Osmundus (315b; 9W23). The festerman referred to as Osulf in the list probably bore the English name Ōswulf rather than cognate Scandinavian Ásulfr. In the list, initial W-survives in OE Wulf- as a first element, Wulger, Wulfeh, Wulfric, whereas W- is lost from this position in GDB, e.g. Vlfac (316b; 9W68), Vluric (330b; 29W20). The Scandinavian second element -ketill survives in uncontracted but anglicised form in all the names in which it appears in the list, Alfcetel (2x), Arcetel, Ascetel (2x), Auðcetel, Grimcetel (4x), Roscetel, Þorcetel, Ulfcetel (2x), whereas in Domesday Book the element has almost always been contracted to [kil] or [kel], e.g. Alchel (GDB 315b; 9W25), Alchil (324a; 14E26) but Alchetel (301b; 6N26), Archil (315b; 9W24), Grimchil (315a; 9W5), Roschil (315b; 9W24), Torchil (308a; 5W19), Vlchil (315a; 9W9). The consistency with which the -cetel of the list is represented by -chil or occasionally -chel in Domesday Book invites comment.

Ásketill is probably the Scandinavian name which appears with the greatest number of different spellings in English sources. In the post-Conquest period there are several men in Yorkshire and in Lincolnshire bearing this name who are referred to by varying, often widely differing forms of it, suggesting that the ultimate identity between Askil, the East Scandinavian mutated form Eskil, the Norman forms Anschetillus, Anschitillus, Asketinus and Anketinus and numerous diminutive forms such as Asti, Hasti, Astin, Hankin and Astil was generally recognised by both English and Norman scribes.[23] There is, however, only one instance of a man being referred to by both the contracted and the non-normanised full forms of the Scandinavian name and this instance is rather doubtful. The Domesday tenant referred to as Aschil (GDB 345b (2x), 346a (3x), 376b; 8/15, 17, 23, 27–28, 71/15) was the brother of Siric, Siworth and Abbot

[22] Farrer, Early Yorkshire Charters vol. 1; H. Lindkvist, 'Some notes on Elfric's Festermen', Beiblatt zur Anglia 33 (1922), pp. 130–44.
[23] Fellows Jensen, Scandinavian Personal Names, pp. 25–32.

Brand and son of *Tochi*. He is named once in a spurious charter as *Askytelo* [1060x1066] 13.[24] There is, in fact, very little evidence at all for the alternation of *ketill* and *kil* in personal names in Lincolnshire and Yorkshire. The abbot of Crowland, however, appears as *Vlchel* in Domesday Book (GDB 377a; 72/48) but as *Wlfketelum* in the Latin *Acts of Lanfranc*, recording his deposition in 1085.[25] Another *Vlfchetel* was an under-tenant in Lincolnshire of Berenger de Todeni in Allington and of Robert of Stafford in Casthorpe (GDB 353b; 19/1, 368b; 59/2). Both these holdings are in Winnibriggs Wapentake and it seems likely that the two entries refer to the same man but there is no way of determining whether he is also to be identified with the tenant or tenants referred to elsewhere in the survey as *Vlchil* or *Vlchel*. The under-tenant of Alfred of Lincoln in Rothwell, Lincolnshire, is named as *Torchetel* (GDB 357b; 27/15). It seems likely that he is to be identified with Alfred's under-tenant in Creeton, Bourne and Rippingale, who is referred to as *Turchil* (GDB 358a; 27/40, 358b (2x); 27/51, 53) but this identification cannot be proved. Finally, a man bearing the French forename *Deuleward* is noted as being *filius Arketil* and *filius Arkel* in two grants of land in Lincolnshire dated to about 1225 and recorded in the fourteenth-century Thurgarton cartulary.[26]

In the Scandinavian homelands the personal names in *-ketill* mostly occur in the surviving records with contracted forms in *-kell* or *-kill*, although the full forms do appear in some Icelandic literary sources, in an eleventh-century Norwegian runic inscription (*arnktil* NIYR no. 230), in a few Norwegian documentary sources and in a number of eleventh-century runic inscriptions from Sweden.[27] That the uncontracted forms must also have been current in Denmark in the late ninth and early tenth centuries is shown by their occurrence among the Danish settlers in the Danelaw and Normandy. There are only three compounds in *-ketill* which occur in Norman sources: *Arnketill*, *Ásketill* and *Þorketill*[28] and of these only *Ásketill* and *Þorketill* are at all frequent. Both names occur in normanised forms, as *An(s)ketil*, *An(s)kitil*, rarely *Anskil*, and *Torketil*, *Turketil*, *Torkitil*, *Turkitil* respectively. The small number of *ketill*-compounds introduced into Normandy and their conservative forms are to be explained by the fact that the Viking settlement of that province took place in the tenth century and that reinforcements would not seem to have arrived from the Danish homelands after the development of the contracted spellings.

There are many more compounds in *-ketill* recorded in the English sources and the forms these names take show great variation but all of them are recorded

[24] S. 1059.
[25] C. Plummer and J. Earle, eds, *Two of the Saxon Chronicles Parallel*, vol. 1 (Oxford, 1892–99), p. 290.
[26] F. M. Stenton, 'The Free Peasantry of the Northern Danelaw', *Bulletin de la Société royale des Lettres de Lund* (1925–6), nos. 201–2.
[27] Fellows Jensen, *Scandinavian Personal Names*, p. cv; J. Insley, 'Scandinavian Personal Names in Norfolk', unpublished Ph.D. thesis for the University of Nottingham (1980), pp. 41–3, and the works cited there.
[28] J. Adigard des Gautries, *Les noms de personnes scandinaves en Normandie de 911 à 1066*, Nomina Germanica 11 (Lund, 1954), pp. 77–8, 81–4, 163–5, 275, 287–94, 322–6.

with uncontracted forms of the second element, except for one which is only found with a shortened form -ket that presupposes introduction of the name to England in the uncontracted form -ketill. The names I have noted in English sources are: Alfketill, Arnketill, Ásketill, Auðketill, Brúnketill, Grimketill, Gunnketill, Holmketill, Hrafnketill, Hrossketill, Ormketill, Sigketill, Steinketill, Þorketill, Ulfketill and *Unnketill or *Húnketill. For many of these names the forms recorded in pre-Conquest sources show anglicisation of the second element by substitution of cognate West Saxon cytel for Scandinavian ketill, for example Alfcytel (coin of Æthelred, Torksey),[29] Arncytel (coin, York),[30] Oscytel (recorded in the ASC as the name of a Danish king 875, a Danish hold 905 and the Archbishop of York, and found on a coin, Chester),[31] Grymcytel (ASC 1038–47, Bishop of Selsey) and Grimcytel (coin, Lincoln),[32] Steigncytel (in a charter dated [972x992] 12),[33] Purcy-tel (recorded in the ASC as the name of a Danish jarl 915, the Abbot of Bedford 971, and others), Ulfcytel (coin, York)[34] and Ulfkytel (in the ASC 1004–16 as the name of the chief man of East Anglia). Several of the names also appear with anglicised forms of their first elements. Alf- is replaced by Ælf- and Elf- in Ælfcetel (coin, Lincoln)[35] and Elfkitil (1046).[36] Arn- is replaced by Earn- in Earcytel (1038),[37] Erncytel (coin, York),[38] Ás- is replaced by Os- in several instan-ces of Oscytel, Stein- is replaced by Stan- in Stannechetel (GDB 243a), Þor- is once replaced by Purh- in Purhcytel (ASC 1016), Ulf- is once replaced by Wulf- in Wulkitele (1046).[39] It is clear that these names showing anglicised elements had been adopted into the English nomenclature. Although it seems likely that they were generally borne by descendants of the original Scandinavian settlers, since they occur most frequently in northern and eastern England and often in families whose other members bear Scandinavian names, an eleventh-century bearer of such a name would not necessarily be of Danish descent. That such names could be borne by men who felt themselves to be English is shown by Ulfkytel, the renowned defender of East Anglia, who died fighting against the Danes at the Battle of Ashingdon in 1016. Six years earlier, however, the Danes were victori-ous in a battle because their East Anglian opponents had taken to flight and the Anglo-Saxon Chronicle (E version) notes that the flight was instigated by Purcytel

[29] V. Smart, Cumulative Index of Volumes 1–20, Sylloge of Coins of the British Isles xxviii, p. 13.

[30] Smart, Cumulative Index, p. 14.

[31] Smart, Cumulative Index, p. 15.

[32] Smart, Cumulative Index, p. 43.

[33] A. J. Robertson, Anglo-Saxon Charters (Cambridge, 1939, 2nd. edn 1956), no. 39; S. 1448.

[34] V. J. Smart, 'Moneyers of the late Anglo-Saxon coinage 973–1016', Commentationes de nummis saeculorum IX–XI in Suecia repertis vol. 2, ed. M. L. Rasmusson and B. Malmer (Stockholm, 1968), p. 230.

[35] Smart, Cumulative Index, p. 13.

[36] D. Whitelock (ed.), Anglo-Saxon Wills (Cambridge, 1930), no. 32.

[37] S. 1392.

[38] Smart, Cumulative Index, p. 14.

[39] Whitelock, Anglo-Saxon Wills, no. 32; S. 1535.

Myran heafod. Florence of Worcester calls *Purcytel* a *Danicus minister*[40] but his name and by-name suggest rather that he was an Englishman of Danish descent and divided loyalties. After the Conquest, another man bearing this Scandinavian name in its contracted form, *Turkil* of Harringworth in Northamptonshire, abandoned his estates and, according to the Red Book of Thorney, went over to 'the Danes who were his kinsmen'.[41] Is it in fact more reasonable for the Red Book to have assumed that *Turkil* was a kinsman of the Danes than for Florence of Worcester to call *Purcytel Myran heafod* a Danish *minister*? The form *Turkil* taken by the name of the former suggests that it is.

The date of the contraction of the element -*ketill* to -*kel(l)* and its further development to -*kil(l)* in Denmark cannot be fixed with any exactitude. The introduction of the uncontracted forms to England and Normandy at the end of the ninth century and beginning of the tenth century forms the *terminus post quem*, while the *terminus ante quem* can be deduced from the fact that the contracted form is the only one to be found in Danish runic inscriptions and that the earliest relevant inscriptions, namely Hune (*DR* no. 161) and Flejsborg (*DR* no. 132), belong to the Jelling-type and can thus probably be dated to before the year 1000.[42] That the development to -*kil* had certainly taken place by the year 1000 is confirmed by the occurrence of the contracted form in the names of Danes whose activities in England at the beginning of the eleventh century are recorded in the *Anglo-Saxon Chronicle*.

The famous Jómsborg viking, jarl Thorkell the Tall, makes his first appearance in the *Anglo-Saxon Chronicle* under the year 1009, when the C version glosses a reference to *se ungemetlica unfrið here* with the comment *þe we heton Ðurkilles here*. From then on until his outlawing by Cnut in 1021 and subsequent reconciliation with Cnut in 1023, jarl Thorkell is frequently mentioned in the Chronicle, where his name takes such forms as *Purkil*, *Purcyl* 1013E, *Purkyl* 1020D, *Porkyll* 1021D, *Purkil* 1021E. In the West Scandinavian sources he is referred to as *Porkell*[43] and in Danish sources as *Turkil(lus)*, *Turchil(lus)*,[44] while the uncontracted form of his name, *þurktil*, appears in a single Swedish runic inscription (*SRU* no. 344). More or less contemporary with the references to Thorkell in the *Anglo-Saxon Chronicle* are a number of coins of Æthelred whose moneyers bear *ketill*-names in contracted form: *Stencil*, *Stgncil* (Lincoln), *Ascil* (London) and *Oscel* (York).[45] Of these, the coins bearing the inscriptions *Ascil* and *Oscel* have been thought possibly to be Scandinavian imitations.[46] After

[40] Plummer and Earle, *Two of the Saxon Chronicles Parallel* vol. 2, p. 188.
[41] D. Whitelock, 'Scandinavian Personal Names in the *Liber Vitae* of Thorney Abbey', *Saga-Book* 12 (1940), p. 140.
[42] J. Brøndum-Nielsen, *Gammeldansk Grammatik* vol. 1 (Copenhagen, 1928), 146, n. 3; H. Andersen, 'Nogle runedanske Navneled', *Namn och Bygd* 24 (1936), p. 85.
[43] E. H. Lind, *Norsk-isländska personbinam från medeltiden* (Uppsala, 1920–1), col. 139.
[44] *Danmarks gamle Personnavne*, ed. G. Knudsen, M. Kristensen and R. Hornby (Copenhagen, 1936–64), col. 1389.
[45] Smart, 'Moneyers of the late Anglo-Saxon coinage', pp. 235, 254; id., *Cumulative Index*, pp. 15, 68.
[46] Smart, 'Moneyers of the late Anglo-Saxon coinage', p. 255; id., *Cumulative Index*, p. 68.

Cnut became king in England, the number of moneyers bearing names with the contracted form of -*ketill* increased, although moneyers bearing the full forms of the names continue to function even after the Norman Conquest. Veronica Smart has commented that in order to exercise effective supervision, the moneyers would have needed to have a knowledge of the mint, even if they did not actually strike the coins themselves, and that it would therefore not have been possible for Cnut to have rewarded his followers with the lucrative office of moneyer before they had had time to achieve the necessary expertise.[47] It is thus not surprising that it is generally the old established Anglo-Scandinavian names in -*ketill* that occur on the coins rather than the new introductions in -*kil*.

The contracted forms of the names begin to appear in charters and writs in England from about the second quarter of the eleventh century. About 1024 a man called *Thurkil Hoche* made a grant of a moneyer at Stamford and land there, a grant which is recorded by Hugh Candidus in his twelfth-century chronicle of Peterborough Abbey.[48] This *Thurkil* has been identified with the *Turkyl Ho3e* who appears in the Thorney *Liber Vitae*[49] and the *Thurkyl hoga* who witnesses a charter of Cnut in 1024.[50] Thurkil's by-name has been explained as the OE adjective *hoga* 'prudent'[51] but in view of the fact that he was probably a recent Danish immigrant, it is perhaps more likely to be an anglicised form of a Scandinavian adjective such as *hógr* or *hœgr* 'tall' or *hægr* 'amenable'. A document dating from about 1032 is witnessed by a man called *Þorð* who is said to be *Þurkilles* or *Þurcylles nefa*,[52] while a *Đurcil(l) hwita* is recorded as a participant in a lawsuit about land in Herefordshire which was being conducted some time between 1016 and 1035.[53] This man and his wife *Lēofflǣd* still held property in the county at the time of the Domesday Survey and John Insley has suggested that *Đurcil(l) hwita* was probably a Danish follower of Cnut who had been granted land in Herefordshire and married into the local landed aristocracy.[54]

The occurrence of Scandinavian personal names outside the areas of Scandinavian settlement is considered by John Insley to be 'largely a consequence of the establishment of Scandinavian landowners throughout England by Cnut and his sons' and the consequent social prestige enjoyed by the Scandinavian personal names.[55] It is tempting to believe that it was also a consequence of the establishment of the followers of Cnut and his sons on land in the areas already

---

[47] V. Smart, 'Scandinavians, Celts and Germans in Anglo-Saxon England: the evidence of the moneyers' names', *Anglo-Saxon Monetary History. Essays in memory of Michael Dolley*, ed. M. A. S. Blackburn (Leicester, 1986), pp. 180–1.

[48] C. R. Hart, *The Early Charters of Eastern England* (Leicester, 1966), no. 351.

[49] Whitelock, 'Scandinavian Personal Names', p. 140.

[50] S. 961.

[51] G. Tengvik, *Old English Bynames*, Nomina Germanica 4 (Uppsala, 1938), p. 347.

[52] Robertson, *Anglo-Saxon Charters*, no. 86; S. 1465.

[53] Robertson, *Anglo-Saxon Charters*, no. 78; S. 1462.

[54] J. Insley, 'Some Scandinavian personal names in South-West England from post-Conquest records', *Studia Anthroponymica Scandinavica* 3 (1985), p. 46.

[55] J. Insley, 'Some Scandinavian Personal Names from South-West England', *Namn och Bygd* 70 (1982), p. 77; K. Mack, 'Changing Thegns: Cnut's Conquest and the English Aristocracy', *Albion* 16 (1984), pp. 375–87.

settled by men of Scandinavian descent that the contracted forms of the names in -*ketill* begin to appear side by side with the full forms in the eleventh century. Danes would seem to have continued to enter the service of the English king in the reign of Edward the Confessor and to have been rewarded for their services by grants of land. Several of the tenants with names in -*kel* or -*kil* in Domesday Book are specifically said to be *tegnus regis*, e.g. *Aschil teignus regis* Hertfordshire (GDB 139a; 31/1), *Turchil teignus regis Edwardi* Bedfordshire (GDB 213a; 23/18), *Turchillus teinnus* Suffolk (LDB 417a; 34/7). A few of the Domesday tenants are specifically stated to be Danish and among these is numbered *Turchillus danus* Huntingdonshire (GDB 203b; 2/8).

Although there is thus good reason to believe that many of the Domesday tenants with names in -*kel* or -*kil* were recent Danish immigrants, this does not mean that they all were. There is some evidence that the English confused the -*kil* ending with the OE element -*cild* so that *Purkil* became *Purcild* in a document from about 1075 concerning the purchase of slaves in Cornwall,[56] while the [tʃild] ending in the OE name *Leofcild* was replaced by [kil] in the name of the Domesday tenants *Lefchil* YW (GDB 308a; 5W21) and *Lufchel* Nottinghamshire (GDB 285a; 9/34). The resulting hybrid name was accepted into the nomenclature of eastern England. A *Lefchetel*, in whose name the -*kil* had in turn been replaced by -*ketill*, is recorded in Suffolk at the end of the eleventh century[57] and a *Luuechil* in Lincolnshire in 1202.[58] While -*kil* from -*cild* was replaced by -*ketill* in this name, -*ketill* was replaced by -*kil* in some old established Scandinavian names in England. The names of Ælfric's festermen, for example, would seem to have been 'modernised' in this way in Domesday Book. In a will that can be dated 1043x1045 and which survives in a thirteenth-century transcript, an East Anglian called *Purstan Wine sune* with a Scandinavian forename and an English patronymic, reveals himself to have been in partnership (*felagescipe*) with a man called *Vlfketel*.[59] The name of this partner makes one appearance in the will in the genitive case as *Vlfkeles*, suggesting that the uncontracted and contracted forms of the name were already being identified as representing the same name. Two men called *Vlfketel* witness the will and their names are both spelt thus, while another man with whom Thurstan jointly owned land is called *Askil*, gen. *Askilles*. *Askil* may have been a recent Danish immigrant and the two or three *Vlfketels* of Anglo-Danish stock. It is, however, possible that the name *Ulfketel* had a greater tendency to survive in uncontracted form than had the other *ketill*-compounds. A grant by Cnut of land in the East Riding of Yorkshire in 1033, for example, has among its witnesses *Purcyl* and *Ulfkitel*,[60] while of all the names in -*ketill* borne by Domesday tenants, it is *Ulfketill* which most frequently survives in uncontracted form.[61] The name was of comparatively infrequent

---

56 J. Insley, 'Some Scandinavian Personal Names from South-West England', p. 88.
57 von Feilitzen, *Pre-Conquest Personal Names*, p. 313.
58 Fellows Jensen, *Scandinavian Personal Names*, p. 186.
59 Whitelock, *Anglo-Saxon Wills*, no. 31; S. 1531.
60 Farrer, *Early Yorkshire Charters*, no. 8; S. 968.
61 von Feilitzen, *Pre-Conquest Personal Names*, pp. 399–400.

occurrence in the Scandinavian homelands. It was borne by one of the original settlers in Iceland whose nationality is doubtful[62] and is otherwise not recorded in the West Scandinavian area. It is found in a few Swedish runic inscriptions (cf. SRU nos. 100, 160–61, 479, 633). The bearer of the name referred to in three of these inscriptions belonged to the family of Ulv of Borresta, a great yeoman-farmer from Uppland who had served with both Thorkell the Tall and King Cnut in England and it is perhaps significant that his name appears in uncontracted form ulfkitel on no. 160 but as ulfkel on no. 100 and ulfkil on no. 161. It has been suggested that this man may owe his name to the Danelaw connections of his family (SRU no. 100). In Denmark the first recorded instance of the name Ulfkil is the owner's name inscribed in runes on a walking stick found in Lund and dated by its ornamentation to c.1025.[63] This name and the Ulfkil on some late eleventh-century coins may well have been borne by men from the Danelaw.[64] It is possible that the compound Ulfketill arose in the Danelaw and later spread from there back to the Scandinavian homelands. In this connection it is perhaps relevant to mention that the majority of the personal names in -ketil which are found in the Danelaw are not of very common occurrence in Scandinavia and are first recorded there in late sources. It is possible that both these and some of the other Scandinavian names recorded in the Danelaw also arose in England and spread from there back to the Scandinavian homelands or across the Atlantic to Iceland.

If it is accepted that the names in -ketill were introduced to England at two different periods, firstly in their uncontracted forms at the time of the original settlements in the late ninth and early tenth centuries and secondly in contracted form in the early eleventh century, then a study of the form taken by these names in place-names in England might be able to reveal something about the date of the coining of the place-names. Place-names containing uncontracted forms of the personal names cannot, however, provide much information, since these forms are known to have continued in use even after the Norman Conquest, being of particularly frequent occurrence in East Anglia,[65] while the uncontracted forms of Ásketill are also very common in post-Conquest sources in both Lincolnshire and Yorkshire, probably because they were reinforced by the Norman forms of the name, Ansketillus and Anketillus.[66] It must surely be significant, however, that the uncontracted forms are of rare occurrence in place-names. The only major settlement names to have recorded forms showing uncontracted forms of the personal names are Arkston in Herefordshire (Archelestune c.1170, Arketeleston 1212; DEPN), Thurcaston in Leicestershire (Turchitelestone GDB 230a; C/11, Tvrchitelestone 232a; 13/19, Turchilestone 235b (2x); 29/1, 15, Tvrchilestone 235b; 29/20), and Ilketshall in Suffolk, which apparently

[62] E. H. Lind, Norsk-isländska dopnamn och fingerade namn från medeltiden (Uppsala, 1905–15), col. 1053.
[63] E. Moltke, Runerne i Danmark og deres oprindelse (Copenhagen, 1976), p. 379.
[64] Danmarks gamle Personnavne, col. 1528.
[65] Insley, 'Scandinavian Personal Names in Norfolk', pp. 114–24.
[66] Fellows Jensen, Scandinavian Personal Names, p. 31.

contains an *i*-mutated form *Ylfketill* of *Ulfketill* (*Ilcheteleshala* LDB 300b; 4/20, *Ilcheteshala* 300b, 301a (3x), 301b, 356a; 4/22–24, 28, 32, 13/7, *Elcheteshala* 301a; 4/26, *Ilketeleshal* 1186, *Hulketeleshal* 1228; *DEPN*). In addition there are the now-lost Domesday settlements of *Thurketeliart* in Norfolk (*LDB* 230a; 20/36) and *Tvrchetlestuna* in Suffolk (*LDB* 420a; 36/6). It is striking that in the three of these names that survive, the uncontracted forms of the personal names alternate with contracted ones: *Arketel* with *Archel*, *Turchitel* with *Turchil* and *Ilchetel* with *Ilchet*, and that the uncontracted forms are obscured in the modern forms of the place-names. This means that the possibility has to be taken into account that uncontracted forms may have been shortened after the coining of some of the place-names whose only recorded forms have contracted forms of the personal names. This would probably have been done in order to avoid tongue-twisting formations. It should be noted, however, that Ilketshall, *Thurketeliart* and *Tvrchetlestuna* are all in East Anglia and that Thurcaston is a so-called Grimston-hybrid and was probably among the earliest names to be coined by the Scandinavian settlers in Leicestershire. The occurrence of uncontracted forms of the personal names in these four place-names is therefore quite natural.

Uncontracted forms of the personal names are also found in some minor names which are first recorded in post-Conquest sources and whose date of coining cannot be determined. John Insley has noted several instances in Norfolk[67] but elsewhere they are of rare occurrence. I have noted *Asketelhage* 1189 and *Arketelesneuland* 1360 in Lincolnshire,[68] and there is *Asketillesdal* 1220 in Hertfordshire.[69]

The contracted forms of the personal names are of frequent occurrence in both major and minor names in Yorkshire. Settlement names recorded in Domesday Book include the name of a lost place in Pickering Marishes YN (*Aschilesmares* GDB 299a; 1Y4, *Aschelesmersc* 380b; SND12), Asselby YE (*Aschilebi* GDB 304b (2x); 3Y4, 306b; 5E25, 381b (2x); SEHow4, 7), Exelby YN (*Aschilebi* GDB 313a; 6N151, 381a; SNCtA41), Haisthorpe YE (*Aschiltorp* GDB 299b; 1Y14, *Ascheltorp* 304a; 2E16, 382a; SEBt4, *Haschetorp* 332b; 31E1,[70] a lost settlement in YN (*Roscheltorp* GDB 305a; 4N2, 380b; SNL10), Thirkleby YN (*Turchilebi* GDB 327a; 23N1), Thirtleby YE (*Torchilebi* GDB 323b; 14E6, 382a; SEHol11), a lost settlement in YE (*Vlchiltorp* GDB 303a; 2B18), Uncleby YE (*Vnchelsbi* GDB 301a; 1E51, *Vnglesbi* 314b; 8E1, *Vnchelfsbi* 382a; SEAc3), a lost settlement in YW (*Hvnchilhvse* GDB 315b; 9W21, *Hunchilhuses* 379a; SWBA5). In marked contrast there is not a single Domesday settlement name in Lincolnshire whose specific is a contracted form of a personal name in -*ketill*, although Grimblethorpe is recorded as *Grinchiltorp* in the Lindsey Survey of 1115x1118.[71]

67 Insley, 'Scandinavian Personal Names in Norfolk', pp. 38, 96, 827, 873.
68 Fellows Jensen, *Scandinavian Personal Names*, pp. 14, 25.
69 J. E. B. Gover, A. Mawer and F. M. Stenton, *The Place-Names of Hertfordshire*, English Place-Name Society 15 (1938), p. 252.
70 i.e. the Bruce fief of 1120x1129, cf. G. Fellows Jensen, 'The Domesday Book Account of the Bruce Fief', *Journal of the English Place-Name Society* 2 (1969–70), pp. 8–17.
71 Fellows Jensen, *Scandinavian Personal Names*, p. 107.

None of the other East Midland counties has a Domesday settlement name whose specific is a contracted form of a personal name in -*ketill* but Oakerthorpe in Derbyshire is first recorded in a late twelfth-century document in the fourteenth-century Darley cartulary as *Ulkilthorp* and has been associated with a *Hugo filius Hulfchetel* who is named in the same cartulary.[72] Contracted forms of the personal names occur in a few other settlement names scattered around the country. In the North-East, *Ulkil* is found in two Oustons, one in Durham and one in Northumberland.[73] In the North-West, *Arkil* occurs in Arkleby in Cumberland and Arkleton in Dumfriesshire, and *Ulkil* in Brotherilkeld in Cumberland.[74] *Thurkil* is found in two Thruxtons in areas where Scandinavian names are of rare occurrence, Hampshire and Herefordshire (*DEPN*).

It is, of course, possible that the *ketill*-compounds in these names were contracted after the coining of the place-names but since no trace of the uncontracted forms survives in the recorded forms, even when these are as early as Domesday Book, it seems more likely that it was in their contracted forms that the personal names were incorporated into the place-names. This would suggest that the bearers of the personal names were Danish immigrants of the eleventh century or descendants of such late arrivals. Some support for this view is provided by the fact that the pre-Conquest tenant of *Hvnchilhvse* was a man called *Hunchil*, i.e. *Unnkell* or perhaps *Húnkell*, who probably gave his name to the settlement. I would look upon the presence of these eleventh-century nameforms in the Yorkshire settlement names as a reflection of the substitution of the name of a new tenant for that of the outgoing tenant at the time when the property changed hands. There is hardly any certain evidence for this practice in England but there is the much-quoted example of Buslingthorpe in Lincolnshire, in which the Norman name, *Buselin*, of an early twelfth-century tenant displaced a Scandinavian personal name, *Esi*, as specific of the Domesday place-name *Esetorp* (GDB 352b; 18/3; cf. *DEPN*) and I have earlier suggested that the place-names in Cumberland and Dumfriesshire which consist of a Norman personal name plus the Scandinavian generic -*bý* reflect an outward movement from Carlisle of settlers with Norman names, who took over pre-existing settlements with names in -*bý* and imposed upon these their own personal names as new specifics.[75] The main reason for the comparative paucity of evidence for the changing of specifics in place-names is probably the fossilising effect on the nomenclature of the compilation of Domesday Book.

Even though I certainly do not look upon the presence of late forms of personal names in the Scandinavian settlement names in Yorkshire as evidence that these settlements were founded as late as in the eleventh century, I have to admit that the names are unlikely to have taken the forms they display in

---

[72] K. Cameron, *The Place-Names of Derbyshire*, 3 vols, English Place-Name Society 27–9 (1959), pp. 335–6.
[73] A. Mawer, *The Place-Names of Northumberland and Durham* (Cambridge, 1920), p. 153.
[74] G. Fellows-Jensen, *Scandinavian Settlement Names in the North-West*, Navnestudier 25 (Copenhagen, 1985), pp. 26, 189, 63.
[75] Fellows-Jensen, *Scandinavian Settlement Names*, pp. 21–4.

Domesday Book earlier than about the year 1000. This implies that many of the other Scandinavian place-names in the county may also not have received their lasting form until this late date, even when there is nothing about their phonological or lexical content to necessitate such an assumption. In the light of this realisation, I am obliged to confess both that the scepticism with which I once viewed Peter Sawyer's opinion on the date of the coining of the place-names in -bý was unwarranted and that there is still much that we do not understand about the significance of the Scandinavian settlement names in England.

A DOMESDAY POSTSCRIPT AND
THE EARLIEST SURVIVING PIPE ROLL

Alexander R. Rumble

Some forty years after the suspension of work on the primary text of Great Domesday Book, a brief summary of the constituents of the fief of Robert de Bruce I, created by Henry I, was added to its Yorkshire folios.[1] The orthography of the place-name forms in this document was carefully analysed by Gillian Fellows Jensen in 1970, while the text as a whole has lately been discussed in detail by the county editors of the Phillimore edition of Domesday Book.[2] The present note attempts to add a palaeographical dimension to our appreciation of this Domesday postscript, a consideration of its external features having been omitted from the author's recent publications on Domesday palaeography.[3]

The addition to Great Domesday Book of details concerning this Yorkshire fief is datable to after 17 May 1103 and probably to 1120 × 1129.[4] The text lists the number of carucates and/or bovates at each place belonging to the fief in the

---

[1] GDB (London, PRO, E 31/2), fos 332v–333r. Work on entering the edited version of the Domesday returns into this volume came to a halt either soon after the death of William I on 9 September 1087 or with the exile of William of Saint-Calais, bishop of Durham, in 1088. See A. R. Rumble, 'The palaeography of the Domesday manuscripts' in *Domesday Book: A Reassessment*, ed. P. Sawyer (London, 1985), pp. 28–49, at 46–7; and P. Chaplais, 'William of Saint-Calais and the Domesday survey' in *Domesday Studies*, ed. J. C. Holt (Woodbridge, 1987), pp. 65–77, at 77.
[2] 'The Domesday Book account of the Bruce fief', *Journal of the English Place-Name Society* 2 (1969–70), pp. 8–17; *Domesday Book*, gen. ed. J. Morris, vol. 30, *Yorkshire*, ed. M. L. Faull and M. Stinson (2 parts, Chichester, 1986), notes on Robert of Brus and on ch. 31.
[3] 'The palaeography of the Domesday manuscripts' (see above, n.1); 'The Domesday manuscripts: scribes and scriptoria' in *Domesday Studies*, ed. J. C. Holt, pp. 79–99; and 'Methods of textual abbreviation in Great Domesday Book', Appendix II of the Alecto Facsimile Edition, ed. A. Williams (London, 1987).
[4] It is certainly later than *Regesta Regum Anglo-Normannorum 1066–1154*, vol. 2, *Regesta Henrici Primi 1100–1135*, ed. C. Johnson and H. A. Cronne, (Oxford, 1956), no. 648, to which it refers (see below). It seems also to be later than the death of Nigel Fossard c.1120, since it refers to the lands of his son Robert, but earlier than the addition to the fief, by 1129, of lands previously held by Richard Surdeval from the count of Mortain, see Fellows Jensen, 'The Domesday Book account of the Bruce fief', p. 9; W. Farrer, *Early Yorkshire Charters*, vol. 2 (Edinburgh, 1915), pp. v–vi, 11–12, 16, 327; and I. J. Sanders, *English Baronies* (Oxford, 1960), p. 66. It is also earlier than Robert de Bruce's foundation of Guisborough Priory (?1129), cf. *Regesta*, vol. 2, 1582; Farrer, ibid. no. 671. Note that both Fellows Jensen and Farrer misdate *Regesta*, vol. 2, 648 to Whitsuntide 1107.

East, West and North Ridings of Yorkshire in turn; a further paragraph at the end relates specifically to an exchange made with the king on 17 May 1103 concerning lands in the North and East Ridings.[5] The character of the text is reminiscent of the abbreviated entries in the so-called Yorkshire Summary,[6] although that document is thought to pre-date the Domesday Survey in composition; both were probably first composed by local agents of the king in Yorkshire and were intended as a guide to future taxation assessment.[7]

The text of the description of the Bruce fief consists of 80 written lines added as a postscript to previously blank pages at the end of the Yorkshire Domesday survey in Great Domesday Book.[8] The writing occupies two columns (each of 35 lines) on fo. 332v, and 10 lines of a left-hand column on fo. 333r. An *ad hoc* horizontal ruling, with c.8 mm. between the lines, has been added to guide the writing. There are no page-headings and no form of rubrication.

Most of the text is written in a fairly formal documentary version of protogothic minuscule script of s.xii[1] (see Plate 1). Rustic capitals are used, however, not only for the initial letter of names and of clauses but also to highlight a few parts of the text. Thus they occur in the first three words (HIC EST FEVDVM fo. 332v, col. 1, line 1) and in two of the Riding-headings (IN WESTREDINC ibid. line 26; IN NORTREDING 332v, col. 2, line 5).[9] Elsewhere, they are only found in the name of the important soke-centre of Burton Agnes (BORTONA 332v, col. 1, line 4) and twice in the name of Harpham (HARPEIN ibid. line 6 and 333r, line 4); in the latter they serve to highlight the paragraph containing detailed additional statistics concerning Harpham and other places (in both the East and North Ridings) which were the subject of the exchange of 1103 (see above).

The writing is bold, well spaced, and inscribed with a thick nib. It is the fluent hand of a professional scribe used to writing at speed without any loss of legibility. Quickness is reflected by the fact that final upstrokes on letters are often exaggerated in length, and by the presence of some overlapping joins on curved letters (for example, at the top of the bowls of **a** and **d** or at the top or bottom of **B, C, D,** and **O**) and at the meeting of the bar of **t** with its stem. The ascenders of **b, h, l** and the ascending stems of **H** (uncial), **I, L,** and **N** are normally notched at the top; however, the top of *b* in *Vsebruna* (332v, col. 1, line 28) and of *l* in *Laclum* (333r, line 10) are completed by a transverse hairline. The bottoms of

---

[5]   *Regesta*, vol. 2, 648. Note however that in this notification of the exchange the number of bovates stated to be at Lealholm is 16, while in the Domesday postscript it is 10; likewise, the total number of carucates at Eskdale is given as 12 in the notification (*recte* 13) while in the Domesday postscript it is 12 carucates, 2 bovates.

[6]   It is especially similar to the summary of Count Alan's lands which is arranged by landholder rather than by Yorkshire wapentake, see *GDB*, fo. 381r; ed. Faull and Stinson, section SN, CtA.

[7]   For the whole Summary, see *GDB*, fos 379–382r; ed. Faull and Stinson, sections SN, SW, SE and Appendix 5; also S. P. J. Harvey, 'Domesday Book and Anglo-Norman governance', *TRHS*, 5th series, 25 (1975), pp. 175–93, at 177–8.

[8]   For the codicological context of fos 332v–333r, see *Domesday Re-Bound* (London, PRO, 1954), Appendix IA.

[9]   But not in *In Oustredinc* 332v, col. 1, line 4.

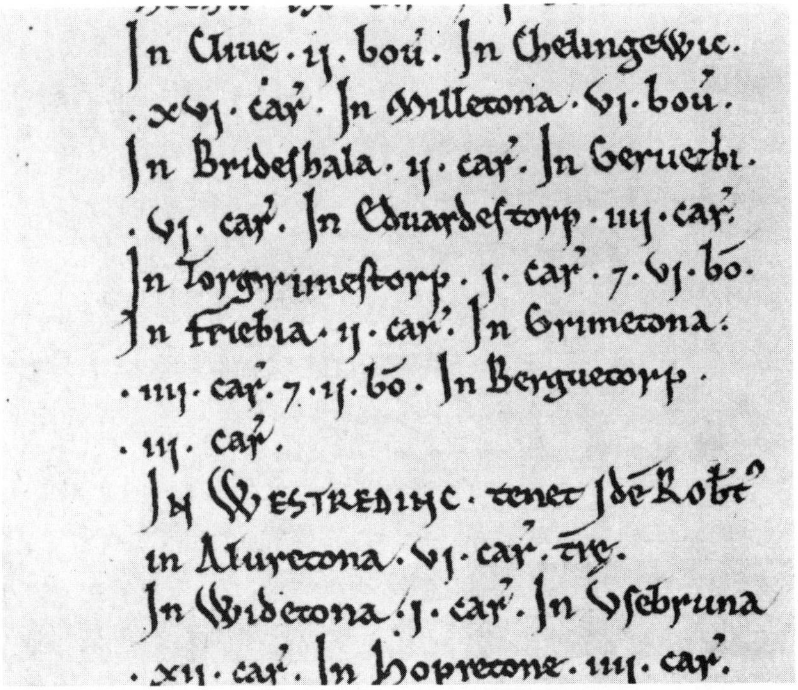

Plate 1. Great Domesday Book, fo. 332v, col. 1, lines 18–29. The description of the Bruce fief. *Reproduced by permission of Alecto Historical Editions*

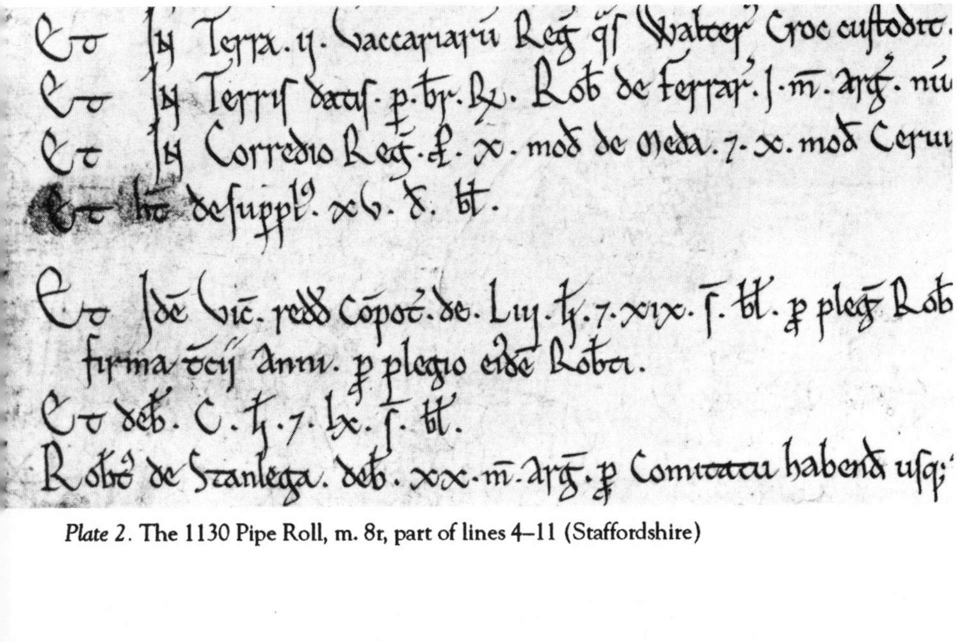

Plate 2. The 1130 Pipe Roll, m. 8r, part of lines 4–11 (Staffordshire)

minims are finished off by the addition of a long oblique serif which rises to the right. The letters **f**, **r**, and **s** are usually long; their descenders, as well as those of **p**, **q** and **I** (long), curve to the left. The following individual letters have characteristic forms:

a is nearly always in the caroline minuscule shape but a simple triangular form also occurs (for example, the final letter of *Danebia* 333r, line 8). In both varieties a very marked feature is the long upward finishing stroke, particularly noticeable at the end of a word. There is a single occurrence of high initial a (*alia* 332v, col. 2, line 11).

d is always round-backed and its long ascender curls to the right at the top.

e has a long protruding tongue, particularly noticeable at the end of a word.

g leans forward, has a pointed top to its bowl and a descender which is usually closed by a hairline rising at 45°.

ę has a narrow, ovoid spur (for example, *terrę* 332v, col. 1, line 27).

B is constructed from two unequal lobes, the upper one narrower than the one below.

E occurs both in a rustic capital form and in an enlarged minuscule shape, the latter one complete with protruding tongue.

F is a rustic capital form, with its top bar extended forwards into an upward-rising ribbon (FEVDVM ibid. line 1; *Foxtun* 332v, col. 2, line 16).

G is 6-shaped.

M is an angular uncial form (*Milletona* 332v, col. 1, line 19; *Morhusum* 332v, col. 2, line 30).

N is a rustic capital form; it has a large foot at the base of its left vertical and a long descender to its right vertical; the cross-piece descends obliquely from left to right.

O is a pointed oval.

R has a narrow head and a prominent foot on its left leg.

S leans backwards and is constructed from two opposed semi-circles, one placed above the other.

T has a cross-bar whose right arm curves upwards.

The only display capital is **H**, the first letter of the text, which is two lines high. There are several instances of the ligature of **s** + **t** but no opportunity occurs for the use of a ligature of **c** + **t**. The 2-shaped form of **r**, usually found at this time after o, is avoided. In roman numerals i-*longa* is used for *i*, as well as for the last minim of larger numbers.

The word *et* is nearly always represented by the tironian nota, which has a straight bar and a long thin descender which is drawn at an angle of 45°; on occasions, this descender was at first made shorter than usual but was then extended by the addition of a further stroke (332v, col. 1, lines 14 and 30). The ampersand is used only for the first occurrence of *et* in the text (ibid. line 4). The abbreviation for the final syllable -*bus* is the letter *b* followed by a jagged diagonal line (*duabus* ibid. line 10 and 333r, line 9).[10] Other abbreviations to be noted are ħ for *hoc* (332v, interlined between lines 8 and 9); *s;* for *sed* (ibid. line 14); *scilic[7]* for *scilicet* (333r, line 8); and either *bõ* or *bou[7]* for *bouate.* Suprascript a is open-topped (*postquam* 332v, col. 1, line 2). The overline is commonly either 7-shaped or in the form of a long diagonal.[11]

The most frequent mark of punctuation is the single point; this occurs between clauses and also on either side of numerals. The *punctus elevatus* also appears (ibid. line 9). A single hyphen, rising from left to right, is used to indicate run-overs at the end of a line. There is some offsetting of the initial letter of *In* (ibid. line 30; 332v, col. 2, lines 5, 7, 9, 11, 13, 27; 332r, line 2); this feature may be intended to mark some fiscal sub-divisions of the fief, but this is not certain. A single example of the *paragraphos* occurs (ibid. line 4), before the additional information concerning the exchange of Harpham, etc. (see above).

Orthographic conventions in the name-forms of the text include Anglo-Norman *ch* for *k* (*Haschetorp* = Haisthorpe, 332v, col. 1, line 7; *Buschebia* = Little Busby, 332v, col. 2, line 15) and *z* for *ts* < *ds* (*Geruezbi* = Garrowby Hall 332v, col. 1, line 20; *Tormozbia* = Thornaby, 332v, col. 2, line 17).[12] The form *Rotbertus*, etc. (five occurrences) is also favoured as against *Robertus* (once). It is not certain, however, whether these and the many other spelling conventions which were analysed by Fellows Jensen were the ones normally used by the scribe or were those of his source(s).[13] The frequent addition of Latin endings to vernacular place-name forms in this text is similar to the convention found in Little Domesday Book and the Exon Domesday and may point to the use of a now-lost provincial Domesday document as the source for place-name forms,[14] but it should be remembered that this was also a common feature of most twelfth-century documents.

Two copying-errors which may probably be attributed to the scribe of the Bruce fief, rather than to his source(s), are *Gerou* for *Geron* (ibid. line 8) and *Galmetona* for *Galmetorp* (ibid. lines 34–5).[15]

Some of the palaeographical features of the scribe of the Bruce fief are similar to those of Scribe A of Great Domesday Book.[16] These include the form of r

---

[10] See Chaplais, 'William of Saint-Calais and the Domesday survey', plate IIIh.

[11] The generic term 'overline' is used here to refer to the basic abbreviation-mark added above a letter to signify the omission of an unspecified letter or letters at that point in a word.

[12] Cf. A. H. Smith, *The Place-Names of the East Riding of Yorkshire and York*, English Place-Name Society 14 (Cambridge, 1937), pp. 89 (Haisthorpe), 130 (Garrowby); and idem, *The Place-Names of the North Riding of Yorkshire*, English Place-Name Society 5 (Cambridge, 1928), pp. 169 (Little Busby), 172 (Thornaby); also G. Fellows Jensen, *Scandinavian Personal Names in Lincolnshire and Yorkshire* (Copenhagen, 1968), sections 126 and 105, 107, respectively.

[13] 'The Domesday Book account of the Bruce fief' (as above, n. 2), *passim.*

[14] Ibid. pp. 13–17.

[15] DB, ed. Faull and Stinson, notes to 31N2 and 31N8.

[16] For descriptions of Scribe A's handwriting, see Rumble, 'The Domesday manuscripts: scribes and scriptoria', pp. 82–5 and plate Va; and Chaplais, 'William of Saint-Calais and the Domesday survey', pp. 72–3 and plates IIIc–g, IVb.

(with descender), ȩ, F, G, I (long), M, T; the avoidance of 2-shaped r; the transverse line sometimes added to ascenders of b and l; the nota for et (with straight bar); and the abbreviations for hoc, sed and -bus.[17] Such features seem, however, to be naturally executed by the scribe of the Bruce fief and may have been due to his training in a writing-office influenced by Scribe A, rather than being directly imitative of the latter's work in Great Domesday Book itself.

The occasional use of the abbreviation bó for bouate, which is the form used in the Yorkshire Summary but which is rare elsewhere in the Yorkshire survey in Great Domesday Book, may have been carried over in copying from a local draft of the Bruce fief text.

At the time that the description of the Bruce fief was added to Great Domesday Book, the latter was normally kept in the royal treasury at Winchester, which by 1135 was located in the castle.[18] The first sentence of the text refers to Domesday Book as liber de Wintonia. It is very probable that the only individual who would have been allowed to add new information to the Domesday volumes was the treasurer's scribe. In this context, it is significant to note the similarities between the handwriting in the Bruce fief and that of the main scribe of the earliest surviving royal Pipe Roll, that for 1130 [31 Henry I] (see Plate 2), who has tentatively been identified as the treasurer's clerk.[19] Although there is a marked difference in the width of the nib used in each of these documents, and perhaps a few years' gap between their inscription, there are so many identical letter-forms and such a great similarity in the duct of the writing that it is virtually certain that both are the work of the same scribe. Particularly to be noted are the following comparable features: the exaggerated final upstrokes on letters (especially on final a, on the enlarged minuscule form of E, and on minims); the overlapping joins on letters (particularly on the bowls of a and d, and at the top of the stem of t); the treatment of ascenders and descenders (see above); the letters d, e, g, r, ȩ, B, E (enlarged minuscule), F, N, O, R, S, T; the use of i-longa for the numeral i; the usual avoidance of 2-shaped r; the shape of the tironian nota for et; the abbreviations for -bus and sed; and the use of a long rising overline.

If it is accepted that the scribe of the Bruce fief was also the main scribe of the 1130 Pipe Roll, then this adds a further detail to the career of the royal scribe whom T. A. M. Bishop designated as scriptor viii in his study of the palaeo-

---

[17] On the latter abbreviation, see Chaplais, ibid. pp. 72 foll. Note however that the sign as used in the description of the Bruce fief is rather shorter and less slanted than that of Scribe A, cf. Chaplais, ibid. plate IIIh; it may merely be an independent development from the abbreviation -b; rather than an imitation of Scribe A's own symbol.

[18] E. M. Hallam, Domesday Book through Nine Centuries (London, 1986), p. 34; F. Barlow, M. Biddle, O. von Feilitzen, D. J. Keene, Winchester in the Early Middle Ages, Winchester Studies 1, ed. M. Biddle (Oxford, 1976), pp. 304–5. Cf. Regesta, vol. 2, 1000, 1500, 1515. On the office of treasurer at this time, see C. Warren Hollister, 'The origins of the English treasury', EHR 92 (1978), pp. 262–75.

[19] London, PRO, E 372/1. For a preliminary description of the hands in the roll, see J. A. Green, The Government of England under Henry I (Cambridge, 1986), pp. 52–3.

graphy of early twelfth-century royal charters.[20] Besides the 1130 Pipe Roll, Bishop identified the work of **scriptor viii** in charters issued by Henry I in favour of the following beneficiaries: the abbot of Jumièges (dated at Westminster, 1105 × 1107); Miles of Gloucester (at Winchester, 1121); Walter of Gloucester (at Cheddar, 1121); the abbot of Ramsey (at Woodstock, 1115 × 1122, ?1121); the bishop of Lincoln (at Guildford, 1120 × 1122, ?1121); St Paul's, London (at Woodstock, 1107 × 1127); and Holy Trinity, Aldgate, London (at Winchester, 1123 × 1129, ?1127).[21] He also wrote a charter of Queen Matilda in favour of the church of Durham (dated at Windsor, 1107 × 1116).[22] Most of these documents were probably written while **scriptor viii** was a member of the itinerant royal household, presumably while on the immediate staff of the chancellor. The charter in favour of Holy Trinity, Aldgate, dated at Winchester, may however have been written as part of treasury business,[23] as indeed was the Pipe Roll, and, it is here suggested, the description of the Bruce fief. The scribe appears to have been one who retired from the itinerant royal secretariat to become stationed at the treasury in Winchester at some time in the later 1120s.[24] Although his name is not known, his career provides an interesting sidelight on the organization of royal writing-services in the reign of Henry I. We do not know how typical his career was, but its course suggests a continuing close connection between the staff of the itinerant household and that of the treasury. If he both added the description of the Bruce fief to Great Domesday Book and wrote most of the 1130 Pipe Roll, he also represents a human link between two financial documents which are of supreme importance for the administrative history of Anglo-Norman England.[25] If, indeed, this writer were the treasurer's scribe he was in a position to influence the external characteristics of the Pipe Rolls in their infancy, and it is possible that his first-hand acquaintance with Great Domesday Book may have had some effect on the general palaeographical features of the new royal financial record. There is, for example, a basic similarity of physical arrangement by local administrative unit in both Great Domesday Book and the Pipe Rolls. In the former, such units are represented by county textual booklets and in the latter by county or shrieval 'pipes' or rotulets;[26] both types of unit are capable of being of any length and of being placed in any order; both types are ideally suited to a national financial summary which is constructed from a number of individual textual sub-sections of varying size. There is also the fact

[20] *Scriptores Regis : Facsimiles to Identify and Illustrate the Hands of Royal Scribes in Original Charters of Henry I, Stephen, and Henry II* (Oxford, 1961), pp. 28–9 and plate XIIIa.
[21] *Scriptores Regis* S50, 679, 411, 356, 469, 250, 515, 443; *Regesta*, vol. 2, 842, 1280, 1268, 1262, 1254, 1531, 1514. See also Green, *Government of England*, p. 30.
[22] *Scriptores Regis* S15; *Regesta*, vol. 2, 1143.
[23] Green, *Government of England*, p. 30.
[24] Ibid.; *Scriptores Regis*, pp. 28–9.
[25] For fiscal comparisons between the two documents, see J. Green, 'William Rufus, Henry I and the Royal Demesne', *History* 64 (1979), pp. 337–52.
[26] Rumble, 'The palaeography of the Domesday manuscripts', pp. 28–9, 34–40; R. L. Poole, *The Exchequer in the Twelfth Century* (Oxford, 1912), pp. 150–1; and Green, *Government of England*, p. 55.

that the inscription of the final version in each case was almost all effected by a single skilled scribe.[27] This feature would have given added authenticity to (the greater part of) the text since unauthorized additions should have been easily discovered. Such a feature would have helped the convention of the use of a distinctive script for the Pipe Rolls that soon developed and which continued, in an increasingly artificial form, until the eighteenth century.[28]

It has been shown elsewhere that the text of Great Domesday Book (and, to a lesser extent, of Little Domesday Book) has had a continuous history of consultation for one purpose or another since its inscription.[29] Its reputation as a document has been owed not only to the magnitude of its conception but also to its unbroken custody as a public record; its mystique has also been helped by the monumentality of its external appearance. It is possible that certain of its external characteristics were deliberately copied when the question of the arrangement of the Pipe Rolls was first discussed and likely that the scribe of the earliest surviving Pipe Roll had first-hand knowledge of Great Domesday Book, having himself added a postscript to it. If so, this would represent a long-lasting and basic way in which the senior record of the Anglo-Norman treasury influenced some of its junior companions in the royal financial archives.

---

[27] Rumble, 'The Domesday manuscripts: scribes and scriptoria', p. 81; Green, *Government of England*, pp. 52–3.

[28] See L. C. Hector, *The Handwriting of English Documents*, 2nd edn, (London, 1966), p. 66 and plate XXIa (1628 Pipe Roll); also C. Johnson and H. Jenkinson, *English Court Hand A.D. 1066 to 1500, Illustrated Chiefly from the Public Records*, 2 vols (Oxford, 1915), vol. 2, plates V (1156 Pipe Roll), VIII (1167), XI (1214), XVI (1256), XXVI (1346). Note also that exemplifications of entries from Domesday Book were usually written in an imitative script from the 1470s, see Hallam, *Domesday Book through Nine Centuries*, pp. 60–1 and plates 30–1.

[29] Hallam, ibid. chapters 2–6.

NORSE SETTLEMENT IN THE HEBRIDES:
WHAT HAPPENED TO THE NATIVES
AND WHAT HAPPENED TO THE NORSE IMMIGRANTS?

Per Sveaas Andersen

On 26 April 1915 D. J. MacLeod, inspector of schools in the island of Lewis of the Outer Hebrides, was visiting the school of Valtos, a windswept village on the west coast facing the Atlantic. During the visit the headmaster of the school drew his attention to 'certain articles of brass and bronze' which some of the school children had recently unearthed from a small sand mound. About 150 yards from the school in a patch of sandy soil a boy had noticed a bone sticking out of the ground, and together with his friends he started digging and made one of the more exquisite Viking-age finds in Scotland.[1] The objects belonged to a woman's grave and consisted of a pair of tortoise brooches of an early Norse type,[2] a circular bronze brooch, ornamented in Celtic style, and with a setting for amber or a stone in the middle, a bronze belt-buckle, a penannular brooch, a bronze chain, an oblong bead of reddish-brown amber, and some remains of iron objects. The Valton find clearly evinces the mingling of Norse and Celtic cultural influences and has been dated to the second half of the ninth century.[3] At the same time this grave of an immigrant woman from the north raises the question whether the meeting between the native Hebrideans (Picts and Dalriadic Scots) and the Norse was peaceful or violent; and, if more or less peaceful, whether there occurred an integration process between the two peoples. These two questions call for some additional information: When did the settlement take place? What would be the conditions of the native population at the time of the Norse immigration? What would be the extent of the Norse settlement in its primary and secondary phases? And finally, what happened politically to these habitations and tunships throughout the early and high Middle Ages?

It is obviously a well-nigh impossible task to penetrate the historical mist which enshrouds these western Scottish islands during the Middle Ages. From neighbouring regions, the Scottish mainland littoral, the Northern Isles of Orkney and Shetland, the Isle of Man and coastal Ireland, however, some con-

---

[1] PSAS 50 (1916), pp. 181 f.
[2] O. Rygh, *Norske Oldsager* (Christiania/Oslo, 1885), 647.
[3] H. Shetelig, 'The Viking Graves in Great Britain and Ireland', *Acta Archaeologica* 16 (1945), pp. 9, 49.

temporary information may be gleaned. References to Norse immigrants into and emigrants from the Hebrides may also be found in Icelandic medieval literature – *Landnámabók*, some of the family sagas (*Njál's saga*, *Eyrbyggja saga* and *Laxdæla saga*). The *Orkneyinga saga*, *Heinskringla*, and *Hákonar saga Hákonarsonar* throw a few gleams of light on the Hebridean scene in the eleventh, twelfth and thirteenth centuries. Nevertheless the written sources are quite insufficient for the reconstruction of the main outlines of Hebridean political history. Fortunately other categories of source material – environmental sources, archaeological material, and place- and personal names in combination with the fragmentary written sources enable the historian to recreate certain aspects of Hebridean social and cultural history during the Norse period.

There seems to be a general agreement among scholars about the scale and extent of the Norse land-taking in North-western Scotland. It varied from a large-scale initial settlement in the northern Hebrides to a more shortlived and less extensive immigration into the southern isles. At the same time in modern research, especially in place-names studies, there is a growing realization of a certain and not insignificant immigration into the western mainland littoral of Scotland. The real difference and the more heated debate between Scottish scholars, however, have been concerned with the *encounter* problem. What happened to the native population as a result of the Norse invasion and settlement in Scotland? The two main views in this debate are respresented by two archaeologists – Iain A. Crawford and Anna Ritchie. According to Ritchie 'there can be no doubt that some forms of social integration between Pict and Norseman existed at least in the ninth century and probably into the tenth century [in Orkney]',[4] whereas Crawford vehemently asserts that the Norse colonization in the ninth century 'was sudden and totally obliterative in terms of local material culture'. On the basis of his Udal site excavation (North Uist) he is convinced that 'the message is one of compulsive dispossession or expulsion' of the natives.[5] There remains, however, an indisputable fact, which no historian can disregard: During the late Middle Ages the Hebrides were Gaelic-speaking, although with certain dialect peculiarities, most likely as a result of influence from Old Norse.[6] So far no historical monograph has been written on the Norse period (800–1266) in the Hebrides. This does not imply, however, that the study of the western islands of Scotland during the Middle Ages has been neglected, but that research has been concentrated on certain localities – islands and parts of islands and carried out by place-name researchers, archaeologists and other specialists.[7]

---

[4]   A. Ritchie, 'Excavation of Pictish and Viking-age farmsteads at Buckquoy, Orkney', *PSAS* 108 (1976–7), p. 192.
[5]   I. A. Crawford, 'War or Peace – Viking colonisation in the Northern and Western Isles of Scotland reviewed', *Proceedings of the Eighth Viking Congress* (1981), p. 267.
[6]   C. H. Borgstrøm, 'The Dialects of the Outer Hebrides', *NTS*, Supplementary vol. 1 (1940); 'The Dialects of Skye and Rosshire', *NTS*, Supplementary vol. 2 (1941); M. Oftedal, 'The Gaelic of Leurbost, Isle of Lewis', *NTS*, Supplementary vol. 4 (1956).
[7]   A. W. Brøgger, *Ancient Emigrants* (Oxford, 1929); H. Shetelig, 'Vikingeminner i Vest-Europa', *Instituttet for sammenlignende kulturforskning*, serie A – forelesninger 14 (Oslo,

There seems to be considerable agreement about the date of the Norse invasion both of the Western Isles and the western mainland littoral. Nor have great divergences arisen from the discussions about the actual landtaking or settlement in these regions of Scotland. The invasion of the Norsemen from the sea must have taken place during the decades before and after AD 800. The original raiders fairly soon and perhaps in the course of a few decades more or less changed the sword for the plough or the spade and became farmers (and fishermen) in these islands, evidently without relinquishing inveterate raiding habits. The settlement process belongs to the ninth century and was possibly terminated before 870, when a new wave of emigration from Norway, the western isles of Scotland, and most likely from other Viking settlement areas in the British Isles and Ireland started for the islands in the Atlantic Ocean, and primarily for Iceland.

From Lewis in the North to Arran in the South between thirty and forty grave-finds have so far been registered by laymen and archaeologists. The graves, and especially their contents, leave no doubt as to their Scandinavian character. Although the number of graves may not seem impressive, it probably only represents a fraction of the total number of pagan Norse graves in this region. From North Uist and the neighbouring isles members of the Mackenzie family during the period 1880–1934 collected a great amount of artifacts from house-sites and graves. Most of these items have an indisputable provenance in the Viking period.[8] The general chronology of the Norse graves found in the Hebrides seems to indicate that the first Norse interments took place during the second half of the ninth century. Another certain indicator of permanent settlement is the relatively great number of female graves found. Characteristic of the artifacts from these graves, are the pair of tortoise brooches. Of the thirty-two graves in which the sex of the interred could be decided, fourteen were female graves. Even at the distant island group of St Kilda, approximately forty miles west of North Uist, a pair of tortoise brooches bear witness to the sometime presence of a Norse woman in these rugged isles.[9]

1933); S. Grieg, 'Viking Antiquities in Scotland', in H. Shetelig, ed., Viking Antiquities in Great Britain and Ireland, part 2 (Oslo, 1940); M. Oftedal, 'The village names of Lewis in the Outer Hebrides', NTS 17 (1954); A. C. O'Dell and K. Walton, The Highlands and Islands of Scotland (London, 1962); B. Gordon, 'Some Norse Place-Names in Trotternish, Isle of Skye', Scottish Gaelic Studies 10 (1963), pp. 82–112; I. A. Crawford, 'Scot (?), Norseman and Gael', Scottish Archaeological Forum 6 (1974), pp. 1–16; J. A. Graham-Campbell, 'The Viking-age silver and gold hoards of Scandinavian character from Scotland', PSAS 107 (1975–6), 114–35; A. MacLaren, 'A Norse House on Drimore Machair, South Uist', Glasgow Archaeological Journal 3 (1974), pp. 9–18; W. F. H. Nicolaisen, Scottish Place-Names. Their Study and Significance (London, 1976); id., 'The Viking Settlement of Scotland: the place-name evidence', in R. T. Farrell, ed., The Vikings (London, 1982), pp. 95–115; A. Small, 'Norse Settlement in Skye', in R. Boyer, ed., Les Vikings et leur civilisation: problèmes actuels (1976), pp. 29–37; D. M. Wilson, 'Scandinavian Settlement in the North and West of the British Isles – an archaeological point of view', TRHS, 5th series, 26 (1976), pp. 95–113.
8   J. Close-Brooks and S. Maxwell, 'The Mackenzie Collection', PSAS 105 (1972–4).
9   A. B. Taylor, 'The Norsemen in St. Kilda', Saga-Book 17 (1967–8), pp. 116–44.

The geographical distribution of the grave-finds in the Hebrides does not point out any main concentration of the Norse settlement. And the dating of the different graves makes it impossible to indicate a chronological progression of the settlement from north to south. Furthermore, little is known about Norse settlement conditions during the ninth and tenth centuries. However, a few investigations of Norse sites have been carried out by archaeologists since the Second World War. The two more interesting were the excavations undertaken by A. MacLaren on Drimore Machair, South Uist, in 1956[10] and by I. A. Crawford at Udal, North Uist, throughout more than ten years and concluded in 1976.[11] Firstly these excavations show that the Norse immigrants did nor arrive in an uninhabited archipelago, and secondly that they were attracted by the same soil which was the main subsistence basis of the native Picts and Gaels – the so-called *machair*, a Gaelic word for the flat or low-lying coastal strip of arable land, chiefly consisting of shell sand and therefore easily tillable, selfdraining and quite fertile. Is it possible to consider this location of the Norse settlements along the western coastal littoral of the Outer Hebrides and some of the coastal fringes of the inner isles as indicating that the primary activity of the Norse must have been agriculture? And were the stability and continuity of settlement dependent on agricultural resources? The location of thirty-one of the Norse grave-finds in areas with agricultural potential seems to support the theory of a settlement type of predominantly agricultural character. But it is always important to bear in mind other subsistence factors which are difficult to quantify: What part did the resources from the sea and the cliffs play in the daily economy of the settlers? The geographer A. Small is probably right when he maintains that the extent and scale of the Norse settlement would be dependent on soil and tillage conditions in the areas invaded.[12] And Small draws our attention to what may be considered the main problem in the study of the Viking-age settlement in these islands (and in all Scandinavian-settled regions of Great Britain): to what extent can the place-names put us in a position to localise and quantify the immigrant population? He is optimistic as to the possibility of localising the Norse settlements, but is more cautious with respect to methods of quantifying the number of immigrants arriving from the North during the Viking period. 'One aspect where place-names are important, is in indicating the local areas settled by the Norse. For example, in Barvas parish [Lewis] there is a very high density of Norse place-names, whereas in the island of Jura there are very few. Parts of Barvas are very well suited to agricultural settlement, whereas there is very little cultivable land in Jura'.[13]

The old place-names of the Hebridean landscape are undoubtedly the only

---

10 MacLaren, 'A Norse House on Drimore Machair'.
11 Crawford, 'War or Peace'.
12 A. Small, 'The Viking Highlands – a geographical view' in E. Meldrum (ed.), *The Dark Ages in the Highlands: 95th Anniversary Conference of the Inverness Field Club* (1971) (1972), pp. 69–90; L. Scott, 'The Norse in the Hebrides', in (*Proceedings of the First*) *Viking Congress, Lerwick, July 1950*, Aberdeen University Studies 132 (1954), pp. 189–215.
13 Small, 'The Viking Highlands', p. 81.

substantial source material available for the study of early settlement and its development in a locality or a district and thus for the whole archipelago. At the same time their composite ethnical background does imply different and difficult problems, which frequently have proved insurmountable even to Gaelic-Norse philologists. As already mentioned above, Small accepts place-names as a means of localising Norse settlement in certain areas, but he has no comments on the implications of an absence of Norse names in a nearby district. Such an absence should not necessarily be taken to signify that immigration did not take place in such areas. The absence of Norse place-names in regions of the Hebrides, where such toponymy might be expected, may be explained in different ways: political changes in the Western Isles during the twelfth and thirteenth centuries, due to Scottish political pressure, and coupled with growing influence from the Irish church, may account for the decline of the Norse dialect in the isles. The establishment of Somerled's (ON *Sumarliði's*) kingdom about the middle of the twelfth century in the southern and Inner Hebrides, including his own territorial basis of Argyll, brought a stronger Gaelic-Irish influence to bear on the islands and may also explain the victorious advance of the Gaelic language throughout these parts of the archipelago. The transition from Norse to Gaelic seems to have taken its course at an accelerating pace throughout the twelfth century, and the cultural and linguistic transformation was carried further north to the outer isles during the thirteenth and fourteenth centuries. G. W. S. Barrow refers to 'a resurgence of Gaelic culture and an intensification of the old links with Ireland, . . .' And he looks upon the attempt to 'restore and revive the greatest Christian shrine of the west, Iona' as a clear indication of this process.[14] The slower progress of Gaelic culture and language in the Outer isles and in the region north of the Ardnamurchan Peninsula generally may be due to ethnic and political differences with deep roots in the Hebridean past. Whereas, on the eve of the Norse invasion, the greater part of the native population of the North seems to have been Picts, interspersed with some pockets of Gaelic-Irish monks and priests, the southern region with the adjacent mainland littoral was inhabited by Gaelic-spealing people with Irish background. The southern Hebrides had been invaded during the late fifth and early sixth centuries by an Irish tribe, the Scots. And the Irish tribal king of the Scots moved his seat to Argyll, and thus the kingdom of Dalriada was established. Its religious and cultural centre was St Columba's monastery on Iona after its foundation in 563. During the 730s and 740s this petty kingdom was almost on the verge of being conquered by the Picts from the East, but it survived the onslaught, and took the offensive against the Pictish kingdom in central and eastern Scotland during the late eighth and first half of the ninth centuries, leading to the unification of the two peoples c.843 by the Dalriadic Scottish king Kenneth macAlpin. It is difficult to assess the part played by the invading Norse in this unification process, but it cannot have been without significance. How the resources of the southern Hebrides were mustered for military operations in mainland Scotland, we do not know. What we may

[14] G. W. S. Barrow, *Kingship and Unity. Scotland 1000–1306* (London, 1981), p. 107.

establish with some certainty at the beginning of the ninth century, is the following: the southern Hebrides, including the Ardnamurchan Peninsula, constituted the island-part of the kingdom of Dalriada, whereas the northern region, although with a predominantly Pictish population did not seem to have any political unity and obviously was only loosely connected with the Pictish kingdom. St Columba's mission had undoubtedly been active among the Hebridean Picts from its very beginning. And monastic seats or stations have left a scatter of *papa*-names along the coasts of the northern Hebrides, either in the form of island names – Pabbay More & Beg (Lewis), Pabbay (Harris), Pabbay (two small islands, South Uist), Pabbay (Barra), Pabay (Skye), and habitation names – Bayble (ON *papa-býli*; Lewis), Paible (Harris), Paible (North Uist). Finally there is a single *dalr*-name – Papadil (Rhum). All these place-names have been coined by Norse settlers, living in the neighbourhood and probably after some time of permanent settlement. According to A. Macdonald '. . . *papar* was a colloquial blanket-term' and 'as a place-name [element] only applied to church sites of all kinds which had been (temporarily) abandoned . . . . When conditions became less turbulent [after the Norse immigration], they were reoccupied . . .'.[15]

The initial double question included in the title of this paper – what happened to the natives and what happened to the Norse immigrants during the Norse period – has now to be approached more closely. And I would like to propound a threefold hypothesis:

1. The native Pictish and Gaelic population did survive, but it was reduced to a minority and can hardly have composed a numerous element in the total population.

2. The Norse settlement had its centre of gravity in the North, but even the southern and Inner Hebrides had a considerable population of settlers with a Norse background.

3. The integration process was chiefly of cultural and linguistic character and took place among the settled population. It did *not* imply, at least not to a great extent, the immigration of more Gaelic-speaking people from Ireland and Scotland.

I. A. Crawford on the basis of his archaeological material does argue for the 'compulsive dispossession' or the 'expulsion' of the native population in the Outer Hebrides.[16] Archaeological sources, however, are usually insufficient for drawing such drastic conclusions. Most of the non-archaeological material leaves the door open for an interpretation of some survival of the natives. Above we have mentioned the *papa*-names, which clearly indicate that the Norse immigrants were in contact with Christian people (*papar*-priests) and not only with church structures (*kils*). Whether these *papar* were driven away or not, is an open question. If they were, the probability is that they fairly soon reoccupied their

[15] A. Macdonald, 'On "papar" names in N. and W. Scotland', *Northern Studies* 9 (1977), pp. 25–30.
[16] Crawford, 'War or Peace', p. 267.

seats and were permitted to carry on their Christian activity, possibly with some effects on the immigrant population. We should note that some of the Norse settlers from Ireland and the Hebrides were already Christian when they arrived in Iceland. In this connection we should not disregard the Gaelic personal-names among the immigrants in Iceland. But as most of these names are con-nected with Norse patronymics (*Konáll Ketilsson, Kýlan Kárason, Njáll Þorgeirsson,* etc.) we cannot establish a pure Gaelic ancestry. What we can say, is that their fathers, or mothers (or grandparents) must have been in rather close touch with Gaelic-speaking people in Ireland or the Hebrides during their stay there. In *Landnámabók* there is a reference to two immigrant brothers with Gaelic names coming directly from the Hebrides – *Kalman enn suðreyski* and his brother *Kýlan.* They may have had a Gaelic background from where they came.[17] Moreover, the author of *Orkneyinga saga* mentions Hebrideans with Gaelic names in the twelfth century – *Anakol*, 'a viking of good family', 'the foster-father of [Jarl] Erlend' (ch. 92), and *Dufgall Sumarliðison*, king in the *Suðreyjar* (ch. 100).

Finally imtermarriages between Gaels and Norse are known from the Irish annals; and there is a particular reference to a group or a host of men of a mixed Gaelic-Norse background – the *Gall-Gaedil*. In the Fragmentary Annals of Ire-land they are mentioned sub anno 856; their fleet was defeated by Áed, king of Ailech. It is tempting to assume that a great number of these vikings had been recruited in the Hebrides.[18]

Is it possible to maintain that the Norse settlement had its centre of gravity in the northern isles, and at the same time take the reservation that a considerable part of the population in the southern Hebrides seems to have had a Norse background? The distribution of habitative plave-names of Norse provenance may be a gateway to the problem. We should bear in mind, however, that they only leave us the later and present-day vestiges of what was once a more wide-spread Norse place-name flora. My presentation of Norse habitation names will to a great extent be based on the results arrived at by my former graduate student, cand.philol. David K. Olson, who in 1983 wrote a thesis on 'Norse settlement in the Hebrides, an interdisciplinary study'. He has selected five areas with rather heavy concentration of Norse and Gaelic-Norse place-names for a study of settlement conditions in depth: North Lewis from Tolsta on the east coast to Shader on the west coast, western Uig parish in Lewis, western Trotternish in Skye, The South Rhinns and the southwestern Oa of Islay. His platform of observation is the present-day toponomy, but he has of necessity made use of a wide range of sources – old rentals, early maps, soil and topographical material and a thin scatter of written sources. Having mapped all the settlement names of medieval and later provenance in the five districts mentioned above, Olson tries to evaluate the status of the farms as 'primary', 'secondary' and 'peripheral'.[19] For

---

[17] Landnámabók, ed. F. Jónsson (Copenhagen, 1925), pp. 42 f.
[18] B. E. Crawford, *Scandinavian Scotland* (Leicester, 1987), p. 47.
[19] Olson's criteria for evaluation are the quality of the soil (parent-material), approximate amount of arable land, rental value in the earliest rentals, distance of steading from the

our purpose it will be sufficient to present his discussion of three farm-name generics – the name-elements *-staðir*, *-bólstaðr* and *-setr*. Farm-names containing these generics are well represented in the Northern Isles of Scotland and are among the most numerous in Norway during the Viking period. In addition I would like to add a few words on the settlement-names in *-boer* (*-býr*) in order to recreate the more essential features in the quantitative distribution of Norse settlement-names in the Hebrides.

It might have been desirable to have included the Norse topographical settlement-names (Uig, Eyre, Dell, Haclete, Stromnish, Ildrigill, etc.) in this survey, but their inclusion would not to a significant degree change our impression of the overall distribution of Norse settlement-names.

W. F. H. Nicolaisen considers the generic *staðir* to be a place-name element 'productive in the naming of farms from the very beginning of Viking settlement' in the Hebrides; and he continues: 'There is little doubt that the *staðir*-map represents the extent of Scandinavian settlement within the first generation or two of settlers from Norway'.[20] His arguments for the early presence of *staðir*-names in the Hebrides seem to rest on the assumption that the majority of the recorded *staðir*-names, according to Nicolaisen twenty-five, are to be found from Skye and northwards, and that almost every *staðir*-farm had a coastal situation. Olson cannot subscribe to Nicolaisen's early dating of the *staðir*-names as a group. From his detailed study of the farm settlement areas in Lewis, Skye and Islay, comprising ten or one-third of his recorded thirty-two *staðir*-settlements, Olson comes to the conclusion that Nicolaisen's statement about the *staðir*-settlements' primary status cannot be sufficiently documented.[21] Moreover, he also draws our attention to the possibility of an earlier existence of a greater number of *staðir*-names in the southern Hebrides, especially in Islay. Among his ten *staðir*-settlements Olson only finds three farms worthy to be classified as 'primary' – Tolsta and Skigersta in Lewis and Monksta in Skye. Six are included in the class of 'secondary' farms, whereas Olistadh or Olista in Islay is the only one classified as 'peripheral'.[22] Besides the latter settlement-name he also points to the occurrence of this generic in Coll, Tiree, Morvern, the Ross of Mull and Islay, where Olson (in addition to Olista) on the basis of local pronunciation suggests that Ellister, Kelsay and Greamsa might have been *staðir*-names – *Eilifsstaðir* (?), *Kjólstaðir* (?) and *Grimsstaðir* (?).[23] Olson might also have added another possible *staðir*-name in the same district – Cultorsay. The first element is definitely Gaelic, whereas torsay is a corrupted Norse name, which may originally have had the form *þórs-* or *þorisstaðir*.

A closer study of the transformation of the generic *staðir* into Gaelic forms on

---

sea, the quality of the nearest harbour, proximity to traditional overland routes, possible connection with church or chapel.

[20] Nicolaisen, *Scottish Place Names*, p. 90.
[21] D. K. Olson, 'Norse Settlement in the Hebrides, an interdisciplinary study', Graduate thesis in History, University of Oslo (1983), pp. 226 f.
[22] ibid., p. 226.
[23] ibid., pp. 137, 141, 153.

Distribution of the ON generic
staðir (after D. K. Olson)

50 MILES

the basis of a registration of all possible name-forms in old rentals and on local maps might uncover further *staðir*-names in the southern archipelago.

In his discussion of the generic *setr*, Olson introduces it with a few comments on its Gaelic variant *airigh/airidh*. As a loan-word into Old Norse it is rendered *ærgi* (see *Orkneyinga saga* ch. 103). He finds it a productive settlement-name during the Norse period and also a difficult word for students interested in ascertaining 'the ethnic origin of the name-givers'.[24] The majority of the *ærgi*-names are to be found in two areas: the Outer Hebrides from North Uist south-ward and the Inner Hebrides from southern Skye to Kintyre and Arran. (But the spread of *ærgi-* (*erg-*, *ary-*) names does extend to Galloway, Cumbria, Lancashire, Cheshire and the Isle of Man and a scatter along the northwestern and northern littoral of mainland Scotland, Orkney and Shetland, even to the distant Faroes.)

The distribution of the *setr* generic in the Hebrides is essentially a northern phenomenon from Skye to the Butt of Lewis. It is usually found in the Gaelic form *shader*. In his five areas of investigation Olson has registered nine *setr*-names, and only the simplex *Shader* in Lewis is accepted as a primary settlement, a *setr*-farm. The remaining *setr*-settlements 'are rarely mentioned in the rentals; they generally lie on poor, peaty soil; only one of the 45 examples has a church of some antiquity. Their predominantly secondary and peripheral nature indicates a pastoral origin for the group as a whole'.[25] We might ask whether there should be a functional difference between the use of the generics in *ærgi* and those in *setr* (*shader*). But so far none has been found. The only conclusion which might be drawn with some certainty from the copious material, is that Norse settlers in the Hebrides also adopted a Gaelic word as a useful name in their shieling economy along with names in *setr*, which during the Viking period was most common in north-western Norway. It is also tempting to indicate that the Norse settlers in this region of Scotland not only accepted this Gaelic word as part of their Old Norse dialect, but after a while learned to speak the language of the remaining natives and thus for a period became bilingual.

One of the more interesting Norse generics in the Western Isles is *bólstaðr*, which the Gaelic language has transformed into a selection of name elements – *bost*, *bus*, *bol(l)*, *bolls*, *poll*, *pool*. Olson has listed 106 settlement names in his inventory of this class, also including the names found in the mainland littoral from Cape Wrath to Arran. This is a greater number than in any other Norse-speaking region, including Norway (approximately 90 names with the majority along the western coast). But he takes the reservation that some of the names may be derived from ON *ból*, which he rightly considers a synonym to *bólstaðr*.[26] Looking at the distribution of these place-names, it is of some interest to note the similarity with the spread of the *setr/ærgi* generic. Almost all the *-bost-* names are found in the northern Hebrides north of the Ardnamurchan Peninsula, whereas

[24] ibid., p. 209.
[25] ibid., p. 218.
[26] ibid., p. 236.

Distribution of the ON generics
setr and *ærgi*   (after D. K. Olson)

• setr
◇ ærgi

the -bus, -boll/-bolls, -pol/-poll, -pool-elements dominate in the southern archipelago, and with a concentration of -bus-names in Islay.

Olson has studied more closely nineteen bólstaðr settlements in his five areas in Lewis, Skye and Islay. They represent slightly more than twenty percent of the total number of bólstaðr names (106). According to his 'favorability factors',[27] six places have qualifications to be ranked as 'primary' settlements – Suaineabost and Kirkebost in Lewis, Skeabost and Hunebost in Skye, and Lurabus and Nereabols in Islay. Nine are supposed to be secondary settlements – Habost, Ulbost and Bosta in Lewis, Carbost, Prabost and Heribost in Skye, Cragabus, Asabus, and Kinabus in Islay. Only four farms are listed as 'peripheral' – Leabost in Skye and Bolsay, Risabus and Coilabus in Islay. Olson's general impression of the bólstaðr-group is that it is 'superior to the setr- group, when comparing location, geology and fiscal value'. He goes on to point out a peculiar aspect of the bólstaðr settlements – 'a large number of bólstaðr holdings, share common boundaries with other bólstaðr settlements . . . Suaineabost in Lewis abutting Habost, Skeabost bordering Carbost in Skye, and in Islay Asabus adjoining Kinnabus, as well as Lurabus bordering Cragabus'. Olson's explanation of this 'frequent contiguity is that bólstaðr may have meant a divided farm or a special section of a farm'. Finally he puts a most pertinent question: What would then have been 'the common word used for "farm" in the Hebrides during the Viking period and the years up to 1266?'[28] His answer, suggesting bólstaðr as such an appellative, is hardly acceptable. We shall return to this question below in connection with the discussion of the generic boer/býr.

Whether the compounded bólstaðr-names in their recorded forms can be said to have an entirely Norse etymology or not, has some bearing on one of our main problems, the integration process. It is conceivable that some were transformed into Gaelic-Norse hybrids, some were converted into pure Gaelic names, representing a translation of the Norse settlement names, and some farms received entirely new names, quite simply renamed by some Gaelic speakers. We do not know how many of the bólstaðr-names were replaced by Gaelic names (translated from Old Norse or renamed), but there is some documentation in the rentals of this change. Olson has given an example from Islay: Stanepolls (ON Steinaból-staðr) is supplanted by Bally-martin (Martin's farm) some time between 1507 and 1686.[29] The use of the bally (baile) generic with a Norse specific seems to have been a widespread practice during the late Middle Ages. The general impression of the compounded bólstaðr-names, however, is that their specifics can be traced back to Norse words, indicating position or direction, to personal names, name-elements like kirkju- and kross-, and to habitative and topographic appelatives. In approximately twenty bólstaðr-names it is impossible to decide the linguistic derivation of the word.[30]

This general characteristic of the bólstaðr specifics also applies to the setr and

[27] See above, note 19.
[28] Olson, 'Norse Settlement', p. 241 f.
[29] ibid., p. 198.
[30] ibid., p. 243.

staðir names. The majority have a Norse background. Totally the settlement names of the three classes constitute a formidable number (approximately 165) as compared to the most numerous Gaelic group, the *bally* (*baile-*) names (approximately 130). One reservation has to be taken: the *bólstaðr*-names seem to have been productive during the entire Norse period, and possibly even after 1266 in its corrupted forms.

The fourth group of Norse settlement-names – the *boer-*(*byr-*) names – has been excluded from Olson's analysis. His argument is that it is rare in settlement names in the Hebrides both as a simplex and as a compound. This may be true, if the examination is confined to *by*-names only (Europie, Conisby, etc.), but we should bear in mind that the west Norse form of *býr* is *boer*. In Orkney H. Marwick has registered no less than twenty six *boer*-names in the rentals of the fifteenth and sixteenth centuries, and in these rentals and on later maps the generic has been corrupted into a variety of forms – *bae, bie, by, bea, bay*. Marwick finds the number of *boer*-farms not too impressive, but his explanation of the relative scarcity of such farm-names is quite interesting: 'Some [of these names] still denote large important farms, but others now survive merely as names applied to fields, an old house-site, a boatnoust or even a small district – the farm association being entirely forgotten. The explanation of course is that the original units have been broken up, fresh names have been applied to the component parts, and the original name has survived only by chance, if at all . . .'.[31] A closer study of the generic in the Hebrides in its corrupted forms, would probably disclose more settlement names of this class. An interesting cluster of names is found on a 1768–69 map of the island of Tiree – supposedly the *Sorby*-primary settlement on the south coast. In 1768 this originally habitative name was only retained as the name of the bay outside (Sorby Bay). During the Norse period it must have comprised the following settlements – Balemartine, Quyeish, Balinioe, Heylipoll (ON *Helgibólstaðr*) and Crossapoll (ON *Krossbólstaðr*). Besides the two settlement names, mentioned by Olson (Europie in Lewis and Conisby in Islay), the *boer*-name appeared in Coll (now lost), in Ulva, in Skye (Sourbie/Sourby near Staffin),[32] Lorne and Craignish (spelt Soroba). The *ba*-form of the *boer*-generic is not uncommon in the Hebrides. It is found as a simplex in connection with a loch in Mull – Loch Ba, and Loch Bee in South Uist may possibly contain the generic *boer*. It also appears that the settlement name Lorgba in Islay contains this generic. In the King's Rental of 1541 it is spelt Lorgbay[33] and in 1627 Lergbey.[34] In Islay we also find another peculiar *boer*-name, spelt differently: Ereby in 1507,[35] Nerebie in 1722,[36] and Nerby in

---

[31] H. Marwick, *Orkney Farm Names* (Kirkwall, 1952), pp. 243 f.

[32] Personal communication of Ian A. Fraser in a letter of 19th February 1988.

[33] *Exchequer Rolls of Scotland*, vol. 17, ed. G. P. McNeill (Edinburgh, 1897), p. 619.

[34] *Registrum Magni Sigilli Regum Scotorum*, vol. 8, 1620–33, ed. J. M. Thomson (Edinburgh, 1894), p. 401.

[35] *Exchequer Rolls of Scotland*, vol. 12, ed. G. Burnett (Edinburgh, 1889), p. 587.

[36] *Rental of the Parishes of the Island*, in G. G. Smith, ed., *Book of Islay. Documents illustrating the History of the Island* (Edinburgh, 1895), p. 529.

Distribution of the ON generic
bólstaðr (after D. K. Olson)

0 _____ 50 MILES

Settlement-Names in *bólstaðr* (-bost, -bus, -bolls, -poll, in the Hebrides and on the western coast of Scotland (after D. K. Olson)

ISLAY
- Bolsay
- Lurabus
- Kinnabus
- Coillabus
- Culabus
- Chollebus
- Cornabus
- Asabus
- Risabus
- Grobolls
- Robols
- Carrabus
- Skerolsay
- Kepolse
- + Stanepols
- + Brannabus
- + Tosabus
- Torabus
- Persebus
- Nereabolls
- Eorabus
- Ealabus
- Cragabus
- Skarabus
- Crosspol?

LEWIS
- Habost
- Swanibost
- + Ulbost/Mealabost
- Labost
- Shawbost
- Bosta
- Kirkibost
- Leurbost
- Crossbost
- Garrabost
- Melbost
- Calbost

HARRIS
- Nisabost
- Seilebost

- Horgabost
- Frobost
- Meall Challibost

NORTH UIST
- Kirkibost
- + Husabost

BENBECULA
- + Cornbust
- + Kirkbust

SOUTH UIST
- Frobost

MINGULAY
- Swansibost

SKYE
- Heribusta
- Breabost
- Husabost
- Leabost
- + Hunebost
- Prabost
- Carbost
- Skeabost
- Heribost
- Orbost
- Eabost
- Colbost
- + Boust
- Colbost
- Carbost
- Meabost
- Abost
- Kirkibost
- Harrapool?
- + Skelbost
- + Torgabost
- + Trabost
- Garrabost
- Habost

- Nisabost
- Shawbost
- Stirbista

MULL
- Sunipol?
- Eorabus
- Assapol?
- Crossopol?
- Tabol?
- Scobull?

TIREE
- Biosd
- Bhasapool?
- Heylipool?
- Barrapool?
- Crossapool?
- Kirkepool?
- Bhircapol?

COLL
- Arnabost
- Bousd
- Grishipoll?
- Crossapoll?

LUING
- Cullipool?

KINTYRE
- Killipool?

WESTERN COAST
- Erbusaig
- Ullapool?
- Resipol?
- Unapol?
- Arnipol?

+ Names no longer in use

? From either *bólstaðr* or *ból*

Farm names of Islay

(after D. K. Olson)

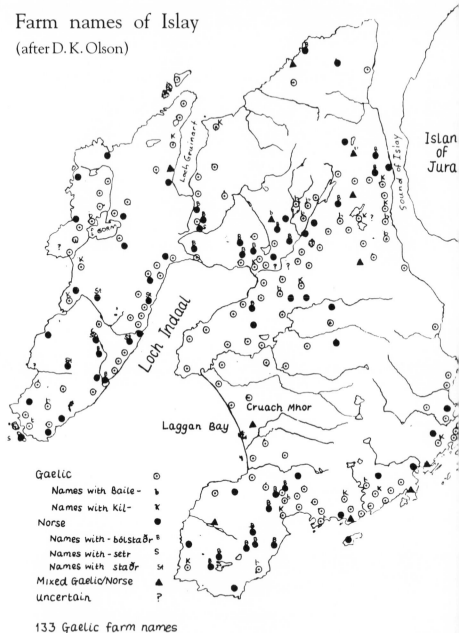

Islan
of
Jura

Loch Gruinart

Sound of Islay

Loch Indaal

Cruach Mhor

Laggan Bay

Gaelic ⊙
   Names with Baile- ♭
   Names with Kil- ⋉
Norse ●
   Names with - bólstaðr ᴮ
   Names with - setr ˢ
   Names with staðr ˢᴧ
Mixed Gaelic/Norse ▲
uncertain ?

133 Gaelic farm names
67 Norse farm names

1750.[37] In the King's exchequer roll AD 1507 there are references to two more settlements in Islay (in addition to Ereby and Conasbe), which may have been boer-names – the simplex Bar and the hybrid Ballenabe.[38]

The relative scarcity of boer/býr-names in the Hebrides can probably be ascribed to

1. the primary status of farms of this class ('land-taking' farm of considerable size), later exposed to a division process, and to

2. the appelative use of this word as the common term for a farm, which implied that it was less useful as a designation of the separate farm units.

And even so, there are at least twelve names which in early rentals and old maps are listed or appear to be listed with a corrupted boer-generic. And it would not be surprising if more names of this class surfaced after a careful study of settlement-names and place-names generally compounded with ba, be, bie, bey.

It is time to conclude the discussion of Norse and Gaelic-Norse settlement-names and return to the historical scene of the twelfth century, the time of Somerled and the establishment of the Gaelic lordship of the isles. He and many of his toiseachs or hofðingjar (chieftains) were descended from mixed ethnic roots – Gaelic and Norse. But they were steeped in Gaelic culture and probably spoke Gaelic more fluently than the Norse dialiect of the Hebrides. The Gaelic renascence of the twelfth and thirteenth centuries was partly due to political leaders like Somerled, but even more to the constant influence of the church. The transition of the Norse immigrants started with its missionary and conversion activity. During the twelfth and thirteenth centuries the Norse population of the isles became Gaelic speakers, even though they hardly forgot their old tongue.

The cultural intermingling which the ninth-century grave-find from Valtos, Uig parish in Lewis, bears witness to, was the beginning of a complete transformation of the Norse settlers. They became gradually totally imbued with different cultural and social values. The key to understanding this process is to be sought in Christian monastic centres in Ireland and above all on Iona.

---

[37] S. McDougall's Map of the Island of Islay, in Smith, Book of Islay.
[38] Exchequer Rolls of Scotland, vol. 12, pp. 587 f.

JELLING FROM IRON AGE TO VIKING AGE

Steen Hvass

The noblest monument from the Viking period of Denmark – and probably from the whole Viking period – is to be found in Jelling in the middle of Jutland. It consists of several elements: the two biggest burial mounds of Denmark, the North Mound with a burial chamber is built on top of an early Bronze Age mound, and the South Mound which has no burial chamber. Under the South Mound parts of two lines of monoliths have been found, maybe the remains of a big ship setting extending as far as the Bronze Age mound underneath the North Mound. Best known are the rune stones: the smaller one erected by Gorm to his queen Thyra, but only put in its present position in modern times, and the larger one, erected by their son Harald, which because of its ornament and inscription is often called the birth certificate of Denmark. It stands in its original position precisely halfway between the two big mounds. Underneath the present church, built in calcareous tufa around 1100, there had been three successive wooden churches. The first of these was very large and contained a chamber grave; it is thought to have been built by Harald Bluetooth when he transferred to it the remains of the body first buried in the North Mound. Through the inscriptions on the two rune stones the Jelling monuments are thus related to King Gorm and Queen Thyra and to their son Harald Bluetooth. Here in Jelling Harald Bluetooth built the greatest royal monument known from the Viking period (Fig. 1).[1]

The Jelling monuments have always occupied a key position in Viking studies. The first archaeological excavation was undertaken in 1704; further excavations took place in 1820–21, 1861, 1941, 1947–48, and 1965. In particular, Jelling has attracted fresh interest after the latest excavations, carried out in 1976–79.[2] Dendrochronology has now made it possible to date some of the monuments very precisely, namely the construction of the North Mound with the burial chamber to the winter 958–59, and that of the South Mound, begun just after 960 and completed only about 970 (Fig. 2).[3]

Until the early 1970s only two older gravefinds had been made in the

---

[1]   K. Randsborg, *The Viking Age in Denmark. The Formation of a State* (London, 1980); E. Roesdahl, *Viking Age Denmark* (London, 1982); E. Roesdahl, *Vikingernes Verden. Vikingerne hjemme og ude* (Copenhagen, 1987).
[2]   K. J. Krogh, 'The Royal Viking-Age Monuments at Jelling in the Light of Recent Archaeological Excavations', *Acta Archaeologica* 53 (1982), pp. 183–216.
[3]   K. Christensen and K. J. Krogh, 'Jelling-højene dateret. Kristendommens indførelse og Gorm den Gamles død', *Nationalmuseets Arbejdsmark* (Copenhagen, 1987), pp. 223–31.

Fig. 1   The two runic stones at Jelling. To the right King Gorm's memorial to his
wife Thyra. To the left King Harald's memorial to his parents and to his own
achievements. *Photo Erik Moltke 1973*

environs of Jelling, one at Knabberup approximately 6 km south of Jelling and
one at Ødsted approximately 10 km south of it, both having, among other things,
a couple of oval brooches. These burials are both found on the edge of the broad
and deep valley of Vejle river.[4]

In Ravning Enge in the Vejle river valley about 10 km southwest of Jelling a
huge bridge had previously been noticed. Its construction was established
through excavations in 1972–77 and dendrochronology indicated that it had
been built c.979, a date pointing to Harald Bluetooth's later years. The bridge is
just under 1 km long and 5½ m wide; it required an enormous amount of
manpower and timber, and to this was added the construction on land of paved
roads and deeply dug-in sunken roads in the steep hill north of the bridge.[5] The
Ravning Enge bridge is the biggest and maybe one of the earliest Viking age

[4] J. Brøndsted, 'Danish inhumation graves of the Viking Age', *Acta Archaeologica* 7
(1936), pp. 81–228.
[5] Th. Ramskou, 'Vikingetidsbroen over Vejle fdal', *Nationalmuseets Arbejdsmark*
(Copenhagen, 1980), pp. 25–32.

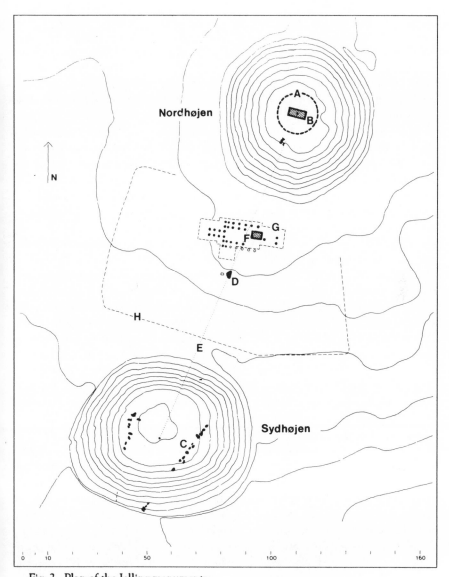

Fig. 2 Plan of the Jelling monuments
A Contour of the Bronze Age mound on top of which the North Mound was built. **B** The burial chamber that was dug into the Bronze Age mound. **C** The South Mound with parts of the two lines of monoliths. **D** King Harald's runic stone, in its original position, and King Gorm's stone after Thyra, put here in modern times. **E** Line connecting the centres of the two mounds. **F** Burial chamber and post-holes in the first wooden church at Jelling. **G** Contour of the present church from c.1100. **H** Contour of present churchyard.
After *Nationalmuseets Arbejdsmark* 1987.

bridges in Denmark. It belongs to the great engineering achievements of the Danish Viking period and was built with very great accuracy. The bridge could only have been in use for a short time, however, since no repairs seem to have been made to it. The magnitude suggests that the king must have been involved in its construction, and as the dating points to the later years of Harald Bluetooth's reign, he is likely to have been involved in this impressive bridge so close to Jelling.

The bridge in Ravning Enge is evidence of a powerful kingship; in its regularity, its dimensions and its short term of service it brings the circular *Trelleborg*-type fortresses to mind. The fortresses of this type are Trelleborg near Slagelse on Sjælland, Nonnebakken in Odense on Fyn, Fyrkat in northern East Jutland, and the greatest of them all, Aggersborg on the Limfjord in North Jutland. The connection between the bridge and the circular fortresses seems even more obvious when the dates are considered. Trelleborg and Fyrkat have been tree-ring dated to c.980, and the finds and the similarities of layout suggest that Nonnebakken and Aggersborg must be of the same date, again towards the end of Harald Bluetooth's reign. These fortresses are normally regarded as garrison forts, regional centres of royal power intended to control a recalcitrant population.[6]

The Jelling monuments, the Ravning Enge bridge approximately 10 km away and the circular fortresses distributed over the country leave no room for doubt that in the second half of the tenth century the king, Harald Bluetooth, had very considerable power and control of a very large area centred on the royal seat of Jelling. After Harald Bluetooth Jelling lost its importance completely. Throughout the Middle Ages and modern times Jelling has been an ordinary village but the king retained it as a royal estate until 1743 when it was auctioned off to the peasants.

But was there any previous settlement in or around Jelling, before the place emerged as a powerful royal seat with the greatest monuments of the Viking period? Until less than ten years ago no settlement sites from the preceding Iron Age or from the Viking Age had been found in the environs of Jelling, but within recent years several new settlements have come to light which show that the area was settled through major parts of the Iron Age, and two Viking period settlements have been localized just outside Jelling.

Jelling is situated on a largish, fairly flat, high plateau which extends approximately 1–1½ km south of present day Jelling. From here some steep hills descend to Lake Fårup which falls eastwards via Grejs River into Vejle Fjord. Grejs River flows in the bottom of a 40–50 m deep valley with high, flat plateaux on both sides of it. On the 1–1½ km wide plateau between present Jelling and Lake Fårup and the Grejs river valley late Bronze Age and early Iron Age settlements have now been identified (Fig. 3).

During the building of a new school some late Bronze Age habitation pits, indicating a settlement from this period, were found just south of Jelling (Fig.

6   E. Roesdahl, 'The Danish Geometrical Viking Fortresses and their Context', *Anglo-Norman Studies* 9 (Woodbridge, 1987), pp. 209–26.

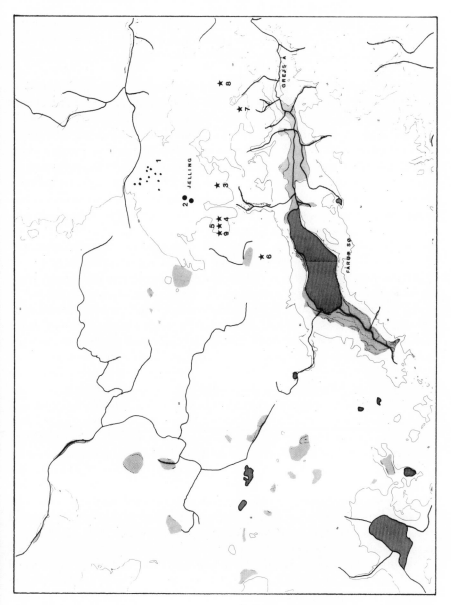

Fig. 3 The cultural land-
scape around Jelling.
1 Group of Bronze Age
mounds, 'Mangehøje'.
2 The Viking Age monu-
ments. 3 Late Bronze Age
settlement. 4 Settlement
from fourth to fifth
centuries BC.
5–8 Settlements from first
to second centuries AD. 9
Stray find of late Iron Age
quern.

3.3). During road and development works parts of a fair-sized settlement from the early pre-Roman Iron Age were found approximately 500 m southwest of Jelling; a house and several pits from the fifth to fourth centuries BC were excavated (Fig. 3.4).

On the 1–1½ km wide, flat plateau between Jelling and Lake Fårup and Grejs river there was in the early Roman Iron Age, the first two centuries AD, a cluster of four settlements, which is interesting in the context of other settlements from this period found in Jutland (Fig. 3.5–8). In the centuries around the birth of Christ there were in Jutland settlements both consisting of only 2–3 farms and big villages with up to 27 farms,[7] but these four settlements from the first to second centuries AD just south of Jelling are, according to preliminary examinations, contemporary, most of them consisting of small settlements with only one or two farms to each. One of these settlements, situated approximately 500 m southwest of Jelling, was excavated completely in 1986 (Fig. 3.5). On the evidence of fences the settlement could be defined on all sides; it covered an area of 75 × 50 m and consisted of only two farms separated by fences (Fig. 4).

The houses were traceable only through the post-holes left by the posts carrying the roof and the posts of the entrance. Each farm had a longhouse in the centre, approximately 20 m long, which would, by analogy with other better preserved house sites, have had human habitation in the western part and a stable with boxes in the eastern part. To these longhouses, which were the main buildings of the farms, belonged several smaller buildings with two, three or four pairs of posts carrying the roof; their length varied from 4 to 12 m; several of these small buildings cut across each other and have therefore replaced each other. The larger of the farms, covering an area of 50 × 40 m delimited by fences and small houses, was found to the west. In addition to the 20 m longhouse it had at least six contemporary small houses between 6 and 12 m long, serving as outbuildings. This farm is demarcated towards the west by a strong post-built fence. Towards the east is the other farm which covered an area of 23 × 40 m. In addition to the 20 m longhouse it had at least five contemporary small houses with lengths ranging between 4.5 and 9 m. The fences delimit this farm both towards the west from the neighbouring farm and towards the east. Just outside the enclosures of the two farms several large rubbish pits with an abundant content of ceramic material were found.

By virtue of the size of its fenced area and the number and size of its outbuildings the western farm at Jelling is the largest farm belonging to the first two centuries AD identified in Denmark.

From the Jutlandic settlements of this period so far examined it is clear that in some of the settlements having a variable number of farms, no differences in the size of farms can be established that might suggest economic and social differences. Marked social and economic differences in society are found only in the previously studied large village of Hodde in south Jutland, belonging to the first

---

[7]   S. Hvass, *Hodde. Et vesjysk landsbysamfund fra ældre jernalder. Arkæologiske Studier* 7 (Copenhagen, 1985), p. 137.

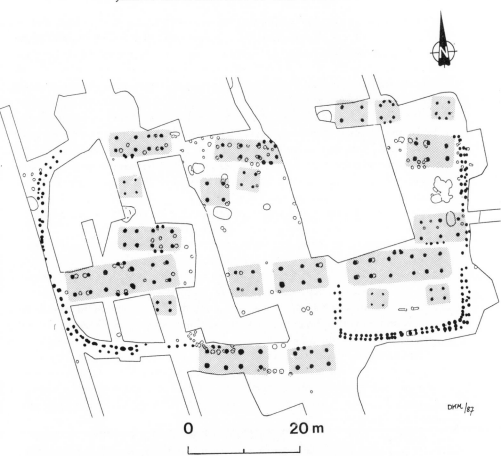

Fig. 4 Two undetached big farms from first to second centuries AD, from Jelling.
Vejle Kulturhistoriske Museum VKH 1262

century BC.[8] To this may now be added the large farm in Jelling, where the
settlement consists of only two contemporary farms. It is possible, therefore, that
the socially and economically prominent farms also occupied at this period a
politically prominent position in society, that magnates living in the manor in
Hodde and the large farm in Jelling exercised a political influence, and that the
inhabitants of settlements with farms of relatively equal size were dependent
upon them. This became even more obvious when a very large contemporary
grave, which by virtue of its size must be regarded as a chamber grave, was found
50 m away from the large farm at Jelling. This burial was solitary. It was dug into
the ground on the highest spot close to the two farms mentioned, without other
graves nearby. The coffin itself, or the chamber, was made of broad planks and
measured 400 × 175 cm and was at least 70 cm high. In the western end of the

8   Hvass, *Hodde.*

grave there was a man buried in *hocker* position with a gold-plated fibula, a silver ring, a belt buckle with strap end and at his feet a set of spurs. By the side of the dead body there was a lance head and an arrow head. In the middle of the grave there was a big 120 cm diameter shield with a very large, partly silver plated, shield boss. By the side of the interred there was also a complete dinner set made up of eight earthenware vessels.

Within a small area in eastern Jutland, with a clear centre of gravity in the Vejle area a number of contemporary, richly furnished burials with weapons have been found.[9] Precisely around Vejle (Jelling is 10 km northwest of Vejle), these rich burials also contain foreign imports in large burial chambers of the same dimensions as the above-mentioned, newly found Jelling burial, suggesting that in this very area there must have been in the first two centuries AD a concentration of social, economic and, therefore, presumably political power in Jutland.

On the same plateau as the above-mentioned two large farms (Fig. 3.5), and 700 m southwest of them, a contemporary settlement presumably consisting of several farms was found; trial excavation suggested a length of 150 m (Fig. 3.6). 2.5 km to the east on the plateau there are two contemporary smaller settlements (Fig. 3.7–8), one of which has been almost completely excavated. On the basis of what has so far been found, it consisted of a farm with a house 20 m long in the middle and on both sides of this main house there were smaller houses 6 and 9 m long, respectively (Fig. 3.8).

Just south of Jelling there was, then, in the first and second centuries AD a concentration of at least four contemporary settlements. Most of them consisted of only a few farms, and one of them stands out as the largest farm so far found in Jutland. To this may even be connected one of the very big and rich chamber graves from the same period.

From this point the Iron Age settlements near Jelling are difficult to trace. It is quite normal for settlements from between the third century and the Viking period to be very difficult to localize by field survey. The settlements of this period are characterised by their lack of potsherds, and potsherds are what normally reveal a settlement in the ploughed field. But the find of a bedstone from a quern shows that the area south of Jelling was also inhabited in the late Iron Age. Unfortunately, a closer localization of the find spot of the quern has proved impossible, except that it was found in the fields south of Jelling in the vicinity of the two excavated first to second century farms (Fig. 3.9). Similar querns are found exclusively in settlements from the third to seventh centuries AD.[10] The find of the quern shows conclusively that we have a settlement succeeding the settlements from the first and second centuries. The excavation

[9] L. Hedeager and K. Kristiansen, 'Bendstrup – en fyrstegrav fra ældre romersk jernalder, dens sociale og historiske miljø', KUML (1981), pp. 81–164.
[10] S. Hvass, 'Vorbasse – eine Dorfsiedlung wshrend des 1. Jahrtausends n. Chr. in Mittel-jütland, Dänemark', Bericht der römisch-germanischen Komission 67 (1986), pp. 529–42.

of other sites in eastern and middle Jutland shows that these late Iron Age settlements can even be very large.[11]

As indicated above Viking Age settlements are also very difficult to recognize on the surface, but at Vorbasse approximately 25 km south-west of Jelling a series of settlements spanning from the third to the eleventh century AD have been completely excavated, and among them a village from the eighth to the tenth century.[12] Here a lot of lessons were learnt about what indicators can betray a Viking Age settlement in a field survey.

In the Jelling area two large Viking period settlements, which can as yet only be dated broadly within the period have now been traced (Fig. 5). About 2 km east of Jelling a Viking Age settlement with a north/south extension of approximately 300 m was found during the installation of North Sea gas pipes; a house with some Viking Age finds was partly excavated. On the basis of its construction and a comparison with the Vorbasse material this house must be dated within the eighth to the tenth century. Further excavation of this site is foreseen in 1988 in order to establish its extent and to assess its state of preservation and, hopefully, its structure. Also on the west side of Jelling, about 3.5 km away, a similarly large Viking Age settlement with finds of, among other things, soapstone vessels, has now been localised. It is premature to express any opinion whether or not these two settlements may be related to the royal sepulchral monument in Jelling but they do show that in the actual Jelling area there were large settlements, probably forming villages contemporary with the royal residence in Jelling itself.

The above-mentioned settlements from different periods of the Iron and Viking Ages in the Jelling area have been found mostly in the last five years; they were not found as a result of any systematic search but they have opened up some promising perspectives of settlement history which will make future work exciting.

Given our present knowledge of Iron and Viking period settlements in the Jelling area, it is possible to look to Vorbasse 25 km south-west of Jelling for a working hypothesis regarding the development of settlement from the Iron Age to the Viking period. In Vorbasse extensive archaeological investigations involving the excavation of more than 260,000 m^2 were carried out between 1974 and 1988. Within 1 km^2 of the fields just north of present Vorbasse it was possible to trace the same village community from the first century BC to the eleventh century AD, and this pre-historic settlement may now be followed further into the Middle Ages in present day Vorbasse. In the settlements from the first century BC to the second century AD preliminary excavations only were made to establish the extent and date of the various settlements but all settlements from between the third and the eleventh century AD have been completely excavated. Excavations have also been carried out inside present day Vorbasse in

[11] S. Hvass, 'Jernalderens bebyggelse. Jernalderens stammesamfund', *Jysk Arkæologisk Selskabs Skrifter* (Århus, 1988).
[12] Hvass, 'Vorbasse'.

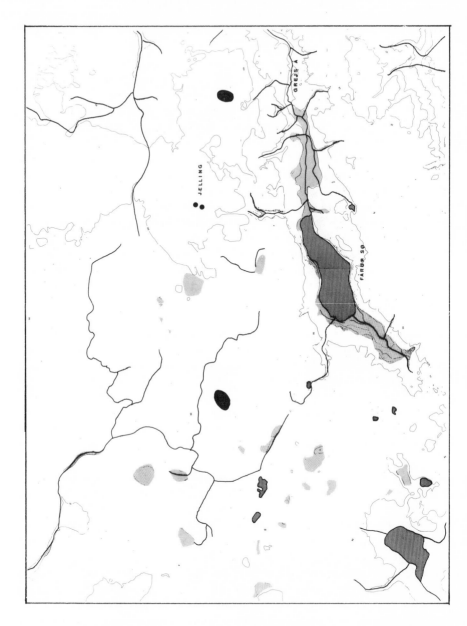

Fig. 5 The cultural landscape around Jelling,
showing the situation of
the two largest Viking
Age settlements.

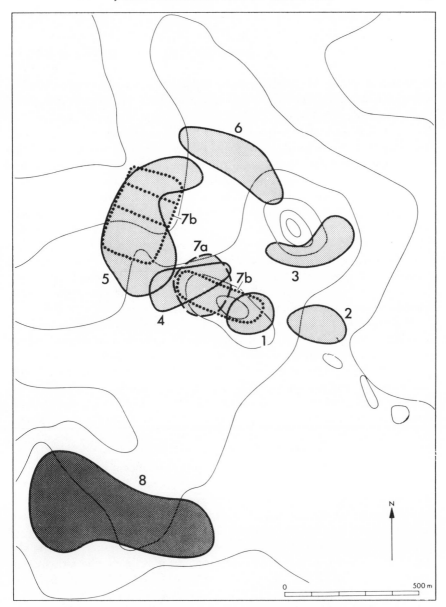

Fig. 6 The villages of Vorbasse from the first century BC to modern Vorbasse

order to establish continuity between the latest parts of the eleventh century settlement in the fields north of Vorbasse and present day Vorbasse throughout the Middle Ages (Fig. 6).

The oldest village studied at Vorbasse belongs to the first century BC (Fig. 6.1). After this a new village emerged about 200 m to the west in the first century AD (Fig. 6.2). Contemporaneously with this village there existed, 600 m to the west of it, two undetached farms. In the second century AD the settlement had moved approximately 250 m to the north (Fig. 6.3). After this there is a major move, about 500 m to the west where a large village comes into being in the third century AD (Fig. 6.4). It is possible to follow how from this village the individual farms moved gradually, one or two at a time, approximately 200–300 m to the west, until a new large village with a very clear village plan emerges in the fourth century AD. It remains in the same position in the fifth century AD (Fig. 6.5). Following this there is a move 100–200 m towards the north, where the village may be followed through the sixth and seventh centuries AD (Fig. 6.6), and another move 400 m towards the south, where a village emerges that may be traced through the eighth, ninth and tenth centuries AD (Fig. 6.7a). This village expanded its area very drastically in the eleventh century when it came to cover an area of approximately 350 × 800 m (Fig. 6.7b). Towards the end of the eleventh century this settlement moved approximately 1000 m southwards and may there be traced further in present day Vorbasse (Fig. 6.8).[13]

In the light of the investigations in Vorbasse it is reasonable, as a working hypothesis, to regard the sites from different parts of the Iron and Viking Ages localized near Jelling as traces of a similar development of settlement to that found in Vorbasse, involving moves from one place to another.

At present the Viking Age settlement in and near Jelling should probably be regarded as the result of a local development of settlement originating in the preceding Iron Age, during which it asserts itself as a particularly strong centre of political power. Jelling first stood out in relation to its surroundings in the early Roman period, the first and second centuries AD, with the largest farm so far excavated and to which a burial was related. This together with other contemporary large and richly furnished graves in the modern county of Vejle goes to show that in this period this very area constituted a powerful local centre of gravity.

In the Viking period Jelling re-emerges as a magnificent centre of political power with the king Gorm the Old and his son Harald Bluetooth. From Gorm the Old at Jelling Denmark has an unbroken royal succession; the throne remained within his kin so that all subsequent rulers of Denmark – even our present queen – are his descendants, although the succession has not always followed the direct line of descent. On the great runic stone in Jelling the inscription runs: 'King Harald had these monuments made after his father Gorm and his mother Thyre, that Harald who won for himself all Denmark and Norway, and christianized the Danes'. The Viking Age monuments in Jelling were put up in memory of Harald's parents. They indicate unambiguously the power of the family over a very great area as well as King Harald's own achievements. At the same time they are closely linked with religion and the introduction of Christianity. Today the Viking Age monuments in Jelling are no longer isolated in the local environment.

---

13 Hvass, 'Vorbasse'.

'DENEMEARC', 'TANMARKAR BUT' AND 'TANMAURK ALA'

Niels Lund

Harald Bluetooth, who died, as Niels Refskou has convincingly argued,[1] on All Saints' Day 987, carved in rock the claim that he won for himself all Denmark and Norway and that he christianized the Danes: . . . *sa haraltr [:] ias : sar · uan · tanmaurk ala · auk · nuruiak · auk · tani [.] (karþi) [.] kristna* (DR 41–42) – and in his reign clearly a lot took place in Denmark which was hitherto unheard of. He built the four great circular fortresses commonly known under the name of the one that was first excavated, Trelleborg on Sjælland, and maybe a fifth now under excavation in Trelleborg in Skåne; he built the impressive bridge at Ravning Enge south of Jelling – and probably was involved in many other improvements to the communications network, other bridges, and roads as well; he set the most impressive monument to his parents ever seen in Denmark at Jelling, where he buried his father Gorm in the North mound in 958 and afterwards exhumed him and buried him in a chamber in his newly erected church between the two mounds there.

This complex is still very enigmatic because it has now been established that the South mound is more recent than the North mound and must have been completed after Harald adopted Christianity, so there is no chance that it could have been erected by Gorm in memory of Thyre. The transhumation of Gorm brings to mind a story in the Russian Primary Chronicle 1044, which records that in this year the bones of Sviatoslav's sons Jaropolk and Oleg were exhumed and baptised and afterwards deposited in Our Lady in Kiev;[2] Oleg was killed by Jaropolk in 977 and, like Gorm, first buried in a mound. Finally Harald carried out great fortification works on Danevirke, the great system of walls protecting Denmark against southerly neighbours.[3]

Harald's reign clearly was a very hectic period, – and it was not as long as used to be thought. Adam of Bremen claimed that he reigned for fifty years and if this were true only a very short span of years would be left into which we could

---

[1] N. Refskou, '*In marca vel regno Danorum*. En diplomatarisk analyse af forholdet mellem Danmark og Tyskland under Harald Blåtand', *Kirkehistoriske Samlinger* (1985), pp. 31–2.

[2] *The Russian Primary Chronicle*, trans. and ed. S. H. Cross and O. P. Sherbowitz-Wetzor (Cambridge, Mass., 1953), p. 139.

[3] H. H. Andersen, H. Madsen and O. Voss, with H. Steuer and H. Tauber, *Danevirke*, Jysk Arkæologisk Selskabs skrifter 13 (Copenhagen, 1976).

squeeze his father Gorm, whose epithet 'The Old' would be difficult to account for, since we seem to have a king Gnupa ruling in Denmark in 934. Harald was, however, one of Adam's heroes, the first Christian king of Denmark and, unlike his immediate successors, one who respected Hamburg-Bremen and its claims. Adam would have liked to see him sanctified: *at ille noster Haroldus, qui populo Danorum christianitatem primus indixit, qui totum septentrionem predicatoribus et ecclesiis replevit, ille, inquam, innocens vulneratus et pro Christo expulsus martyrii palma, ut spero, non carebit,*[4] so he must be suspected of boosting his role beyond the truth, at the expense of the pagan Gorm. Adam indicates himself that he did not care much about the pagan kings of Denmark,[5] and why should he? His subject was the deeds of the archbishops of Hamburg and pagan kings did not speak volumes for them.

The solution most often adopted for this problem has been to limit the area ruled by Gnupa, and by the other kings belonging to the so-called Swedish dynasty, to the Hedeby area in south Jutland and to make the Jelling dynasty start modestly as petty kings of North Jutland.

Another solution has been sought in cutting the Swedish dynasty short and introducing the Jelling dynasty in the second decade of the tenth century rather than the fourth,[6] and that road is not necessarily barred. The end of the Swedish dynasty is normally established by reference to Widukind, who informs us that the king conquered by Henry the Fowler in 934 was Gnupa, but, as demonstrated elsewhere,[7] Widukind is no reliable authority on this point. Gnupa would then in all reason have to be the last of the Swedish kings, but this conflicts with the evidence of the runic inscriptions; they appear to imply not only that Gnupa's son Sigtryg succeeded him as king but also that his widow was able to live on in the area sufficiently undisturbed by any new ruler, to erect her two stones. Professor Lukman's suggestion that the Gorm mentioned as the carver in the longer inscription is indeed King Gorm himself hardly deserves serious consideration.

However, dendrochronology has recently demonstrated that the burial chamber in the north mound at Jelling in which Gorm was first buried, is constructed from trees felled no earlier than 958. Gorm is therefore unlikely to have died twenty years before, and Adam's reliability regarding the length of Harald's reign is undermined. The late Erik Moltke disapproved strongly of my attempts to cast aspersions on Adam's credibility,[8] but there seems to be every reason to persevere.

[4]   Adam Bremensis, *Gesta Hammaburgensis Ecclesiae Pontificum. Quellen des 9. und 11. Jahrhunderts zur Geschichte der hamburgischen Kirche und des Reiches*, ed. W. Trillmich and R. Buchner (Darmstadt, 1978), II 28.
[5]   Adam, I 52.
[6]   P. H. Sawyer, *Da Danmark blev Danmark*, Gyldendal og Politikens Danmarkshistorie, ed. O. Olsen, vol. 3 (Copenhagen, 1988), pp. 218–19.
[7]   N. Lund, 'Svenskevældet i Hedeby', *Aarbøger for Nordisk Oldkyndighed og Historie* 1980 (1982), p. 117, with references in n. 28.
[8]   E. Moltke, 'Det svenske Hedebyrige og Danmarks samling', *Aarbøger for Nordisk Oldkyndighed og Historie* 1985 (1986), pp. 18–21.

This dating, of course, opens new perspectives on a whole lot of old problems, like the date of the inscription on Harald's stone – it has been hotly debated whether it was made in one or more rounds:[9] the first part of it commemorates his parents who were thought to have died before 940, the latter records deeds performed by Harald himself probably at a somewhat later stage of his reign. An affectionate son could not well postpone the erection of a monument to his parents for decades. The new chronology also affects the question of what in fact was Harald's achievement in winning for himself all Denmark: what was re-covered or added to what? Was it a question of recovering South Jutland from the Germans who had taken it from the Swedish dynasty in 934, or from Harald himself in 973? Was it a question of suppressing a great number of petty kings in all Denmark apart from his own heartlands around Jelling, an achievement more often, following *Jómsvíkinga saga*, credited to Gorm's account, but recently re-at-tributed to Harald by Stig Jørgensen,[10] one of many amateur historians whom this period has attracted, who thinks it unlikely that Denmark was a united kingdom before the tenth century and reminds us of the regionalism that persist-ed for several centuries after? Was it, as la Cour claimed,[11] the reconquest of Sjælland from the Norwegians? Or was it something else?

There are very few references to Denmark at this period, mostly because kings were kings of peoples, not of countries. We have numerous references to kings of the Danes, but none to kings of Denmark. In Danish the name Denmark occurs in just four runic inscriptions, those at Jelling by Harald, claiming that he won for himself all Denmark, and by his father Gorm, who describes his wife Thyra as 'tanmarkar but', the 'pride of Denmark' (DR 41–42),[12] and on the Skivum stone in Jutland and the Karlevi stone on Öland, the island in the Baltic now belong-ing to Sweden and then, according to Wulfstan, to the Swedes. The Skivum stone refers to someone who is described as the 'best and first of *landmen* in Denmark' (DR 133), and the Karlevi stone is erected in memory of one Sibbe and predicts that no worthier man will ever be lord of land in Denmark (DR 411).

The etymology most often given for the name *Denmark* regards it as a com-pound of the name of the people, the Danes, and the word *mark*, meaning

[9]   A. E. Christensen, *Vikingetidens Danmark* (Copenhagen, 1969); id., 'The Jelling Monu-ments', *Medieval Scandinavia* 8 (1975), pp. 7–20; K. M. Nielsen et al., 'Jelling Problems', *Medieval Scandinavia* 7 (1974), pp. 156–234; P. V. Glob, 'Jellings bautasten', *Kuml* (1969), pp. 97–109; E. Moltke, *Runerne i Danmark og deres oprindelse* (Copenhagen, 1976); id., 'Kong Haralds mishandlede Jellingsten', *Kuml* (1979), pp. 205–17; E. Johansen and A. Liestøl, 'Jellingsteinen – Steinhogger og runerister', *Kuml* (1977), pp. 64–85; A. Bolvig, 'Harald Blåtand i ideologiens tjeneste', *Den billedskabte virkelighed* (Copenhagen, 1978), pp. 126–48.
[10]   S. Jørgensen, *Danmarks kongemagt og dens fødsel* (Aarhus, 1987), pp. 53–4.
[11]   V. la Cour, 'Kong Haralds tre Storværker', *Aarbøger for Nordisk Oldkyndighed og Historie* (1934), pp. 55–87.
[12]   K. M. Nielsen, *Jelling-studier og andre afhandlinger* (Copenhagen, 1977).

'frontier'.[13] Wadstein also considered the interpretation *dan*, 'wet' or 'damp', thus getting 'damp frontier area'. In both cases the name *Denmark* is thought to have been coined from a German point of view. The Germans would regard Denmark as a frontier inhabited by Danes, and this interpretation could borrow some strength from the fact that in a charter of Otto II from 865, Denmark is referred to as *marca vel regno danorum*. There is, though, no reason to believe that the Germans regarded Denmark as a field of expansion more or less under their domination like the Slav territories to their east.[14]

An alternative explanation has, however, been suggested by the Swedish philologist Richard Ekblom. He claimed that the name had been given from a Swedish point of view to those areas which the Danes originally occupied,[15] and which he thought were Sjælland and Skåne, i.e., as will be discussed below, North-Danish territory, and claimed that Ottar distinguished between the land of the Danes and Denmark. A similar line of thought had, in fact, been adopted by Anna-Maria Freiin von Liliencron who in her 1914 Kiel dissertation *Beziehungen des Deutschen Reiches zu Dänemark im 10. Jahrhundert* has this passage:

> Das Land, das die Dänischen bewohnten, und bis an dessen Grenze die fränkischen Truppen (815) vordrangen, war eben nicht Dänemark, sondern ein Gebiet, in dem noch keine dauernden Besiedlungsverhältnisse geschaffen waren. Von Schweden her sind wandernde Dänenzüge auf die Inseln und die jütische Halbinsel gekommen. So muß man auch die Bemerkung Ohteres verstehen, daß die Inseln Laaland, Seeland, Langeland, Moen, Falster usw. zu Dänemark gehören, sie sind Kolonialgebiet, in das sich der rasch entwickelnde nordgermanische Stamm der Dänen, der im südlichen Schweden ursprünglich saß, den Strom seiner überquellenden Kraft ergoß.

The fact that the Skivum stone is solidly in the middle of Jutland raises some difficulties to this theory which, although Janet Bately found no support for it, pointing out that there is a similar duality of naming in Ottar's use of both *Norðmanna land* and *Norðweg* for Norway,[16] is otherwise rather attractive. It is based on a literal interpretation of a voyage through Danish waters, from Kaupang in south Norway to Hedeby in south Jutland, given in the late ninth century by Ottar. He makes a curious distinction between *Denemearcan* and 'lands belonging to the Danes' and this distinction corresponds to the one made between North-Danes and South-Danes in the description of northern Europe appended to the Old English Orosius. In her contribution to *Gyldendals Danmarks Historie I*, published in 1977, Inge Skovgaard-Petersen noted that the

---

[13] K. Hald, 'Daner', *Kulturhistorisk leksikon for nordisk middelalder* 2 (Copenhagen, 1957), p. 645; id., *Vore Stednavne*, 2nd ed. (Copenhagen, 1965), p. 178.

[14] Refskou, '*In marca vel regno Danorum*', pp. 19–33.

[15] R. Ekblom, 'Ohthere's Voyage from Skiringssal to Hedeby', *Studia Neophilologica* 12 (1939–40), pp. 177–90.

[16] *The Old English Orosius*, ed. J. Bately, Early English Text Society, supplementary series 6 (Oxford, 1980), p. 196.

Anglo-Saxon text leaves open the possibility of regarding the islands and the Scanian landscapes as that Denmark which Harald won for himself (p. 110), and regarded the shifting of the royal burial place from Jutland to Roskilde, where Harald Bluetooth himself was buried, as part of an eastward extension of the power of the Jelling dynasty (p. 166). More recently Ole Crumlin Petersen has taken the text at face value on this point[17] and Peter Sawyer has suggested that such understanding also holds the clue to Gorm's stone at Jelling:[18] the meaning of *tanmarkar but* has nothing to do with either Thyra mending the national defences or with Gorm himself but simply refers to a princess from *Denamearc*, *tanmaurk* who got married to a prince of Jutland.

It is therefore worth having a fresh look at the concept of Denmark in the ninth and tenth centuries in order to explore if the achievement of Harald Bluetooth could have been the unification of these two areas.

Ottar's account runs like this:

> To the south of *Sciringes heal* a great sea penetrates the land; it is too wide to see across. Jutland is on the far side and after that *Sillende*. This sea flows into the land for many hundred miles. From *Sciringes heal* he said that he sailed in five days to the trading town called Hedeby, which is situated among the Wends, Saxons and Angles and belongs to the Danes. When he sailed there from *Sciringes heal* he had Denmark to port and the open sea to starboard for three days. Then two days before he arrived at Hedeby he had Jutland and *Sillende* and many islands to starboard. The Angles lived in these districts before they came to this land. On the port side he had, for two days, those islands which belong to Denmark. (16.9–20)

The distinction is remarkably sharp: on his starboard is Jutland, *Sillende* and many islands, on his port is Denmark and those islands belonging to it. And some corroboration of this division is to be found in the geographical description of northern Europe attached to the *Old English Orosius*; it makes a distinction between the South-Danes, who occupy *Sillende* and Jutland, and the North-Danes, who are found to the east and north of them, both on the mainland and on the islands.

The account of Europe in the seven books of history against the pagans by Paulus Orosius did not include Germania or Slavonic eastern Europe. Therefore, when Alfred the Great had his translation of Orosius made, he also had the text supplemented on these points; the voyages of Ottar and Wulfstan serve the same ends.

The description of Europe is organized round a number of pivotal points. One such pivotal point is the area of the Old Saxons; they are themselves first located in relation to the Thuringians, and next a number of peoples are located in relation to them:

[17] O. Crumlin-Pedersen, 'Ships, navigation and routes in the reports of Ohthere and Wulfstan', *Two Voyagers at the Court of King Alfred*, ed. N. Lund et al. (York, 1984), pp. 30–1.

[18] Sawyer, *Da Danmark blev Danmark*, pp. 220–1.

West of the Old Saxons is the mouth of the river Elbe and *Frisland*, and northwest from there is the land which is called Angeln and *Sillende* and part of the Danes (*sumne dæl Dene*). North of them are the *Afdrede* and northeast the *Wilte* known as the *Hæfeldan*; east of them is the lands of those Wends who are called *Sysyle*, and southeast the *Maroara* who extend over a wide territory. (12.29–13.3)

The South-Danes are introduced as a pivotal point without having been placed in relation to anything else; they must, however, be that 'part of the Danes' referred to:

West of the South-Danes is the arm of the ocean surrounding Britain, and north of them is the arm of the sea called *Ostsæ*. To the east and north of them are the North-Danes both on the main lands and on the islands. To the east of them are the *Afdrede*, and south of them is the mouth of the Elbe and part of the Old Saxon lands. (13.14–19)

The North-Danes, having been placed in relation to the South-Danes, serve as the next pivotal point:

The North-Danes have to their north the same arm of the sea which is called *Ostsæ*, east of them are the tribe the *Osti*, and to the south the *Afdrede*. (13.19–21)

This all looks very curious but the description given is coherent enough. The South-Danish area is Jutland from the mouth of the Elbe to the north tip; the *Ostsæ*, as becomes clear from Ottar, included all Kattegat and part of Skagerrak, both of which names are much younger. The Abodrites are made eastern neighbours of the South-Danes, and if Jutland as far south as the Elbe was South-Danish it makes sense to place the Abodrites, who lived in East Holstein and West Mecklenburg, to their east.

The North-Danes are located east and north of the South-Danes, both on the main lands and on the islands. The main lands must be the coastal provinces in present day western Sweden and maybe also modern Norwegian Østfold and this falls well in line with Ottar's information that from the time he left *Sciringes heal* he had Denmark to port. How the islands should be distributed between South- and North-Danes is not clear from the text; in fact, no islands at all are assigned to the South-Danes, and the location in relation to the neighbouring peoples suggests that such southerly islands as Lolland and Falster should be reckoned as belonging to the North-Danes. From their point of view it makes sense to describe the Abodrites as southerly neighbours and the *Osti* as easterly ones.

It rather baffles a modern Dane that what we jokingly refer to as our South Sea Islands are here assigned to the North-Danes but Wulfstan, as Ove Jørgensen has recently pointed out,[19] in his account of his journey from Hedeby to Truso

---

[19] O. Jørgensen, *Alfred den Store – Danmarks geografi. En undersøgelse i fire afsnit af den gamle engelske Orosius* (Odense, 1985), p. 112.

duly assigns the islands of Langeland, Lolland and Falster to Denmark: *þas land eall hyrað to Denemearcan.* (16.24–25)

If one looks at the map of possible and likely routes for Ottar from Kaupang to Hedeby, Denmark to him clearly consisted of the landscapes on the west coast of present day Sweden plus Sjælland and a number of adjacent islands; the only problem seems to be whether Fyn belonged with Denmark or with *Sillende/* Jutland. Ottar could have gone through either the Great Belt or the Little Belt – from a navigational point of view these routes, as Ole Crumlin-Petersen has shown,[20] make equally good sense – but it would seem difficult, if he went through the Little Belt, to find enough islands on his starboard to justify Ottar's phrase *iglanda fela*, many islands. But whichever route he took there seems to be a striking identity between what he describes as Denmark and the lands of the North-Danes, and between his Jutland/*Sillende* and the areas occupied by the South-Danes.

Ottar is remarkably silent about the political conditions of Scandinavia. He was a contemporary of Harald Fairhair but does not mention any king of Norway. Neither does he comment on the political situation in Denmark; Wulfstan, however, informs us that Bornholm had its own king – it was also made a separate pivotal point in the survey of northern Europe – and that Blekinge, later to emerge as a Danish province, and Öland, with the Karlevi stone, belonged to the Swedes.

A distinction between North-Danes and South-Danes is suggested in Danish material too, but so vaguely that – *pace* Lis Jacobsen who in 1929 did a study of the end of the Swedish dynasty in Hedeby which has since baffled scholars with its lack of accord between the evidence quoted and the views arrived at – nobody has seriously tried to exploit it. A very obscure inscription from Sædinge on the island of Lolland (DR 217) was erected by one Thyre after her husband Krok. It belongs to a group of inscriptions that have often been adduced in favour of some Swedish presence in the area; Moltke, apparently modelling his notions of the kingdom of Sweden on those of Birger Nerman, indeed came close to regarding Lolland as a Swedish outpost in the Baltic guarding the route between Birka and Hedeby.[21] Just how arbitrary and contradictory this whole business is can be seen from Moltke's comments on one of these stones, the Sønder Kirkeby stone (DR 220). This stone has a ship on it which shows some similarities with that on the Tullstorp stone in Skåne, and in *Danmarks Runeindskrifter* (Text: 271) as well as in *Runerne i Danmark* (188) we are told that this is an indication of the close links existing between Falster and Skåne and, together with the Sædinge and Tirsted stones, a hint of the route followed by the Swedish colonists to Hedeby. The Sønder Kirkeby stone is, however, post-Jelling, Moltke himself dated it between Jelling 2 and 1000 AD,[22] and the Tullstorp stone, with its ornament in a style more Ringerike than anything else, he puts more than a generation later

---

[20] Crumlin-Pedersen, 'Ships, navigation and routes', pp. 35–8.
[21] Moltke, 'Det svenske Hedebyrige', p. 25.
[22] Moltke, *Runerne i Danmark*, p. 188.

than Jelling 2,[23] that is, well into the eleventh century. What can such late evidence possibly tell us about events or conditions a century or more earlier? – And what do links between Falster and Skåne tell us about the presence of Swedes in Denmark? Skåne only began to be Swedish in 1658 and is hardly yet recognized as such by the *uppsvear*!

The inscription on the Sædinge stone is incompletely preserved and inadequately understood, but the point of it seems to be that Krok was a powerful opponent of the *sutrsuia : auk : suþrtana :* – the 'particular Swedes' and the 'South-Danes' – and he was the best of *nurminum*, which might just be a reference to North Danes, although it is of course possible that he was a Norwegian instead. Attempts to demonstrate Norwegian influence in this inscription or even to prove that it was indeed Norwegian must, however, be regarded as misguided. But in any case the interpretation of this inscription is so conjectural and its date and historical context so uncertain that no hypothesis can safely be based upon it.

The only other text that distinguishes between North-Danes and South-Danes is the Beowulf epos. This seems to have a time-honoured claim to consideration as historical evidence which is, though, very difficult to respect. Swedish scholars, certainly, have been very fond of it.[24] True, this story about a supernatural hero, who first kills a monster and then the monster's mother on the bottom of a lake, is set in a historical scene, but the historical material has been used with great license to create the sort of setpiece that the poet wanted for poetic reasons.[25] He has not cared a brass farthing about historical truth, and we should expect that historical fact is as impossible to reconstruct from this as Diabelli's little waltz would be from, say, Beethoven's 27th variation of it. This has been recognized by most translators of Beowulf; realizing that when the text gives North-Danes, South-Danes, East-Danes, Spear-Danes and many others the reason is invariably to be found in the need for a certain alliteration, they render them, in prose translations at least, as simply 'Danes'.[26]

The information supplied by Ottar and Wulfstan cannot be precisely dated, no more precisely than probably in the last quarter of the ninth century. This is a period in the history of Denmark about which we are very poorly informed, we don't know more than the name of many kings, and for some years not even that, nor do we know whether Denmark was united.

Now, we must not forget that almost a century may separate the conditions described by Ottar from those in which Harald Bluetooth lived, nor that even a thousand years ago a hundred years was a long time during which many changes could take place. Still, the clearcut division between South-Danes in Jutland and

---

[23] ibid., p. 203.

[24] See C. Weibull, 'Die Geaten des Beowulfepos', *Acta Societatis scientiarum et litterarum Gothoburgensis. Humaniora* 10 (Gothenburg, 1974), pp. 3–7.

[25] I. Skovgaard-Petersen, 'Oldtid og vikingetid', *Danmarks historie*, ed. A. E. Christensen et al., vol. 1, *Tiden indtil 1340* (Copenhagen, 1977), p. 33.

[26] *Beowulf*, A prose translation with an introduction by D. Wright (Harmondsworth, 1957), p. 117.

some adjacent islands, and North-Danes on other islands and some parts of the Scandinavian mainland, together named Denmark, does offer a tempting explanation to Harald's claim that he won for himself all Denmark. Based at Jelling he would be a South-Danish king, and Denmark was the lands of the North-Danes. And his father Gorm would seem to have prepared the way for him by marrying a princess from Denmark, thus giving his son a hereditary claim to it. An obvious parallel would be Æthelred II's first marriage, to a daughter of earl Thored, one of the most powerful men in Northumbria.[27]

The main obstacle to this interpretation is the inscription of Skivum which seems to imply that Jutland belonged to Denmark; the only way round this seems to be to assume that runic inscriptions are not necessarily erected on the deceased's grave or near his home but could be put up where-ever he found sudden death. Sibbe might then not have been a chieftain in Öland, and Öland not part of Denmark, and the landman commemorated at Skivum may have belonged elsewhere – although a landman is probably, as suggested by the Turinge stone, the antithesis of a viking chieftain leading his lið abroad.[28] But whereas we have quite a few inscriptions in Scandinavia commemorating people who died abroad, like the Sjonhem stone on Gotland,[29] there are not many like the London St Paul's stone commemorating abroad Scandinavians who died abroad.

Another possible stumbling block may be that the word Denimarca was used, but used, unfortunately, in such a way that we cannot tell whether the reference is to Denmark in a modern sense or in the Ottarian sense, by Regino of Prüm, who completed his chronicle in Trier in 908. In his entry for the year 884 he informs us about some Nortmanni who had come to Kennemerland in Holland ex Denimarca and were permitted by Godfred, who in 872 had been given Rurik's former fief, to carry out an attack up the Rhine. It is possible that Regino used Denimarca in the same sense as Ottar but it is as possible that he used it in a modern sense.

The interpretation of Gorm's memorial inscription to his wife in the light of the geographical framework that we can deduce from the accounts in the Old English Orosius, a geographical framework which we tacitly turn into a political one, is a very attractive one. The Skivum stone and Regino should probably only be allowed to remind us that there are hardly any temptations that one can succumb to unreservedly. Well – what would Paradise be without the serpent?

---

[27] N. Lund, 'King Edgar and the Danelaw', Medieval Scandinavia 9 (1976), p. 192.
[28] SRSö, n. 338.
[29] SRG, no. 135.

DANES AND WENDS:
A STUDY OF THE DANISH ATTITUDE
TOWARDS THE WENDS*

Tinna Damgaard-Sørensen

THE LOLLAND-FALSTER ISLANDS

Being the southernmost of Denmark's numerous islands, Lolland and Falster are
also the closest to the Baltic coastlines of Germany, separated from them at the
narrowest point by a stretch of water no wider than the Great Belt between
Zealand and Funen to the North. During the Viking Age, this was a frontier
zone, a dividing line between two cultures, the Slavonic and the Nordic. Ships
from both plied the watery border, making it less distinct, intermingling and
establishing more or less friendly relations. The southern islands of Lolland and
Falster were among the places where the two cultures met.

THE FIND AT FRIBRØDRE BROOK

Archaeological confirmation that this was in fact the case seems given by the
find made along the banks of Fribrødre Brook on North Falster. Excavations have
shown that ships were repaired, and possibly constructed here in Viking and
Early Medieval times. The large body of material brought to light shows many
affinities with Slavonic culture.

As so often happens, the site was discovered quite by chance. In 1981, a
farmer dredging mud from the bottom of the brook to raise the height of the
dykes along its banks, came across well preserved timber imbedded in the brink.
Archaeological authorities were alerted and the find was judged to be of
eleventh- to twelfth-century date, belonging to a vessel of Nordic or Slavonic
type, and worth further examination.

During the first season of excavation, in 1982, it became clear that what had
been found wasn't the remains of just one ship, but of several. A thick, com-
pacted layer was encountered, made up of shrub and branches and containing

* This contribution is based on parts of a more comprehensive study in the form of an
unpublished thesis. I should like to thank Niels Lund, Institute of History, University of
Copenhagen, for his valuable support. The translation was kindly taken care of by Jan
Stubbe Østergaard.

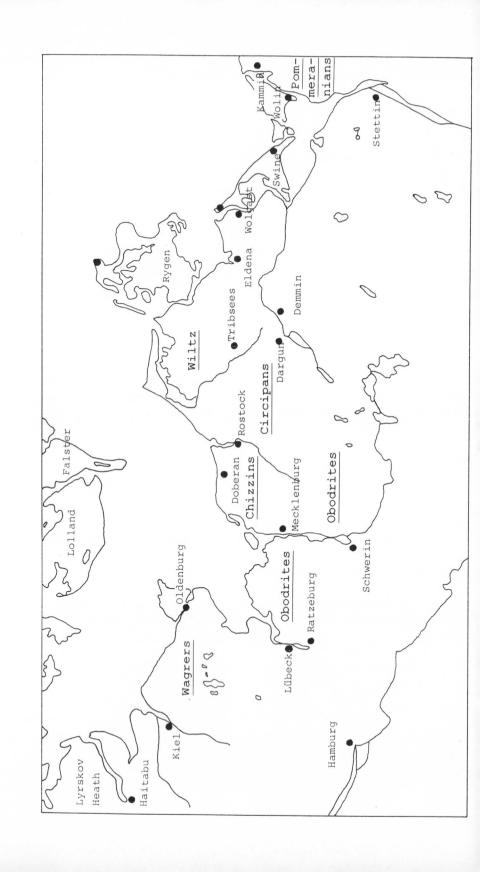

partly destroyed, discarded ships fittings and timbers, tools, chippings, pottery, animal bones and much else besides. All organic materials were in an excellent state of preservation. The site was interpreted as having been the scene of both the repair and the building of ships; dendrochronology established a date of felling of 1050–1055 AD for the wood of one of the timbers found. This would also be the approximate date of construction, but as most of the ships' parts seemed old and worn, they may be assumed to have been discarded some thirty to forty years later, indicating a late eleventh-century date for the activities on the site.

The vessels broken up or repaired or actually built there, were double-prowed, clinkerbuilt ones, of a type wellknown from other Nordic sites. In certain constructional details, however, the vessels deviate from the Nordic tradition. Nordic ships were assembled by means of iron nails, whereas those from Fribrødre have planking held together by wooden pegs. Furthermore, they were caulked with a moss-based substance, rather than cattle hair as in Nordic ships. Though these differences may seem insignificant, they are nevertheless sure signs of the Fribrødre ships being more closely related to Slavonic, than to Nordic tradition – as their builders may be assumed to have been as well.

Pottery constitutes the other major group of finds, and it has a similar orientation towards Slavonic culture. With few exceptions, the sherds are of a coarse, gritty ware, fired to grey, brown and black hues. Several are coated with a more finely levigated clay slip. The pots were hand made, but given a finish on a slow wheel, a tool being used on some to shape the rim. Most sherds carry a decoration of some kind, the commonest being incised lines running round the pot; incision was also used to produce wavy lines, hatching and bands of comb dotting. Impressed decoration occurs and some bottom sherds have cruciform 'makers' marks'. Such pottery may with great certainty be classed as belonging to the Late Slavonic group which in the course of the Viking Age reached all parts of the Baltic region, earning it the rather vague name of 'Baltic Pottery'.

Finally, a number of individual finds with unmistakable Slavonic traits must be mentioned, such as a knife with decorated handle, a hammered bronze ornament from a knife sheath and an earring of twisted silver.[1]

Though the excavations at Fribrødre Brook have yet to be concluded, there can be no doubt of the Slavonic element in the activities at the site. This raises the question of whether there was actually Slavonic presence on the island at the time.

---

[1] Part of the material from Fribrødre Brook has been briefly described by J. Skamby Madsen, 'Et skibsværft fra vikingetid/tidlig middelalder ved Fribrødre å på Falster', Hikuin 10 (1984), pp. 261–74; id., 'Snekkeværft', Skalk 2 (1984), pp. 3–9; id. and M. Müller, 'Musik til arbejdet', Skalk 1 (1986), pp. 8–11; N. Bonde, 'Dendrokronologiske undersøgelser på skibstømmer fra Fribrødre å ved Maglebrænde på Falster', Hilkuin 10 (1984), pp. 275–8.

THE STATE OF RESEARCH

The question is one of long standing. The presence or not of those Slavs known under the name of Wends has been debated since the 1850s. Written sources offer no direct evidence of Wends settled in Denmark, but the possibility is suggested, indirectly, by such names as Gnemer and Dobicus, of Wendish origin, and belonging to men mentioned by Saxo in his *Gesta Danorum* as active on the ships of the Danish fleet of war; added to which we have quite a number of Wendish-sounding toponyms. This explains why students of onomastics have led the debate, while historians have concentrated on the written sources dealing with Wendish piracy in Danish waters, with the glorious action taken by Absalon and Valdemar against Wendish freebooters. That Wends may have settled as farmers and craftsmen on the Danish islands is mentioned in passing with reference to onomastic studies, and, in more recent years, to archaeological evidence. An unfortunate situation results from this, in which students of onomastics and historians are not aware of the character of the evidence involved on either side. A third source, that of archaeological finds, is now beginning to play its part. Consequently, we need to clarify the nature of the evidence available from three distinctly different types of sources, speaking independently, on their premisses, in order to assess the contribution they have to make. In the following, I shall attempt to show that there are some reasons for optimism among historians as regards the contribution of our written sources towards resolving the problem in question.

THE WRITTEN SOURCES

When making use of the written sources in dealing with the present problem, a number of circumstances must be taken into consideration. The Wends had no written language, and have therefore left no written records. We must make do with the writings of neighbouring regions, which tended to regard the Wends as a population in need of missionary attention; sympathetic comments about such heathens are not to be expected. Several sources mention the Wends in short reviews of past events, but the tribes seldom play any part in accounts of contemporary developments – and nowhere is there any talk of Wends settling in Denmark.

Even so, I suggest that the written sources may contribute. Providing, of course, that one does not insist on posing the question in the terms of 'Did the Wends settle in Denmark?', some indirect light may fall on the problem at hand. One might, for example, ask 'Were there any reasons for the Wends to leave their country in favour of foreign lands?' Do our written sources allow us to trace any factors which may have motivated such emigration? Or we might ask, 'Would it be at all possible for Wends to find a home on Danish territory?' What was the attitude of Danes towards the Wends? Are we to believe Helmold, when he says that Wends fleeing to Denmark were sold as slaves?[2] What were the practical and legal possibilities of Wends acquiring land in Denmark?

I shall concentrate on just one of these several questions, namely that of Danish attitudes to the Wends.

THE ATTITUDE TOWARDS WENDS AMONG THE DANES

Saxo's *Gesta Danorum* contains the amplest information on relations between Danes and Wends. In the final six of his books in the *Gesta*, Wends are very much in evidence. In his description, the Wends are almost without exception barbaric, greedy, dissolute and arrogant, serving their purpose as foils to his account of the Danish kings, whether weak or strong. He shows us the weak kings as powerless witnesses to the violence and brutality of the Wends, laying waste the countryside – only to enhance the glory of stronger kings, triumphing over the enemy. Such compositional effects all went to achieving Saxo's aim of giving his wholehearted support to the policy of the Valdemars. He tells us how Denmark lay open to the incursions of the Wends during the period of civil strife and how Valdemar the Great, with the able assistance of bishop Absalon, went from strength to strength after coming to power, beating down the Wends and making them pay for their ill deeds in their own homeland.

Saxo wrote his history after the final defeat of the Wends. During the 1160s Valdemar and Absalon had made repeated seaborne assaults on the Wends. They took Rügen in 1169, the lords of Rügen recognizing Valdemar as their king and the inhabitants being baptized. The final subjegation was carried through by Canute IV in 1185; heavy raids on Pommerania had forced the *dux* Bugislav I and his allies to sue for peace and hail Canute as lord. 'King of the Wends' thereafter became part of Canute's title, the Wends being regarded as defeated.

Against such a background, Saxo was free to present a picture of the enemy, full of scorn, rather than of fear. The Wends had been subdued, militarily, culturally and politically.

Taking Saxo's attitude as one's basis, combined with Helmold's statement that Wends arriving in Denmark were sold as slaves, Wends would not seem to have much chance of settling there. But then, both Saxo and Helmold were writing against the background of twelfth-century events and opinions. Other factors determined attitudes of times before theirs. An evaluation of what possibilities Wends had of settling on Danish territory, based on a Danish point of view, must rest on earlier sources, and discard the hostility evident in Saxo.

Below I shall review the sources, progressing chronologically century by century, centuries being chosen for reasons of clarity, not because they necessarily reflect historical divisions of time. I shall begin with the tenth-century, the date of the earliest written sources of any value, and end with Saxo's account, of the

---

[2] *Helmoldi presbyteri Bozoviensis Chronica Slavorum* II 5, ed. G. H. Pertz, *Ex Monumentis Germaniae* (1868).

late twelfth-century. As far as possible, attitudes to the Wends will be isolated and their historical background discussed.

THE TENTH CENTURY

In the beginning of the ninth century, relations between Denmark and the western Wends were strained. Godfred, the Danish king, had allied himself with the Wilz, further to the East. He attacked the Obodrites, and destroyed the trading settlement of Reric, where he had levied tax on earlier occasions; his men murdered the Obodrite chieftain Trasco.[3] During the following century relations gradually improved.

In the late tenth century a runic stone was raised by Tove, daughter of the Obodrite lord Mistivoi, in memory of her mother. The runic inscription read: 'Tove, daughter of Mistivoi, wife of Harald the Good, son of Gorm, had these runes made for her mother'.[4] Not only does the stone preserve the memory of Tove's mother (whose name is not given), it also tells of a marriage relation entered into by the Danish and Obodrite royal families. The Danish king Harald Bluetooth enjoyed friendly relations with the Obodrites. From these he profited when taking up arms in 970s against the German emperor Otto, who had seized the territory between the rivers Schlei and Eider. The Wends fought as Harald's allies and with their help he was able to retake the lost lands.[5] There have also been suggestions of the Danish kings being involved in the stronghold of Jomsborg,[6] possibly situated in the territory of the Wilz tribe.

In Norwegian-Islandic skaldic epics of the tenth century we meet the Wends as the equals of the Danes. Danish warriors are given such epithets as 'Vinds Myrdi' ('Killer of Wends'), and 'Vindun Hattr' ('Danger to Wends'). It would be wrong to see such names as demeaning to the Wends; just as fierce fights do not

---

[3] Annales Regni Francorum, s.a. 808–9, ed. R. Rau, Quellen zur karolingischen Reichsgeschichte 1 (Darmstadt, 1977).
[4] For the runic stone from Sdr. Vissinge see DR no. 55.
[5] Thietmar of Merseburg, Chronik III 24, ed. R. Holtzmann, MGH SRG 9 (Berlin, 1935).
[6] Sven Aggesen, Brevis Historia Regum Dacie 8, ed. M. Cl. Gertz, Scriptores Minores Historiae Danicae Medii Aevi 1 (Copenhagen, 1970); Saxo Grammaticus, Gesta Danorum X 1, 1; 4, 2; 8, 3–4, ed. J. Olrik and H. Ræder (Copenhagen, 1931); Knytlingesaga 1, in Sogur Danakonunga, ed. C. af Petersens and E. Olson (Copenhagen, 1919); Adam of Bremen, Gesta Hammaburgensis Ecclesiae Pontificum II 27, ed. B. Schmeidler, MGH SRG (Hannover, 1917); Helmold, I 15. The existence of Jomsburg has been debated since both the castle and its viking warriors were discarded as figments of the imagination by Lauritz Weibull, Kritiska undersökningar i Nordens historia omkr. år 1000 (Copenhagen, 1911). Others disagree, cf. S. Ellehøj, 'Olav Tryggvesons fald og venderne', Historisk Tidsskrift 11, række 4 (1953), pp. 1–55; A. E. Christensen, Vikingetidens Danmark paa oldhistorisk baggrund (Copenhagen, 1977), pp. 255–6; I. Skovgaard-Petersen, 'Oldtid og vikingetid', Danmarks historie, ed. A. E. Christensen et al., vol. 1, Tiden indtil 1340 (Copenhagen, 1977), p. 183. The reality of the castle has recently been questioned again by L. Sobel, 'Ruler and Society in Early Medieval Western Pomerania', Antemurale 25 (1981), pp. 19–142.

necessarily reflect any permanent tension. Fighting is the essence of skaldic poetry; courage and deeds of battle are glorified, and foreign peoples are usually described as trembling victims of heroic fury. Besides 'Killer of Wends', we meet 'Enemy of the Danes' and 'Opposer of the British'.[7] These nick-names indicated warrior status.

The sources outline an equality, accompanied by changing alliances and skirmishes. The Vikings of the North tested their strength on the Wends, but no enduring enmity seems to have resulted. Wends are not met with as aggressors on Danish soil, they were no threat, and there seems to be no reason why a hostile image of them should have been created, detrimental to any Wendish immigrants.

THE ELEVENTH CENTURY

Danes do not appear to have been particularly preoccupied with the Wends during the eleventh century. Initially, attention was directed westwards. Danish kings were attempting to get a foothold in England with a view to creating Viking dominion over both shores of the North Sea. On the death of Hardeknud in 1042, the dreams were shattered, the North Sea Empire broke down and Denmark was weakened.

The same period saw leading families wanting to turn Denmark into a modern state with an independent standing within the European cultural ambit. Svend Estridsen and his sons worked to free Denmark from the influence of the German archbishops; in other spheres they sought to organize affairs in Denmark on a more advanced European model. The Wends were of no great interest in this connection, though the long established relations with the Obodrite lords were maintained. Thus, Gotskalk, grandson of Mistivoi, whose daughter had been married to Harald Bluetooth, went into the service of King Canute the Great and his sons in England. Gotskalk fought under Svend Estridsen as well, winning the hand of Estridsen's daughter.

One particular event in the mid-eleventh century may to some degree have affected Danish attitudes to the Wends. This was the incursion into Southern Jutland of Wendish forces led by the sons of one Ratibor, in 1043. They were defeated by Magnus the Good at Lyrskov Heath, a battle which the written sources talk of a lot. According to Adam of Bremen, it cost more than 15,000 dead,[8] and Snorre says the loss of life was the greatest ever in the North.[9] Remarkably, contemporary skaldic poets do not agree with later sources in seeing

---

[7] Tindr Hallkelsson, *Drape om Hakon Jarl* v. 6 (dated c.987), in F. Jonsson, *Den norsk-islandske skjaldedigtning*, 2nd ed. (Copenhagen, 1973), vol. 1B, p. 137; Hallfrøðr Ottarsøn Vandrædaskald, *Olafsdrapa* v. 11 (dated c.1001), in Jonsson, op. cit., p. 152.

[8] Adam of Bremen, II 79.

[9] Snorre Sturlason, *Uphaf Magnús konungs góda* vv. 26–8, in id., *Heimskringla*, ed. F. Jonsson (Copenhagen, 1911), pp. 436–8.

the battle as something out of the ordinary – there is just the usual mention of cloven heads and dead being left for the ravens to feed on.

If Adam of Bremen and Snorre are exaggerating, why might that be? Do their reports reflect the shock effect on Danes of meeting the Wends as aggressors for the first time? Or are they a witness to successful public relations on the part of Magnus the Good?

We know nothing of how the population reacted to the Wendish attack; but we do know that Magnus was not in a particularly strong position at the time. After the death of Hardeknud in 1042, a struggle for power in Denmark had been going on between Magnus and Svend Estridsen. Glorifying his efforts against the Wends could give him the political support he so desparately needed. Exaggerating the number of dead and stressing the violence of the battle might make it look as if Magnus had averted a threat to the nation, making him the saviour of the kingdom. Such manipulation of the facts cannot be proved, but for the first time we have a situation in which a Danish king may arguably have had a reason to make the population take a definite, unfavourable, view of the Wends. The importance given to the battle in later sources might be taken to mean that Magnus had some success in this respect: Adam of Bremen had much of his information from Magnus' arch rival, Svend Estridsen, but nevertheless gives an unreservedly favourable impression of him. He tells us how the great battle brought peace and happiness to the Danes for the duration of Magnus' reign, and how the people loved him for his bravery and justice.[10] We cannot know how widespread this opinion of Magnus actually was. In assessing the population's reaction to the battle, we can only make surmises. Thus, one would suppose people in Southern Jutland to be receptive to Magnus' version of the battle and its import, having themselves been the object of Wendish plundering and therefore being the more afraid of repetitions; these would also be the people who had gloried most in the sweetness of victory, the ones to tell others of death-defying exploits. In other parts of the country, there would have been no direct involvement and nothing to fear as long as the Wends did not attempt seaborne raids; consequently, opinions on the battle – if any – would perhaps depend on which side one supported at home, Magnus or Svend Estridsen.

According to Ælnoth, the 1080s saw Canute the Holy attempting to improve the legal status of foreigners in Denmark. They were to have the same rights as Danes, provided they had committed no crimes.[11] An anonymous source brings us concordant evidence, reporting that Canute forbade the Danes to look down on Christians from abroad.[12]

Since Weibull's review of the sources,[13] Ælnoth's hagiography has usually been seen as a literary construction, conforming to established conventions with

[10] Adam of Bremen, II 79.
[11] Ælnoth 14, ed. M. Cl. Gertz, *Vitae Sanctorum Danorum* (Copenhagen, 1908–11).
[12] *Vitae Sanctorum Danorum* 66.
[13] C. Weibull, *Källkritik och historia* (Stockholm, 1964), pp. 178–206.

the aim of making Canute appear in the guise of an augustinian *rex iustus*. Recently, however, some authors have taken Ælnoth's statements at face value.[14]

If we were to believe Ælnoth, his account would illustrate the dislike Danes had of foreigners; the animosity was such that people passing through the country were forced to seek the protection of the Crown or of local nobles to avoid being treated as outlaws.[15] Since Canute felt prompted to deal with the problem, it would be reasonable to assume that there was quite a number of non-Danes resident in the country. Some of them may have been Wendish refugees, fleeing for religious or political reasons. The great Obodrite alliance was split during the eleventh century, the internal power struggle culminating in 1066. That year, Gotskalk, who had led the Christian faction, friendly towards the Germans and interested in developing a state along European lines, was murdered. His wife and son fled to Denmark,[16] and they can hardly have been the only ones to do so. The new Obodrite regime wanted Wendland free of German dominance and encouraged traditional Wendish practices and beliefs. This shift in power and the ensuing persecution of Christians may have caused a wave of emigration, that brought more Christian Wends to Denmark,[17] and a wave of immigration may have caused Canute to consider the legal status of foreigners. There may be some truth to what Ælnoth tells us.

In the very last years of the eleventh century, during the reign of Erik Ejegod, the Wends enter the stage once more. They came by sea this time, and for the first time we hear of them entering Grønsund, where they captured and killed Auden, brother of Skjalm Hvide. Saxo goes on to recount the subjugation of the Wends by Erik, how he conquered the island of Rügen and gave it in fief to Skjalm Hvide.[18] A lay from 1104 dedicated to Erik to some extent supports this account. In it, Markus Skeggjason praises Erik for defeating and conquering the Wends, laying them under tribute.[19]

As to what actually happened, we cannot be certain. Erik may have added Rügen to his possessions, and he may have invested bishop Asser with ecclesias-

---

[14] N. Skyum Nielsen, *Kvinde og Slave* (Copenhagen, 1971), p. 4; C. Breengaard, *Muren om Israels hus* (Copenhagen, 1982), pp. 136–9, esp. p. 137, sees the good deeds catalogued by Ælnoth as concrete examples of political initiatives taken by Knud. He thus disagrees with Weibull; in characterising Knud's various steps to curb the negative effects of the institutions of society on certain social groups as being christian policy and therefore qualifying him for canonisation, our sources from Odense are not the victims of literary convention. On the contrary they must be interpreted in the light of the fact that the Church, its clergy and its congregation were the victims of the ancient social order of Denmark (op. cit., p. 138).

[15] N. Lund, 'Peace and Non-Peace in the Viking Age', *Universitetets Oldsaksamlings Skrifter*, ny rekke nr. 9 (1987), pp. 255–69.

[16] Adam of Bremen, III 50; 51; Helmold, I 22; 24; 25.

[17] Helmold, I 25–6.

[18] Saxo, XII 4, 1–2; 6, 5.

[19] Markus Skeggjason, *Eriksdrápa* vv. 15–23, ed. Jonsson, *Den norsk-islandske skaldedigtning*, pp. 416–18.

tical authority.[20] At any rate, this was undoubtedly the first of those expeditions against the Wends which were to become so characteristic of the twelfth century.

Our very sparse written sources do not allow us to say what people thought of Erik's expeditions. It appears, however, that Erik was concerned about the salvation of his soul – or that he was aware of the influence of Christianity on political affairs in Western Europe.[21] He might, with an undertone of contempt for barbarians, have wanted to depict the Wends as heathens fit for conversion, thus turning his campaigns into a crusade. In that case, Erik stands as an early exponent of a movement which did not really make itself felt until the middle of the twelfth century.

THE TWELFTH CENTURY

In the course of the twelfth century, Denmark established itself as a nation on the periphery of Western Europe. Early hagiographical literature bears witness to the endeavours made to place Denmark within the sphere of European culture. The favourable effect on the internal politics of Denmark achieved through the canonization of Canute the Holy, go to show that Christianity had taken root to an extent that made it politically potent. This was to influence Danish attitudes to the Wends in the second half of the century. The Wends began causing difficulties for Denmark at the beginning of the century. The Obodrite *Rex* Henrik Gotskalksøn carried on piracy along the Danish coast up to Schleswig[22] and in the eastern reaches of Wendland the Pommeranians were stirring. Niels attempted to counter the troubles by having his son Magnus marry a daughter of the Polish king Boleslau and organizing joint Danish-Polish raids on the eastern Wends.[23]

In 1135, the Wends attacked once again. Kongshelle, a prosperous town on the Norwegian coast, was destroyed.[24] The following year Erik Emune headed for Rügen, took the island and forcibly baptized the inhabitants. Erik installed bishops to keep a grip on the island, but no sooner had he sailed away than the bishops were removed and Rügen proclaimed its earlier independence.[25] These hostilities may be supposed to have made some impression in Denmark, but their precise effects cannot be gleaned from the sources. Early hagiographies make absolutely no mention of the Wends. The Roskilde Chronicle, of about 1138–1140, speaks only of the Wends in connection with events in the past: the flight of Harald Bluetooth to the Wends as well as the abductions and returns by ransom to which Sveyn Forkbeard was subjected (increased from two to three by

---

[20] Asser was granted missionary rights on the island in 1127; *Diplomatarium Danicum* I, 2 (Copenhagen, 1938–), nos. 50–1.
[21] He went on pilgrimage with his wife; Sven Aggesen, 12; Saxo, XII 7, 1–6; Markus Skeggjason, *Eriksdrápa* vv. 28–31.
[22] Saxo, XIII 2, 1–9.
[23] Saxo, XIII 5, 2.
[24] Snorre Sturlason, *Uphaf Magnús blinda* vv. 9–11, in *Heimskringla*, ed. Jonsson, pp. 561–6.
[25] Saxo, XIV 1, 6–7.

the author of the Chronicle).[26] This episode in the Chronicle is dependent on
Adam of Bremen's account and the story is told in a matter of fact fashion which
reveals not a glimmer of passion with regard to the Wends. The second part of
the Chronicle, dealing with the author's own times, does not have a word on the
Wends. It would be reasonable to conclude that at the time the Wends did not
constitute a problem of national importance. Descriptions of what the kings had
accomplished against those southern neighbours were not obligatory. Nation-
wide, an image of the Wends as being an enemy did not yet exist.

The sources deal at length with internal political problems, which abounded.
It had not yet been decided who was to succeed the ageing king Niels. His son,
Magnus, felt his rights threatened by Knud Lavard;[27] relations between them
went from bad to worse, and Magnus finally killed off his rival in 1135. The
murder of Knud Lavard initiated a struggle for power destined to last for more
than 25 years without interruption and involving all leading families. Many lost
their lives.

The middle of the century saw a critical development of events. Magnus,
Niels, Harald Kesje and Erik Emune had fallen, with many of their supporters.
Erik Lam stepped from power voluntarily, to become a monk. The realm was
divided between two kings making war on each other: Svend Grathe and Knud.
The German emperor, Frederick Barbarossa, was not slow to take advantage of
the situation. The two kings had to cede the country to him in 1152, after which
Svend received it back as a royal fief. As for Knud, he was given extensive
estates, to be his thereafter. The net result was continued strife in the realm.
Denmark had lost its independence and the civil war now entered a decisive
phase.

Prior to this, Wendish incursions had been few and far between; among the
population as a whole, they would hardly have made much of an impression
considering the tumultuous events at home. 'The enemy' would be thought of as
someone belonging to the other side in the Civil War. As we come near the
middle of the century, we see the heathens to the south becoming the object of
rather stronger attention. When the Pope exhorted the Christian world to crusades, in 1147, Svend and Knud set aside their differences for a while and joined
forces in an expedition against the Wends. Two of the fallen – Asmund and
Gudmund – are remembered in the Libri Memoriales of the Chapter of Lund as
having died under the sign of the Holy Cross.[28] The idea of crusades had thus
come to Denmark, though some time was to pass before it came to fruition.

---

[26] Chronicon Roskildense 4, ed. M. Cl. Gertz, Scriptores Minores Historiae Danicae Medii
Aevi (Copenhagen, 1970).
[27] Knud Lavard was a dangerous rival. Being the son of Erik Ejegod he clearly had a claim
to the throne and his position was stronger than that of other rivals. He had the support of
the emperor Lothar, whose vassal he had become, receiving the title of knés of the
Obodrites and holding Schleswig in fief. The circumstances are described by H. Paludan,
'Flos Danie', Historie, Jyske samlinger, ny række 7 (1966–7), pp. 497–525.
[28] Libri memoriales capituli Lundensis – Lunde Domkapitels gavebøger, ed. C. Weeke (Copenhagen, 1884–9), p. 195.

These were just the years in which Wendish attacks on Denmark – enfeebled by civil war and incapable of organized defence – became more daring. The Annals of Colbaz carry reports of raids on Skåne in 1150.[29] The following year, Svend Grathe approached the German emperor, entreating him to make his nobles take action against the Wends.[30] Along the Danish coasts there was lively activity, stockades being erected both on land and underwater to prevent the Wends from landing.[31] Where noble families may still primarily have been preoccupied with the fight for the throne, ordinary people living on the coast must have been increasingly afraid of the Wends, who time and again appeared on the beaches, robbing the inhabitants and taking people away into slavery.[32] One may assume that a direct consequence of such acts would be that parts of the population came to see the Wends as synonymous with the enemy. As we shall see this was soon to have political repercussions.

The civil war came to an end in 1157, with the death of both Svend and Knud. Valdemar was on the throne, sole ruler. After such a long period of internal strife the Crown was, however, weak. Valdemar needed a cause to strengthen it. By their repeated plunderings, the Wends had become just the external threat Valdemar needed. They menaced the population living on the coasts and this had to be stopped. Wendish territory and the fight against the Wends became vital issues in the policy put foreward by the new regime; both home and foreign affairs stood to profit from officially declaring the Wends to be the enemy.

At home, Valdemar needed to boost his power and create national unity. To start with, he appointed one of his staunchest supporters, Absalon, as bishop in Roskilde. In doing so he ensured the powerful Hvide-family an influential position in Danish politics and created an alliance between Crown and Church which had ramifications in his foreign policy.[33] Together, Valdemar and Absalon took on the Wends; in succeeding, the two of them would hold the reins of power and an aggressive foreign policy might divert the attention of other powerful factions from the home scene.

Danish independence and Denmark's position in relation to European culture were the major issues in foreign policy. As it was, Denmark was considered a German fief, forcing Valdemar to accept the policies of the German emperor; he took his oath of fealty to Frederick Barbarossa in 1162. The long term goal was to liberate Denmark from this German sovereignity. In the short term, fighting the

---

[29] Colbaz Annals, s.a. 1150, ed. E. Kroman, *Danmarks middelalderlige annaler* (Copenhagen, 1980).
[30] *Diplomatarium Danicum* I, 2, no. 103.
[31] Saxo, XIV 5, 1; 6, 1; 15, 5.
[32] Saxo, XIV 44, 6; XV 6, 11; Helmold, I 65; 83; 92; II 13.
[33] The election of two popes in 1159 affected Danish politics. Archbishop Eskil had ties with the gregorian Alexander III, while circumstances forced Valdemar to follow the policy of the German emperor in supporting Victor IV. Absalon chose to support the Crown rather than the Church, and his position in Roskilde therefore helped to avoid a break between Church and Crown.

Wends with success would improve Denmark's position in relation to the German emperor.

As already stated, Denmark had found its place as a state on the European fringe. Gone were the dreams of a North Sea Empire, to be replaced by the dream of Denmark as the leading power in the Baltic. Being on the periphery of Europe had the advantage of being in the immediate vicinity of heathen lands not yet within the compass of European culture. These it would be possible to acquire with the Pope's blessing.

Thus, the idea of crusading was politically beneficial in more ways than one; the obvious way to point was towards the Wends, describing them as barbaric heathens who needed to be cowed with the Cross and the sword. Having taken the island of Rügen in 1168 or 1169,[34] Denmark approached pope Alexander III, requesting permission to make the conquered island part of the See of Roskilde. The Pope's reply, of 4 November 1169, shows that Denmark described its action against the Wends as just retribution for repeated wrongs, and as a crusade.[35] The Pope was pleased to grant Denmark the missionary rights to Rügen, thus no doubt encouraging further campaigns.

At home, Valdemar was at pains to support this official view of the war on the Wends, as when issuing coins carrying the royal portrait and the Banner of the Cross[36] to enhance his image as a just defender of the true faith. Thanks to Saxo's full account, we may, for the first time, have an opinion on the extent to which an official attitude was accepted by leading families in various parts of the country.

From Saxo's narrative concerning the numerous expeditions against the Wends one gets the impression that the various detachments of the army behaved differently. The Zealanders were an aggressive lot, eager to attack; those from Skåne less eager, so that they occasionally had to be threatened with excommunication to get on the move. The Jutes had no feeling of solidarity with the others and wanted to go home whenever things got rough. Worst of all were those from Falster, who actually tried to thwart Valdemar by informing the enemy of his plans.[37]

These differences in attitude to the fighting are used by Saxo for compositional effect: Valdemar and Absalon are the more to be honoured for having led the strongest and most enthusiastic contingents. The subjugation of the Wends is due to their merit. Their feat is highlighted when Saxo describes the passive, unwilling conduct of detachments from other parts of the country.

---

[34] There is some uncertainty as to the precise date. Danish research has usually dated the conquest to 1169, partly because of arguments adduced by J. C. H. R. Steenstrup, *Venderne og de danske før Valdemar den Stores Tid* (Copenhagen, 1900), pp. 199 ff. However, a date of 1168 is preferred by A. E. Christensen, 'Tiden 1042–1241', *Danmarks historie* vol. 1, p. 334. In this, he follows Helmold.

[35] *Scriptores Minores Historiae Danicae Medii Aevi*, no. 189.

[36] P. Hauberg, 'Danmarks Myntvæsen i Tidsrummet 1146–1241', *Årbøger for Nordisk Oldkyndighed og Historie* 5 (1906), p. 347 no. 61, and plate III no. 61.

[37] Saxo, XIV 22, 2; 23.

Even so, Saxo's account must to some degree reflect the facts of the situation. There were undoubtedly different opinions on the Wendish venture according to which region of Denmark you came from. Not necessarily differences due to diverging attitudes to the Wends, nor differences to be explained merely by lack of courage and fighting spirit. These detachments were led by nobles whose views were determined by the political situation at home. The success of these campaigns would increase the power of Valdemar and his companion, the noble families on Zealand, giving them even more influence on other affairs of the realm. That was not to everybody's liking and for some meant putting a lower priority on the defeat of the Wends.

To what extent the noble families influenced the population as a whole in their attitude to the Wends, and how this affected the possibility of Wends settling in Denmark, we cannot tell. Most, one would suppose, relied more on their own experiences than on what some more or less distant lord might have to say. But this is beyond our means to ascertain. Saxo's writings do, however, give us a glimpse of what things were like in one particular part of the country, the one in which we have a special interest: Falster.

Saxo does not think too highly of the people of Falster. They do not appear to have supported the official view of the Wends, but tried instead to solve the problems arising from their geographical position by considering both Wendish and Danish interests.

To be sure, there were contingents from Falster in the Danish army, but they were ready to resort to compromise to keep off the Wends.[38] What the Wends stood to gain by leaving Falster in peace is made clear by Saxo, who tells us that people on Falster were willing to hold prisoners taken by the Wends, and that from time to time the Wends were informed about attacks being planned by the Danes.[39] The Danish commanders took steps against this leaking of information by making sure that people from Falster and Lolland were told about military moves only in the very last minute.[40]

The accommodating attitude towards the Wends met with on Falster may not have been entirely dictated by necessities of self-defence. Relations of long standing between these southern islands and Wendland may have played a part. One, Gnemer, from Falster is mentioned by Saxo as being an officer on the Danish fleet. He was familiar with the area around Rügen and Barth, and he had a farm on Falster.[41] Now, Gnemer is a name of Slavonic origin, but the way Saxo talks of him, he must have been born on Falster. He may have belonged to a Wendish element in the population which had been there for some time. We also have a Niels from Falster among Absalon's men, and he was well versed in the Wendish language,[42] he had left his home island, where he may have learnt

---

[38] Saxo, XIV 15, 5.
[39] Saxo, XIV 22, 2.
[40] Saxo, XIV 23, 20.
[41] Saxo, XIV 23, 20; 54, 9.
[42] Saxo, XV 1, 4; XVI 4, 9. He is probably identical with the Niels who witnesses a number of charters from the late twelfth century. He heads the laymen witnessing

Wendish from people like Gnemer, to take up an influential post in Absalon's entourage.

The policy of accommodation not withstanding, Falster was not always spared when the Wends were on the attack.[43] The explanation for such apparently arbitrary behaviour may be that Saxo sometimes neglects to distinguish between the various Wendish tribes. Falster may have had friendlier relations with some than with others.

Valdemar's expeditions against the Wends culminated in the Pommeranian campaign of 1185. The Pommeranians were defeated and *dux* Bugislav I was forced to swear an oath of fealty, together with all his allies, to Valdemar's son and heir, Knud IV. Thus, combined Danish and German efforts had succeeded in subduing the Wends militarily, politically and culturally. They no longer constituted a threat to Danish coastal regions. Knud IV was able to add 'King of the Wends' to his title, and attitudes to the Wends might now contain a touch of contempt. Twelfth-century attitudes are clearly revealed in the writings of the two chroniclers, Saxo Grammaticus and Sven Aggesen, both viewing events in the light of the final defeat of the Wends and Bugislav's oath-taking. Even so, they mirror two different points of view.

Sven Aggesen wrote his chronicle of Denmark around 1185–87. The relations which Harald Bluetooth and Sveyn Forkbeard had with Wendland are prosaically described.[44] The Wends do not appear as enemies in this part of Aggesen's account. With later events he deals more briefly, referring the reader to Saxo. The merits of Knud Lavard and Valdemar in fighting the Wends are mentioned in the passing,[45] and it appears that Aggesen himself took part in the expeditions. He saw Absalon levelling the walls of Jomsborg and witnessed Bugislav taking the oath to Knud IV.[46] But what really concerns him are the dealings with the Germans; they are the ones he directs himself against. This may be due to his background, belonging as he did to one of those noble houses in Jutland which took a dim view of Valdemar's repeated and successful shows of power. The Jutish nobles were not inclined to accept the official view of the Wends, which promoted the idea that they were the ultimate enemy.

Saxo, on the other hand, holds the Wends in contempt, as powerful but defeated enemies. They are an instrument in the composition of his work: Under weak kings they behave like wild animals, only to be tamed by the strong. His description serves to illuminate the eulogy of Valdemar's and Absalon's deeds, makes the harshness of the campaigns against Wendland seem legitimate; Here we have the most detailed exposition of the official view on the Wends, on which Valdemar and Absalon based their policies.

Absalon's exchange of property with Esrom Monastery in 1164–78 (*Diplomatarium Danicum* 1, 2, no. 162). Later on, together with other men from Absalon's house, he witnesses a transfer of estates to the monastery, in a charter of 28 August 1167–74 (ibid., no. 185).

[43] Saxo, XIV 22, 1.
[44] Sven Aggesen, 8.
[45] Sven Aggesen, 13; 17–18.
[46] Sven Aggesen, 8; 20.

CONCLUSION

Posterity has seen fit to accept Saxo's opinion of the Wends. A review of the written sources at our disposal shows that in the period prior to the accession of Valdemar, this attitude cannot be traced; and even at the time of Valdemar's campaigns opinions demonstrably differed as to the neighbours to the south. Only later generations – wielding Saxo – were able to create a uniformly negative opinion of them as evil and barbarian, not to be compared with our Nordic Vikings. This is something which must be discarded when assessing the possibility of Wends settling in Denmark during the Viking and Early Middle Ages.

I hope to have shown that our written sources, though meager, can in fact contribute to a discussion of Wendish presence in Denmark. I am quite convinced that this is a direction in which progress may be made. Thus, a careful reading of the sources results in a comparatively detailed picture of conditions among the Wends; the probability of several waves of immigration may be suggested. As to the situation in Denmark, several questions must be introduced and studied: How was the society of the time equipped to deal with problems arising from large scale immigration? What was the legal status of foreigners wanting to settle in Denmark? What provisions regulated right of ownership? – Could foreigners come to own land? Might land be alloted to a foreigner or would he have to acquire it himself? Was the common land reserved for Danes or might foreigners profit from it as well? Are we able to find circumstances that would be especially attractive to immigrants? – Were the southern Danish island thinly populated, for example? An unequivocal answer to these, and other, questions are not to be expected. But pose them we must, if we are to prepare the ground for facing the really fundamental question of whether it was at all practically possible for foreigners – Wends among them – to make a living in Denmark, and if so, on what conditions? The answers we seek demand the cooperation of historians, students of onomastics and archaeologists – all working on their own premisses. It is for the historians to mobilize the written sources, in readiness for future discussions; we can no longer just quote the results of other branches of historical research. With a little help from imagination, we will make progress.

ON THE EARLY COINAGE OF LUND

Brita Malmer

Coins arguably form the most important source for the history of Scandinavia in the Viking and early Medieval periods. About 250,000 Oriental, Byzantine, German and English coins from the Viking period have been found in the Scandinavian countries. In addition to this there are a few thousand domestic coins, mostly from the late Viking period.

Coins differ from other sources for the Viking period in several respects. The coins are *contemporary*, they are *written*, and they appear in *very great quantity*. Other written evidence from the Viking period is extremely scarce and rarely contemporary. The archaeological sources are contemporary and sometimes numerous but they are not written. No other type of evidence permits in the way the coins do a three dimensional analysis of a problem: chronological, spatial and quantitative analysis. By virtue of their great numbers the coins are well suited to statistical treatment. Research results may therefore be tested to a degree that is unusual within the humanities. The fundamental research technique in Viking and Medieval numismatics, the comparison of dies, is a method of objective recording. Other important qualities of the coins as research objects are their fineness and weight, their die axis and their secondary treatment of pecking and fragmentation. These qualities, too, may be recorded objectively. The numismatic evidence for the history of the Viking period, thus, is not only contemporary, written and numerous, it may also be studied through objective methods to a degree that renders numismatics comparable to the natural sciences.

Sture Bolin was one of the first to realize the importance of coins as historical evidence for those periods for which other written evidence is scarce or non-existent. In recent decades it is Peter Sawyer above all who has championed the cause of numismatics to the general public. In *The Age of the Vikings* there is a broad survey of numismatic finds, supplemented with a dozen analyses of finds. In *Kings and Vikings* the numismatic material has been integrated in the text and account has been taken of the most recent research. There is an unmistakable connection between the increased attention paid in recent years to Viking age numismatics and the writings of Peter Sawyer.

Unfortunately, this extraordinary source material has one very big handicap. The methods based on objective recording mentioned above are time-consuming and physically exhausting. This applies in particular to the comparison of dies. No scientific research laboratory with a big and well trained staff is at the disposal of numismatists. In fact only a few persons are engaged in the kind of work mentioned and they generally work alone. Even the great publication projects are progressing slowly. The Swedish series, *Corpus nummorum saeculorum IX–XI qui in Suecia reperti sunt*,[1] has so far produced eight volumes with descriptions of just over 50,000 coins, or barely a quarter of the Swedish Viking period material. We may not expect to see the series completed this side of the year 2000.

Among the Viking period finds Anglo-Saxon, Scandinavian and Samanid coins are particularly suited to die analysis. The relief is sufficiently high and the individual features sufficiently numerous to make the dies distinguishable. Within Viking numismatics die analysis was first applied to Anglo-Saxon coins and it has yielded particularly interesting results in this area of study. Some of these results have direct importance for the Scandinavian coins which are to a large extent imitations of Anglo-Saxon coins. Those parts of the numismatic evidence which it has been possible to subject to die analysis – be it an Anglo-Saxon mint in the period of Æthelræd II, the pseudo-Samanid coinage of the Volga Bulgarians in some decades of the tenth century, or parts of the oldest Sigtuna coinage – appear as small clearly lit spots in a landscape still largely shrouded in obscurity. One area where darkness is slowly being dispelled by on-going die analysis is the first coinage of Cnut the Great in Lund.

P. Hauberg's *Myntforhold og Udmyntninger i Danmark indtil 1146*, published in 1900,[2] still serves as the work of reference for the oldest Danish coinage and its inscriptions, fig. 1. There is a single type with the name of Sven Forkbeard, a *Crux*-imitation from the 990s. No mint is given. According to Hauberg a gap of more than twenty years follows. Cnut's coinage begins in 1018, the year in which he inherited Denmark from his brother Harald. As Cnut no. 1 Hauberg puts an imitation of Æthelræd II's *Last Small Cross*-type (LSC). As no. 2 comes a coin with an obverse imitating Cnut the Great's first English type, *Quatrefoil* (Q). The reverse is the same type, LSC, as no. 1. Cnut's third Danish type imitates the *Quatrefoil* type on both sides. All these were, according to Hauberg, minted in Lund in Skåne.

The twenty year gap between Sven Forkbeard and his son Cnut is now beginning to be bridged by Scandinavian imitations of contemporary Anglo-Saxon coins. Through die analysis it is at best possible to establish long chains linking imitations, with incomprehensible, barbarized legends, with legible and datable coins. Particularly problematic are those imitations which are so well made that it is difficult to distinguish them from the genuine coins. An English scholar, Mark Blackburn, has discovered a chain linking no less than 92 dies, mainly *Long-Cross* (LC) imitations. Some coins in this chain have been struck from original English dies exported to Scandinavia, others are close to the

---

[1] *Corpus nummorum saeculorum IX–XI qui in Suecia reperti sunt* (CNS), ed. B. Malmer (Stockholm, 1975–).
[2] P. Hauberg, *Myntforhold og Udmyntninger i Danmark indtil 1146*, in Det Kongelige Danske Videnskabernes Selskabs Skrifter, 6:te række, historisk og filosofisk Afdeling, 5. 1 (Copenhagen, 1900).

SVEND TVESKJÆG (985—1014)

Lund

KNUD DEN STORE (1018—1035)

Lund

Fig. 1 From P. Hauberg, *Myntforhold og Udmyntninger*, Copenhagen 1900, Tab. I

originals, some are barbarized. Blackburn dates this chain to the very first years of the eleventh century, before the succeeding type, Helmet (H), began to be struck in England c.1003. Regarding the location of the mint Blackburn is very cautious, suggesting 'somewhere east of the North Sea and north of the Danevirke'.[3] The mint must be in Denmark. It could be Lund.

Other Scandinavian die-chains are connected with the change from Æthelræd's last type, Last Small Cross (LSC) c.1009–1017, to Cnut's first type as king of England, Quatrefoil (Q) c.1017–1023. There are two major chains containing dies with Cnut's Danish regal title (23, resp. 68 dies, with at least 43, resp. 125 specimens) and a closely related die-chain with Cnut's English regal title only (39 dies, at least 91 specimens). All these chains are a mixture of imitations of Æthelræd's three last types, LC, H, LSC, and Cnut's first English type, Q. According to the chronology of R. H. M. Dolley the four English prototypes, LC, H, LSC, and Q, cover the period c.997–1023. A closer study of these chains suggests that Cnut's Danish coinage began before 1018, before the death of his brother Harald.[4]

By means of the terminus post quem of the finds (the earliest possible date of the youngest coin) it may be established that the English coin types were normally copied very soon in Scandinavia, within that short period of about six years during which each type was legal tender in England. The first type struck for Cnut as king of Denmark therefore ought to be Quatrefoil (in England c.1017–1023) and not Last Small Cross (in England c.1009–1017). Attention has been drawn to this problem by Marion Archibald who suggests a later date for Quatrefoil.[5] It is, however, unlikely that the minting of Quatrefoil in England should have started as late as 1018, more than a year after Cnut's accession. The extremely well organized English coinage could hardly have been not functioning for such a long period. But it is equally unlikely that an older type no longer current in England should have been taken by Cnut as a model for his first Danish coinage. Mark Blackburn explores the remaining alternative, that Cnut's first Danish coinage was minted before the introduction of Quatrefoil in England, but prefers not to commit himself.[6]

It is impossible in this context to show those die-chains which demonstrate that Cnut's first Danish coins, the Last Small Cross imitations, Hauberg no. 1, are in fact just part of a considerable coinage which probably began long before 1018. Instead, a smaller section of the longest of the above-mentioned die-chains must serve to illustrate the present state of numismatic affairs. In the autumn of

[3]   M. A. S. Blackburn, 'An imitative workshop active during Æthelræd II's Long Cross issue', in Studies in Northern Coinages of the Eleventh Century, ed. C. J. Becker (Copenhagen, 1981), p. 56.

[4]   B. Malmer, 'On the Danish coinage of Cnut, Hauberg type 1', Nordisk Numismatisk Unions Medlemsblad 1986: 9, pp. 219–22.

[5]   M. Archibald, 'Coins and Currency', in Viking Artefacts: a select catalogue, ed. J. A. Graham-Campbell (London, 1980), p. 119.

[6]   M. A. S. Blackburn and S. Lyon, 'Regional die-production in Cnut's Quatrefoil issue', in Anglo-Saxon Monetary History: essays in memory of Michael Dolley, ed. M. A. S. Blackburn (Leicester, 1986), pp. 258–9.

1987 the entire chain comprises 29 obverse dies and 39 reverse dies – these numbers are likely to increase gradually. The distribution of types of these 68 dies is shown in this table:

Type:	LC	H	LSC	Q	Total
Obv.:	10	2	11	6	29
Rev.:	9	2	26	2	39

Twenty-seven reverse dies (69%) but only four obverse dies (14%) have blundered legends. The twenty-five legible obverse dies are distributed like this:

Æthelræd	English title	16 dies
Cnut	Danish title	1
Cnut	English title	8

The twelve legible reverse dies have the following legends:

Ascetel mo Lund
Asthrith mo Nor
Ælfsige mo Cesth
Brethnoth mo E
Brithnoth mo Lud
Eadwold m Lun
Leofn mo Unta
Leofric mo Cntwa
Lyfinc on Lund
Thorcetl mo Lund
Thorcl mo Lund
Wulfwine mo Lunde

The Ascetel die is linked with the only obverse die in the chain which has Cnut's Danish regal title. Ascetel might have been active in Lund in Skåne. The remaining eleven reverse dies are either imports from England or they are Scandinavian imitations of English dies. This means that *Lund* denotes London, *E* (*Eoferwic*) York, etc.

The section of the long chain described above, which is illustrated on fig. 2, includes five legible obverse dies, I–V, with *Cnut rex Dænor* as die I. Reverse die no. 1 is the Ascetel die from Lund in Skåne just mentioned. The remaining reverse dies, nos. 2–10, have all meaningless combinations of letters. Fig. 3 illustrates the corresponding obverse dies, I–V, and the reverses nos. 4, 5, 6, 8 and 10.

The list of dies and coins below describes the twenty-five coins belonging to the chain section in fig. 2. Sixteen specimens derive from eight different finds

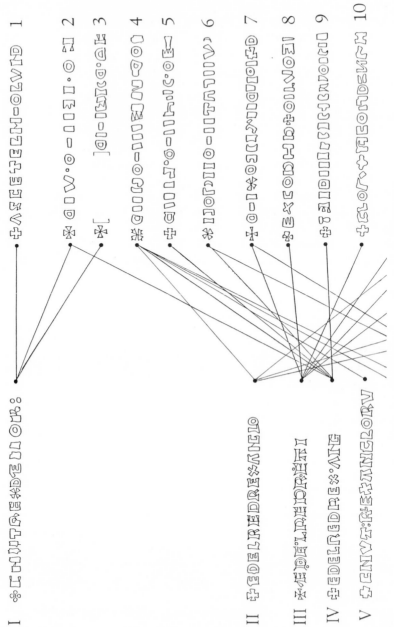

Fig. 2 Part of a Danish die-chain. Inscriptions and die-links

with a known *terminus post quem*. The dates of these eight hoards are 1018–, 1018–, 1021–, 1024–, 1056–, 1102–, 1106–, 1120–. It may be assumed that coins belonging to the same die-chain have all been struck within a limited period. Coins from the same chain tend to appear in hoards a short time after being struck. Consequently the oldest hoards were buried in 1018 or slightly later. Other coins may then stay in circulation a century or more. The cluster of finds from the beginning of the twelfth century may be due to the fact that towards the end of the Viking period hoards get fewer but also larger, which increases the chance of survival of single specimens.

In this section of the long chain the median weight is 1.48 g. The youngest type, *Quatrefoil*, is represented by a single die. In the chain referred to above with Cnut's English title (39 dies) *Quatrefoil* contributes one fifth of the dies. In this latter chain one finds a chronologically related difference of weight between the older part of the chain (without *Quatrefoil*) and its younger part (with *Quatrefoil*). The median weight is 1.49 g for the older part, 1.21 g for the younger part.[7] For the English coinage, on which the Danish was modelled, the introduction of *Quatrefoil* also implies a weight reduction, in this case from 1.32 g to 1.06 g. Danish *Last Small Cross* imitations with a high median weight should at least partly have been struck before the introduction of *Quatrefoil*, before the death, that is, of Harald Svensson.

The detailed study of Danish coinage in the second decade of the eleventh century has only just started. As the study of dies progresses an increasingly exact knowledge will be gained. It is already clear that the numismatic evidence is going to increase our knowledge about economic and political conditions in Denmark not only in the reigns of Sven Forkbeard and Cnut the Great, both of whom are already fairly familiar in a numismatic context, but also in that so far rather obscure reign of Harald Svensson 1014–1018.

---

[7]   B. Malmer, 'Coinage and monetary circulation in late Viking Age Scandinavia according to recent die-studies', 10th International Numismatic Congress, London, 1986 (forthcoming).

Fig. 3   Part of a Danish die-chain. The corresponding coins are marked with * in the List of dies and coins. Photo: Gert Rispling, Stockholm. Enlarged, 1.5:1

List of Dies and Coins[8]

English prototypes: *Long Cross* (LC), c.997–1003; *Helmet* (H), c.1003–1009; *Last Small Cross* (LSC), c.1009–1017; *Quatrefoil* (Q), c.1017–1023.

Obverse I = LSC; I–III = LC; IV = H; V = Q.
Reverse 1–10 = LSC. * = reproduced in fig. 3.

I/1 (a) Skåne, 'Everlöv', *t.p.q.* 1018. CNS 3.4.59.888. 1.48 g.

I/2 (a) Gotland, Hall, Gannarve, *t.p.q.* 1120. BJ G 185. 1.43 g.
    (b) Gotland, Rute, Fardume, *t.p.q.* 1024. BJ G 94. 1.24 g.
    (c) KMK Syst. Coll. 1.79 g.

I/3 (a) KMK Syst. Coll. 1.46 g. Obv.*

II/4 (a) Gotland, Lye, Mannegårda, *t.p.q.* 1102. BJ G 181. 1.24 g.
    (b) KMK Syst. Coll. 1.41 g.

II/– (a) Gotland, Närd, Hallsarve, *t.p.q.* 1106. BJ G 183. 1.72 g.
Reverse not described in this connection. Obv.*

III/7 (a) Skåne, 'Everlöv', *t.p.q.* 1018. CNS 3.4.59.853. 1.52 g.

III/8 (a) Gotland, Lye, Mannegårda, *t.p.q.* 1102. BJ G 181. 1.48 g.
    (b) Gotland, Rute, Fardume, *t.p.q.* 1024. BJ G 94. 1.14 g.
    (c) KMK Syst. Coll. 1.48 g. Rev.*
    (d) KMK Syst. Coll. 1.07 g. Obv.*

III/10 (a) Medelpad, Indal, Stige, *t.p.q.* 1021. BJ S 45. 1.70 g.
    (b) Gotland, Lye, Mannegårda, *t.p.q.* 1102. BJ G 181. 1.34 g. Rev.*

IV/2 (a) Skåne, 'Everlöv', *t.p.q.* 1018. CNS 3.4.59.861. 1.62 g.

IV/4 (a) Blekinge, Edestad, Gärestad, *t.p.q.* 1056. BJ D 110. 1.12.g.

IV/5 (a) Gotland, Lye, Mannegårda, *t.p.q.* 1102. BJ G 181. 1.36 g. Rev.*

IV/6 (a) Skåne, 'Everlöv', *t.p.q.* 1018. CNS 3.4.59.860. 1.49 g.

IV/9 (a) KMK Syst. Coll. 1.31 g. Obv.*

[8] The abbreviations used in the following list are:
BJ M. A. S. Blackburn and K. Jonsson, 'The Anglo-Saxon and Anglo-Norman element of north European coin finds', in *Viking-Age Coinage in the Northern Lands: The Sixth Oxford Symposium on Coinage and Monetary History*, ed. M. A. S. Blackburn and D. M. Metcalf, BAR, IS 122 (Oxford, 1981), pp. 147–255.
CNS *Corpus nummorum saeculorum IX–IX qui in Suecia reperti sunt.*
KMK Royal Coin Cabinet, Stockholm.

V/4   (a) Medelpad, Indal, Stige, *t.p.q.* 1021. *BJ* S 45. 1.46 g.

        (b) Gotland, Lojsta, Kvie, *t.p.q.* 1018. *BJ* G 81. 1.00 g. Rev.*

        (c) KMK Syst. Coll. 1.54 g. Obv.*

        (d) KMK Syst. Coll. 1.46 g. Fragment.

–/6   (a) KMK Syst. Coll. 1.76 g. Rev.* Obverse not described in this connection.

THE ORIGIN OF THE *TUNA*-NAMES RECONSIDERED

Thorsten Andersson

The word Swedish *tun*, English *town*, German *Zaun* etc. exists in all Germanic languages except Gothic; the fact that it is missing there is probably accidental. The word, which has an equivalent in Celtic languages (cf. below), originally meant 'fence' (as still in German), and also, secondarily, 'enclosure'. It is only natural that such a word should have been used frequently in the formation of place-names. The English place-names in -*ton* are particularly numerous, but also in other parts of the Germanic language area the name element is well represented, although with different densities of distribution.[1]

A group of names appearing in plural form has attracted particular attention, namely the Scandinavian *tuna*-names. Their core area is in the Mälar region in middle Sweden, the country of the *sviones*, but they exist also in other Swedish areas, partly as simplicia, *Tuna*, OSw. (i) *Tunum*, partly as second elements, -*tuna*, OSw. (i) -*tunum*. Finally, plural names also occur in Denmark and Norway, though more by way of exception.[2]

The *tuna*-names are among the most discussed Scandinavian place-names. For a long time they have been in the focus of interest for linguists, especially place-name scholars, and also archaeologists and historians. The reason is that special functions in prehistoric society have been attributed to places with *tuna*-names. It has been suggested that they were cult places, trading places, fortified places, castles, or administrative centres in general.

It is true that in Karl Axel Holmberg's substantial monograph on *tuna*-names, to which reference is made for earlier research,[3] it is maintained that these names had no special meaning but, like the word *tun*, only meant 'fence' and 'enclosure' in general.[4] As I have tried to show in a review of Holmberg's book, this conclusion is premature.[5] Purely linguistic reasons clearly indicate that certain *tuna*-places did have a special function in society; this is confirmed by the intimate connection between – in Old Swedish form – *Solændatunum* and *Solænda hundare*, *Valændatunum* and *Valænda hundare* in Uppland, where *Solænda* and *Valæn-*

---

[1] K. A. Holmberg, *De svenska tuna-namnen*, Studier till en svensk ortnamnsatlas 12 (Uppsala, 1969), pp. 244 ff. on conditions outside Sweden; K. Cameron, *English place-names*, 3rd. ed. (London, 1977), pp. 141 ff.
[2] Holmberg, *De svenska tuna-namnen*, pp. 249 ff.
[3] ibid., pp. 9 ff.
[4] ibid., p. 279.
[5] T. Andersson, '*Tuna*-problem', *Namn och bygd* 56 (1968), pp. 111 ff.

da (gen. pl.) are old inhabitant designations, referring to the people in *Soland* and *Valand* respectively, two old districts (*land*) that had been arranged in the old *hundare* ('hundred') organization. Sollentuna and Vallentuna, as the places are called today, were each apparently centres of a *hundare* district.

Holmberg's total zero position on the *tuna*-names has not gained any support. The question is no longer *whether* the *tuna*-places did have a special function, but *to what extent* was this the case. There are, however, different opinions about this. Against the background of his own research on the *tuna*-names, spanning several decades but published only in preliminary surveys Lars Hellberg has maintained that, by and large and apart from a few exceptions named after other names, the *tuna*-names denoted administrative centres in ancient society;[6] thus *tuna* is interpreted as a *terminus technicus*, meaning '(public) main centre of territorial administration (in a broad sense)'.[7] Also Ingemar Olsson, who has published an excellent summary of the recent *tuna*-debate, considers the *tuna*-names as normally carrying a special meaning.[8] According to Harry Ståhl, however, these names probably do not constitute a uniform group.[9] A wait-and-see attitude is represented by Sölve Göransson and the present writer in a survey of ancient territorial organization.[10]

This question, only briefly touched upon here, will not be discussed more closely in this context; we have every reason to await the results of Lars Hellberg's investigation of the *tuna*-names. It should be pointed out, however, that there is a risk of circular reasoning in assuming *a priori* that *tuna* has a special signification. Assuming that the *tuna*-names have developed out of compounds with the element *tun* 'fence', 'enclosure' (which, tacitly, I have done above), it would indeed be remarkable if, contrary to the *tun*-names in singular (*Tun, -tun*), they generally refer to centres of some kind. Thus we have reached the quite decisive question from a linguistic point of view: how has *tuna* come to develop a special meaning? – a question that is still unanswered[11] and has hitherto been much neglected. The answer to this question is decisive for our understanding of the *tuna*-names as a group, as well as of individual *tuna*-names. The discussion about the origin of the *tuna*-names runs along two main lines, one taking influences from outside into account, the other preferring a vernacular develop-

---

[6] L. Hellberg, 'Ortnamnen och den forntida sveastaten: Presentation av ett forskningsprojekt', *Inledningar till NORNAs fjärde symposium Ortnamn och samhälle på Hanaholmen den 25.–27.4.75* 1. *Namngivning* (Helsingfors, 1975), pp. 92–110, 110a–d (duplic.); id., 'Aktuell forskning om tuna-namnen', *Ortnamnssällskapet i Uppsala. Namnspalten i UNT 3. 9.10 1984–24.9 1985* (Uppsala, 1985), pp. 20–4.
[7] Hellberg, 'Aktuell forskning om tuna-namnen', p. 21.
[8] I. Olsson, 'Tuna-namnen i Sverige – forskningsläget', *Fornvännen* 71 (1976), pp. 71–81.
[9] H. Ståhl, 'Tun. Ortnamn: Sverige', *Kulturhistoriskt lexikon för nordisk medeltid från vikingatid till reformationstid* 19 (Malmö, 1975), col. 48.
[10] T. Andersson and S. Göransson, 'Forskning om äldre territoriell indelning i Sverige. En introduktion', *Bebyggelsehistorisk tidskrift* 4 (1982), p. 5.
[11] Hellberg, 'Aktuell forskning om tuna-namnen', pp. 20, 24.

ment.[12] We are, thus, faced with a question that is always important when dealing with ancient social organization.

It has been suggested that *tun* in the *tuna*-names refers to a special fence or defense work.[13] This idea has no support in the Scandinavian material of appellatives, however, nor is there any archaeological evidence to support it. On the other hand, Continental Germanic material shows that *tun* was also used for fortifications, which in itself is only natural. Especially interesting is that derivations of *tun*, medieval Latin *tuninus, tuninum, tunimus*, are known for instance from a document, issued by Charlemagne, where it denotes a special fence around his demesnes.[14] Of course the possibility cannot be excluded that, in the Swedish core area, Scandinavian *tun* was influenced by the usage of the equivalent word on the continent or, for that matter, that we are here dealing with a purely vernacular development of a special fortification meaning of the word *tun*. There is nothing, however, that speaks in favour of this explanation of *tuna*, nor does it occupy any central interest in current research.

What *is* of central interest is a hypothesis about Celtic influence on the *tuna*-names. This hypothesis, suggested a long time ago by Sune Lindqvist[15] and Magnus Olsen[16] has never been abandoned in the discussion, and it still has its advocates. Sune Lindqvist, who sees early trading centres in the *tuna*-places, wants to explain *tuna* as a popular etymological transformation of *-dūnum*, known in Roman Iron Age-Scandinavia (the first four centuries AD) from names of fortified towns in the Celtic provinces that were subdued by the Romans. For the dating he refers particularly to the newly created name *Augustodūnum* (Autun) in Gallia, founded some years BC on the command of Emperor Augustus.

An essay on the name *Sigtuna* by Magnus Olsen[17] has been particularly important for the continued discussion, even though it is a mere outline. In this name he sees an equivalent to the four examples of the Gallic *Segodūnum*, where the second element is a latinized form of the Gallic *-dūnon* 'castle'. According to Olsen's opinion we are here dealing with a Gallic appellative **segodūnon* 'strong castle', which is said to have been taken over by the Germanic peoples, who are supposed to have etymologically associated the first element with Germanic **segi(z)-*, ON *sigr* 'victory'. Olsen assumes a general Celtic influence on Germanic *tun* (according to certain authorities it was even borrowed from Celtic languages[18]), so for example in Engl. *town*, in the name of Norway's oldest town,

---

12 Andersson and Göransson, 'Forskning om äldre territoriell indelning i Sverige', p. 5.
13 Holmberg, *De svenska tuna-namnen*, pp. 21 ff.; Andersson, '*Tuna*-problem', p. 123.
14 Andersson, '*Tuna*-problem', p. 123.
15 S. Lindqvist, *Den helige Eskils biskopsdöme. Några arkeologiska vittnesbörd om den kristna kyrkans första organisation inom mellersta Sverige* (Stockholm, 1915), later published as *Antikvarisk tidskrift för Sverige* 22:1 (1917), pp. 142–3, 161, n. 1; id., 'Åker och Tuna. En ortnamnsstudie', *Fornvännen* 13 (1918), pp. 25 ff.
16 M. Olsen, 'Sigtuna', *Namn och bygd* 5 (1917), pp. 90–2.
17 loc. cit.
18 Holmberg, *De svenska tuna-namnen*, p. 244.

ONorw. *Túnsberg* (Tønsberg), and in the plural Norwegian *Tune*. In particular he points to Gallic names like *Lugudūnum* (Lyon), *Virodūnum* (Verdun) and, as we have seen, *Segodūnum*.[19]

According to Olsen a word borrowed from Gallic thus forms the basis of *Sigtuna*, in the first place the well-known *Sigtuna* in Uppland, but also of some of the other Scandinavian *Sigtuna*-names which, consequently, he does not regard as named after the historically well-known Upplandic name – probably the most widely held opinion.[20]

Jöran Sahlgren, who wants to connect the *tuna*-names with the ancient sea-war organization (OSw. *leþunger*), alternatively joins Sune Lindqvist and Magnus Olsen in assuming influences from the Celtic *dūnon* 'castle' and he thinks that *Sigtuna* might be borrowed directly from the castle name *Segodūnum*.[21]

The idea of a Celtic loan in *Sigtuna* and in the *tuna*-names on the whole is rejected by Karl Axel Holmberg,[22] but has otherwise never been totally dismissed. Lately, Ingemar Olsson in particular has pleaded for a test of this hypothesis,[23] which Stefan Brink, too, finds interesting.[24] According to Olsson an unforced interpretation of 'fortified place, trading centre' or the like is possible. Recently Olsson has briefly outlined how the Celtic hypothesis could be supported.[25] He makes a connection with another hypothesis, that, during the early Roman Iron Age, leather in large quantities was being exported from Sweden to the Roman army along the *Limes*,[26] and he is of the opinion that, if this idea is right, there were good opportunities for Scandinavians to accept and bring home the Celtic name element. In its Latin form, *-dunum*, with an ending that fits with the predominant Old Swedish dative form, will easily pass into Old Swedish morphology; the idea that *Sigtuna* is named after *Segodūnum* may possibly be supported by early runic evidence, **til sihtunum**.[27] Olsson's idea is undoubtedly interesting and well worth closer scrutiny. Already at this stage, however, it

---

[19] See further, Holmberg, *De svenska tuna-namnen*, p. 244.
[20] Holmberg, *De svenska tuna-namnen*, pp. 40 ff., 149; J. P. Strid, 'Sigtuna i myt och verklighet. De språkliga källorna till Sigtunas äldsta historia', *Avstamp – för en ny Sigtunaforskning. 18 forskare om Sigtuna. Heldagsseminarium kring Sigtunaforskning den 26 november 1987, Gröna ladan, Sigtuna*, ed. S. Tesch (Sigtuna, 1989), p. 112.
[21] J. Sahlgren, *Vad våra ortnamn berätta*, Studentföreningen Verdandis småskrifter 351 (Stockholm, 1932), 2nd ed. (Stockholm, 1963), pp. 39 ff.; id., 'Sigtuna', *Ortnamnssällskapets i Uppsala årsskrift* 1960, pp. 29–34.
[22] Holmberg, *De svenska tuna-namnen*, pp. 24, 146 ff.
[23] Olsson, 'Tuna-namnen i Sverige', p. 79.
[24] S. Brink, *Ortnamn i Hälsingland* (Stockholm, 1984), p. 57.
[25] I. Olsson, Referee's assessment of applications for an extra lectureship in Scandinavian languages at Uppsala University, April 21 1988 (unpublished), p. 5.
[26] U. E. Hagberg, *The archaeology of Skedemosse 2, The votive deposits in the Skedemosse fen and their relation to the Iron-Age settlement on Öland, Sweden* (Stockholm, 1967), pp. 121 ff.; id., *Skedemosse. Studier i ett öländskt offerfynd från järnåldern* (Stockholm, 1967), pp. 21 ff.
[27] C. Åneman, 'Runbelägget **til sihtunum**', *Studia onomastica. Festskrift till Thorsten Andersson den 23 februari 1989*, ed. L. Peterson and S. Strandberg with L. Elmevik, L. Moberg and A. Rostvik (Stockholm, 1989), pp. 441–5.

ought to be mentioned that the leather is supposed to have been exported from Götaland in southern Sweden, while the *tuna*-names have their centre in eastern Svealand around Lake Mälaren.

The hypothesis that *tuna* is a borrowed element undoubtedly owes its origin to the difficulty of explaining the special meaning of the name element out of the basic meanings 'fence' and 'enclosure'. The main question then will be whether it is really necessary to look outside Scandinavia in order to explain the special status of the *tuna*-names. Since the appellative material does not give us any support,[28] we have to turn to the place-names.

As has been pointed out, the place-name element *tun* is well evidenced all over the area of Germanic languages. It is quite natural that a word meaning 'enclosure' is used in the formation of place-names and that the names can refer to enclosures of different kinds, for example farmsteads, as in lots of English -*ton*-names and in several Norwegian -*tun*-names, or enclosed pasture land for cattle, as in the Danish *Galten* < *Galtatun 'enclosure for boars'.[29] Of course we must expect such a natural usage of *tun* also in Sweden; the opposite would be remarkable, to say the least. It is from such a natural usage of *tun* that, in the first place, we must try to explain the special function of the *tuna*-names. The plural form does not in itself need a special explanation; *Tuna*, -*tuna* is on much the same lines as normal place-name patterns, *Berga*, -*berga*, *Dala*, -*dala*, from the words *berg* 'mountain', *dal* 'valley', etc. We must not assume *a priori* that the plural form implies a special function (cf. below on *Tun* and *Tuna* in Västergötland). The roots of *tuna* as a *terminus technicus* for a centre of some kind can thus be looked for in the *tuna*-names as well as in the *tun*-names.

Two different ways have been tried in order to explain a vernacular development of a special meaning of *tuna*. Already at an early stage attention was drawn to the fact that it is not rare for the names of gods to form the first element in *tuna*-names, for example *Frö* (ON *Freyr*) in *Fröstuna* (Frustuna), *Fröja* (ON *Freyja*) in *Frötuna*, *Tor* (ON *Þórr*) in *Torstuna*, *Ull* (ON *Ullr*) in *Ultuna*.[30] Karl Henrik Karlsson is of the opinion that, in theophoric names of this kind, *tun*, which he otherwise interprets as a designation of the enclosed farmyard, may have referred to a sacrificial place or a place, consecrated to the god.[31] Similar ideas about enclosed cult places have been published by Oskar Lundberg,[32] Adolf

---

[28] Olsson, '*Tuna*-namnen i Sverige', p. 79.
[29] Holmberg, *De svenska tuna-namnen*, pp. 249 ff.; Cameron, *English place-names*, pp. 141 ff.; *Norsk stadnamnleksikon*, ed. J. Sandnes and O. Stemshaug, 3rd ed. (Oslo, 1990), pp. 323–4.
[30] Holmberg, *De svenska tuna-namnen*, pp. 10 ff., 16 ff.; Andersson, '*Tuna*-problem', p. 104.
[31] K. H. Karlsson, 'Några bidrag till Sveriges uppodlingshistoria hemtade från ortnamns-forskningens område', *Svenska fornminnesföreningens tidskrift* 10 (1900), p. 46.
[32] O. Lundberg and H. Sperber, *Härnevi*, Uppsala universitets årsskrift 1911. Filosofi, språkvetenskap och historiska vetenskaper 3:4 (Uppsala, 1911), pp. 23, 30 ff.

Noreen,[33] Otto von Friesen,[34] Erik Brate[35] and also by Jöran Sahlgren.[36] The latter, however, changed his mind later.[37]

It is a very attractive idea to regard the theophoric *tuna*-names as at least one of the sources for the special meaning of centre; the cult places formed important centres for the people of the district. I have pointed to this possibility in oral discussions, for example in a symposium on the age of settlements and settlement-names in Copenhagen in 1982,[38] and it is suggested in a survey of territorial organization by Sölve Göransson and myself.[39]

Names like *Fröstuna, Frötuna, Torstuna* and *Ultuna* can be supposed to have denoted enclosed cult places, of course without the word *tun* itself necessarily having meant 'cult place'.[40] Against this argument it has been objected that, for example, *Ultuna* in Uppland can be seen as an elliptic formation from *Ulleråker*, the name of the cult place proper, 'Ull's acre', or that, in any case, the first element in *Ultuna* possibly emanates from the cult on the acre.[41] To this it may be objected that, firstly, there is no reason why several cult places of a certain god could not have existed close to each other (at *Torstuna* and *Torsåker* in Uppland there is also *Torslunda* 'Tor's grove'), secondly, we are here concerned with the origin of the type of name, not with the formation of particular, preserved place-names. Circular reasoning lies dangerously near at hand if we assume that each *tuna*-name denotes an administrative centre.

The idea that, among other things, *tun* may have referred to precisely enclosed cult places seems to be supported by names like *Hovtun* in Norway and *Vitten* in Denmark, provided that they contain designations of cult places, *hov* and *vi*, as first elements;[42] according to Magnus Olsen *Hovtun* goes back to an

[33] A. Noreen, *Spridda studier. Populära uppsatser* 3 (Stockholm, 1913), pp. 113–14.
[34] O. von Friesen, 'Upländska sockennamn', *Upsala nya tidning*, Christmas number, 1915, p. 3; id., 'Bynamn på de uppländska runstenarna', *Namn och bygd* 18 (1930), p. 98.
[35] E. Brate, 'Åker och Tuna', *Fornvännen* 13 (1918), pp. 209–10.
[36] J. Sahlgren, 'Forntida svenska kulturprovinser och kulturvägar', *Rig* 3 (1920), p. 162, reprinted in id., *Valda ortnamnsstudier (Opuscula toponymica selecta)*, Acta Academiae regiae Gustavi Adolphi 43 (Uppsala/Copenhagen, 1964).
[37] See above, n. 21.
[38] Following a lecture by Lars Hellberg which was not published in the proceedings of the symposium, *Bebyggelsers og bebyggelsesnavnes alder. NORNAs niende symposium i København 25–27 oktober 1982*, ed. V. Dalberg, G. Fellows-Jensen, B. Jørgensen and J. Kousgård Sørensen, NORNA-rapporter 26 (Uppsala, 1984).
[39] Andersson and Göransson, 'Forskning om äldre territoriell indelning i Sverige', p. 5.
[40] Cf. Holmberg, *De svenska tuna-namnen*, pp. 273 ff.; Andersson, 'Tuna-problem', p. 109.
[41] Hellberg, 'Ortnamnen och den forntida sveastaten', p. 100; id., 'Hedendomens spår i uppländska ortnamn', *Ortnamnssällskapets i Uppsala årsskrift* (1986), pp. 52 ff.; cf. Olsson, 'Tuna-namnen i Sverige', p. 80.
[42] Andersson, 'Tuna-problem', pp. 100–1, 103, 109; B. Jørgensen, *Dansk stednavneleksikon* 2, *Jylland – nordlige del* (Copenhagen, 1982), p. 144; on *hov*, T. Andersson, 'Germanisch Hof – Hügel, Hof, Heiligtum', *Sprache und Recht. Beiträge zur Kulturgeschichte des Mittelalters. Festschrift für Ruth Schmidt-Wiegand zum 60. Geburtstag*, ed. K. Hauck, K. Kroeschell, S. Sonderegger, D. Hüpper and G. von Olberg (Berlin/New York, 1986), pp. 1–9.

appellative meaning 'enclosed cult place'.[43] Another Norwegian name, *Logtun* (to ON *lǫg* n. pl. 'law'), directs the attention to another natural starting point for the development of *tun* into a term for a centre, namely the 'thing' places; *Logtun* was the name of the place for the Frosta Thing in Trøndelag.[44] The close connection between administrative division and *tuna*-names[45] can speak in favour of enclosed 'thing' places having played a role for the origin of a *tuna*-term.[46] Direct indications like the ones regarding the theophoric *tuna*-names are, however, missing.

A totally different way of explaining a special meaning of *tuna* has been suggested by Ivar Lundahl. He assumes that the *tun* that we encounter in the village names *Tun*, *Tuna* and *Sätuna* in Västergötland meant 'farm', and, *Sätuna* consequently, 'the farm by the lake'.[47] This is a very plausible assumption; it would actually be strange if *tun* had not developed this meaning also in Sweden.[48] Lundahl draws particular attention to the fact that, in the Edda, the plural of *tun* is used meaning 'farm', for example *Freyjo túna* (gen. pl.) 'Freyja's farm'.[49] Following Magnus Olsen's interpretation of ONorw. *Bœr*, *Býr* (to ON *bœr*, *býr* 'farm'),[50] Lundahl sees the meaning 'the farm par préférence' in the simplex *Tuna*. This interpretation of *tuna* undeniably opens up another way of understanding the special meaning of 'administrative centre' or the like.

What is interesting with these two possible explanations of the origin of the *tuna*-names is that they do not exclude each other: both of them have a natural basis in ancient society with local chieftains and certain cult and 'thing' places. In this prehistoric society *tuna* might well have developed its special meaning in a purely domestic context. Beside *tuna*-names which have developed naturally, we can then expect new names, formed with a *terminus technicus tuna*; simplicia *Tuna* meaning 'administrative centre' or the like might have succeeded other, genuine place-names, in the same way as names of the type OSw. *Kirkioby* 'church village' and *Mølnoby* 'mill village' have sometimes replaced older names.[51] In that case we must expect to find *tuna*-names of different character

[43] M. Olsen, 'Kultminne i stadnamn. Norge', *Religionshistorie*, ed. N. Lid, Nordisk kultur 26 (Stockholm/Oslo/Copenhagen, 1942), p. 60.
[44] Andersson, '*Tuna*-problem', p. 101; J. Sandnes, 'Stadnamn i Trøndelag', *Trøndermål. Språkarv og språkforhold i Trøndelag og på Nordmøre*, ed. A. Dalen and O. Stemshaug (Oslo, 1972), p. 70.
[45] See above pp. 197 f.
[46] Cf. Ståhl, 'Tun. Ortnamn: Sverige', col. 48.
[47] *Sveriges ortnamn. Ortnamnen i Skaraborgs län*, vol. 1 (1972), pp. 30–1; vol. 4 (1954), pp. 73–4; vol. 11: 1 (1969), pp. 110–11; vol. 16 (1965), pp. 30–1; see also Holmberg, *De svenska tuna-namnen*, p. 23.
[48] Cf. Andersson, '*Tuna*-problem', pp. 110–11.
[49] *Sveriges ortnamn. Ortnamnen i Skaraborgs län*, vol. 11: 1, p. 111.
[50] M. Olsen, *Ættegård og helligdom. Norske stedsnavn sosialt og religionshistorisk belyst*, Institutt for sammenlignende kulturforskning, Ser. A. Forelesninger 9a (Oslo et al., 1926), pp. 213 ff.
[51] T. Andersson, 'Bebyggelsenamn givna efter fornlämningar', *Bebyggelsers og bebyggelsesnavnes alder* (see above, n. 38), p. 309.

and status side by side, names that cannot be separated from each other in a purely formal way.

Two main lines along which attempts have been made to explain the origin of the *tuna*-names have been presented here: one presupposing foreign influence and the other assuming a vernacular development from a normal usage of *tun* 'fence', 'enclosure' as a place-name element. It is still too early to draw a final conclusion. There are no cogent reasons for assuming loans. The complete picture of names formed with the element *tun*, in Scandinavian as well as in Germanic areas on the whole, rather speaks in favour of the special meaning having grown out of a natural name usage, i.e. *tuna* as *terminus technicus* has a secondary origin in the Swedish area. The hypothesis about foreign influences cannot, however, be rejected. It is also possible that vernacular development tendencies in OSw. *Tunum*, *-tunum* can have been hastened and strengthened thanks to influences from a foreign element *-dunum*. It is highly desirable that the loan hypothesis be critically tested, not least because such a test would cast light on the big question to what extent foreign influences in general affected pre-Christian Scandinavia.[52]

The question about the origin of a special *tuna*-term is of fundamental importance for the understanding of the *tuna*-names. If we assume a successive, vernacular development from certain types of names (simplicia and certain compounds), we should expect to find several normal place-name formations among the *tuna*-names, with *tun* referring to enclosures of various kinds. If, on the other hand, we consider the *tuna*-names to have been modelled on foreign names, we can to a higher degree regard them as referring to centres. Consequently, the understanding of the origin of the *tuna*-names leads directly into another question, already mentioned in the introduction, a question that appears as central for current *tuna*-research, namely to what extent *tuna*-names denoted special centres and to what extent they are names of farmsteads and other enclosures which have developed naturally.

This question, which must be kept open for the time being, is also intimately connected with the question of the distribution of the *tuna*-names and their relation to the singular *tun*-names, a question that can be given a concrete form with a reference to *Tun* and *Tuna* in the *Wahlheimat* of the *Jubilar*. Is it necessary or even appropriate to regard them as essentially different? That question cannot be answered until the problems presented here have been thoroughly aired. The purpose of my presentation has been precisely to emphasize and to specify central questions that are relevant for the assessment of the origin of the *tuna*-names.

---

[52] Cf. Andersson, 'Germanisch *Hof* – Hügel, Hof, Heiligtum', pp. 6 ff.

ICONOGRAPHY AND RUNE STONES: THE EXAMPLE OF SPARLÖSA

Åke Hyenstrand

The symbolic character of Viking art, for example on rune stones, is an important key to the understanding of early Christianity in Scandinavia and of Scandinavia's connections with central and Western Europe. This topic has recently been discussed in a substantial volume from a conference in Marburg, which includes Signe Horn Fugelsang's analysis of 'Iconographie der scandinavischen Runensteine der jüngere Wikingerzeit'.[1] The starting point in her discussion is the important Jelling stone.

The main 'rune stone period' in Scandinavia is 975–1100. The Jelling stone provides an important model for understanding this material in general and its close connection with mission and state formation. The pictures on the stone can be apprehended as forming a symbolic scheme with a religious, christian background. We can follow the process of and need for mission in the distribution of rune stones; from the many stones in the Lake Mälaren area in Sweden, especially in the province of Uppland, we may assume the 'need' to be great in this region in the eleventh century; the stones may be a mirror of the need of control.

In this paper my aim is to discuss an example of such a symbolic scheme, almost two hundred years older than Harald's stone at Jelling, the pictures on the famous stone at Sparlösa, Västergötland, western Sweden. This stone, one of the most discussed in Scandinavia, is a regular, scare sandstone, with pictures and runes on each of its four main sides. The pictures can be systematised as follows:

---

[1] S. Horn Fugelsang, 'Iconographie der skandinavischen Runensteine der jüngere Wikingerzeit', in *Zum Problem der Deutung frühmittelalterlicher Bildinhalte*, ed. H. Roth (Siegmaringen, 1986), pp. 183–210.

The Sparlösa rune stone, Västergötland

Side	Man	Animal	Artefact	Sign
I	face			cross
II		birds, snakes		
III	equestrian	birds	building	cross
		cat-like animals	ship	
		(lions ?), deer?		
IV	face			spiral

The text (as interpreted in *Sveriges runinskrifter*) is (in Swedish):

Öjuls, Eriks son, gav, (likaså) gav Alrik . . . i gengäld . . . Då (?) satt fadern i Uppsala (?), fadern som . . . Nätter och dagar . . . Alrik LU(BI)R fruktade (?) ej (?) Öjuls. . . att Sigmar (el. segerfrejdad) heter (el. kallas, må kallas) Eriks son . . . väldig strid (?). . . Efter Öjuls (är minnesvården rest). Och tyd runorna där, de från gudarna stammande, som Alrik LUBU ristada . . .

(in English):

Öjuls, Erik's son gave, (also) gave Alrik . . . in return . . . At that time (?) was the father in Uppsala (?) the father who . . . Nights and days . . . Alrik LU(BI)R did not fear (?) Öjuls . . . that Sigmar (or victorious) is named (may be named) Erik's son . . . glorious battle (?) . . . in memory of Öjuls (the stone is erected) And interpret the runes originating from the gods that Alrik LUBU carved

The meaning is vague. Three persons are mentioned: Öjuls (the subject), Alrik and Erik. The text indicates battles, glory, gods and so on. The Sparlösa stone is a monument in the full sense of the word. Its contemporary importance seems manifest. The pictures have been analysed by Bertil Almgren, who compares them with West European art, the Tours school and the Oseberg find.[2] The Sparlösa stone has been dated to about 800 or the later part of the eighth century. The pictures seem to form a symbolic scheme. Many parallels can be found in early Christian art in Europe.

The main figures, the rider and the ship, are common in the composition of the Gotlandic picture stones from the late Vendel period or early Viking Age, as has often been pointed out. Also a building and birds can be found on these stones. A similar symbolic scheme, without the rider, is found on early Nordic coins, which have the building, the ship, the face and the deer.

A closer analysis of the Gotlandic picture stones reveals very strict schemes with figures, scenes and signs; ships and riders occur, as do processions, birds, men in front of each other, a man lying below a horse, scenes of welcome, small

[2] B. Almgren, 'Den arkeologiska dateringen av Sparlösastenen', in O. von Friesen, *Sparlösastenen*, Kungl. Vitterhets Historie och Antikvitets Akademien Handlingar 46/3 (1940), pp. 114–27.

animals and so forth. They seem to illustrate a transition, involving a long journey, to paradise or Valhalla. This pattern may be compared with myths about Odin. The characteristic shape of the stones, the regular narrowing and the wide, round shaped 'tympanum' may be considered as part of the scheme; as a symbol of a door,[3] as in the building on the Sparlösa stone, the door of life or the portal of death?

The symbol schemes on picture stones on Gotland can also be found in another archaeological context; the boat graves in Uppland, Vendel and Valsgärde. On the helmets discovered there we find such figures as the rider, birds, processions, two men in front of each other, a man below a horse, men carrying swords upside down et cetera. The construction of the grave itself, the boat (compare the ship figures on the stones) and the grave gifts with horses and equipment for a rider (helmet, sword, shield etc.) underline the symbolic scheme of transition.

This world of symbols also seems to connect Sparlösa, Gotland and Uppland with the continent and Western Europe, and with the leadership of the early Germanic kingdoms of the fifth to eighth centuries AD. At the courts of early medieval Europe the borderline between christianity and traditional heathendom was very vague, and a particular form of christianity, arianism, was widespread in the Germanic states of this period, particularly those of the Goths. In addition, the Germanic states were important transmitters of Greek and Classical myths to northern Europe and Scandinavia.

One of these myths is 'the hunt for the deer (or hind) with the golden antler'. This myth can be found in widespread figures and contexts, even in forge iron figures on church doors in Sweden from the twelfth century.[4] The deer is also represented on Gotlandic picture stones and on early Nordic coins. As a symbolic figure the deer is widespread, and is also to be found in early christian contexts. The myth of the hunt has been associated with several important leaders in Europe, including Theodoric,[5] Charlemagne and Henry the Lion.

Theodoric, the sixth-century king of the Ostrogoths, who ruled from Ravenna, was one of the great leaders of early medieval Europe. In legend he is known as 'Didrik of Bern', an early crusader for God and arianism. He is mentioned on the most famous rune stone in Sweden, at Rök in Östergötland, from about 800. In this text he is described as a rider with a shield over his shoulder.

Returning to the Sparlösa stone, the symbolic scheme here is interesting in the context of myths of Didrik of Bern and the hunt, German arianism, and such early christian symbols as the lion, the birds, the door and, probably, the ship.

---

[3]   B. Arrhenius, 'Tür der Toten. Sach- und Wortzeugnisse zu einer frühmittelalterlichen Gräbersitte in Schweden', *Frühmittelalterliche Studien* 4 (1970), pp. 384–94.
[4]   L. Karlsson, 'Die Hindin mit dem goldenen Geweih', *Acta Archaeologica* 51 (1980), pp. 1–68.
[5]   S. Nancke-Krogh, 'Den oheldige helt', *ICO. Der Iconographiske Post* 7 (1976), 3, pp. 3–13.

Also the faces must be mentioned;[6] are they faces of Christ? The key problem is the animal behind the rider; is it a deer or not? It looks like a deer with a large antler.

The names of Erik and Alrik are also of central importance for the interpretation of the Sparlösa stone. The *rik* element of their names designate a ruler or king, as in the names Theode*rik* (Theodoric) and his successor Atala*rik* (Athalaric). Alrik and Erik are also mentioned in the famous Ynglinga saga, perhaps of the ninth century. Equally, one might note the existence of a king, Ericus, one time king of the Svear, who is mentioned as a candidate for deification in the *Vita Anskarii*,[7] and who must have died sometime before 830, that is suggestively close to the period to which the Sparlösa stone is assigned.

What is the meaning of the Sparlösa stone? Does the monument represent an early stage of Christianity, connected with kingship in the eighth century in Vastergötland? The monument is very interesting for the discussion of early christianity in Scandinavia. We cannot argue in terms of pure Christianity or pure paganism. The relations must have been much more complex, a result of a long process of contacts, social and economic changes and the development of authority.

[6]   B. Arrhenius, 'Einige christliche Paraphrasen aus dem 6. Jahrhundert', in *Zum Problem der Deutung*, ed. Roth, pp. 129–51.
[7]   Rimbert, *Vita Anskarii* 26, ed. W. Trillmich, in *Quellen des 9. und 11. Jahrhunderts zur Geschichte der hamburgischen Kirche und des Reiches* (Darmstadt, 1961).

WOMEN AS BRIDGE-BUILDERS; THE ROLE OF WOMEN IN VIKING-AGE SCANDINAVIA

Birgit Sawyer

The Uppland widow Inga honoured her dead husband Ragnfast with no fewer than four rune stones, and one of them relates that she had also built a bridge in his memory (fig. 1).[1] In order to pay for all this Inga must have had considerable wealth at her own disposal. The question how she had reached such a position is partly answered by one of the stones that explains that she had inherited from her child.[2] A very detailed runic inscription on a rock at Hillersjö (fig. 2) supplements that answer; Inga also inherited property from her father. The Hillersjö-inscription reads in full:

> Read! Germund took Gerlög, a maiden, as wife. Then they had a son before he (Germund) was drowned and then the son died. Thereafter she had Gudrik as her husband. He . . . this . . . (damaged part; the reference is probably to Gudrik as the owner of Hillersjö) Then they had children but only one girl survived, her name was Inga. Ragnfast of Snottsta had her as his wife. Thereafter he died and then the son. And the mother (Inga) inherited from her son. Then she had Erik as her husband. Then she died. Then Gerlög inherited from Inga her daughter. Torbjörn skald carved the runes.[3]

Thus:

$$
\begin{array}{ccc}
& 1 \quad\quad 2 & \\
\text{Germund} = \text{Gerlög} = \text{Gudrik, of Hillersjä} \\
\quad\quad | & \quad\quad\quad\quad | \\
\text{son} & \\
& 1 \quad | \quad 2 & \\
\text{Ragnfast} = \text{Inga} = \text{Erik} \\
\text{of Snottsta} \quad | \\
\text{son} &
\end{array}
$$

---

[1] SR U330. Inga's four inscriptions, SR U329–32, are at and near Snottsta, which is about 30 km north-east of Hillersjö. They show that Ragnfast inherited Snottsta from his father Sigfast, that he had two sisters, Gyrid and Estrid, and that Inga inherited after the death of her child.

[2] SR U332.

[3] SR U29.

Fig. 1   Rune stone in Snottsta, Uppland (U330): 'Inga had these stones raised and this bridge built after Ragnfast, her husband. Assur was his *huskarl*'. *Photo ATA*

Fig. 2 The Hillersjö-inscription, Uppland (U29). Photo Bengt A. Lundberg, Riksantikvarieämbetet

In these inscriptions we meet women with considerable wealth and can see how paternal inheritance time and again passed from one family to another by means of 'reverse inheritance' (i.e. when a parent inherits from a child), and how Inga's mother, the widow Gerlög, in the end was the heiress of three different families. These two cases raise many questions about the condition of women in Viking-Age Scandinavia: how representative are Inga and Gerlög? How common was reverse inheritance? How often did daughters inherit from their fathers? Did other women build bridges? What do we know about the right of women to own and dispose of property or, indeed, about their role in society in general?

Most comments on women in prehistoric Scandinavia, like comments on pre-Christian circumstances in general, are based on Christian texts written several centuries later. Two very different, indeed contrasting views of Viking-Age women have been drawn from these late sources. One, based on Icelandic sagas, represents women as free, proud and independent, whose characteristic roles are as powerful wives or queens, or even as the much-feared amazons or 'shield-maidens'. The other view, based on the provincial laws, is of women as oppressed and powerless, indeed almost outside the protection of the law, whose role is by and large only to be an object of the activity of men. Both these views must be seriously questioned. As far as the sagas are concerned, we must allow for a large element of literary construction and recognize that a number of quite different purposes further complicate interpretation. As regards the provincial laws, even if they undoubtedly contain some ancient provisions, most only survive in manuscripts of the thirteenth and fourteenth centuries, and so far no sure way has been found to distinguish what is old from more recent additions. Further, an often overlooked complication is that the situation must have been very different in different areas. Circumstances in barren coastal areas were fundamentally different from those in areas with well developed arable cultivation; natural resources, forms of land ownership or use, social structures etc., must have had a profound influence on attitudes and norms that regulated women's lives. Variations in this respect were significant throughout Scandinavia, and generalisations are therefore misleading.[4]

Yet, generalisations are often made, particularly about women's inheritance rights, and here, again, we encounter contrasting views: one holds that women in the Viking Age had extensive inheritance rights that were later *reduced*, but according to an opposing view, now widely accepted, women's rights to inherit were steadily *increasing*. There is, however, no evidence for the first interpretation and the second involves circular reasoning: the medieval laws that most restrict women's rights are interpreted as reflecting an older stage – thus 'proving' that women originally had no inheritance rights at all – and by arranging the different law codes in a chronological sequence according to the extent of female inheritance rights, a 'development' has been traced.[5]

---

[4]   B. Sawyer, 'Women and the conversion of Scandinavia', in *Frauen in Spätantike und Frühmittelalter*, ed. W. Affeldt (Sigmaringen, 1990).
[5]   For the first view, see P. Nyström, 'Hatt till och huva ifrån', in *Historieskrivningens*

Considering the problems involved in using all this late evidence for condi-tions during the Viking Age it is remarkable that more attention has not been paid to the contemporary evidence of the runic inscriptions. These inscriptions, of which there are about 2000 in Scandinavia,[6] provide, for the first time, written evidence produced in the North that casts some light on contemporary circum-stances. Most of them are on raised stones, but some are on earth-fast rocks. They are very unevenly distributed: about 1750 in Sweden, over half of which are in Uppland, about 200 within the bounds of medieval Denmark, and only about 50 in Norway. Most attention has been paid to the inscriptions that mention voyages east or west, although these are less than a tenth of the whole material. Virtually all the inscriptions, however, provide information of historical interest. In the vast majority of cases, we learn who commissioned the inscription, who was commemorated, and the relationship between them. Sometimes we hear about inheritance and property, or about particular achievements of the erectors or the dead, and a Christian prayer is included in many inscriptions.

What, then, can be learnt about Viking-Age women from a study of the rune stones? Admittedly only a few inscriptions explicitly refer to property and inhe-ritance, but most of them – indirectly – yield very useful information. In the first place, the proportion of stones commissioned by women shows how common it was for them to possess and dispose of property at that time. To raise a stone was a costly business, and women who did so on their own must have had resources, whether inherited or acquired through marriage as dowry or 'morning-gift', and/or a share of the property jointly held by husband and wife.

Before discussing further the question of female property owners in Viking-Age Scandinavia and their ability to act independently the material on which this study is based requires some comment.[7] Of the approximately 2000 inscrip-tions from this period only the 'complete' ones have been used, i.e. the cases where the sex of the erectors as well as of the deceased can be determined. This principle of selection has yielded a corpus of more than 1620 inscriptions, the geographic distribution of which well reflects that of the total number: almost half of the cases are to be found in Uppland (approx. 745), about 260 in Söder-manland, about 160 in Östergötland and Denmark respectively, less than 100 in Västergötland, about 75 in Småland, about 40 in Norway, about 30 in Öland, 15 in Gotland, and fewer in Närke, Västmanland and Gästrikland. For the sake of comparability proportions will be presented, generally expressed as percentages, and only exceptionally – above all for areas that are poorer in inscriptions – will absolute figures be given.[8]

Even if most of the Scandinavian rune stones were erected by men for men,

---

dilemma, ed. T. Forser (Stockholm, 1974), pp. 74–81. For the second, see Å. Holmbäck, Ätten och arvet enligt Sveriges medeltida lagar (Uppsala, 1919).
6   This number refers to the Viking-Age inscriptions.
7   This study is based on runic inscriptions published in SR, DR and NIYR.
8   All figures given here are based on my preliminary investigation (see note 23). When all the inscriptions are taken into account these proportions and figures will need some slight adjustment.

women are represented everywhere. Most often we meet women as erectors, on their own (12.5 per cent) or together with men (15 per cent); only seldom have stones been erected in memory of deceased women (7 per cent, of which almost half commemorate both women and men). The proportion of female erectors is especially high in Uppland, Södermanland and Öland, but this is due to the fact that so many of the stones in these areas were commissioned by men and women together. In Denmark, Västergötland, Östergötland and Småland women and men rarely acted together, and in Norway never. I will later return to the question whether the women who joined men in erecting stones also owned property that they could dispose of, but to begin with I will focus on those cases where women acted on their own, i.e. the cases that give us a minimum measure of female ownership in Viking-Age Scandinavia.

WOMEN WHO ERECT STONES ON THEIR OWN

In Scandinavia as a whole more than 12.5 per cent of the rune stones were commissioned by women to commemorate men, but with some significant variations; while it seems to be equally common in most areas, in Norway and Småland, Öland and Gotland this category is very rare. How is this pattern to be understood? If we exclude chance, the variations can of course reflect demographic differences, but considering the very low figure for Småland (4 per cent) it is more likely that the variations are due to different customs regulating when it was appropriate for women rather than men to erect rune stones.

All stone erectors – male and female – are most often (on average in 90 per cent of the cases) very careful to point out how they were related to the deceased. The majority were close family members, and an investigation of the frequency of all relations shows that stones in memory of men were most often erected by the very closest male relatives: *sons*, *brothers* or *fathers*. Leaving out for the moment the mixed category of men and women acting together, common only in eastern Sweden, the next two groups, roughly equal in size, in the order of frequency are:

(1) *male relatives* other than sons, brothers and fathers, i.e. in-laws, nephews, grandsons etc. or male connections, e.g. friends or partners

(2) *women* – mostly family members, but also other female relatives.

The interesting thing is that where group (2) is small, group (1) is big, and vice versa. It is in fact only in Östergötland that these groups are of equal size; in the rest of Scandinavia the proportions vary significantly. In Västergötland group (1) (other male relatives or connections) is somewhat bigger than group (2) (women), in Småland group (1) is twice, in Denmark two and a half times, and in Norway three times as big as group (2). In Uppland, Södermanland and Öland, on the other hand, it is the other way round; here the group of women erecting stones on their own is *twice as big* as the group of more distant male relatives and male connections.

How were these female erectors related to the deceased? In most cases it is *the wife* who commemorates her husband, but very often we also meet *the mother*, commemorating a son. There are, however, important regional variations; in Småland as in Gotland there is only one example of these two categories, and in both cases the woman acted both as a wife and a mother, commemorating her husband and her son on the same stone. Throughout Scandinavia *daughters* and *sisters* seldom erect stones after their fathers and brothers, and the majority of these cases are to be found in Uppland and Södermanland. Outside these provinces there are, in all, five examples of daughters and nine of sisters acting on their own. The occurence of stones erected by men in memory of their in-laws indicates that married daughters and sisters of a deceased were represented by their husbands. It can thus be deduced that women who commissioned rune stones on their own were normally either unmarried or widows.

IN WHAT SITUATIONS DO WOMEN ACT ON THEIR OWN?

The pattern described can be interpreted in the following way: in the whole of Scandinavia women seem not to erect stones as long as sons, brothers or fathers of the deceased were alive. In Denmark, Norway, Småland and Gotland it seems as if they only did it if there were no male relatives, however distant – or friends/partners. When the situation called for a woman to erect a stone, it was apparently in the first place for the widow of the deceased to do so, in the second place his mother, in the third place for his daughter, and in the last, his sister. These independently acting – and economically self-sustaining – women were apparently all single; it is clear that most of them were widows.

Since on average every eighth rune stone in Viking-Age Scandinavia was erected by women on their own, it was not unusual for women to possess and dispose of property. Gerlög and Inga were not unique; all over Scandinavia – with the important exceptions of Småland, Gotland and Norway – it was fairly common that widowed and single women stepped into the shoes of men, commissioning memorials, sometimes of great splendour. How most of these women acquired their property is unknown, but at least it is clear that paternal inheritances quite often reverted (via a child) to the mother – again with the exceptions of Småland, Gotland and Norway.

Most stones erected by women were commissioned by one person; with very few exceptions (one in Närke and two in Östergötland) it is only in Uppland and Södermanland that two or more women act together (e.g. a widow together with a daughter in memory of a deceased husband/father). This difference between eastern Sweden and the rest of Scandinavia reflects a general difference in stone-erecting habits: in Norway, Denmark, Småland, Västergötland and Östergötland most stones have only *one single erector* (on average in 75 per cent of all cases), but in Uppland, Södermanland, Öland and Gotland it is the opposite: here as many as 65% of the stones were erected by groups, consisting of (a) only men, (b) only women, or (c) of men and women together.

WOMEN WHO ERECT STONES TOGETHER WITH MEN

There are more cases of women acting together with men than on their own, but the average, 15 per cent, is very misleading, since this mixed category is very unusual outside Uppland, Södermanland and Öland. In Uppland 24 per cent of all rune stones were jointly commissioned by men and women, in Öland 17 per cent, and in Södermanland 13 per cent. In Norway, on the other hand, there are no examples of this category, in Denmark the proportion is 2.5 per cent (4 stones), in Småland 4 per cent (3 stones), in Västergötland 5 per cent (5 stones), and in Östergötland 5.5 per cent (9 stones).

In most cases the stones belonging to this category were commissioned by *the son and the wife* of the deceased (there is, though, no example in Småland), and it quite often happened that *parents* jointly commemorated their son. Outside Uppland and Södermanland it is only in Östergötland that *sons and daughters* act together (in all 3 cases). Most of the other combinations are only in Uppland, e.g. brother and mother, male relative and wife etc. There are several examples where even more people are involved, each related in a different way to the deceased, e.g. as in this inscription from Överselö:

> Ingjald and Visäte and Stenulv, they raised the stone after Karl, their father, and Gillög after her husband, and Inga after her son, and Ärnger after his brother. Äsbjörn and Tidkume cut the runes – Orökja painted them.[9]

In Södermanland the women of this mixed category were most often mothers, in Uppland wives. Only seldom were they sisters (in Södermanland once, in Uppland 6 times), but daughters are slightly more common (in Södermanland 7 times, in Uppland 28 times), and normally appear together with their brothers.

Thus, even if there are examples of men and women erecting stones together from the whole of Scandinavia – apart from Norway, Västmanland and Närke – they are very few outside Uppland, Södermanland and Öland. This indicates that in these east-Swedish provinces other ideas about the representation of relatives in the inscriptions were prevailing than those elsewhere. Women who in the rest of Scandinavia had, so to speak, been hidden behind their male relatives here appear together with them as stone erectors. They appear in the same order of frequency as the women who act on their own, i.e. in the first place *wives*, in the second *mothers*, in the third and fourth places *daughters* and *sisters* respectively.

Did women in this mixed category possess and dispose of property? It is highly likely that the majority – as widows – did, but it will be argued below that all stone erectors, women as well as men, either owned or administered property.

[9]   SR Sö205.

RUNIC INSCRIPTIONS AS STATEMENTS OF INHERITANCE AND PROPERTY RIGHTS

All over Scandinavia the stone erectors were most often the closest relatives of the deceased, i.e. they were people who owned something together with the deceased, and who could claim the whole or part of the property left following the death. My hypothesis is that it was in fact inheritance that determined who was to erect the stone and how the inscription was formulated. If the only purpose of the inscription was to honour the memory of the deceased, it remains to be explained why the survivors were so carefully named – something which seldom occurs on medieval and modern tomb stones – and, above all, why they are always mentioned first in the inscription. The prominent position of the commissioners suggests that the rune stones were as much monuments to the survivors as to the dead, and when further (in 90 per cent of the cases) such an emphasis is put on the nature of their relationship or connection with the deceased it strongly suggests that a concern to protect inheritance and rights of ownership was an important factor. Considering the limited space normally available for inscriptions and the difficulty of carving them, there can be little doubt that *everything in them was significant*; redundant information cannot be expected.

This point is well illustrated by an inscription from Säby in Uppland: 'Otrygg and Bonde and Alvrik raised this stone after Kåre, their father, and Gunned after her husband. God help his soul. Torbjörn cut the runes'.[10] The inscription is both lengthened and complicated by the description of the relationship between those who raised this stone and Kåre, but it was, nevertheless, clearly considered important to state it. The explanation is presumably that, because of their different relationships with Kåre, the survivors had different claims. The inscription thus states these different relationships which gave the sons the right to their paternal inheritance, the widow the right to her share of what the spouses jointly owned as well as her own property, of course, and – if she survived the sons – the right to reverse inheritance.

Many inscriptions give not only the relationship between those who raised the stone and the dead person but also between the dead and other kin who appear to have died earlier. So, for example, an inscription at Valsta in Södermanland reads: 'Signjut raised this stone after Sigröd, his father, Sibbe's brother'.[11] This suggests that Sigröd had already inherited from Sibbe, and that his son, Signjut, now inherited it all.

This interpretation of runic inscriptions as declarations of inheritance and ownership is supported by the results of the investigation of frequency of mention in inscriptions; it is, above all, difficult to see in what context other than inheritance and ownership women were often excluded but sometimes included, and occasionally appear as the only named survivors. When a wife commemorated a husband we cannot presume inheritance – in no Germanic law did

---

10 SR *U37*.
11 SR *Sö273*.

spouses inherit from each other.[12] She was, rather, taking charge of her own property (dowry and 'morning-gift'), perhaps together with her share of the property she had jointly owned with her husband. If there were children, by making her status known, she also safe-guarded her right to future reverse inheritance. That inheritances often did revert to women in most parts of Scandinavia can be deduced from the stones that were erected by mothers in memory of their sons. But how common was it that daughters and sisters inherited from their fathers and brothers? The number of rune stones erected by daughters and sisters is certainly very low, but it is important to point out that this is only a minimum figure for the number of heiresses; some inheriting daughters and sisters may be 'hidden' behind their husbands who commissioned stones in their wives' place.

There is also another way of tracing inheritances; references to the dead person's father, mother etc. must often have had exactly this function. So, for example, Sibba in Gotland was very careful to point out who was the father of his dead wife: 'Sibba erected this stone after Rodiaud, his wife, daughter of Rodgair in Anga. She died young from her small children'.[13] The fact that Rodiaud is described as Rodgair's daughter suggests that she was his heir and the additional information that she died 'from her small children' makes it clear that there were descendants who had a legal claim to their mother's paternal inheritance. The fact that Sibba so carefully stated this suggests that, as far as inheritance was concerned, childless marriages were treated in much the same way as in the rest of Europe, i.e. where there were no direct heirs, the inheritance of a spouse went back to his or her family. The Hillersjö inscription shows, for example, that this happened after the death of Inga, whose second husband, Erik, clearly had no claim. In his inscription on the stone after Rodiaud, Sibba stated the rights of his children. We do not know how many children he and Rodiaud had, but on a second stone he obviously commemorated the last of them: 'Sibba had this stone erected after his and Rodiaud's daughter'.[14]

Thus:

Rodgair in Anga
|
Rodiaud = Sibba
|
daughter

These inscriptions illustrate how paternal inheritance, from Rodiaud's family, could pass in the form of maternal inheritance, through Rodiaud, and then by

---

[12] A. C. Murray, *Germanic Kinship Structure. Studies in Law and Society in Antiquity and the Early Middle Ages* (Toronto, 1983), pp. 58 ff.
[13] *SR* G111.
[14] *SR* G112.

reverse inheritance via Rodiaud's daughter, to the child's father, Sibba, and so into another family.

From Gotland we also have the interesting Sjonhem inscriptions (3 stones, erected by parents in memory of each of their sons), which can be interpreted as describing a case where two un-named sisters had to give precedence to the uncles of the dead men, whereas the daughter, named Hailvi, of one of the sons seems to have inherited.[15] The similarity between this case and the regulations in the later law of Gotland ('Gutalagen') is striking.[16]

If the interpretation of most Viking-Age inscriptions as declarations of inheritance and ownership is correct, they constitute an entirely new body of material for the study of rights of ownership in Scandinavia in the tenth and eleventh centuries. A preliminary analysis of this material indicates that in all parts of Scandinavia women's rights to paternal inheritance was postponed, but with great variations between regions, and even between neighbouring localities. Much remains to be done before any attempt can be made to explain the variations that appear at different times and in different places. Treating the material very generally, however, it appears that the situation in Småland, Gotland and Norway was most restrictive to women, Denmark and Västergötland only a little less so. In Uppland, Södermanland and Öland, on the other hand, women often appear together with men, e.g. mothers and fathers, daughters and sons etc. How is this difference to be explained? If in these eastern provinces women were more generously treated, being allowed to inherit together with men, is this due to differences in the resources available? Was there in eastern Sweden more personalty available to distribute among all adult members of the family? Is the difference possibly due to the fact that the runic inscriptions in eastern Sweden tend to be later than in the rest of Scandinavia? We know that female inheritance was encouraged by the church, and it is at least worth asking whether stones jointly erected by men and women reflect a later stage, when ecclesiastical influence had begun to make its mark.

In this context it is interesting that women are over-represented among the rune stones that refer to bridge building. During the missionary era to build a bridge and so improve communications was considered a meritorious act, earning Divine favour. Stones mentioning bridge building are especially common in Sweden. I have studied the approximately 100 inscriptions dealing with bridges in Uppland, Södermanland, Östergötland and Västergötland and found that no less than 16 per cent of them are in commemoration of women (either alone or together with men) (fig. 3), while in the whole material (approx. 1620 inscriptions) only 7 per cent commemorate women. Also as commissioners women appear more often among the bridge builders than in the material as a whole: 42 per cent of the bridge building stones were commissioned by women (on their

---

[15] SR G134–6.
[16] *Gutalagen* 20: 4, ed. Å. Holmbäck and E. Wessén, *Svenska Landskapslagar*, vol. 4 (Uppsala, 1979), p. 220.

Fig. 3 Inscription from Vickeby, Uppland (U475): 'Finnvid had the stone memorial and bridge made after Fastlög, his mother'. *Photo ATA*

own or together with men), while only 27.5 per cent of all inscriptions were commissioned by them.

This female over-representation in the 'bridge stones' points in the same direction as many other signs of women's interest in Christianity and their readiness to obey exhortations to support the church and give alms. There is much to indicate that in Scandinavia, as elsewhere, women were among the first to accept and encourage the Christian faith. From the very beginning it was women who were particularly attracted by Christian teaching, and among the earliest Christians the percentage of women, especially of the upper classes, was larger than that of men.[17] Women's Christian zeal and greater piety is also testified to by late antique and early medieval stories about wives who prepared the way for the conversion of their pagan husbands.[18] From all over Europe there are many examples of women, above all widows, who were generous almsgivers and donors to the church.[19] It is probably significant that in describing Anskar's mission in ninth century Sweden, Rimbert has *women* represent pious generosity.[20] And in Birka, the scene of the first known Christian mission to Sweden, the earliest objects that can be associated with the new faith, namely cross-shaped pendants, have all been found in women's graves.[21]

This is not the place to discuss the reasons for women's particular interest and involvement, suffice it to say that in Viking-Age Scandinavia there were many independent women who could exercise pious generosity if they wished, and we have seen that there were indeed many who did. Apart from giving alms or improving communications Christian charity could also be expressed by building a *siluaus* ('soul-house'). Such a house was apparently intended as a resting place for travellers; to build one was a charitable act that would benefit the builders' souls. It is interesting that the only one mentioned in runic inscriptions was built by a husband in memory of his wife. We know about this thanks to the couple's two daughters, who commemorated their father by raising a stone and building a ford:

Ingrid (?) and Ingegärd had this stone erected and a ford built out in (?) the

---

[17] A. von Harnack, *The Mission and Expansion of Christianity in the first three centuries*, vol. 2 (New York, 1908), p. 73.

[18] S. Farmer, 'Persuasive wives; clerical images of medieval women', *Speculum* 61 (1986), pp. 517–43, esp. pp. 532–3.

[19] D. Herlihy, 'Land, family and women in Continental Europe, 701–1250', *Traditio* 18 (1962), pp. 89–120; K. Leyser, *Rule and Conflict in an Early Medieval Society* (London, 1979), pp. 49–73.

[20] Rimbert, *Vita Anskarii*, c. 20, ed. W. Trillmich and R. Buchner (Berlin, 1961). See also B. Sawyer, 'Familjen, förmögenheten och fromheten', in *Manliga strukturer och kvinnliga strategier. En bok till Gunhild Kyle*, ed. B. Sawyer and A. Göransson (Gothenburg, 1987), pp. 62–78, esp. pp. 62–3.

[21] A-S. Gräslund, *Birka IV. The Burial Customs. A Study of the Graves on Björkö* (Stockholm, 1980), p. 82; id. 'Pagan and Christian in the age of conversion', in *Proceedings of the 10th Viking Congress. Festskrift for Charlotte Blindheim on her 70th birthday* (Oslo, 1987), pp. 81–94, esp. pp. 90–2. See also Sawyer, 'Women and the conversion of Scandinavia'.

strait in memory of Tore, their father. Tore had a 'soul-house' made in memory of Ingetora, his wife and of . . .[22]

These road-improving sisters are an appropriate example with which to conclude this survey. In a real as well as figurative sense they symbolize very well all the bridge-building functions of women in the runic material.[23] In the first place we have met women who took an active part in society, erecting stones and building bridges; a more detailed study will no doubt cast light on the role of women as bridges between paganism and Christianity. We have seen how women themselves formed bridges between different families over which property passed by means of reverse inheritance. Above all, a further study of women's representation in the material can contribute to the building of the bridge we need between the rules governing inheritance in the Viking Age and in the later medieval law codes – a bridge between prehistoric and historic times, between archaeologists and historians.

[22] SR U996.
[23] For a fuller discussion of the results of my preliminary investigation see B. Sawyer, *Property and Inheritance in Viking Scandinavia; the Runic Evidence* (Alingsås, 1988).

WOMEN AND JUSTICE IN NORWAY
C.1300–1600

Grethe Authén Blom

In the wake of political feminism there was a flood of superficial women's studies, the point of which was to produce as many examples as possible of the age-old disregard for and oppression and degradation of women. These prejudiced samples having gradually given way to serious empirical research, a long series of interesting studies and books have now been published about the role of women and their contribution to society in many countries and in many periods. The myth about the defenceless and grossly exploited female sex has been exploded. It has been understood that the position of women in former times was above all *different* from what it is today. Modern students of women's history do not just emphasize the elements of violence and domination, but explain woman's long-standing bonds to the home as a necessary division of labour in pre-industrial society, and they stress her biological task. This role made such heavy demands on the female sex that emancipated west European or American women of the twentieth century can hardly comprehend it.

The greatest difficulty for serious scholars of women's studies has been the need to liberate them from so-called male attitudes supposed to exist everywhere. In addition to the fact that up to our own century women must necessarily have had a different kind of daily work, a whole range of intolerant male attitudes, rooted in the time when woman was defined as an inferior creature destined by nature to assume a passive role, are even today, it is claimed, stopping her from assuming her place in a modern society of equality.

'Shut up, you old cow' may have been daily fare in many homes with a brutal husband bullying his wife and children, but I think it is probably wrong to interpret domestic violence or rape as indications of a society in which women counted for less than men and therefore did not get equal treatment or help.

Without intending to generalize and without trying to defend or take a roseate view of the very hard and difficult life of women in the past I shall in this paper draw attention to some source material which in my opinion demonstrates that intolerant male attitudes were neither general nor massive. Women, in fact, stood good chances of slipping through the net that surrounded them. I refer to the interesting legal material, first of all diplomas, which begin to appear in Norway towards the end of the thirteenth century and increase greatly as we approach modern times. Records of judgements, however, are not available until just before 1600. Information about women can be derived from the evidence of several types of courts. I have selected a handful of documents from the fourteenth to the sixteenth centuries, with the intention of casting light on women in different social positions, as well as different types of cases. I have, however, stayed away from witch trials, both because they are very special and because they hardly occur in Norway before 1600. My examples are not unique, they could all be multiplied several times. Common to the women that I have selected is the fact that they themselves appear to have taken the initiative to have their case heard in court, and judgements were without exception to their advantage. The adversary was in every case a man, usually of higher social standing than the women involved.

Before starting it may be useful to remind ourselves that before 1600 there was no fixed sequence of appeals in Norwegian litigation. If mediation or judgement at the local court, the *ting*, did not settle the matter the case would normally be brought before the *lagmann*, the royal justice of the peace, who occupied a key position in the Norwegian judicial system for many centuries. From the *lagmann*, but also directly, a case could be brought before the king who would then set up a committee consisting of one or two *lagmenn* and a group of royal councillors. The judgement of such a committee was final and was normally affirmed by royal writ. In addition to the courts of the *lagmenn* there were ecclesiastical courts hearing among other cases those involving matrimony, wills and morality; in the face of strong royal opposition they also challenged the right of the *lagmenn* to hear cases involving landed property to which an ecclesiastical institution was party. The spiritual judge could be the bishop himself, or his *officialis*. After the Reformation this court was superseded by a collective ecclesiastical court, *Kapittelretten*, the Chapter Court.

Since, at the same time, Norway entered into an 'eternal' union with Denmark, with the common king resident in Copenhagen, the old Norwegian supreme court had to be reorganized. From about 1570, people in Norway might appeal to the *Herredag*, a court of lords, which in Norway was mobile and sat every three years. The court consisted of four to six Danish nobles appointed by the king, all members of the *Rigsråd*. On their arrival in Norway they were joined by Norwegian *lagmenn* who would serve as legal advisers, particularly as experts on Norwegian law, but who would not formally participate in the collegiate judgements of the lords.

Norwegian women knew how to use the whole range of legal possibilities. Procedure was not simple in any of the courts. It took drive and perseverance and preferably the support of kin or other influential persons to institute proceedings against somebody. Since so many women still did, it must be due to their certainty that the judicial system was available for them as well, and that they could expect a fair deal.

The legal self-esteem of the women was nourished by the laws of inheritance which permitted them to own property, not just movables. The majority of the women encountered in the legal material are therefore representatives of the better social classes who went to court to secure their lawful inheritance. I shall provide just a couple of examples of such women. My intention is to demonstrate that even women of the lower classes could succeed in their litigation if they felt abused or trampled upon.

Obviously, I am not claiming that all women who wanted to take their case to court had the opportunity to do so. We have no means of picking up all those who did not dare to or were not equal to the task of having their case heard. But it was probably the same within the men's sphere too. Many women, however, probably had to refrain from litigation for fear of their husbands. We see a lot of them coming to court once they were widowed. According to the law, the husband administered the property of his wife and he undertook any litigation on her behalf. But there are several examples of a woman appearing in court with her husband's power of attorney to prefer her own claims, or even his.

INGEBJØRG PÅLSDATTER AGAINST ASLAK OF LYNG AND COMPANY. 1313

About 1300 Ingebjørg, the daughter of Baron Pål Sure in Trøndelag and the widow of a local magnate, Audun Vigleiksson, was having a dispute with Aslak, Klemet and Ottar, all of whom were co-owners with her of the estate of Lyng in Verdal.

The matron Ingeborg claims 32 *helgdeland*, the equivalent of a sizeable Norwegian average farm. Aslak and his ilk denies the lady this land, they sow and they reap the crops, etc. Ingebjørg first seeks help from the local courts, the *ting* and the *lagmann*, and she possesses several judgements establishing her ownership of the land. Her adversaries completely disregard the judgements given against them. They exploit her as a lonely woman, but their acts cannot simply be regarded as a reflection of misogynist attitudes typical of a male dominated society. Aslak, the most aggressive of her adversaries is concurrently running an equally bitter dispute with the cathedral chapter of Nidaros, so he is after land irrespective of the opposition.

The documents preserved, five of them, come from the year 1313, when, as a last resort, the matron Ingebjørg has brought her case before King Håkon V. This year he pays a personal visit to Nidaros, the metropolitan see and regional capital of middle and northern Norway, to sort out the old dispute over the Lyng estate and restore respect to the legal system.

The king and his councillors leave no stone unturned. A case is brought against each of Ingebjørg's adversaries. In each case the king sets up a committee of four to six members, two of them holding high office in his household: Bjarne Audunsson, the Lord privy seal, and Hauk Erlendsson, *lagmann* of Gulating. The others belong to the aristocracy of Trøndelag. The matron Ingebjørg wins all her cases. The previous judgements are confirmed: Ingebjørg shall hold 'eternally' the 32 *helgdeland*. Her adversaries and co-owners of Lyng must pay heavy compensations, and in addition fines for their contempt of previous judgements. Aslak had to fork up 40 marks, Ottar 150 marks (1 mark = 240 penning). These are huge sums by Norwegian standards. All those convicted are forbidden to bring new cases about the land to dispute. King Håkon confirms the judgements of the committee in royal writs and adds that the sheriff shall outlaw anybody who presumes to violate his judgement. This is an unusually stiff sanction in cases of this type.

And not only that: in a separate writ the king commands twelve local landowners to muster at Lyng on a set date and there measure out, course and mark the boundaries of the 32 *helgdeland* that had been awarded to the matron Ingebjørg. These twelve men will be responsible to God and the king if their task is not performed according to the judgements. King Håkon's own men could not have hoped for better support in court than was extended to the matron Ingebjørg on this occasion.[1]

GUDRID JONSDATTER AGAINST TWO CANONS AT THE CATHEDRAL CHAPTER IN OSLO. 1345

Gudrid, the daughter of a knight and married to a medium landowner in southeast Norway discovers that her dowry – the income from Stofnerud farm – has been usurped by two canons at the cathedral chapter in Oslo, Tollef and Øivind, the latter on behalf of an altar in the cathedral. The lady has tried, apparently in vain, to bring the two ecclesiastics before the available local courts, those of the *officialis* and the *lagmann*, but sees a fresh possibility when the archbishop of Nidaros, Pål Bårdsson, spends the winter following Christmas 1345 with his suffragan the bishop of Oslo. 'She has complained to us repeatedly', the archbishop states;[2] and he accepted the case, to which according to canon law he was perfectly entitled by virtue of his office. Archbishop Pål was probably the sharpest legal brain in the country, a doctor of canon as well as Roman law, having studied in Orleans and Paris, and having paid long visits to Avignon. He had also been chancellor to the king.

The court was opened in the bishop's palace in Oslo, and Gudrid Jonsdatter appeared with her husband's power of attorney to conduct her own case. She could produce both witnesses and documents to show that her father had given her the land in dispute as her dowry. Canon Tollef could produce nothing but vague and unproven claims that he thought the land had been sold back to Jon and then, via intermediaries, been bought by Tollef privately. Archbishop Pål stipulated a period of five months, which was customary in such cases, for Tollef to substantiate his claims. In the meantime the rent was to be collected by a neutral person who would then surrender it to the person to whom the land was finally awarded.

The other half of the property was awarded then and there to lady Gudrid with full rights, and Øivind was to pay her the rent for all the time he had been in possession of the land.

---

[1]   *DN* 1, no. 137; 2, nos. 116–17; 5, nos. 57–8.
[2]   *DN* 1, no. 292.

The reason why the archbishop treated the two canons differently is that he, the legal luminary, was shaken by the way Øivind conducted his case. The copy of the judgement here abandons dry legal terminology and describes the lamentable performance of Gudrid's adversary in court. Himself presumably ill, Øivind sends the official Ogmund, the episcopal regional justice, to conduct his case: 'And although Ogmund appeared and said that he was Øivind's proxy he was unable to produce any evidence; he did not even wish to produce any witnesses, but carried on with sighs and cries without referring to any regulation, or anything that might take the case further. Once he got the impression that the judgement would go against him or against Øivind, he ran out, against our will and orders. And although we recalled him he refused to come back'.

The archbishop had this priceless account of the official's cowardice during a case in which his adversary was a woman, recorded by his own notary, in his official copy of the judgement, a document that would be read aloud to many, both in the cathedral and to the peasants of Stofnerud, and not least within Gudrid's family. The weakness was certainly not concealed within a confined and closed forum of men. The judgement, now in the Norwegian public record office, was in private hands in the district of Follo, of which Stofnerud is part, and was preserved by the owners for five centuries.

KING HÅKON VI HELPS WOMEN TO THEIR RIGHTS

In the the year 1358 the eighteen year old king is travelling the districts of eastern Norway. In his wake there is a copy of a judgement with an introductory account of the background of the case: during his stay at Norderhov, the main district of Ringerike, a certain Margrete, a woman belonging to the lower ranks to judge by her surname, managed to obtain an interview with the king. She might quite easily have been turned away by the royal guards or other followers, and of course by Håkon himself. But the young monarch, who is making his first tour as an adult, ruling king, is probably keen to act as the ideal medieval king, the *rex iustus*, protector of widows, orphans and other weak members of society. Solemnly king Håkon sets up a committee similar to the one set up by his predecessor in 1313. It consists of a couple of the councillors accompanying him and, for the rest, of good men acquainted with the locality. The apparatus appears oversized, for, although awkward enough for the woman herself, this case, in the eyes of the ruler, is a mere trifle. Her complaint is that an *ombuds-mann* has kept her under arrest and (on a suspicion of larceny?) deprived her of a costly mantle. The committee arrives at the conclusion that the arrest has been utterly unwarranted. Their verdict is that the slightly over-zealous *ombudsmann* shall not only return the mantle to her but shall also pay Margrete a handsome compensation of eight marks.[3]

And it was not just in his youth that king Håkon behaved so obligingly when

---

[3]   *DN* 2, no. 340.

a woman complained to him. Ten years later, in 1368 during a tour of Valdres with his Lord Privy Seal and councillors, an appeal by the widow Ingebjørg is placed before the king. She states that her late husband had, against her will and against the law, sold her allodium. According to the law a husband needed his wife's explicit and witnessed permission to sell or exchange her property. Ingebjørg had already achieved at least two judgements in her favour, evidence that in a case as clear as this the courts did play strictly by the law. But the buyer, Torgils, refuses to give up the land. On the spot king Håkon sets up a committee of good men to select other lands from the husband's estate so that the buyer shall not be injured. That done, the king, before travelling on, issues a crystal-clear letter: because it is our will that Ingebjørg and her child enjoy their allodium, Torgils is ordered to accept the land awarded him in compensation. For additional security Håkon confirms in every respect the title of Ingebjørg and her heirs to the disputed land, as well as the previous copies of judgements which are all fastened together with the king's writ.[4]

Since practically all cases from the fifteenth century involving women relate to property, we shall now jump a full two centuries ahead.

In the sixteenth century we find a marked tendency towards stiffer sentences in criminal cases, including 'disobedience to the authorities'. The number of death sentences increases. At the same time the central government as well as the royal *lensherrer* (district governors with administrative, military and execu-tive functions) are attempting to increase public income through extraordinary taxes or through the extortion of extra services like transport services or labour on fortresses from the peasants.

THE WIDOWS OF FIVE HANGED MEN AGAINST THE JUDICIAL SYSTEM IN 1578

In 1574 five peasants from Gauldal in Trøndelag were hanged, having been found guilty of rebellion and mutiny at the municipal court in Trondheim. Their bodies were not buried, but broken on the wheel where their remains were still to be seen in 1578. This was a cruel additional strain on the widows who, with the support of 'all the district', formally summons the chairman of the municipal court before the court of lords which in the year 1578 sat in Trondheim, in the presence of the *lagmann*, the mayor and other 'good men'.

The five women submit that the acts of their husbands and the law as well were misinterpreted in 1574. The court of lords consequently calls in all mem-bers of the court that passed the death sentence; they were peasants from other districts in Trøndelag. The lords must act with extreme caution in this case. One of the justices, his majesty's viceregent in Norway, Ludvik Munk, must step down from the committee as disqualified. In 1574 he was the governor of Trøndelag.

The law report is, however, not censored, since it is clear from the explana-tions of the peasants that, at the municipal court four years before, they had been

4   *DN* 10, no. 70.

ordered, bullied, and consciously mischarged by Ludvik Munk to pass the sentence of death. The matter of the rebellion, as quietly represented by the widows, was no more serious than the destruction of a bridge to prevent the arrest of Rolf of Lyng who had gone on behalf of all of them to Denmark to complain to the king about new oppressive burdens. Such journeys of complaint were perfectly legal, but Rolf had advanced strong complaints against Ludvik Munk! The women also permitted themselves to remind the court how willingly their districts had obeyed the king's orders to put up soldiers for the last war.

The court of lords studied the circumstances very thoroughly and found that a judicial murder had been committed. The municipal court of 1574 had to admit that it had passed a sentence of death without checking Ludvik Munk's accusations, but had taken guidance exclusively from his summing up and interpretations of the law. The lords stated powerfully that it could not by any law be demonstrated that Rolf of Lyng and his neighbours were traitors. And on the grounds that the assessors from 1574 had not interpreted or understood the law correctly the lords resolved that the remains of the poor Gauldal peasants should be taken down and buried in the churchyard.

Obviously the reason for the court of lords not ordering the unfortunate peasant assessors to pay compensation to the widows is that it was tacitly acknowledged that they had been grossly abused by Ludvik Munk; but he was only brought to trial in 1597, having committed a series of new injustices.[5]

At this stage specialists in women's history might ask whether male dominated society and the judicial system would ever care to reverse death sentences passed on women? Yes, this did occur. In the early seventeenth century a couple in southern Norway were beheaded. As far as the man was concerned there was no point in protesting against the sentence. He had committed a notorious crime in plundering wrecks. Wreckage devolved upon the king. But the son wanted to clear the memory and soul of his mother. In the past the loss of honour together with life was the worst stain for the family. The mother had done nothing but to hide her husband on the farm when he had been exposed and was being searched for.

This case, too, was taken before the court of lords in 1604. The justices ruled that it would be against the order of nature for a wife to betray her husband's hiding-place when his life was at stake. A milder sentence ought as a result to have been passed on her. The sentence of death on the wife was therefore declared void and the *lagmann* who had passed it was ordered to pay compensation to the heirs.[6]

A third case involving a husband and wife was heard by the court of lords in 1613.

---

[5]   *NHD* 1, pp. 228–32.
[6]   *NHD* 1604, p. 19.

The Widow Katrine Andersdatter against the Judicial System

After the Kalmar war of 1611–1613 Katrine, a widow with several small children, took her case before the court of lords. During the war her husband, Jens Christensen, a citizen of Bergen, following cursory proceedings in the municipal court – confirmed by the *lagmann* – had been sentenced to death and promptly executed. The charge: Jens had arrogated to himself an officer's command over a company of 600 local men, peasants levied for military service; while waiting in Bergen for officers and transport to the theatre of war they were on the verge of mutiny.

Katrine had accused and summonsed the municipal court as well as the *lagmann*, the sheriff of Sunnmøre and the governor of Bergenhus himself: none of them had realised that poor Jens had tried to save the town from being flooded with frantic mutineers! He ought to have been rewarded; instead he had to perish.

The court partly sustained the claim of the indignant and despairing wife. As in Trondheim in 1578 the chief administrative officers were protected to make sure the authorities did not lose face. The justices ruled that her accusations against the governor and the sheriff at Sunnmøre were groundless. And both of these had in fact immediately counter-summonsed her for baseless accusations, and that could have proved expensive for her. Further the court of lords regarded it as manifest that Jens had both overstepped his powers and showed disobedience towards the authorities when he refused to relinquish his command *immediately*.

But the judges admitted, albeit indirectly, that the arraignment of Jens had been premature and the sentence of death far too severe. Consequently Katrine was entitled to a fair compensation. She was awarded that partly in the form of pardon for her ill-advised actions against the governor and the sheriff; both waived their costs – a long journey to Skien in south-east Norway where the court of lords was held that year. After this fine amicable settlement the superior court placed the full liability for damages on the inferior courts in Bergen. Katrine's arrangement with these authorities was, however, also described as an amicable settlement. We are told that because of the straitened circumstances of the widow and her small children the *lagmann*, the mayor and the city council had given and donated to her 500 *riksdaler*, payable immediately. Such a sensationally huge sum can only be explained as the tacit acknowledgement of judicial murder.[7]

The fact that codes of morality grew much stricter after the Reformation also had a more oppressive effect on women. This was partly due to the fact that the Lutheran church did not regard marriage as a sacrament and that priests were allowed to marry; this acted as a solvent on the lower classes. Many dispensed with marriage altogether. Co-habitation prevailed until the government reacted

[7]   *NHD* 1613, pp. 128–43.

with a law on marriage and engagement in 1582. This was followed up by public persecution with heavy fines for living in immoral relationships. It was only after this time that the birth of unconjugal children really stigmatized a girl; unmarried mothers, therefore, often went to court to accuse the father either of breach of promise or rape. If the man was convicted in such cases, the honour of the girl was regarded as restored. Many an adulterer was fined heavily by the sheriff for having made a girl pregnant, and in the chapter court, a man who had promised a woman marriage might be ordered to raise her child if she did not want to do so herself. If she was prepared to raise it herself the court generally regarded a cow and ten *riksdaler* as a suitable compensation (as in several bastardy cases in Stavanger cathedral court rolls).[8]

From the reformation until the end of the eighteenth century, cases of morality, marriage and engagement were heard by the ecclesiastical courts in the towns, the chapter courts. These courts could not impose any secular punishments but had the duty to examine the matter carefully and appreciate whether there was any breach of marital law, or if a divorce might be granted. If public fines for adultery or the violation of a virgin came into question, the chapter court would hand over the accused to the secular authorities. Flagrant cases of this kind were heard by the secular courts in the first place.

THE GIRL LISBETH AGAINST HER STEPFATHER. 1619

In 1619 a case of fornication was taken as far as the court of lords. The reason was that a convicted man refused to pay the fines he had been ordered to pay. Lisbeth Rasmusdatter, whom her stepfather had repeatedly taken advantage of, had the courage to bring charges against him. She appeared first before six men at the district court, later before twelve men in the same court, and finally before the *lagmann* in Trondheim. All these courts took her accusations seriously and the stepfather was ordered to pay fines, not to Lisbeth but to the public. For a long time he tried to avoid doing it, complaining about various errors in the legal proceedings, but the court of lords cut the cackle, affirmed the *lagmann's* interpretation of the law and his affirmation of the ruling of the court of twelve and sustained the fine payable by the stepfather to the king for adultery, as well as thirty *riksdaler* payable to the *lagmann* for false accusations against him. Lisbeth herself was not awarded anything but she emerged from the case with her honour intact and undoubtedly rose in public esteem because of her dauntless behaviour.[9]

Of the many interesting cases heard by the chapter courts one will have to serve as an example.

---

[8]   *Stavanger Domkapitels Protocol 1571–1630*, ed. A. Brandrud, Udg. for det Norske Historiske Kildeskriftsfond (Christiania/Oslo, 1897).
[9]   *NHD* 1619, pp. 36 ff.

INGEBORG HELLESDATTER AGAINST MR FRANS. OSLO CATHEDRAL CHAPTER. 1616

Ingeborg serves in the rectory with Mr Frans, the incumbent of Asker, one of the rich rural parishes near Oslo. Her nearest guardian is her mother, a widow of straitened means living in a more remote district. Having served a short time Ingeborg suffers the fate of thousands of maids before and after: the master of the house takes advantage of her repeatedly, almost under the very eyes of his wife and children and the other servants. In desperation she runs away home twice but is brought back. When she becomes pregnant the clergyman and his wife attempt to provoke an abortion through phlebotomy and other drastic but unsuccessful means. The child is born, and it is not clear whether it was stillborn or died soon after. After the birth Ingeborg personally informs the cathedral chapter of Oslo of this fact. According to the law all charges against clergymen must be brought before this court in the first instance. The chapter hears this case for several months during the autumn of 1615 and the spring of 1616. Several investigations are made and witnesses are questioned. Ingeborg also appears in person at Akershus castle to hand in her accusations in writing (probably drafted for her by someone else), in the presence of Mr Frans. Those receiving her account were none other than Enevold Kruse, the vice-regent of Norway, and Jens Bjelke, the chancellor of Norway. These gentlemen were supervising the chapter court in Oslo in the name of the king.

The records preserved from this case amount to between ten and fifteen pages in modern print. The descriptions of the attempts at foeticide, for example, are very detailed and realistic. The girl's mother and guardian are summonsed to be present at the final meeting of the court. In the court Mr Frans conjures up many lies, and it is also gradually revealed that he has tried to influence Ingeborg as well as other servants to give false evidence. He said that Ingeborg had seduced him, coming to see him at night in her shift, and that her fiancé fathered the child. But the court traces all sorts of people who can testify against Mr Frans: the bleeder, the midwife, his own wife, the servants in the rectory, and neighbours from her native place, who vouch for her spotless reputation before she went to serve in the rectory. This had a decisive influence. In cases of morality the courts of this time only accepted charges brought by women of good reputation. Women of notoriously easy virtue could not prefer charges against men for sexual abuses.

The chapter court finds that Ingeborg's own written and oral statements as well as the evidence of the witnesses militate strongly against Mr Frans. But since the rector avows his innocence, at least as far as violation of a virgin is involved, the law affords him one more chance. He can take an oath of denial with eleven unprejudiced men who are willing to vouch for his honesty and swear with him on the gospels. The court orders Mr Frans to submit to this ceremony, an ancient medieval legal institution, which must take place before a secular court. If the oath fails it will fall to the secular authorities to punish him for violation of a virgin. The chapter court could only admonish or remove a clergyman for re-prehensible discharge of his office.

Knowing full well that he would be unable to find eleven people willing to swear with him, Mr Frans chooses to give up his office to the viceregent but he implores him for another living so that he can support his wife and children. Faced with this solution the chapter court in Oslo can do nothing more in the case of Mr Frans. The Records of the Court conclude with his resignation. We are not told whether the girl Ingeborg got any public satisfaction. But what is most important in this context is the fact that Mr Frans publicly suffered an abject defeat in the case brought against him by his maid. And the whole congregation had sided with her; this was no small achievement in a time when the clergymen were generally the most respected and influential men in the districts. Ingeborg Hellesdatter had a high social barrier to climb when bringing charges against her master and rector Mr Frans.[10]

On the basis of my knowledge of the entire evidence of Norwegian legal history from the fourteenth to the sixteenth century I suggest that the small selection of cases here presented are representative of the attitudes of courts and authorities towards women preferring cases. Whether their social standing was higher or lower, they got as fair a deal as men did. In the cases above we have seen that the men did not benefit from their sex. That women were excluded from public functions and offices and did not have equal rights of inheritance did not imply any total repression of the female sex. All courts in the country, throughout the period, seem to have been working with one object in mind, to award justice to whosoever, be they man or woman, could adduce the best evidence in favour of their case. Or, in a criminal case, to sentence the person who had committed one or more crimes. Accusations brought forward by a woman were taken as seriously as those preferred by a man.

---

[10] Oslo Kapittel, *Forhandlingsprotokoll* 1616, pp. 154–62; Copiebog, pp. 253–65, *Oslo Kapitels Protokoller 1606–1618*, ed. O. Kolsrud, Udg. for Kjeldeskriftfondet (Christiania/Oslo, 1913–49).

ANCIENT MONUMENTS ACT – EXPLOITATION – MEDIEVAL ARCHAEOLOGY – RESEARCH THOUGHTS ON MANIFEST CONNECTIONS

Hans Andersson

THE ARCHAEOLOGIST AND THE LAW

There are probably not many humanists who are seen out in society as much as the archaeologists. When new houses or new roads are being built, whether in the country-side or in the middle of towns, archaeologists emerge to examine the ancient monuments in the area, monuments that would otherwise be destroyed. What the archaeologists do is to see to it that the source material hidden in the ground in the shape of remnants of buildings, streets, graves, and all kinds of objects left from various building activities, is taken care of. This documentation can be done in many different ways: by descriptions, or drawings, but also through the preservation of objects, bones, parts of plants, or building constructions. Sometimes a whole structure is preserved and made into a museum.

The archaeologists' work is thus very important, yielding new source material for our early history. In Sweden ancient monuments are protected by *The Ancient Monuments Act*, dating in its present form from 1942 but following traditions from the seventeenth century.[1] This law states that ancient monuments must sometimes be removed, and there are clear rules regulating the documentation of the removal. According to the law it is for the County Administration (Länsstyrelsen) to decide whether an ancient monument may be removed because of development, and, if so, on what conditions. These conditions almost always contain a demand for documentation, i.e. in most cases an excavation. Then it is for the developer to pay the costs.

Because of the expansion of building activities in Sweden since the 1960s the kind of archaeological work made necessary by development has become very extensive: so extensive that rescue archaeology has totally overshadowed excavations in which archaeologists have been able to choose their investigation objects themselves. This is also true of other countries, if not exactly in the same way, since legal regulations vary from country to country. In their demands that, certain exceptions apart, the developer shall pay and in their legislation that

---

[1] For general information on the Swedish laws for the preservation of the cultural heritage, see 'The Cultural Heritage in Sweden', *ICOMOS BULLETIN* 6 (1981).

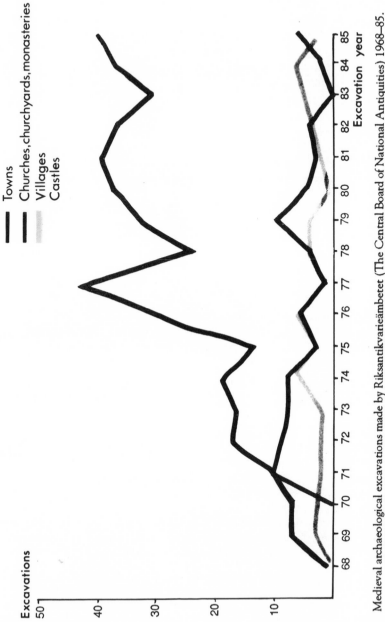

Medieval archaeological excavations made by Riksantikvarieämbetet (The Central Board of National Antiquities) 1968–85. The dominance of urban excavations is very evident. *After A. Bennett, K. Svensson, A. Åkerlund Pilotstudie för bearbetning av UV-material. Prel. Report 1987. Also in Lundaforskare föreläser 19. Lund 1987*

gives general protection to all ancient monuments, Sweden, Norway and Finland form one extreme, while other countries with weaker legal protection – or none at all – form the other extreme. In the former case there are more excavations but also stronger control over objects to be examined, while in the latter case there is more freedom of choice – if there is money.

There have always been different opinions as to whether, from a scientific point of view, the Swedish system is good or not. In many cases it is important that researchers can choose their problems themselves, and so direct their investigations to solve precisely the problems they find essential. According to one view there is a risk that such possibilities are reduced in a system like the Swedish. – Is this really so? There may obviously be conflicts in the present situation, above all if one is not aware of it, but it can at the same time be maintained that precisely the possibilities provided by the *Ancient Monuments Act* are unique and of crucial importance to prehistoric as well as medieval archaeologists. It is a question of awareness and consideration of how to investigate and how to handle the recovered material scientifically.

TOWN ARCHAEOLOGY AND EXPLOITATION

In order to develop these thoughts on law, archaeology and research, my obvious starting-point is medieval archaeology. The extent of medieval archaeological investigations in Sweden has grown enormously since the 1960s, especially from about 1970. Essentially, however, only one area has expanded, namely the investigations of medieval town centres. This is of course due to extensive slum-clearances – whatever one thinks/feels about this term – in the central parts of towns. Most of the remains are hidden under the ground, even if in some towns there are a few medieval buildings and, of course, in most cases a church of medieval origin. In many places, however, an astonishing amount is still under the ground, not only objects but also building foundations, streets, enclosures, and other deposits. Some of the remains have naturally been destroyed by foundations from the nineteenth century, but still much has survived down to our own day, to the time when more radical changes are taking place. This is the primary material of the urban archaeologist.

Some Swedish towns have quite a long archaeological tradition, above all Lund. There is no other Scandinavian town with such a long continuity of investigative activity, dating back to the nineteenth century. Lund has come to mean a great deal to the development of medieval archaeology because of such scholars as Ragnar Blomqvist and Anders W. Mårtensson from the Museum of *Kulturen* in Lund and Erik Cinthio, the creator of the very subject in the Historical Museum of the University. When big building projects began to appear about 1960, readiness in Lund made it possible to start investigations on a large scale. The so-called Thule excavation in 1961 was besides Bryggen in Bergen the most extensive investigation in Scandinavia, indeed in Northern Europe, hitherto, and it came to found a school for many following investigations not only in Sweden and Scandinavia but also in, for example, England.[2]

There were also other places where important archaeological work was done: Uppsala, Stockholm, Söderköping, and Lödöse, but never in such a continous way as in Lund. Thus the 1960s and 70s were dramatic for town archaeology and its development. Several circumstances contributed.

When, after the second world war, building activity started again on a larger scale, it soon developed radically, not least as far as techniques for digging foundations were concerned. Large scale planning was very common, and this caused big problems for the archaeologists. Up till then they had been able to work, at least tolerably well, in parallel with the digging of foundations, and to document the finds; much of the digging was manual and the machines used were small. Suddenly, however, mechanised work took over, and the large excavating machines did not pay any regard to the archaeologist who tried to keep pace with them. It came to a crisis even in places where there was some form of archaeological control. Investigation technique had to be changed completely; the only solution was to anticipate and investigate before areas were exploited. The Thule excavation in Lund served as a guide in this respect.

The crisis was particularly apparent in the Mälar area (in middle Sweden) with all its important medieval towns. In some of these towns many of the cultural layers disappeared before new forms of investigation were embarked upon, in about 1970. At the same time awareness about what the town archaeological material could mean and be used for was increasing. In the somewhat chaotic situation that prevailed at this time it was also obvious that nobody had a real survey of the material or the archaeological possibilities at hand in different places. What cultural layers did still exist? How much had been destroyed?

In connection with the re-organization of excavations, led by the Central Board of National Antiquities, the Medieval Town Project was created and commissioned to put together and analyze the archaeological material from all medieval towns in Sweden. The costs for this were covered by the Central Board of National Antiquities (Riksantikvarieämbetet), the Bank of Sweden Tercenary Foundation, the Swedish Council for Research in the Humanities and Social Sciences, and, finally, by the Swedish Council for Planning and Coordination of Research. The full, though somewhat clumsy, title of the project 'Implications of Early Urbanization for Modern Planning', clearly marks the connection between research and application. The project has published its results in about seventy reports dealing with both specific towns and comparative studies.[3]

---

[2] R. Blomqvist and A. W. Mårtensson, Thulegrävningen 1961, Archaeologica Lundensia 2 (Lund, 1963).
[3] Medeltidsstaden 1–76, Riksantikvarieämbetet och Statens Historika Museer: Rapport (Stockholm, 1976–89). We hope a summary report of the project will be published in English in 1989.

A COMPLETE MOBILIZATION

What was important was the complete mobilization that was achieved, partly by rearranging excavation routines and creating a survey, partly thanks to the scientific discussion that developed in close connection with the organization of the practical work. Much of this could be done because the enterprise had a firm base in the Ancient Monuments Act. Perhaps another observation is important: since this Act is general, that is, it applies to all ancient monuments, investigations also included objects that did not at first sight look too promising. In the historical and archaeological literature of towns it is natural to deal with the bigger towns and places that are important in a political-economical perspective. We cannot, however, fully understand the urbanization process if we do not take the smaller places into account. In all medieval towns of Sweden investigations are now being made, naturally on very different scales, with greater or lesser results. This also applies to towns founded in the seventeenth century. We will, therefore, have a wide range of material which is important in our attempts to write the history of Swedish urbanization.

ARCHAEOLOGICAL EXAMPLES

It might be asked what results all this hectic activity has yielded. Much of the material has still not been worked up; a vast amount has been recovered which is still awaiting final treatment. There is, however, already quite a lot to say about general features, as well as matters of detail.

We now have a much clearer idea of the urbanization process itself, its course and chronology, not least during the early Middle Ages. The development of towns can roughly be divided into four stages: we talk about Viking-age, early medieval, high medieval, and late medieval towns. The time limits are (very approximately) 1000, 1200 and 1350. Common to all towns is the fact that they are central places with permanent, dense settlements. High and late medieval towns had a special legal status and certain privileges. There are hints that the early medieval towns might also have had them, but that is uncertain. In some towns there were in any case special urban taxes which may indicate a special status in relation to the surrounding countryside. On the other hand it is worth emphasizing that, at this early stage, the differences between town and country were not particularly marked, though the towns had a bigger concentration of different kinds of institutions, ecclesiastical and royal. This has been stressed by Anders Andrén in his thesis on medieval urbanization in Denmark.[4] Lund, in particular, is a very clear example.

---

[4] A. Andrén, *Den urbana scenen: städer och samhälle i det medeltida Europa*, Acta archaeologica Lundensia, series in octavo 13 (Bonn, Malmö, 1985).

LUND

Thanks to the archaeological evidence from Lund it has been possible to follow development over different periods. The oldest urban phase at Lund has been found in the latest excavations around the early medieval church of *Drotten* with its large church yard. About 1050 the picture changes; within a hundred years Lund becomes a town with the many churches, more than twenty, and at the same time the whole settlement pattern changes. In the middle of the twelfth century the settlement alongside the through road of the town, *Södergatan* (South Street), becomes more concentrated. Signs of market trade become clearer through remnants of market squares, shops and other finds. The predecessor of the cathedral of Knut the Great's days is gradually replaced by a church during the first half of the twelfth century. In its main features the town plan of today developed at this early stage.

SÖDERKÖPING

Another example is Söderköping, where settlement can be traced back to the early twelfth century, though it does not seem to have been permanent. Later in that century, however, a permanent settlement does appear, and its pattern undergoes considerable changes in the beginning of the thirteenth century.

The archaeological evidence shows great rearrangements; the buildings are closer to each other, the street system is now fixed and new types of finds emerge.

Through dendrochronological examination this change can now be dated fairly exactly: it took place during the first decade of the thirteenth century. Everything did not, of course, happen at once, but we can say that the period from the beginning of the thirteenth century to 1210 is very important in Söderköping. We find the same kind of rearrangements in other places along the Baltic coast; in Visby stone houses were being built from about 1230, and in Lübeck we also find great changes and extensions during the first decades of the thirteenth century. Here too archaeology has given information of crucial importance.

THE EARLY MEDIEVAL TOWNS

The nature of the material suggests that early medieval towns differ in character very much from later towns. Early and later medieval towns had different kinds of economies; while the earlier towns were used by kings in their attempts to rule and control the surrounding areas, towns of later periods, though still controlled by the king, were part of an international economy with other kinds of organizations. Parallel developments in the Baltic area are very instructive in this respect. Comparisons with material from various places and of course also with different kinds of written sources now make it possible for us to discuss these wider perspectives.

THE TOWN ENVIRONMENT

The town environment in its different aspects ought to attract more research work than is currently the case. Much of the evidence that has been recovered from archaeological excavations offers good opportunities to reconstruct medieval town plans and their rearrangements. This makes it possible to study continuity and discontinuity in the development of town planning. The evidence can also be used to answer the kind of general questions mentioned above, and to help us understand what medieval reality looked like and how it changed.

This is a very important aspect to consider in relation to all preservation work. How far back can we trace the town plans and street systems of today? Even where there are no medieval buildings left, the town plan was often fixed during the Middle Ages. In Sigtuna the main essentials of the town were obviously established by about 1200, but much dates back to the eleventh century. In Söderköping the stabilisation of the street system is contemporary with the great changes of the beginning of the thirteenth century, and Visby's plan dates back to the early Middle Ages, certainly to long before the thirteenth century.

What the buildings looked like, where they were situated, what material they were made of and what function they had, all this is fairly simple to examine. Yet, unfortunately these questions have been somewhat neglected. The many excavations have yielded a vast body of material which deserves a closer analysis. When more such work has been done, perhaps also the social structure of the towns will be more apparent than it is now.

Finds from private houses offer very good opportunities to illustrate how an individual household functioned. Pottery has been used for such studies, and in his thesis Jan Erik Augustsson presents an analysis of ceramic ware from medieval Halmstad. The material has been analyzed with regard to several aspects: production, craft organization, needs of different households etc.[5]

Archaeological investigations have also yielded material of great importance to natural scientists. Most common are of course animal bones which can tell a lot about the subsistence of the town, but there are also other interesting finds, for example parts of plants and insects which can cast light on the physical environment. A problem in this field of research is the lack of theories explaining how the different factors are connected in their historical, environmental setting. In order to develop a theoretical framework cooperation between medieval archaeologists and specialized scientists must expand considerably.

THE ANCIENT MONUMENTS ACT AND RESEARCH

Thus we have gone from the wider perspectives to the narrower, from the urbanization process on a large scale to the individual household. Our source material is first of all material from archaeological excavations, and to return to

---

[5]   J.-E. Augustsson, *Keramik i Halmstad ca 1322–1619: produktion – distribution – funktion*, Hallands länsmuseers skriftserie 2 (Halmstad, 1985).

the starting-point of this article it may be asked whether we would have been able to do much of our work without an Ancient Monuments Act. My answer is that without the Act we would not have gained the breadth and depth we have today. In the completely new situation that arose in the 1960s this Act was very important in sustaining our demands for investigations. It has further given us a wide range of material covering places of totally different kinds, which is essential for our understanding of the development as a whole. The Ancient Monuments Act also demands that investigations are made in a scientific way, and the *Medieval Town Project* should be seen against this background.

The pressures of development has led to the dominance of urban archaeology. The disadvantage of this is that, to a large extent, medieval archaeologists have had to abandon other areas for a long time. This, however, is already changing, partly because of a widening of medieval archaeology as a subject, partly because exploitation now also involves settlements in the countryside. Many exciting things will happen during the next few years. The numerous church restorations, both those underway and those planned, will make it possible to document and analyse the medieval churches and their transformations.

Large-scale investigations make heavy demands upon research work. Have we managed to meet these demands? Sometimes one feels a bit doubtful about that. Undeniably much has happened, but there are difficult problems when it comes to working up the vast material. For a medieval archaeology department like ours in Lund it is naturally a great responsibility to carry on the theoretical debate that is needed and to create an understanding for the importance of such work in teaching and otherwise.

Those involved in the preservation of the cultural heritage also have a great responsibility to work for and engage in the development of this kind of research. If research awareness is not kept alive among those who lead the excavations, there is a risk that a great part of archaeological work will only be a recovering of material, and in that case we will find ourselves in a situation where the connection between scientific research and rescue excavations might pose problems. In such a case we will not have met the demands of the Ancient Monuments Act. It will be exciting to see how this symbiosis between theory and practice develops during the years to come.[6]

[6]   A Swedish version has been published in *Lundaforskare föreläser* 19, Lund University Press (Lund, 1987).

TABULA GRATULATORIA

Kjell G. Åberg, MA
Prof. Dr Werner Affeldt
Agneta Åkermark
Alingsås Kommun
Björn Ambrosiani
Lars Amréus
Hans Andersson, Prof.

Bernard S. Bachrach, Dept of History, University of Minnesota, USA
Professor Richard N. Bailey
Dr Suerre Bagge
Søren Balle, Aarhus
Grethe Authén Blom, Professor, Trondheim
Alf Bråthen
Stefan Brink, Fil. dr
Anders Broberg
Brotherton Library, University of Leeds

J. Campbell
Martin Carver
Ingrid Cederquist
Eivind Claesson Audur Magnusdottir
Margaret Cormack
Ole Crumlin-Pedersen

Siver Dagermark
Merete og Troels Dahlerup, Aarhus
Vibeke Dalberg, Universitetslektor
Prof. Alain Dierkens, Université Libre, Brussels
A. A. M. Duncan, University of Glasgow

Dr Harald Ehrhardt, Oberursel, Germany
Rune Ekre, FD, Lödöse
Alvar Ellegård, Göteborg

Ole Fenger, Professor Dr Jur.
Olle Ferm
Vigdis Finnbogadóttir, the President of Iceland
Christer Flodin

Professor Åke Fridh

Michael H. Gelting, Archivist, Mag. Art.
John Gillingham
Walter Goffart
Göteborgs Universitet
Anna Götlind
Rosemary Graham
Dr James Graham-Campbell
Anne-Sofie and Bo Gräslund
Kaaren Grimstad, Associate Professor
Hedda Gunneng and Börje Westlund

Maja Hagerman
Lotte Hedeager
Professor Knut Helle, University of Bergen
Jan Herbertsson
C. Warren Hollister
N. H. Holmqvist-Larsen, Cand. Phil.

Steinar Imsen
Institut for Navneforskning, Copenhagen

Professor R. Ian Jack
Henrik Janson
Tore Janson
Jenny Jochens, Professor
Bengt R. Jonsson, Professor, Stockholm
Mogens Schou Jørgensen

John Kousgård Sørensen, Professor
Lars O. Lagerqvist
Thomas Lindkvist, Dr
John Lindow
Michael Linton
Lars Ljungmark, Docent, Göteborg
Carl Löfving, Göteborg
Iris and Lars Lönnroth
Professor Henry Loyn
Stig Lundberg

Brita and Mats P. Malmer, Lidingö, Sweden
Rikke Malmros, Cand. Phil.
Göran Malmstedt
P. J. Meertens-Instituut

Michael F. Metcalf
Tor Morisse, Castle Studies
Aare and Magnus Mörner
Dr Alexander Callander Murray
Kungl. Myntkabinettet

Miss Beryl R. Nash
Nationalmuseet, 2. afdeling, København
Tom Neill
Dr Hans F. Nielsen
Professor Thomas S. Noonan
Per G. Norseng, cand. philol.
Numismatic Institute, Stockholm University
Tore S. Nyberg, Lektor
Erik and Lena Nylén
Professor Per Nystroem / Lili Kaelas

Marianne and Anders Ollfors
Rikke and Olaf Olsen
Professor Eva Österberg
Inger Österholm

Leif Påhlsson
Lennart Andersson Palm
Claus Marott Pedersen BA
David Pelteret
Pontifical Institute of Mediaeval Studies, Toronto, Canada
Lena Peterson, Uppsala

Gad Rausing
Riksantikvarens Utgravningskontor i Trondheim
Else Roesdahl, Reader in Medieval Archaeology
Margaret Clunies Ross, Sydney

Inga-Maj and Holger Sandberg
Bengt Schönbäck
Seminariet för nordisk ortnamnsforskning, Uppsala
Lars Sjösvärd
Dr Inge Skovgaard-Petersen
Preben Meulengracht Sørensen
Professor Eric Stanley
Magnús Stefánsson, Ass. Prof., and Gunhild
Stifts- och landsbiblioteket, Skara, Sweden
Professor Berta Stjernquist, Lund
Marie and Bjarne Stoklund

Johnny, Marianne, Karin and Elin Strand
Thommy Svensson, Professor

Mr John Taylor
Christer Thörnqvist

Anna Ulfhielm
University of Aarhus, Department of Medieval Archeology
University College London Library
University of Illinois Library
Historisches Seminar der Universitat Kiel
Historisk Institut, Københavns Universitet
University of Toronto Library
University of Washington Libraries
Uppsala University, Dept of Archaeology

Professor Sally N. Vaughn
The Vikingship Museum in Roskilde
Vitenskapsmuseet i Trondheim, Arkeologisk Avdeling
Vitterhetsakademiens bibliotek
Volker Vogel

Birgitte Wåhlin, Lektor
Martin Wallén, Fil. Kand.
Gerd Wolfgang Weber
David M. Wilson
Christer Winberg

Susan Youngs